Jewish Bible Theology

Jewish Bible Theology
Perspectives and Case Studies

edited by

Isaac Kalimi

Winona Lake, Indiana
Eisenbrauns
2012

Library of Congress Cataloging-in-Publication Data

Jewish Bible theology : perspectives and case studies / edited by Isaac Kalimi.
  p.   cm.
Includes bibliographical references and indexes.
ISBN 978-1-57506-231-0 (hardback : alk. paper)
  1. Bible. O.T.—Theology.   2. Bible. O.T.—Criticism, interpretation, etc.   3. God—Biblical teaching.   4. Judaism—Doctrines.   I. Kalimi, Isaac.
  BS1192.5.A1J478   2012
  296.3—dc23

                                                          2011051244

*This volume is dedicated to the blessed memory
of my beloved teacher*

Professor MOSHE GREENBERG, *z"l*

and to my adored friends

Professor RIMON KASHER
and
Professor BYRON SHERWIN

with appreciation.

Contents

List of Contributors

Ehud Ben Zvi is a professor in the Department of History and Classics and the Interdisciplinary Program in Religious Studies at the University of Alberta. He is a former president of the Canadian Society of Biblical Studies, current general editor of the *Journal of Hebrew Scriptures*, and author of several books and numerous essays on biblical literature.

Marc Z. Brettler is the Dora Golding Professor of Biblical Studies at Brandeis University. He is co-editor of the *Jewish Study Bible*, which has won a National Jewish Book Award. Most recently, he has published *How to Read the Bible*. His other books include *God Is King, Biblical Hebrew for Students of Modern Israeli Hebrew, Reading the Book of Judges,* and *The Creation of History in Ancient Israel.*

Amos Frisch is Associate Professor of Bible at Bar-Ilan University. His main areas of research are: literary study of the Bible (especially biblical narrative), Jewish biblical exegesis (especially in the 16th–19th centuries), and biblical kingship. He is author of *The Bible's View of Labor* (Hebrew).

Zev Garber is Professor and Chair of Jewish Studies at Los Angeles Valley College. He is the series editor of Studies in the Shoah, co-editor of *Shofar*, founding editor of Shofar Supplements, and has served as president of the National Association of Professors of Hebrew. His books include *Shoah: The Paradigmatic Genocide, Academic Approaches to Teaching Jewish Studies,* and *Mel Gibson's* Passion: *The Film, the Controversy, and Its Implications.*

Moshe Greenberg, *z"l*, (Ph.D., University of Pennsylvania), was Professor Emeritus of Biblical Studies at Hebrew University of Jerusalem. His extensive publications include commentaries on Ezekiel 1–20 (AB 22, 1983) and Ezekiel 21–37 (AB 22A, 1997), *Understanding Exodus, Introduction to Hebrew, On the Bible and on Judaism,* and numerous articles on various biblical studies.

Frederick E. Greenspahn is Gimelstob Eminent Scholar in Judaic Studies at Florida Atlantic University. He has published extensively on biblical literature, languages, and Jewish exegesis and translations. He taught for more than two decades at the University of Denver.

Peter J. Haas is Abba Hillel Silver Professor of Jewish Studies and Chair of the Department of Religious Studies at Case Western Reserve University. He was ordained at Hebrew Union College–Jewish Institute of Religion in Cincinnati (1974) and received his Ph.D. in history of religions, Judaism, from Brown University (1980). He has published several books and articles dealing with Jewish moral discourse and with Jewish and Christian thought in the post-Holocaust era.

Isaac Kalimi (Ph.D., the Hebrew University of Jerusalem), The Oriental Institute–University of Chicago. He is editor/co-editor of several volumes and author of numerous books and articles, including *The Book of Chronicles: A Classified Bibliography* (Simor Bible Bibliographies 1), *Zur Geschichtsschreibung des Chronisten* (BZAW 226), *Early Jewish Exegesis and Theological Controversy* (Jewish and Christian Heritage 2), *An Ancient Israelite Historian* (SSN 46), and *The Retelling of Chronicles in Jewish Tradition and Literature: A Historical Journey*. His monograph *The Reshaping of Ancient Israelite History in Chronicles* is the recipient of the 2006 R. B. Y. Scott Award, of the Canadian Society of Biblical Studies "in recognition of an outstanding book in the areas of Hebrew Bible and the Ancient Near East." He has received many awards, for example, from the National Endowment for the Humanities (2007–8) and the Fulbright Distinguished Chair (University of Salzburg, 2011).

Joel S. Kaminsky is a professor in the Department of Religion and Co-Director of the Program in Jewish Studies at Smith College. He teaches courses on the Hebrew Bible and ancient Judaism, and his research focuses on the theology of the Hebrew Bible and its influence on early Christianity and rabbinic Judaism.

Asa Kasher is Laura Scwarz-Kipp Professor Emeritus of Professional Ethics and Philosophy of Practice and was Avraham Horodisch Professor of Philosophy of Language at Tel Aviv University. Among his books is *Judaism and Idolatry*, which is an interpretation of much of the Jewish tradition that he explores in this volume. His other publications include *Military Ethics*, *Spirit of a Man*, *Meaning of Life* (all in Hebrew), and about 200 additional books, papers, and ethical documents. He won the Prize of Israel in general philosophy in 2000.

David Novak has been the J. Richard and Dorothy Shiff Professor of Jewish Studies at the University of Toronto since 1997. Before then, he was the Edgar M. Bronfman Professor of Modern Judaic Studies at the University of Virginia. He is the author of 15 books on Jewish thought and philosophy.

Uriel Simon is Professor Emeritus of Bible at Bar-Ilan University and former director of the Institute for Jewish Biblical Interpretation. He received the Bialik Prize in 2004. His publications include *Seek Peace and Pursue It* (2nd ed., 2004), *Rabbi Abraham Ibn Ezra*, and *The Foundation of Reverence and the Secret of the Torah: An Annotated Critical Edition* (2007).

Benjamin D. Sommer is Professor of Bible at Jewish Theological Seminary of America. For several years he was the Director of the Crown Family Center for Jewish Studies at Northwestern University. He is the editor of the Jewish Publication Society's multivolume commentary on the book of Psalms, of which he authored the first volume.

Marvin A. Sweeney is Professor of Hebrew Bible at the Claremont School of Theology, Professor of Religion at Claremont Graduate University, and Professor of Bible at the Academy for Jewish Religion. He is the author of several books, such as *Reading the Hebrew Bible after the Shoah: Engaging Holocaust Theology*.

Abbreviations

General

CD   Cairo Genizah copy of the *Damascus Document*
DtrH   Deuteronimistic History
KJV   King James Version
NJPSV   New Jewish Publication Society Version
RSV   Revised Standard Version

Reference Works

AB   Anchor Bible
AJSRev   *American Jewish Studies Review*
ATDA   Alte Testament deutsch
BEL   Biblical Encyclopedia Library
Bib   *Biblica*
BJRL   *Bulletin of the John Rylands University Library of Manchester*
BJS   Brown Judaic Studies
BTB   *Biblical Theology Bulletin*
BZAW   Beihefte zur Zeitschrift für die alttestamentliche Wissenschaft
CBQ   *Catholic Biblical Quarterly*
CHJ   Davies, W. D., and Finkelstein, L., editors. *Cambridge History of Judaism*. 4 vols. Cambridge: Cambridge University Press, 1984–2006
ConBNT   Coniectanea Biblica, New Testament
CRINT   Compendia rerum iudaicarum ad Novum Testamentum
DJD   Discoveries in the Judaean Desert
DSD   *Dead Sea Discoveries*
FAT   Forschungen zum alten Testament
HALOT   Koehler, L.; Baumgartner, W.; and Stamm, J. J. *The Hebrew and Aramaic Lexicon of the Old Testament*. Translated and edited by M. E. J. Richardson. 5 vols. Leiden: Brill, 1994–2000
HAT   Handbuch zum Alten Testament
HBT   *Horizons in Biblical Theology*
HSM   Harvard Semitic Monographs
HTR   *Harvard Theological Review*
HUCA   *Hebrew Union College Annual*
IBT   Interpreting Biblical Texts
ICC   International Critical Commentary
IEJ   *Israel Exploration Journal*
Int   *Interpretation*

JAAR	*Journal of the American Academy of Religion*
JAB	*Journal of the Aramaic Bible*
JBL	*Journal of Biblical Literature*
JJS	*Journal of Jewish Studies*
JQR	*Jewish Quarterly Review*
JR	*Journal of Religion*
JSOT	*Journal for the Study of the Old Testament*
JSOTSup	Journal for the Study of the Old Testament Supplement Series
JSQ	*Jewish Studies Quarterly*
JSS	*Journal of Semitic Studies*
KAT	Kommentar zum Alten Testament
LCL	Loeb Classical Library
MGWJ	*Monatsschrift für Geschichte und Wissenschaft des Judentums*
NEB	Die Neue Echter Bibel
NIB	New Interpreter's Bible
NICOT	New International Commentary on the Old Testament
NovTSup	Novum Testamentum Supplements
OTL	Old Testament Library
OPIAC	*Occasional Papers, Institute for Antiquity and Christianity*
PAAJR	*Proceedings of the American Academy for Jewish Research*
PRS	*Perspectives on Religious Studies*
RB	*Revue biblique*
SAC	Studies in Antiquity and Christianity
SBLMasS	Society of Biblical Literature Masoretic Studies
SBLDS	Society of Biblical Literature Dissertation Series
SBLSymS	Society of Biblical Literature Symposium Series
SJOT	*Scandinavian Journal of the Old Testament*
SSN	Studia Semitica Neerlandica
TSAJ	Texte und Studien zum antiken Judentum
VT	*Vetus Testamentum*
VTSup	Supplements to Vetus Testamentum
WBC	Word Biblical Commentary
YJS	Yale Judaica Series
ZAW	*Zeitschrift für die alttestamentliche Wissenschaft*

I

Contemporary Jewish Bible Theology: An Overview

ISAAC KALIMI

The present volume, which is to the best of my knowledge the first of its sort, takes issue with scholars who believe that the terms *biblical theology* and *Jews* contradict rather than approximate each other. Some of them even assert that "there is no Jewish theology of the Old Testament."[1] Without saying so, they automatically confirm the definition of the German theologian Otto Procksch that "alle Theologie ist Christologie."[2] In other words, they are of the opinion that *biblical theology* is an exclusively Christian discipline and that Jews are simply not interested in biblical theology. Hence, all that is left is just to point out the reasons for this situation.[3] Others go even further and claim that the Jewish religion as such lacks a theology, that is, it is a religion without theology!

In recent decades, there is increasing interest in earlier and current Jewish biblical theologies. On the one hand, a new generation of Jewish scholars from North America and Israel show great interest and actively engage in Hebrew Bible theology. They strive to make Jewish Bible theology a legitimate subdiscipline of biblical studies and to develop it separately and independently from Christian theology. On the other hand, many Christian scholars are interested in understanding the Hebrew Bible/Old Testament and its various themes from a Jewish theological perspective(s). The recurrent demand from all sides encouraged me to initiate the present volume for the benefit of all.

This volume comprises a number of essays that raise substantial methodological and historical issues, while others focus on particular topics

---

1. See M. Tsevat, "Theology of the Old Testament: A Jewish View," *HBT* 8 (1986) 33–50, esp. pp. 33–34.

2. See O. Procksch, *Theologie des Alten Testaments* (Gütersloh: Bertelsmann, 1950) 1.

3. See, for instance, J. D. Levenson, "Why Jews Are Not Interested in Biblical Theology?" in *Judaic Perspectives on Ancient Israel* (ed. J. Neusner, B. A. Levine, and E. S. Frerichs; Philadelphia: Fortress, 1987) 281–307; republished in his collection *The Hebrew Bible, the Old Testament and Historical Criticism: Jews and Christians in Biblical Studies* (Louisville, KY: Westminster John Knox, 1993) 33–61.

from the Torah, Prophets, and Writings (Tanak). Altogether they reflect fresh and current thoughts on important issues in Jewish religious and intellectual world views.

The first part of the volume, "Jewish Bible Theology," opens with the essays that deal with the past and present situation of the discipline. In his "Jewish Theologies of Scripture," Frederick E. Greenspahn states that, although the Hebrew Bible's centrality in Judaism is widely acknowledged, it has been described in several different ways. These can be grouped into three broad categories, depending on whether they focus on what it says, what it is, or what it does. The Hebrew Bible is commonly understood as a conduit for revelation. Most often, it is understood as promulgating law (*Gesetz*); however, some have emphasized its teachings (*Lehre*), whether intellectual or moral. A few have even seen it as containing all significant truths. A second group embraces the views that are concerned with the Hebrew Bible's status rather than its contents. Rooted in wisdom theology, this approach sees Scripture as having cosmic status. It has sometimes been equated with God and even, occasionally, elevated above God. The third approach avoids questions about whether the Hebrew Bible is human or divine by treating it as the arena where the two meet. Although this has obvious attractions for our time, it was already evident in rabbinic tradition, which portrayed the Torah as a marriage contract. In addition to demonstrating Judaism's commitment to the Hebrew Bible, these views reflect the diverse ways in which its centrality has been understood.

In the chapter "Constructing the Past: The Recent History of Jewish Biblical Theology," Ehud Ben Zvi details the sources of the current general opinion that Jews were not interested in theology in general and in biblical theology in particular and the images of the past that this opinion creates. He focuses on the circumstances within which this view developed, including the proliferation of works addressing issues of Jewish biblical theology in recent years, and other possible reasons, such as hybridism. Ben Zvi also addresses the possible reasons for marginalization of relatively recent works on a consensus. Among the crucial factors feeding these processes of history/memory-shaping, he mentions implicit constructions of what is Judaic, and self and/or community-produced lines of continuity and identification of present scholars with their predecessors.

The second part of the volume opens with six general theological case studies. Asa Kasher's paper, "Fighting Forms of Idolatry: The Meaning of an Image of Moses in Jewish Theology," embeds an image of Moses that arises from a certain Jewish tradition within the broadest possible meaning framework of Jewish Scriptures. It interprets Jewish texts and practices in terms of a comprehensive, deeply entrenched, and strictly observed opposition to any possible forms of idolatry. In the first part of the paper, Kasher observes a trend manifest in Jewish tradition of pointing out weak elements in what Moses did. In the second part, he interprets those observations and provides a proper understanding of an image of Moses that emerges from elements of the Jewish tradition, showing it to be a gate to understanding Jewish texts and practices in a unified way. The merit of the proposed understanding is discussed in the last part of the essay. Kasher gives attention to related observations about a certain image of Moses in the Torah and midrash. He concludes that the case of Moses shows how biblical verses and a paragraph in the midrash can be interpreted as conveying one of the deepest principles of the Jewish religion—that of the practical commitment to fighting idolatry, whatever form it takes. The idea of fighting idolatry is shown to serve as a cultural common denominator for people who hold different attitudes toward the Jewish religious traditions, that is, both for people who view it from an internal point of view and people who view it from an external point of view.

Moshe Greenberg's chapter "Jewish Conceptions of the Human Factor in Biblical Prophecy" claims that from the

> Talmud to the Renaissance classical Jewish thought and exegesis invests the prophetic writings with divine authority: all were inspired by the Holy Spirit. In the case of the Torah (the prophecy of Moses), the text was ultimately dictated by God. This formal, dogmatic predication of divine inspiration and authorship does not hinder acknowledgment of the literary evidence of human shaping of the text. The Torah even contains extensive tracts formulated by Moses; their inclusion in the Torah means that they were ultimately sanctioned (dictated) by God, but the personal touch of Moses is there "to this day." Outside the Torah, it is freely posited that prophecy is conditioned by the personality and capacity of the prophet: his age, his spiritual level, his education—all affect his message. This alone accounts for the variety of styles and formulations that distinguish the prophets from one another, even when—and particularly when—they communicate similar messages. Therefore, the introductory prophetic formula "thus said the Lord" signifies no more than "this is the substance of the Lord's communication to me, couched in my own language." It also happens that one prophet adopts the wording of his predecessor, with which he was familiar by education, when that wording seemed to him a suitable vehicle for the word of God that came to him. The personal factor may be so dominant that the inexperience and lack of education of a prophet result in faulty language and a disordered text.
>
> Classical Jewish exegetes acknowledged these literary facts in the face of the great temptation to absolutize the authority of Scripture and silence the incessant challenges to its integrity and validity by categorically asserting that all is simply divine dictation. To modern Jewish critics, they are a model of reverence toward the source of religion, which does not entail blindness to the complexity of that source or

the adoption of a far-fetched cloaking of that complexity. The tradition of honest and sober reasoning, accommodating articles of faith to (literary) facts, stands the critics in good stead as they confront a wave of simplistic dogmatic piety that seeks to impose itself on the entire community, stifling curiosity and independence of judgment.

Uriel Simon's paper is, in fact, a response to the dominant theological conception among religious Zionists in the State of Israel and the Diaspora, according to which the foundation of the State of Israel signifies the "beginning of the growth of our (ultimate) redemption." In contrast to the belief that we are assured that "the third [i.e., current] redemption will never end" (*Midr. Tanḥuma*), based on a couple of midrashim, the dominant biblical concept is outlined: divine destinies are conditional promises. The considerable discrepancy between the divine promises to Abraham and their late fulfillment implies a distinction between the normal, *natural* connection of any people to its Land and Jewish *supernatural* or *destiny-oriented* bond with the Land of Israel. A natural connection is continuous, however generally limited, while the destiny-oriented bond is intermittent but eternal. Seemingly, this distinction is the background for Abraham's territorial generosity toward Lot. The conditional aspect of biblical promises is further substantiated through the juxtaposition of the comments of Rashi and Naḥmanides on Gen 1:1 and the analyses of Lev 18:26–28; Deut 4:25–31, 9:4–7, 16:20; Jeremiah 7; and Amos 9:8–11.

The chapter "God and Human Rights in a Secular Society: A Biblical-Talmudic Perspective" by David Novak claims that the concept of human rights is endemic to democracy. Those who wish to be part of democratic discourse today can avoid having to justify what they mean by "human rights." Religious people who affirm the value of democracy, which almost all of them do today, need to find sources in their respective religious traditions that affirm human rights. Thus, they will be able to answer secularist critics who insist that religious traditions are antidemocratic precisely because they do not affirm human rights. Novak attempts to show that human rights are not only affirmed by the biblical-talmudic tradition but that this tradition provides a better foundation for human rights than do competing secularisms.

Amos Frisch discusses the Hebrew Bible's attitude toward human toil. He critically evaluates Engnell's study on the topic and points out that Engnell offers a clear analysis of the Hebrew Bible's perspective on labor. However, Engnell finds that the Hebrew Bible is basically negative toward human work, except for prophetic literature, which is somewhat less negative. Frisch takes a detailed look at the attitude toward work in three passages that represent three different genres of the Jewish biblical corpora: the stories of the creation and of the Garden of Eden in Genesis 1–3, Psalm 127, and Isaiah 40–66. In each of these passages, there are, at first glance, grounds for educing an unfavorable view of human labor. However, a close reading shows that the first two texts are not critical of work, while the third (the importance of which is ignored by Engnell) deprecates it without totally rejecting its value. In order to complete the picture, Frisch briefly reviews three other biblical genres: the legal sections of the Torah, the Deuteronomistic History, and Wisdom Literature. He concludes with two additional issues. First, does the Hebrew Bible evince a different attitude toward various occupations; specifically, is the shepherd better than the farmer? Second, what can we say about the evolution of attitudes toward labor in postbiblical Jewish thought, from the talmudic sages through Hasidism, classic Zionism, and in contemporary times in the State of Israel.

Joel S. Kaminsky's essay "New Testament and Rabbinic Views of Election" closes this section. Kaminsky explores some of the ways that rabbinic Judaism and early Christianity adapted and reinterpreted the concept of election that they had inherited from the Hebrew Bible/Old Testament. He shows many points in common between the two traditions as well as places in which the two traditions move in substantially different directions. Furthermore, Kaminsky seeks to clarify the ways in which each tradition changes or remains fairly close to the theological outlook of the earlier biblical texts with which both traditions wrestle. He reflects on which pieces of the biblical heritage may have been obscured by one or the other of these two traditions, both of which grew out of and continue to claim the Hebrew Bible/Old Testament as their theological heritage. Kaminsky deepens each community's understanding of its own theological position by placing it in relation to its sister tradition and to the Hebrew Bible/Old Testament.

The second section of this part, "Topics from Torah, Prophets, and Writings," opens with Zev Garber's discussion of the problematic issue of Amalek and Amalekut: "Amalek and Amalekut: A Homiletic Lesson." Garber begins with *mitzvah* numerology: Commandment 604 is a warrant for genocide:

> Remember what Amalek did unto these by the way as you came forth out of Egypt: how he met you by the way, and smote the hindmost of you, all that were enfeebled in your rear, when you were faint and weary; and he feared not God. Therefore, it shall be, when the Lord your God had given you rest from all your enemies round about, in the land which the Lord your God gives you for an inheritance to possess it, that you shall blot the remembrance of Amalek from under the heaven; you shall not forget. (Deut 25:17–19)

Garber explains that this commandment challenges observant Jews who are committed to living within the bounds of *halacha* (Jewish law), a system of divinely inspired biblical commandments, as well as rabbinic decrees and derivations, with textual ambiguity and *halachic* conflict. In other words, how does one understand the confrontation with Amalek as a *milhemet mitzvah* (holy war) and yet show empathy for the "other," including the enemy, demanded by the repeated biblical injunction: "Remember, you were slaves in the land of Egypt" (e.g., Lev 19:34). How to reconcile conflicting obligatory *mitzvot* is the focus of this chapter. In this attempt, Garber embraces the hermeneutics of scriptural *peshat* (simple meaning), rabbinic midrash, kabbalistic gleanings, *halachic* derivations, and contemporary example. Among Garber's findings are ways that biblical language molds Jewish character and ways to resolve the enigma of the Amalek without and within (*Amalekut*). A *halachic* excursus on the assassination of Prime Minister Yitzhak Rabin is featured.

Marvin A. Sweeney offers the foundations for a Jewish theology of Tanak/Hebrew Bible. He begins by considering the reasons that a Jewish theology of the Hebrew Bible is both possible and necessary. He considers the distinctive form of the Hebrew Bible as opposed to the Christian Old Testament as a basis for a Jewish biblical theology. One of the two major concerns of his paper is to demonstrate how the Tanak emphasizes the Temple as the holy center of creation, and on that basis, defines Israel's holy life in the created world. The second concern is with the central role that the Prophets play within the structure of the Tanak, insofar as these books examine the questions of the destruction and the projected restoration of the Jerusalem Temple and articulate their respective understandings of the significance of these events for Israel/Judah and creation at large. Sweeney claims that the Prophets engage in dialogue, both with their respective understandings of Israelite/Judean tradition and among themselves, in their efforts to make theological sense out the crisis engendered by the Babylonian destruction of the Temple in 587/6 B.C.E. He begins with the Former Prophets and then turns to each of the Latter Prophets, before concluding with a brief consideration of the means by which the Prophets prepare the reader for the Writings within the framework of the Hebrew Bible as a whole.

In the essay "Psalms and Jewish Biblical Theology," Marc Z. Brettler states that, though there is no consensus about the nature of Jewish biblical theology on the way it differs from "regular" biblical theology, most agree that Jewish Bible theology should use rabbinic models as its basis. As such, a major feature of classical rabbinic interpretation is the *davar aher* (the "alternate opinion")—in other words, the fact that most classic rabbinic texts do not offer a single authoritative interpretation but several alternative views. Thus, in contrast to much "regular" biblical theology, any attempt to construct Jewish biblical theology would not begin by looking for the *Mitte* (center) but would instead relish what has been called polydoxy or polyphony. According to him, the book of Psalms is an ideal starting place for exploring the legitimacy of this perspective, because through superscriptions, form-critical markers, and other features, Psalms is clearly marked as a composite work, coming from various authors and time periods, yet it has been structured and preserved as a single book. By exploring the variations of ideas in Psalms, Brettler argues that a Jewish biblical theology that highlights differences as its central concern has not only rabbinic support but strong support from the Hebrew Bible itself.

Benjamin D. Sommer writes about "Psalm 1 and the Canonical Shaping of Jewish Scripture." He stresses that references to Torah study in Psalm 1 assert the subservience of the Psalms, and by extension all the *Ketuvim*, to the Torah. These references also attempt to define the nature of the book of Psalms: it is not only a collection of prayers, but a book for study. This psalm asserts a particular set of religious values that emphasize study and intellectualization over prayer and spontaneous joy. The psalm implies a judgment on religious leadership, valorizing the sage and priest over the singer and the king. The impact of Psalm 1 on our understanding of the Psalter as a whole becomes especially clear when we compare its attempt to shape the book with other possible introductions and conclusions, such as Psalms 2, 150, or 151. These psalms accentuate the role of the Davidic monarchy or the role of joyous worship rather than study. The questions to which Psalm 1 provides pointed answers continued to be asked later in Judaism, and they play a particularly central role in the midrash on Psalm 1, which notes answers to these questions other than the answers stressed by Psalm 1. This midrash, even when its digressions seem irrelevant to Psalm 1, participates in precisely the debate that Psalm 1 intended to engender. It is only when one views Psalm 1 in relation to Psalms 2 and 150–51 that the midrash turns out to be something other than a series of nonsequiturs. A comparison of Psalm 1 and *Midr. Psalm* 1 provides a vivid example of the way that Jewish Scripture works with Jewish tradition to form a matrix of sacred literature, and only in the context of this matrix is Jewish Scripture sacred.

Moshe Greenberg's "Reflections on Job's Theology" treats the biblical story of a man, Job, who represents the paradigm of piety and integrity founded on happiness with one's children and wealth. However, one day all these are stripped away from Job in a time of utter misfortune. Initially, Job cannot comprehend the moral cause for his disaster after holding God in such great esteem in his life. He begins to view God's moral management as unwarranted and disordered. Job sees no clear relation between just order and the reality of individual destiny. Eventually, he accepts his shift in fortune as an inexplicable evolution of man and finds consolation in his awareness of the complexity of God. Job reasons that no truly righteous man can measure his love for God unless he suffers a great fate: a test of the motives of man. He notes the differences in his outlook on God in times of fortune and misfortune and understands that both represent the work of God, while realizing the limitations of his former viewpoint in his notion of God's nature. In the end, through the character of Job, the idea forms that we must not have total dependence on the erratic nature of moral causality and the doubtful validity for which it stands, but neither may we wholeheartedly deny the force that they represent: a common ground must be found that reveals God's work as eternally reasonable.

"Fear of Annihilation and Eternal Covenant: The Book of Esther in Judaism and Jewish Bible Theology" by Isaac Kalimi states the theological status of a book that is considered one of the strangest in the Hebrew Bible. It briefly reviews the absence of Esther from among ca. 200 Dead Sea biblical manuscripts. However, the absence of the book of Esther among the Dead Sea Scrolls cannot be a model representing the general attitude of all Jews toward it, since the whole Qumran community comprised no more than several hundred members. This small, isolated Jewish community was a marginal minority among the Jewish people in the late Commonwealth. The majority of Jewish people, however, had a very different approach to the book. The absence of God's name from the book of Esther does not mean that the author has no interest in theological issues. On the contrary, his message is intended for Jews in general and for those in the Diaspora in particular—that God is with Israel. Each generation has its "Haman," but God is always there to keep his promise and help Israel, directly or indirectly while acting quietly "behind the curtain." Apparently, Esther's author trusts that God's covenant with Israel is everlasting, for "the Lord . . . is God, the faithful God who maintains *covenant loyalty* with those who love him and keep his commandments to a thousand generations" (Deut 7:9). He holds the prophetic promise of, for instance, Isaiah (Isa 54:9–10, 66:22). Since the existence of the Jewish people is eternal, he believes that the extermination of the Jews by any means or at any time or place is intolerable to God. The author of Esther is confident that "Israel is holy to the Lord, the first fruits of his harvest; all that devour him shall offend: evil shall come upon them" (Jer 2:3). Kalimi concludes that this is the chief theological theme emerging from the book of Esther for everyone, Jews and non-Jews. The story of Esther sends the message that later is expressed by the rabbis in the Passover *Haggadah*. Kalimi evaluates the theological view of Esther against the background of the Jewish reality in the last millennium and concludes with review of the post-Shoah reading of Esther among contemporary Jews.

Peter J. Haas closes this section and the entire volume with his discussion of the book of Daniel, what he calls "The Strange End of Biblical Theology." Haas states that the book of Daniel as an apocalyptic work (particularly chaps. 7–12) stands out as an unusual book to be part of the Jewish Scripture. Although apocalyptic literature does draw on earlier literary forms, its cosmology based on ancient Persian religion (Zoroastrianism) is different from what went before. Despite this fact, the book was accepted as canonical very early on, as evidenced by the Septuagint, the Dead Sea Scrolls, and Josephus. Daniel's inclusion indicates that apocalyptic thinking was part of at least some part of the Judaic community of late Antiquity. Although the book of Daniel came to be accepted as canonical in both the Septuagint and the Tanak/Hebrew Bible, its different placement suggests two different theological perspectives on reading these passages. The Septuagint places the book among the prophets and thus invites us to read Daniel, and Scripture in general, as a prophetic, apocalyptic work looking toward a future consummation of history. This consummation is part of a divine scheme or even a battle between the forces of Good and the forces of Evil. The Hebrew Bible, on the other hand, has "demoted" the book to the Writings, thus marginalizing the apocalyptic character of the whole. This distinction presages the different directions that rabbinic Judaism and early Christianity would eventually follow.

The range of views expressed in the current volume are, of course, the responsibility of their authors. In other words, they do not necessarily represent my own opinion on the topics under review. Nevertheless, it is my hope that the present volume will direct Jewish biblical theology in promising and interesting directions. Hopefully, the studies collected here will stimulate further research and discussion on the topic and attract additional scholars to commit to this enthralling branch of biblical studies.

Part 1

Jewish Bible Theology

Jewish Theologies of Scripture

Frederick E. Greenspahn

The Bible is widely recognized as central to Judaism.[1] According to Franz Rosenzweig, "It is to a book, the Book, that we owe our survival."[2] Therefore, Solomon Schechter spoke of the Bible as Jews' "sole *raison d'être*," while Leo Baeck called it Judaism's "secure and immovable foundation, the permanent element amid changing phenomena."[3] Recently, Isaac Kalimi asserted that "The Bible is the bedrock on which Jewish religion, culture, and literature stand."[4] It is no wonder that Mohammad called Jews the "people of the book (*ahl al-kitab*),"[5] an epithet they have eagerly embraced.

However, characterizing the Bible's role and status within Judaism has proven elusive. There are several reasons for this difficulty. First, modern scholarship has tended to undermine much of the Bible's credibility, while the Oral Law serves as a competing source of authority.[6] At the same time, the Bible has been tainted by Christianity's adoption of what it calls the "Old Testament," despite its universally acknowledged Jewish origin.[7]

In recent years, several thinkers have called on Jews to reappropriate their Bible.[8] In fact, similar efforts have been undertaken for centuries.

1. In detail on this issue, see Isaac Kalimi, "Die Bibel und die klassisch-jüdische Bibelauslegung: Eine Interpretations- und Religionsgeschichtliche Studie," *ZAW* 114 (2002) 594–610, esp. pp. 594–96..

2. Franz Rosenzweig, *Kleinere Schriften* (Berlin: Schocken and Jüdische Buchverlag, 1957) 94, where he also states: "Ein *buch*, das Buch, das wir nicht umsonst auch äußerlich in jahrtausendalter unveränderter Gestalt benutzen . . ."; compare Mordecai Kaplan: "The existential reality of the Jewish people and certainly the religious significance of Its peoplehood, are inconceivable apart from the Bible" (*Judaism without Supernaturalism: The Only Alternative to Orthodoxy and Secularism* [New York: Reconstructionist, 1958] 35).

3. Solomon Schechter, "Higher Criticism—Higher Anti-Semitism," in *Seminary Addresses and Other Papers* (Cincinnati: Ark, 1915; repr., New York: Arno, 1969) 37; Leo Baeck, *The Essence of Judaism* (rev. ed.; New York: Schocken, 1948) 22; F. Rosenzweig described the Bible as "the source and foundation of everything that is alive in Judaism" (*Kleinere Schriften*, 57).

4. Kalimi, "Die Bibel und die klassisch-jüdische Bibelauslegung: Eine Interpretations- und Religionsgeschichtliche Studie," 595.

5. Qur'an 4:153 and 172.

6. See in detail Kalimi, "Die Bibel und die klassisch-jüdische Bibelauslegung," 595–608.

7. See my "Jewish Ambivalence towards the Bible," *HS* 48 (2007) 14–15.

8. Especially Solomon Schechter: "above all . . . it is . . . of supreme importance that

Although individual thinkers do not always fit neatly into one or another category, the results can be arranged in three broad groups. The first encompasses those approaches that emphasize what the Hebrew Bible says, the second is concerned with what it is, while the third category focuses on what it does. In other words, some writers focus on the Bible's contents, others on its metaphysical status, and still others on its function. Each of these includes thinkers and schools of thought from a variety of epochs and locales. We will, therefore, draw on a wide range of sources to characterize each one, without assuming that everything said by the writers cited here belongs under the same heading.

THE CONTEXT OF SCRIPTURE

Easily the most familiar Jewish attitude toward the Bible considers it a conduit for revelation: what matters is what it says. As Rashi's grandson Samuel ben Meir (Rashbam) put it, "the Torah's main purpose is to teach us and to inform us by means of the straightforward meaning as well as lore and law." [9] Over a thousand years earlier, Aristeas called the Bible God's "oracles," expressing a view that has been repeated since Antiquity. [10]

Most often, Jews have taken the content of Scripture to be its legal provisions. In Philo's words, "The sacred scriptures are not monuments of knowledge and of vision but are the divine commands and the divine words." [11] Similarly, *Tiqqunei Zohar* explained that, "without the command-

---

we re-possess ourselves of our Scriptures. The Torah is, as the Rabbis express it, 'the bride of the congregation of Jacob,' but to acquire it through the medium of Christian commentaries means to live by proxy, and never to gain the spiritual nearness which made it so easy for our ancestors to die and even to live for it" (*Studies in Judaism* [2nd Series; Philadelphia: Jewish Publication Society, 1908] 200; idem, *Seminary Addresses and Other Papers*, 3–5 and 38. Others who have expressed a similar concern include Heinrich Graetz ("Zur hebräischen Sprachkunde und Bibel Exegese," *MGWJ* 10 [1861] 21), Benno Jacob (Robert S. Schine, *Jewish Thought Adrift: Max Wiener [1882–1950]* [BJS 259; Atlanta: Scholars Press, 1992] 15), Kaufmann Kohler (*Hebrew Union College and Other Addresses* [Cincinnati: Ark, 1910] 22–24), Max Margolis ("The Jewish Defense of the Bible," *Bnai Brith News* [June, 1915] as cited in Leonard J. Greenspoon, "On the Jewishness of Modern Jewish Biblical Scholarship: The Case of Max L. Margolis," *Judaism* 39 [1990] 82, 83 n. 2), Franz Rosenzweig ("Zeit Ists . . . ," *Kleinere Schriften*, 71), Felix Perles (*Mahu Lanu Mada Ha-Miqra* [Jerusalem: n.p., 1924] 6 and 12), Cyrus Adler (Ira Robinson, "Cyrus Adler: President of the Jewish Theological Seminary, 1915–1940," in *Tradition Renewed: A History of the Jewish Theological Seminary* [ed. Jack Wertheimer; New York: Jewish Theological Seminary, 1997] 1:128), and Mordecai M. Kaplan (*Judaism as a Civilization: Toward an Reconstruction of American Jewish Life* [New York: Schocken, 1967] 549 n. 6).

9. *Commentary* on Gen 37:2.

10. Aristeas 177; cf. Philo, *Moses* 2.35 (LCL 6; Cambridge: Harvard University Press, 1929) 542–43, §188; cf. *De Posteritate Caini* 43.143 (LCL 2; Cambridge: Harvard University Press, 1935) 412–13.

11. Philo, *Quaestiones et Solutiones in Genesin*, 4.140 (LCL sup.; 421–22); therefore, God is identified as "legislator (*nomothetes*)" in *De Fuga et Inventione* 13.66 and 18.99 (LCL 5; 46–47 and 64–65) and *Moses* 2.8 §48 (pp. 472–73); cf. Joseph B. Soloveitchik, *Halakhic Man* (Philadelphia:

ments, the Torah is not the Torah of God."[12] Drawing on Spinoza's view that "the whole Mosaic Law had reference merely to the government of the Jews and merely temporal advantages," Moses Mendelssohn described the Bible as "a book of laws," albeit laws that he believed to be binding solely on Jews.[13]

This approach has a rich and ancient pedigree. It is already apparent in the Septuagint, where the Hebrew word "Torah," which carries a broad range of meanings, is consistently translated with the Greek word *nomos* ('law').[14] The classic expression of this perspective is found in the *Mechilta de Rabbi Ishmael*:

> Why were not the Ten Commandments said at the beginning of the Torah? They told a parable: What does this resemble? someone who entered a country. He said to them, "Let me rule over you." They said to him, "What good have you done for us that you should rule over us?" What did he do? He built the wall for them, brought water in for them, fought wars for them; then he said to them, "Let me rule over you." They said to him, "Yes, yes." Thus, God brought Israel out of Egypt, split the sea for them, brought the manna down for them, brought up the well for them, brought the quail for them, made war with Amalek for them. Then He said to them, "Let me rule over you," and they said to Him, "Yes, yes."[15]

According to this passage, the stories with which the book of Exodus (and, more broadly, the Bible) opens are there to justify the laws that follow. In other words, the Bible's main purpose is to enumerate God's commandments; everything else is subordinate to that goal.[16] As Saadia Gaon explained,

> God has provided us with summary accounts of all that has transpired in order that we might thereby be put into a fit condition for obeying

---

12. *Tiqqunim* 94a as cited by Steven T. Katz, "Mysticism and the Interpretation of Sacred Scripture," in *Mysticism and Sacred Scripture* (ed. Steven T. Katz; New York: Oxford University Press, 2000) 33; that is also the assumption behind R. Zeira's remark in *Ruth Rab.* 2:14.

13. Moses Mendelssohn, *Jerusalem, or On Religious Power and Judaism* (trans. Allan Arkush; Hanover, MA: University Press of New England, 1983) 99; and Eva Jospe, ed., *Moses Mendelssohn: Selections from His Writings* (New York: Viking, 1975) 126; cf. "A Theological-Political Treatise" [part 5] in *The Chief Works of Benedict de Spinoza* (New York: Dover, 1951) 1:76; and Isaac Albalag as described by Julius Guttmann, *Philosophies of Judaism: The History of Jewish Philosophy from Biblical Times to Franz Rosenzweig* (New York: Holt, Rinehart and Winston, 1964) 201.

14. Stephen Westerholm, "Torah, *nomos*, and law: A Question of 'Meaning,'" *Studies in Religion / Sciences Religieuses* 15 (1986) 33 n. 28.

15. *Mek. Yitro* §5 (ed. H. S. Horowitz; Jerusalem: Bamberger & Wahrman, 1960) 219.

16. Cf. Philo, *De Opificio Mundi* 1 (LCL 1:6–7) and *Moses* 2.51 (pp. 472–73), *Midr. Tanḥ.* Genesis 11 (ed. Buber, Vilna; reprinted Jerusalem: Ortsah, 1964) 4a, and Rashi at Gen 1:1.

Him. These accounts were incorporated by Him into His Holy Book. He attached to them also His precepts and appended to the latter a statement of the rewards He would mete out for their observance.[17]

Although widespread within the Jewish tradition, this view is not the only one, even among those who emphasize the Bible's contents.[18] For example, Joseph ibn Kaspi saw Scripture as a vehicle for achieving intellectual perfection, (שלימות השכל),[19] while Hasdai Crescas considered it an avenue to eternal happiness.[20] Others have disagreed. According to Samuel David Luzzatto, "The purpose of the Divine Torah was not to impart scientific knowledge but rather to train the steps of the people in the paths of righteousness" התורה האלהית אשר אין מגמתה ללמד את העם חכמה ודעת אלא (להדריכם במעגלי צדק).[21] Gersonides reflected a similar perspective when he observed that "the Torah guides us towards the [moral] perfection in many of the commandments."[22] Saadia Gaon would have agreed; he noted that the Bible's stories describe behavior that we should strive to emulate.[23]

A broader version of this approach draws on the mishnaic statement that "everything is in it" (הפוך בה והפוך בה דכולא בה, *m. 'Abot* 5:13) to infer that the Torah contains all significant truths. In the words of Judah Messer Leon, "Every science, every rationally apprehended truth that any treatise may contain, is present in our Holy Torah and in the book of those who

17. Saadia Gaon, *The Book of Beliefs and Opinions* (trans. Samuel Rosenblatt; New Haven, CT: Yale University Press, 1948) 3.6, pp. 154–55.

18. According to Jakob J. Petuchowski, 19th-century Jewish theologians debated whether the Torah should be understood as *Gesetz* or *Lehre* (*Ever Since Sinai: A Modern View of Torah* [New York: Scribe, 1961] 11).

19. *Mishneh Kesef* (ed. Isaac Last; Pressberg: Alcalay, 1905; repr. Jerusalem: Sifriyat Meqorot, 1970) 2; cf. Judah Messer Leon, *The Book of the Honeycomb's Flow, Sēpher Nōpheth Ṣūphim* (ed. Isaac Rabinowitz; Ithaca: Cornell University Press, 1983) 1:13 §13, pp. 142–45. Samuel ibn Tibbon rejected this position (Georges Vajda, "An Analysis of the Ma'amar Yiqqawu ha-Mayim by Samuel b. Judah ibn Tibbon," *JJS* 10 [1959] 141 n. 11).

20. Guttmann, *Philosophies of Judaism*, 235.

21. Luzzatto, *Ha-Mishtadel* (Vienna: Il Busch, 1847) 1 at Lev 1:1; cf. Avraham Kuk, *Iggerot Ha-Reayah* (Jerusalem: Mosad Harav Kook, 1985) 1:163; and Yeshayahu Leibowitz, *Yahadut, Am Yehudi, U-Medinat Yisrael* (Tel Aviv: Schocken, 1979) 342, 345.

22. Menahem Kellner, "Introduction to the Commentary on Song of Songs Composed by the Sage Levi ben Gershon: An Annotated Translation," in *From Ancient Israel to Modern Judaism: Intellect in Quest of Understanding—Essays in Honor of Marvin Fox* (4 vols.; ed. Jacob Neusner, Ernest S. Frerichs, and Nahum M. Sarna; BJS 159; Atlanta: Scholars Press, 1989) 2:195.

23. Erwin I. J. Rosenthal, "Saadya Gaon: An Appreciation of His Biblical Exegesis," *BJRL* 27 (1942-43) 177. Others who have seen it as a book of ethics include Joseph Albo ("there is not a word and not a narrative in the law of Moses which is not essential either to inculcate an idea or moral, or to explain one of the commandments," *Sefer ha-Ikkarim* (*Book of Principles*) III 25 [ed. Isaac Husik; Philadelphia: Jewish Publication Society, 1946] 3:221), Maimonides (*The Guide of the Perplexed* 3:50 [trans. Shlomo Pines; Chicago: University of Chicago Press, 1963] 613–14), and Nahmanides (e.g., Gen 9:26), although he noted that it is possible to be "a scoundrel within the letter of the Torah" (נבל ברשות התורה; at Lev 19:2).

speak by the Holy Spirit. . . . all the sciences and truths of reason, including all that were humanly attained, for everything is either latent therein or plainly stated."[24] Some have even gone so far as to assert that the Bible itself is everything.[25]

Reaching this position obviously requires looking beyond the text's literal sense. As Leo Baeck explained, "It was discovered again and again that the words of this Book said more than they appeared to say."[26] Such a position is almost inevitable for those who take the Bible seriously, given the breadth of material in it. As the Zohar points out, "What does it matter to us whether the ark rested in this or in another place?"[27] And so Jews have expended considerable effort and developed countless techniques to find the significance of biblical passages that, at first glance, seem trivial. Sometimes this has involved treating the Bible as if it were in a kind of code, reading phrases as acrostics (*notarikon*) or calculating the numerical value of their letters (*gematria*) or even the intervals between them.[28] One mystical tradition holds that the Bible's real meaning lies not in the letters but in the spaces surrounding them.[29]

Kabbalistic tradition has been particularly energetic in such undertakings. According to one rabbi, "The scroll of the Torah is not vocalized, because it includes all the senses and all the profound paths. All of these may be expounded in each letter," while early Hasidism taught that "the holy

24. *The Book of the Honeycomb's Flow*, 1:13 §§12–13, pp. 142–43. As Abraham J. Heschel put it, the Bible is "an ocean of meaning" (*God in Search of Man* [New York: Farrar, Straus & Cudahy, 1955] 241; Emil L. Fackenheim noted that it includes "an inexhaustible treasure of rational truths and religious doctrines which are simultaneously connected with the laws that they form but one entity" (*The Jewish Bible after the Holocaust: A Re-reading* [Bloomington: Indiana University Press, 1990] x). Similarly, Walter Kaufmann observes that "[w]hat the Jews have traditionally sought in the Torah was not merely a way of life nor truths but—this is scarcely an exaggeration—everything" (*Critique of Religion and Philosophy* [New York: Harper, 1958] 191).

25. Cf. Nahmanides ("הכתוב יכלול הכל" in *Sefer Ha-Mitzvot Leha-Rambam im Hassagot Ha-Ramban* (*Maimonides Book of the Commandments*) (ed. Chaim Dov Chavel; Jerusalem: Mossad HaRav Kook, 1981) *Ha-Shoresh Ha-Sheni*, 44. Similar views have been expressed by Joseph Gikatilla (Torah is "the form of the mystical world," as quoted in Gershom Scholem, "The Name of God and the Linguistic Theory of the Kabbala," *Diogenes* 80 [1972] 180), Gersonides ("Behold, the book that God wrote [Exod 32:32] is all of reality" והנה הספר שכתב השם הוא [המציאו' בכללו], *Peirush al Ha-Torah al Derekh Biur* [New York: Sirkin, 1958; orig. Venice, 1547] 113b), and the Vilna Gaon as quoted by Aryeh Morgenstern, *Messianism and the Settlement of Eretz-Israel* (Jerusalem: Yad Ben Zvi, 1985) 96 [Hebrew].

26. Leo Baeck, *This People Israel: The Meaning of Jewish Existence* (New York: Holt, Rinehart, and Winston, 1964) 59.

27. *Zohar* 3:149b; cf. *b. Hul.* 60b: "There are many verses [e.g., Deut 2:23 and Num 21:26] which to all appearances ought to be burnt like the books of the heretics, but are really essential elements in the Torah."

28. Michael Drosnin, *The Bible Codes* (New York: Simon and Schuster, 1997).

29. Cf. Gershom G. Scholem, "The Meaning of the Torah in Jewish Mysticism," *On the Kabbalah and Its Symbolism* (New York: Schocken, 1969) 49–50, 82.

Torah was created as an incoherent jumble of letters" (כתערובות אותיות).[30] According to the Zohar, "the Torah consists entirely of [God's] Holy name; in fact, every word written there consists of and contains that Holy Name."[31]

The diversity of these positions, which range from law to science and theosophy to ethics, notwithstanding, all see the Bible's contents as what matters. That is a familiar and therefore comfortable position for both those who accept what the Bible says and those who do not, but it is not the only way Jewish tradition has approached the Bible.

THE STATUS OF SCRIPTURE

For many Jews, the Bible's significance lies somewhere other than in its contents. One way in which this has been achieved is by emphasizing its role. For example, the Bible has sometimes been thought of as substituting for the Jerusalem Temple. Aaron ben Asher compared its three-part structure to that of the Temple.[32] Some medieval biblical manuscripts are actually called מקדשיה.[33] In a similar vein, Samson Raphael Hirsch and Heinrich Heine described the Bible as the Jews' spiritual and, fortunately, portable homeland.[34] Even more dramatically, both the ancient Therapeutae and medieval mystics conceived of it as being alive.[35]

30. First quotation: *Responsa of David b. Solomon ibn Abi Zimra* (*Teshuvot Ha-Radbaz*) vol. 3, #643, p. 43c, quoted by José Faur, *Golden Doves with Silver Dots: Semiotics and Textuality in Rabbinic Tradition* (Bloomington: Indiana University Press, 1986) 137. Second quotation: *Ge'ulat Yisrael* 1d–2a, cited by Gershom G. Scholem, "Meaning of the Torah in Jewish Mysticism," 76.

31. *Zohar* 2:87a, 90b; 3:36a, 80b, 89b, 265b; cf. 73a, 159a, and 298b. According to Nahmanides, "the writing was continuous, without a break between words, so that it could be read as divine names or as we normally read it—concerning the Torah and the commandment" (*Commentary to the Pentateuch* [ed. Chaim Chavel; Jerusalem: Mossad Harav Kook, 1991] introduction, 1:7.

32. N. Wieder, "'Sanctuary' as a Metaphor for Scripture," *JJS* 8 (1957) 167; cf. Profiat Duran, *Maase Efod* (Vienna: Holzwarth, 1865; repr. Jerusalem: Makor, 1970) 11. In fact, the destruction of the Jerusalem Temple was probably a significant factor in elevating the Bible's status, so that it could replace the Temple as Judaism's "sacred center" (William Scott Green, "Romancing the Tome: Rabbinic Hermeneutics and the Theory of Literature," *Semeia* 40 [1987] 155).

33. Richard Gottheil, "Some Hebrew Manuscripts in Cairo," *JQR* 17 (1905) 615, 649; and Wieder, "'Sanctuary' as a Metaphor for Scripture," 166; cf. Abraham ibn Ezra, *Moznei Leshon ha-Qodesh* (Ophibeck: Tsvi Hirsch Segal Shpitz, 1891) 1a (שהם ספרי הקדש); and CD 7:15–16 (ספרי התורה הם סוכת המלך).

34. Samson Raphael Hirsch, *Horeb: A Philosophy of Jewish Laws and Observances* (London: Soncino, 1962) 571 (§714), Heinrich Heine ("ein portatives Vaterland") in "Gestandnisse," *Sämtliche Schriften* (ed. Klaus Briegleb; Munich: Hanser, 1975) 6/1:483; also "Aus den Memoiren des Herren von Schnabelwopski," ibid., 1:552. Cf. G. Steiner, "Our Homeland: The Text," *Salmagundi* 66 (1985) 4–25. According to Fritz Bamberger, Leopold Zunz makes a similar point in his *Gottesdienstlichen Vortraege*, p. 322 ("Zunz's Conception of History: A Study of the Philosophic Elements in Early Science of Judaism," *PAAJR* 11 [1941] 18).

35. Philo, *De Vita Contemplativa* 10:78 (LCL 9; 160–61) and *Sefer Ha-Temunah*, according

Genesis Rabbah provides the classic expression of Scripture's importance as lying in what it is rather than what it says when it opens with the statement that:

> The Torah said, "I was the working tool of the Holy One, blessed be He." Normally, when a mortal king builds a palace, he does not build it by himself but with an architect, and the architect does not build it by himself but has plans and diagrams so that he knows how to arrange the rooms and how to arrange the wicket door. Thus, the Holy One, blessed be He, looked in the Torah and created the world. The Torah says, "In the beginning God created" (Gen 1:1); "beginning" (ראשית) refers to the Torah, as in the verse "the Lord made me as the beginning (ראשית) of His way" (Prov 8:22).[36]

Identifying what the book of Proverbs calls "wisdom" (חכמה) with the Torah, the rabbis took the Bible's statement that God had made wisdom as "the beginning of His way" to mean that the Torah was the first thing He created. They then explained that God used the Torah—which, after all, opens with a description of the creative process—as a kind of manual for making the world.[37] They even correlated this with the Bible's opening phrase, which they interpreted as meaning that God had created the world by means of (ב) Torah (ראשית).[38]

---

to which certain scriptural verses "are the limbs of the body, and the *sefirot* are in a human image" (p. 25a, as cited by Elliot R. Wolfson, *Through a Speculum That Shines: Vision and Imagination in Medieval Jewish Mysticism* [Princeton, NJ: Princeton University Press, 1994] 329); cf. Abraham Joshua Heschel, *Israel, An Echo of Eternity* (New York: Farrar, Straus and Giroux, 1969) 46.

36. *Gen. Rab.* 1:1; cf. 1:4, 8; and Philo, *De Opificio Mundi* 4 §§16–20 (LCL 1; pp. 14–17), where God created the world from a pattern.

37. *M. 'Abot* 3:14; *b. Pĕsaḥ.* 54a; *b. Ned.* 39b; *Gen. Rab.* 1:4; *Exod. Rab.* 30:9; *Pĕsiq. Rab Kah.* 12 (ed. B. Mandelbaum; New York: Jewish Theological Seminary of America, 1987) 222; cf. 4Q525 2 ii 3–4; Philo, *De Virtutibus* 62 (LCL 8; 200–201); *Midr. Tanḥ.* Genesis 5 (ed. Buber, p. 2b); as well as Plato, *Timaeus* 28–29 (LCL 7; pp. 48–53). *Tanḥ. Pĕqudē* 3, p. 136a and *Pirqe deRabbi El.* §11 find support for this by taking "we" in Gen 1:26 to be a reference to God and Torah. *2 (Slavonic) Enoch* 30:18 asserts that wisdom was commanded to create man (James H. Charlesworth, *The Old Testament Pseudepigrapha* [Garden City, NY: Doubleday, 1983] 1:150–51), while according to the *Zohar*, the Torah created the angels and all the worlds (3:152a). A medieval *piyyut* describes how God sought Torah's permission to create world (Leon J. Weinberger, *Jewish Hymnography: A Literary History* [London: Littman Library of Jewish Civilization, 1998] 69). According to one tradition, the Torah had been made 2,000 years before creation (*Gen. Rab.* 8:2; *Cant. Rab.* 5:15 §1; and *Tg. Neof.* Gen 3:24). *Pirqe R. El.* §3 identifies Torah's name as תושיה ("wisdom"); cf. *Gen. Rab.* 17:5, 44:17; and *Tanḥ.* Genesis 1 (Jerusalem: Lewin-Epstein) 5a. The introduction to the Gospel of John makes a similar claim regarding Christ (John 1:1); cf. Luke 11:48–49, where a statement attributed to Jesus by Matt 23:34 is attributed to God's *word*; see also 1 Cor 1:24, 30; 2:7; Col 2:3. Islamic tradition ascribes a similar role to the Qur'an.

38. *Gen. Rab.* 1:1; *Frg. Tg.* and *Tg. Neof.* Gen 1:1; cf. *Exod. Rab.* 47:4; and *Midr. Tanḥ.* (ed. Buber) Genesis 5, p. 2b.

If the Torah was involved in the process of creation, then it could not have originated at Sinai, since, according to the Bible, that took place some 26 generations later.[39] What happened there was the transmission of that cosmic "Ur-Torah" (תורה כלולה) from heaven to earth.[40] This idea, too, is rooted in Wisdom teachings that are attested in the intertestamental period.[41]

A Torah that had existed since the beginning of time and participated in the creation of the world would be of universal importance. And, indeed, the rabbis taught that the reason it had been revealed in the wilderness was so that no one nation could claim it.[42] They even said that it was to have been proclaimed in 4 languages, or maybe 70, so that all mankind could benefit from it.[43] However, Adam's sin forced God to reevaluate this plan, giving it to the descendants of Abraham, who had observed the commandments before they had even been revealed.[44] Or, perhaps, it was only after all the other nations had turned it down that God held Mount Sinai over Israel's heads with the warning, "If you accept the Torah it will be well with you, but if not, you will find your grave there."[45]

Yet another tradition suggests that the nations of the world were not the only ones who had missed an opportunity to possess God's Torah. The

---

39. *B. Šabb.* 88b, *Gen. Rab.* 21:9; *Lev Rab.* 19:1; and *'Abot R. Nat.* A 31. The tradition that the Torah was created 974 generations before the world rests on the reference to "the word God commanded for 1,000 generations" (Ps 105:8 = 1 Chr 16:15) in light of the 26 generations from Adam to Moses.

40. E.g., *b. Zebaḥ.* 116a; cf. the reference to Torah as כלי חמדה (*m. 'Abot* 3:14; *'Abot R. Nat.* A 39) and חמדה גנוזה and חמדה טובה (*b. Šabb.* 88b; and *Cant. Rab.* 5:11 §1). Kabbalistic sources distinguished Moses' physical Torah (תורה דבריאה) from the perfect Torah (תורה דאצילות); Gershom Scholem, "The Meaning of the Torah in Jewish Mysticism," 48–49, 66–67; cf. also תורה קדומה (Barbara A. Holdrege, *Veda and Torah: Transcending the Textuality of Scripture* [Albany: State University of New York Press, 1996] 209). According to Shabbatai Zvi, these were exact opposites of each other (Joseph Dan, *Gershom Scholem and the Mystical Dimension of Jewish History* (New York: New York University Press, 1988) 301–3).

41. Sir 24:1–23; *1 En.* 42:1, Bar 3:24–4:1; cf. Wis 9:9–10.

42. *Mek. Haḥodesh* §§1, 5 (ed. H. S. Horowitz, pp. 205, 222). The *Sifra* interprets 2 Sam 7:19 ("this is the law of mankind") as evidence that it had not been intended just for priests, Levites, or even Israelites, but for all of mankind (*Aḥarei Mot* 13:13).

43. *Sifre Num. Korah.* §119; *Sifre Deut* 343; *b. Šabb.* 88b; *Midr. Tanḥ. Exod* 25 p. 69b; *Yitro* 11 p. 96a; *Midr. Tanḥ.* (ed. Buber) *Exod* 22 p. 7a; *Exod Rab.* 28:6.

44. *M. Qidd.* 4:14; *Gen. Rab.* 24:5; cf. *Pirqe R. El.* §12.

45. *Mek. Haḥodesh* §5 (ed. H. S. Horowitz, p. 221); *Sifre Deut* 343; *b. 'Abod. Zar.* 2b; *b. Šabb.* 88a; *Num. Rab.* 14:10; *Lam. Rab.* 3:1.1; *Pesiq. Rab Kah.* 12 (ed. B. Mandelbaum, pp. 449–50); *Pirqe R. El.* §41; cf. *Tg. Ps-J.* Exod 19:17, where the Hebrew has ההר בתחתית ויתיצבו. The belief in the Bible's universal relevance has persisted to the present day, as when Solomon Schechter described it as the Jews' gift to humanity ("Higher Criticism: Higher Anti-Semitism," 37) and the Proclamation of the State of Israel asserts, "The Land of Israel was the birthplace of the Jewish people. . . . Here they wrote and gave the Bible to the World" (*The Jew in the Modern World* [ed. Paul Mendes-Flohr and Jehuda Reinharz; 2nd ed.; New York, Oxford University Press, 1995] 629).

angels had wanted it left in heaven but were forced to give it up when God pointed out that its teachings did not pertain to them.[46] In fact, the Torah itself wanted to stay there but eventually descended, to be accepted by Moses as the heavens wept.[47]

The Torah's role in the universe did not stop with creation. Several rabbinic traditions credit it with keeping the world from reverting to chaos.[48] As Simeon ben Zemach Duran explained, "This round world is suspended in space and has nothing to rest on except the breadth of Torah study from the mouths of students."[49] Or, in the words of Hayim of Volozhin, "Were the entire world, from one extremity to the other, to be voided, even for a single moment, from our study and consideration of the Torah, in that moment all the worlds, upper and lower, would be utterly destroyed—Heaven forefend."[50] Thus, the Jewish people are the unique bearers of an object of cosmic status.[51]

Scripture's lofty metaphysical status first became evident toward the end of the biblical period, when it was mentioned in contexts that had earlier been reserved for God. For example, Chronicles reports God's expectation that Solomon's descendants walk in *God's Torah* (2 Chr 6:16), although its source in 1 Kgs 8:25 had said that they should walk before God.[52] In such an environment, it is not surprising that the Torah was later equated with God himself, albeit usually with qualifications, as when the Zohar states that "[h]e who is occupied with Torah, it is *as if* he were occupied with the Holy One, blessed be He."[53] Similarly, Joseph of Hamadan wrote that "The Torah, *as it were*, is the shadow of the Holy One, blessed be He . . . and inasmuch as the Torah is the form of God He commanded us to study

---

46. *Cant. Rab.* 8:11.2; cf. *b. Ber.* 28b; *b. Šabb.* 88b–89a; *Deut. Rab.* 8:2.

47. *Pesiq. Rab.* §20 (ed. M. Friedmann, 95a).

48. Cf. *Cant. Rab.* 1:9.6; 7:1.1. According to *b. Šabb.* 88a–b, Israelite acceptance of the Torah avoided the world's reversion to chaos (cf. *Gen. Rab.* 8:2; *Deut Rab.* 8:5), while other accounts report that God held off creating the world until he was sure that it would be accepted (*b. Šabb.* 88a; *b. 'Abod. Zar.* 3a, 5a; *Exod. Rab.* 40:1, 47:4; *Deut. Rab.* 8:5; *Midr. Tanḥ. Genesis* 1:1 (ed. Buber, p. 5b), cf. *Pesiq. Rab.* §21 (ed. M. Friedmann, 100a).

49. Judah Goldin, *The Living Talmud* (New York: New American Library, 1957) 47.

50. *Nefesh Ḥayim* 4:11, as quoted by Moshe Hallamish, *An Introduction to the Kabbalah* (Albany: State University of New York Press, 1999) 212.

51. *Sifra Beḥuqotay* 8:10 (ed. I. H. Weiss; Vienna: Schlossberg, 1862; reprinted New York: Om, 1946) 112c.

52. Similarly postexilic texts speak of inquiring of God's Torah where preexilic texts had spoken of inquiring of God (e.g., Hos 10:12 and Ezra 7:10)—faith in God becomes faith in His commandments (Exod 14:31 and Ps 119:66); cf. Isa 2:3 and Mic 4:2, where Torah is parallel to *debar yhwh*, and Sir 32:18, where *'ēl* is parallel to *tôrâ*.

53. *Zohar* 3:9b (כל מאן דאשתדל באורייתא כאלו אחיד בקב״ה, emphasis added); cf. 3:89b and R. Solomon Alkabes, as cited by Moshe Idel, *Kabbalah, New Perspectives* (New Haven, CT: Yale University Press, 1988) 245.

it so that we may know the pattern of the upper form."[54] Elsewhere, it is described as God's cloak, which cannot be separated from divine substance "like the grasshopper whose clothing is part of itself."[55] Judah Ḥayyat even said that the Torah is "the image of the Holy One, blessed be He," while the *Sefer haYiḥud* asserts that "All the letters of the Torah . . . are the shape of God."[56]

In the end, the line separating God from the Torah sometimes disappeared altogether. According to the Zohar, "Torah is the Holy One,"[57] which Menahem Recanati explained as meaning that "God is nothing outside of the Torah, neither is the Torah something outside of God."[58]

Although Franz Rosenzweig warned about idolizing the book (*Buch Vergötzung*),[59] such ideas have persisted, particularly in theological systems influenced by Kabbalah, where the "real" Torah is often identified with one or another of the heavenly emanations (*sefirot*). Thus, the primordial Torah is described as the linguistic expression of the *Ein Sof*, while the written Torah is identified with the *sefirah tiferet* (or *ḥesed*, according to the *Sefer Bahir*) and the Oral Torah with *malkhut* (= *shekhinah*).[60]

Sometimes the Bible is even elevated above God. Followers of Kabbalah are not the only ones to expound such ideas.[61] Although most con-

54. *Sefer Taʿamei haMitzvot* (ed. Meir, p. 58), as translated by Elliot R. Wolfson, *Through a Speculum That Shines: Vision and Imagination in Medieval Jewish Mysticism* (Princeton, NJ: Princeton University Press, 1994) 377 (emphasis added). R. Shemaiah ben Isaac (XII) taught that "God created man in his own image, this [image] being the Torah, which is the shadow of God, blessed be He" (*Sefer Ṣeror Ḥayyim*, 198a, as cited by Moshe Idel, *Kabbalah: New Perspectives* (New Haven, CT: Yale University Press, 1988) 247.

55. Gershom Scholem, *Kabbalah* (New York: New American Library, 1978) 132; cf. *Tanḥ. Va-Yelekh* 2 regarding the Torah's being written on God's arm (cf. Rashi at *b. ʿErub.* 21a s.v. *esrim*).

56. Judah Ḥayyat: Commentary to *Maʿarechet HaElohut*, 95a as cited by Elliot R. Wolfson, *Through a Speculum That Shines*, 377 n. 180. *Sefer haYiḥud*: Moshe Idel, "Infinities of Torah in Kabbalah," in Geoffrey H. Hartman and Sanford Budick, *Midrash and Literature* (New Haven, CT: Yale University Press, 1986) 145.

57. *Zohar* 2:60a (ואין תורה אלא קב״ה).

58. הקדוש ברוך הוא יתברך אינו צד אחד בלתי התורה, ואין התורה חוץ ממנו ואינו דבר חוץ מן התורה. על כן אמרו חכמי הקבלה כי הקדוש ברוך הוא יתברך שמו הוא התורה (*Taʿamei haMitzvot*, 3a as quoted by Isaiah Tishby, *Mishnat Ha-Zohar* [3rd ed.; Jerusalem: Bialik Institute, 1971] 1:145. Moses Hayim Luzzatto expanded this equation, asserting that "the Holy One, blessed be He, and the Torah, and Israel are one" (cf. Isaiah Tishby, *Studies in Kabbalah and Its Branches: Researches and Sources* [Jerusalem: Magnes, 1993] 950–51 [Hebrew]); cf. *b. Ber.* 8a and David Klinghoffer's heading, "No Torah, No God," in "What Do American Jews Believe? A Symposium," *Commentary* 102 (August 1996) 55b.

59. *Kleinere Schriften*, 150; cf. Leibowitz, *Yahadut, Am Yehudi, u-Medinat Yisrael*, 347.

60. Gershom Scholem, *Kabbalah* (New York: Quadrangle, 1974) 132; and *On the Kabbalah and Its Symbolism*, 49; for *Sefer Bahir* §136, see Elliot Wolfson, "Female Imaging of the Torah: From Literary Metaphor to Religious Symbol," in *From Ancient Israel to Modern Judaism: Intellect in Quest of Understanding, Essays in Honor of Marvin Fox* (Atlanta: Scholars Press, 1989) 289.

61. Cf. Edmond Jabès, *The Book of Yukel, Return to the Book* (Middletown, CT: Wesleyan University Press, 1976) p. 231 ("The invisible form of the book is the legible body of God"); Emmanuel Levinas, "Loving the Torah More Than God," in *Difficult Freedom, Essays on Judaism*

spicuous in Elie Wiesel's accounts of God being indicted for violating Scripture, [62] the roots of this theme lie deep within Jewish tradition. The famous talmudic story about the oven of Aɔnai uses Deuteronomy's statement "It is not in heaven" (30:12) to place Scripture above direct communication from God. [63] In other words, the Bible (granting its divine origin) takes on a life and authority of its own.

These doctrines receive physical expression in the way Jews treat their Scripture. The cabinet in which Torah scrolls are kept originated as a portable box that was placed in a niche in the sanctuary wall during worship. [64] Such niches are a common feature in the holy buildings of several religious traditions, where they typically housed the statues or cultic objects that served as the focal point of worship. [65] In other words, the Torah occupies the architectural space historically reserved for idols. It is even treated in much the way that "idols" were—adorned and carried around in dramatic procession. [66]

This point is reinforced by the verses that are recited as the Torah scroll appears during synagogue worship, which typically invoke God rather than the scroll—e.g., Ps 86:8 ("There is none like You among the gods, O LORD, and there are no deeds like Yours"), Ps 145:13 ("Your kingship is an eternal

---

(Baltimore: Johns Hopkins University Press, 1990) 142–45; and Jacques Derrida, *Writing and Difference* (Chicago: University of Chicago Press, 1978) 102.

62. E.g., *Ani Maamin: A Song Lost and Found Again* (New York: Random House, 1973) 54–57.

63. *B. B. Meṣ.* 59b; more precisely, Scripture's meaning is said to be dependent on majority rabbinic vote, based on Deut 30:12. The tradition that nothing of the Torah was left in heaven is expressed in *Deut. Rab.* 8:6; *Tg. Neof.* and *Frg. Tg.* Deut 30:12; cf. *b. Tem.* 16a.

64. An engraving from the ancient synagogue at Capernaum shows the ark on wheels (Erwin R. Goodenough, "The Problem of Method: Symbols from Jewish Cult," in *Jewish Symbols in the Greco-Roman Period* [New York: Bollingen Foundation, 1954] 4:115; cf. Rachel Hachlili, "The Niche and the Ark in Ancient Synagogues," *BASOR* 223 [1976] 49–50).

65. Lee I. Levine, *The Ancient Synagogue: The First Thousand Years* (New Haven, CT: Yale University Press, 2000) 136.

66. Cf. S. Morenz, *Egyptian Religion* (Ithaca, NY: Cornell University Press, 1973) 88; A. L. Oppenheim, *Ancient Mesopotamia: Portrait of a Dead Civilization* (Chicago: University of Chicago Press, 1964) 188–93; and Karel van der Toorn, "The Iconic Book: Analogies between the Babylonian Cult of Images and the Veneration of the Torah," in *The Image and the Book: Iconic Cults, Aniconism, and the Rise of Book Religion in Israel and the Ancient Near East* (ed. Karel van der Toorn; Leuven: Peeters, 1997) 233. Sikhs decorate their holy book, the Adi Granth, and carry it in celebratory procession (Pashaura Singh, *The Guru Granth Sahib: Canon, Meaning, and Authority* [New Delhi: Oxford University Press, 2000] 278). It is also called the *Guru* Granth Sahib because it is regarded as their teacher (guru), indeed, the last in the line of founding authorities. As the embodiment of God's teachings, the Torah is also a teacher of sorts. Although "idols" are not exactly gods, the distinction is not without ambiguity; cf. Frederick E. Greenspahn, "Syncretism and Idolatry in the Bible," *VT* 54 (2004) 481–83. As van der Toorn observes, "Theoretically, god and image are not one. . . . In the actual cult, however, the distinction between god and image tended to blur ("The Iconic Book," p. 235). According to 1 Macc 3:48, Jews "opened the book of the law to inquire into those matters about which the Gentiles were consulting the images of their idols."

kingship, Your dominion is for all generations"), Exod 15:18 ("the LORD will reign forever and ever"), and Ps 29:11 ("May the LORD grant strength to His people; may the LORD bless His people with peace"). Most dramatic of all is the recitation of Deut 6:4 ("Hear O Israel, the LORD our God, the LORD is one") as the scroll is removed from the ark, followed by "Our God is one; great is our lord, holy is His name" and Ps 34:4, with which the leader invites worshipers to "Exalt the LORD with me and let us extol His name together." They then respond with 1 Chr 29:11 ("Yours, O LORD, are greatness, might, splendor, triumph, and majesty, yes, all that is in heaven and on earth; to You, LORD, belong kingship and preeminence above all"). In other words, the scroll's appearance is accompanied by the recitation of numerous passages glorifying God, whose presence it, therefore, seems to represent.[67] Supporting this point, an ancient synagogue inscription identifies the ark as "the receptacle of the Merciful" (תקה רחמנה).[68]

That connection is further reinforced by the designation *'ā-rôn* ("ark") for the cabinet in which the Torah is kept. Originally, that term referred to the chest that held the tablets of the covenant while the Israelites wandered through the desert (e.g., Exod 25:16, 40:20; Deut 10:1–5), the synagogue cabinet, was called a *têbâ*. The connection between the desert ark and the scroll is made explicit by several of the biblical passages that are recited during the Torah service.[69] The Israelites took that chest with them whenever they went into battle or on a journey (Num 10:33–35; 14:44). Its loss was tantamount to losing God Himself, causing the Israelites to lament and bringing severe disruptions to those who captured it, even as its return was cause for great rejoicing (1 Samuel 4–6). Plainly, the ark signified God's presence.[70] That is why God is said to have spoken from between or above the cherubs that were on top of it, making it God's throne or, in the book of Chronicles, his footstool (Num 7:89, 1 Sam 4:4, 1 Chr 28:2). Thus, designating the cabinet in which the Torah is now kept as *'ā-rôn* links it with the biblical ark as symbolizing God's presence.

THE ROLE OF SCRIPTURE

Where the first two Jewish approaches to the Bible focus on its contents and its metaphysical status, the third emphasizes its power, especially

67. See already *b. Ber.* 8a.

68. Joseph Naveh, *On Stone and Mosaic* (Tel Aviv: Israel Exploration Society and Carta: 1978) 144 [Hebrew]; the dedicatory inscription from another synagogue includes the phrase תקא דמרי שומיא (ibid., 41).

69. Viz. Num 10:35–36 and Ps 132:8. Interestingly, John Chrysostom refers to the synagogue chest as κιβοτος (lit. "box"), the very word used by the Septuagint to translate biblical occurrences of *'ā-rôn*; see Shaye J. D. Cohen, "Pagan and Christian Evidence on the Ancient Synagogue," in *The Synagogue in Late Antiquity* (ed. Lee I. Levine; Philadelphia: American Schools of Oriental Research, 1987) 164.

70. Cf. Kaufmann Kohler, *Hebrew Union College and Other Addresses*, 174.

as a way of linking God to the Jewish people. Like the others, this approach is rooted in rabbinic tradition. Preaching on Isaiah's statement, "I, even I am He that comforts you" (51:12), Rabbi Abba bar Kahana said in the name of Rabbi Yoḥanan:

> It is like a king who married a woman and wrote her a large marriage contract: "I am making you so many state rooms, I am giving you so much jewelry, I am giving you so many treasures." He left her and went away to sea, staying there for many years. Her companions taunted her, saying to her, "How long will you sit? Take a husband while you are young and still have your strength." But she would go into her house, take her marriage contract and read it, and be comforted. After a long time the king came back. He said to her, "My daughter, I am surprised. How did you wait for me all these years?" She said to him, "My lord, O king, were it not for the large marriage contract that you wrote for me, my companions would have made me give up on you long ago." Similarly, in this world the nations taunt Israel, saying to them, "How long will you be killed for your God and give up your lives for Him and be murdered for Him? How much pain He causes you; how much contempt He brings over you, how much suffering He causes you. Come with us, and we will make you commanders and lieutenants and governors." But Israel goes into their synagogues and study houses and takes the Torah and reads in it, "I will walk in your midst" (Lev 26:10) and "I will make you fruitful and multiply you and establish My covenant with you" (Lev 26:9), and they are comforted. When the end comes, the Holy One, blessed be He, will say to Israel, "I am surprised; how did you wait for Me all these years?" And Israel will say before the Holy One, blessed be He, "Master of the universe, were it not for the Torah which You wrote for us, the nations of the world would have made us give up on You long ago." That is why it is said, "I call this [the Torah] to mind; therefore, I have hope" (Lam 3:21), and thus David said, "Were not your Torah my delight, I would have perished in my affliction" (Ps 119:92).[71]

Drawing on the biblical metaphor of God's relationship to Israel as a marriage, the rabbis compared the Torah to a marriage contract, in which the bridegroom guarantees payment should the marriage come to an end.[72] Looked at this way, the Torah has no intrinsic value, any more than does the paper on which a contract is written. What matters is what it represents—God's commitment to the Jewish people, which, according to the midrash, can itself bring consolation, even when events seem to contradict

---

71. *Pesiq. Rab. Kah.* 12 (ed. B. Mandelbaum, pp. 305–6); cf. *Lam. Rab.* 3:21 §7.

72. *Deut. Rab.* 3:12, 17; 4Q185:ii.10 describes wisdom as a "good gift (זבד טוב)" for Israel; cf. *Pesiq. Rab. Kah.* 12:11 (ed. B. Mandelbaum, p. 211). The same idea is implied in *m. Taʿan.* 4:8; *Mek. Ha-Ḥodesh* §3 (ed. H. S. Horowitz, p. 214); *Lam. Rab.* proem 33; and *Pirqe R. El.* §41.

the assurances it contains. Put in more contemporary parlance, Jakob Petuchowski observed that "Jewish literature, beginning with the Bible itself, is full of love letters which the partners to this particular union have addressed to each other."[73]

Even more dramatically, the rabbis sometimes described the Torah as God's daughter.[74] A memorable *piyyut* has Him arranging its marriage, while heaven and earth rejoice in the way that wedding guests do.[75] Another midrash compares God to a committed (some might say overprotective) father, who follows his daughter even after she has married; in acquiring the Torah, Israel, therefore, acquired God.[76] In all of these, the Torah's value lies neither in what it says nor what it is but in how it brings God and Israel together. Shifting metaphors, the medieval philosopher Joseph Albo spoke of the Torah as testimony (*'ēdût*), the vehicle for bringing God's presence into the world.[77]

Views such as these grant the Bible no autonomous status. In the words of Abraham Joshua Heschel, "The Torah is not an end in itself,"[78] what is "decisive is that which happened between God and the prophet rather than that which happened between the prophet and the parchment."[79] Like the tablets of old, it symbolizes God's relationship with the Jewish people.[80]

This approach has substantial attractions for our own time, when, as Kaufmann Kohler observed, the divine origin of Mosaic law is "contradicted by all our knowledge and our whole mode of thinking."[81] For this approach allows the Bible to be acknowledged as both human and ancient, recognizing its written character without requiring that it be accepted

---

73. *Ever Since Sinai: A Modern View of Torah* (New York: Scribe, 1961) 27.

74. *Exod. Rab.* 33:1, 6–7; *Lev. Rab.* 20:10, 25:1; *Num. Rab.* 12:4; *Deut Rab.* 8:7; *Cant. Rab.* 8:11.2; *Pesiq. Rab.* §20 (ed. M. Friedmann, p. 95a).

75. Leon Weinberger, "God as Matchmaker: A Rabbinic Legend Preserved in the *Piyyut*," *JAAR* 40 [72] 238–44; cf. *Sifre Deut* 345 and *Pesiq. Rab.* §20 (ed. Meir Friedmann, 95a, where Torah betrothed to Israel. Even more dramatically, *b. Pesaḥ.* 49b portrays Torah as the bride of God.

76. *Exod. Rab.* 33:1, 6, 7; *Cant. Rab.* 8:11.2.

77. השכינה שורה בישראל באמצעות התורה (Joseph Albo, *Sefer ha-Ikkarim, Book of Principles* 1:3, 3:192), drawing on Exod 25:21 and Ps 132:12.

78. Abraham J. Heschel, "God, Torah, and Israel," in *Theology and Church in Times of Change: Essays in Honor of John Coleman Bennett* (ed. Edward LeRoy Long, Jr., and Robert T. Handy; Philadelphia: Westminster, 1970) 76; hence, "One must not be in awe of the Torah but in awe of Him who gives the Torah" (ibid., 77).

79. Abraham J. Heschel, *God in Search of Man*, 257–58; cf. Jakob Petuchowski, "The Supposed Dogma of the Mosaic Authorship of the Pentateuch," *Hibbert Journal* 57 (1958–59) 356–60; and Mordechai Breuer, "Über die Bibelkritik," *Judaica* 58 (2002) 24.

80. Note William A. Graham's description of "Scripture as a Relational Concept" (*Beyond the Written Word: Oral Aspects of Scripture in the History of Religion* [Cambridge: Cambridge University Press, 1987] 5).

81. Kaufmann Kohler, *Jewish Theology Systematically and Historically Considered* (New York: Ktav, 1968) 46.

literally or accorded unique metaphysical stature. In Leo Baeck's words, "Mere scholarship, with all its ingenuity, only concerns itself with the outer shell; that which lives in the book is not yet revealed to it."[82]

It is, therefore, not surprising that modern thinkers have been attracted to the human dimensions of the Bible. As Martin Buber put it, revelation is "the humanized voice of God, resounding in human idiom and captured in human letters," or, in Heschel's classic articulation, "As a report about revelation, the Bible itself is *a midrash*."[83] Some see it in personal terms, as in Leo Baeck's statement that "The books of the Bible . . . are confessions of individual religious quests."[84] Others have emphasized its collective character, as when Mordecai Kaplan described it as "the hypostasis of the civilization of the Jewish people."[85] This approach has the added advantage of effectively reclaiming the Bible from those who would frame it in either Christian or ancient Near Eastern terms.

Seen this way, the Bible is neither purely divine nor wholly human, but rather the arena where the two meet—"the great document of the 'dialogical reciprocity between heaven and earth,'" as Buber put it.[86] Dialogue is,

---

82. Leo Baeck, *This People Israel: The Meaning of Jewish Existence*, 57. According to Franz Rosenzweig, "Each day of the year Balaam's talking ass may be a fairy tale to me, but not on the Sabbath Balak, when it speaks to me out of the open [ausgehobenen] Torah" (*Briefe* [Berlin: Schocken Verlag, 1935] 520); cf. Isaac Breuer, *Neue Kusari, Ein Weg zum Judentum* (Frankfurt a.M.: Verlag der Rabbiner Hirsch Gesellschaft, 1934) 327, 331.

83. Martin Buber, *On the Bible* (New York: Schocken, 1968) 214–15; Abraham J. Heschel, *God in Search of Man*, 185; thus, in it "The spirit of God is set in the language of man" (ibid., 259). The impact of Heschel's characterization is evident in the language of numerous thinkers, including Emil Fackenheim, W. Gunther Plaut, Harold Schulweiss (Milton Himmelfarb, "The State of Jewish Belief: A Symposium," *Commentary* [1966] 87, 123b, 139b), David Singer, Nina B. Cardin ("What Do American Jews Believe? A Symposium," *Commentary* 102 [1996] 83b, 26a), Louis Jacobs (*A Jewish Theology* [New York: Behrman, 1973] 203–4), Elliot Dorff (*Conservative Judaism: Our Ancestors to Our Descendants* [New York: United Synagogue of America, 1977] 115), Daniel Jeremy Silver (*The Story of Scriptures from Oral Tradition to the Written Word* [New York: Basic Books, 1996] 10). Cf. Mordecai Kaplan's view that "the Torah reveals God, not that God revealed the Torah" (*The Future of the American Jew* [New York: Macmillan, 1949]) 382.

84. Leo Baeck, *The Essence of Judaism* (rev. ed.; New York: Schocken, 1948) 41.

85. Mordecai M. Kaplan, *Judaism as a Civilization*, 411; cf. Herman Cohen's description of it as "national literature" (*Religion of Reason out of the Sources of Judaism* [New York: Ungar, 1972] 73); and Eugene B. Borowitz's characterization of it as "the founding religio-ethnic saga of our people" (*Liberal Judaism* [New York: Union of American Hebrew Congregations] 280). According to Franz Rosenzweig, "The Jewish Bible, sprang from the richness of the life of a whole people, of a whole national literature ("bot die aus der ganzen Breute eines Volkslebens und in der ganzen Breute einer Nationalliteratur erwachsende jüdische Bible," *Kleinere Schriften*, 125).

86. Martin Buber, *On the Bible* (New York: Schocken, 1968) 240; cf. idem, *On Judaism* (New York: Schocken, 1967) 214. In Heschel's words, "the Bible is more than the word of God: it is the word of God *and* man" (*God in Search of Man*, 260). Franz Rosenzweig criticized those who see it "as a soliloquy of the people" ("ein Selbstgespräch des Volkes," *Briefe*,

of course, a central feature in Buber's thought. That is why he insisted that the Bible not be read like any other book—an "it"—but used as a vehicle for experiencing God as the eternal Thou.[87] As Heschel explained, "The Bible . . . is not a book to be read but a drama in which to participate; not a book about events but itself an event."[88] As God's voice, it should not be read solely for its content—something we humans have transformed into legislation—but as an expression of revelation.[89]

Despite its distinctly contemporary ring, this approach is not a recent invention. Centuries ago, Shneur Zalman of Lyadi explained, "the Bible is called *Mikra* for it summons (*kore*) and draws down revelation of the light of the *'Eiyn Sof* through the letters, although the reader may grasp nothing of their meaning."[90] Earlier still, Meir ibn Gabbay had described the Bible as mediating the upper and the lower realms, something to be experienced rather than explained.[91]

According to Jewish tradition, the Torah is always being given.[92] Thus, Abraham Joshua Heschel spoke of the Bible as "always being written, always disclosing and unfolding,"[93] while Mordecai Kaplan explained that "studying Torah . . . meant . . . reliving the experience of national revelation."[94]

---

520), explaining that "The Scriptures constitute the first conversation of mankind, a conversation in which gaps of half and whole millennia occur between speech and response" ("Das Gespräch der Mensch heit hat mit diesem Buch angehoben. In diesem Gespräch liegen zwischen Reden und Widerrede halbe, ganze Jahrtausende," *Kleinere Schriften*, 166).

87. Eugene B. Borowitz, *A New Jewish Theology in the Making* (Philadelphia: Westminster, 1968) 137.

88. *God in Search of Man*, 254.

89. Thus Buber: "The Torah of God is understood as God's instruction in His way. . . . It includes laws and laws are indeed its most vigorous objectivizations, but the Torah itself is essentially not law" (*Two Types of Faith* [New York: Harper, 1961] 57); "I do not believe that *revelation* is ever a formulation of Law. It is only through man in his self-contradiction that revelation becomes legislation" and "Revelation is not legislation" (*The Letters of Martin Buber, A Life of Dialogue* [ed. N. N. Glatzer and Paul Mendes-Flohr; New York: Schocken, 1991] 315, 327). So, too, Rosenzweig: "revelation is certainly not Law-giving; it is primarily only—revelation" ("So ist Offenbarung sicher nicht Gesetzgebung; sie ist überhaupt nur—Offenbarung," *Briefe*, p. 535).

90. *Liqqutei Torah, Vayiqra* 5b, as cited in Moshe Hallamish, *An Introduction to the Kabbalah*, 213.

91. *Avodat Ha-Qodesh*, 36d, as cited in Moshe Idel, *Kabbalah: New Perspectives*, 177.

92. "God gave the Torah and He continues to give the Torah at every moment (Isaiah Horowitz, *Shnei Luḥot Ha-Berit, Beit Ḥokhmah*, 25b, as quoted by Tamar Ross, *Expanding the Palace of Torah: Orthodoxy and Feminism* [Waltham, MA: Brandeis University Press, 2004] 197). According to Emil L. Fackenheim, "the Torah is given whenever Israel receives it" (Milton Himmelfarb, ed., "The State of Jewish Belief, A Symposium," *Commentary* [1966] 87).

93. Abraham J. Heschel, *Israel: An Echo of Eternity*, 46; thus, in 1967, "The Bible, we discovered, is not a book sealed and completed; the Bible lives on, always being written, continuously proclaimed" (ibid., 49).

94. Mordecai M. Kaplan, *Judaism as a Civilization*, 44; cf. *b. Ber.* 63b. A similar view regarding the exodus is expressed in *m. Pesaḥ.* 10:5; cf. also *Exod. Rab.* 28:6 and *Pirqe R. El.* §41 (ed. M. Friedmann, 97b).

This concept is rooted in Deuteronomy's assertion that it was "not with our fathers that the LORD made this covenant, but with us, the living, every one of us who is here today" (5:3) and God's later insistence that "I am not making this covenant with its sanctions with you alone, but with those who are standing here with us this day before the LORD our God and with those who are not with us here this day" (29:13–14). [95] And so both of the blessings that accompany the reading of Scripture during synagogue worship end by describing God as the one who *gives* the Torah (*nôtēn hatôrâ*), even as many contemporary synagogues incorporate ceremonies in which the Torah scroll is passed from older to younger generations.

SUMMARY

All in all, no one view of the Bible can encompass all of Jewish thinking on the subject, but Judaism has clearly not avoided theological reflection on Scripture's role. We have here identified three distinct Jewish approaches to the Bible—that it is bearer of divine revelation, object of cosmic stature, and symbol of God's relationship to Israel. Each of these categories incorporates a variety of views as to the Bible's significance. Its content has been understood as law, ethics, science, and truth; its importance has ranged from assisting God in the creation of the world to all but replacing Him in its governance; and its role has been conceived as serving as the vehicle for experiencing God. None of these is limited to any one time or place. Proponents for each can be found in antiquity and modernity, as well the intervening centuries. Nor have individual thinkers been entirely consistent as to which approach they prefer. None of them should, therefore, be written off as too distant or alien for modern consideration. Instead, they provide Jews with a variety of ways to express their own view of Scripture, with the confidence that they will find ample precedent and sophisticated articulation for whichever best suits their world view.

95. Cf. Hermann Cohen, *Religion of Reason out of the Sources of Judaism*, 76.

3

Constructing the Past:
The Recent History
of Jewish Biblical Theology

EHUD BEN ZVI

" There is no Jewish theology of the Old Testament" (1986).[1] "Jewish scholars instinctively shrink back at the very mention of 'theology' in the context of biblical studies" (1987).[2] "'Theology' was something that simply did not exist for Tanak scholarship—neither the subject matter nor the term" (1987).[3] "Why Jews Are Not Interested in Biblical Theology" (1987, 1993).[4] "Jewish biblical theology is just an emerging enterprise"

---

1. M. Tsevat, "Theology of the Old Testament: A Jewish View," *HBT* 8 (1986) 33–50 (quoting pp. 33–34). It is worth noting that Tsevat is using "Old Testament" here not in a theological sense that would have precluded by definition a Jewish theological approach but rather as a *terminus technicus*. In fact, Tsevat clearly used *Old Testament* in this article for what many scholars today would call "Hebrew Bible," and, as such, it refers to a text that at least potentially renders itself as a source for Jewish theology. Note, for instance, that Tsevat uses the term *Old Testament* when he explains his understanding of the meaning of the term *Torah* in the well-known characterization of the deity as the one who נתן לנו תורת אמת וחיי עולם נטע בתוכנו. There, Tsevat states, "I understand Torah here in the broad sense as comprising the twenty-four books of the Old Testament" (ibid., 43). The controversy among Jewish scholars about the propriety of the term *Old Testament* as a *terminus technicus* has no direct bearing on the arguments advanced in this essay and stands beyond its scope.

2. M. H. Goshen-Gottstein, "Tanak Theology: The Religion of the Old Testament and the Place of Jewish Biblical Theology," in *Ancient Israelite Religion: Essays in Honor of Frank Moore Cross* (ed. P. D. Miller Jr., P. D. Hanson, and S. Dean McBride; Philadelphia: Fortress, 1987) 617–44 (quoting p. 618); for an earlier Hebrew version of the essay, see *Tarbiz* 50 (1980–81) 37–64.

3. Goshen-Gottstein, "Tanak Theology," 621.

4. This is the title of an essay by J. D. Levenson, who—on the surface, ironically—is one of the Jewish biblical theologians of this generation; cf. I. Kalimi, *Early Jewish Exegesis and Theological Controversy: Studies in Scriptures in the Shadow of Internal and External Controversies* (Jewish and Christian Heritage 2; Assen: Van Gorcum, 2002) 122. The essay was published first in *Judaic Perspectives on Ancient Israel* (ed. J. Neusner, B. A. Levine, and E. S. Frerichs; Philadelphia: Fortress, 1987) 281–307, and, slightly revised, in J. D. Levenson, *The Hebrew Bible, the Old Testament and Historical Criticism: Jews and Christians in Biblical Studies* (Louisville, KY: Westminster John Knox, 1993) 33–61. References to that essay in this essay will be to the revised edition.

(1997).[5] "Why Jews Should Be Interested in Biblical Theology" (1997).[6] "At one time, not too long ago, writing about 'Jewish biblical theology' would have been considered unthinkable" (2000).[7] "Very few Jews have been engaged in the field of biblical theology until relatively recent times" (2000).[8] This collection of titles and introductory statements reflects a particular and highly interesting scholarly consensus, according to which Jews have not been involved in biblical theology. To be sure, there was not a consensus that this state of affairs was praiseworthy. On the contrary, most if not all of the scholars cited above wished for, called for, or were actively involved in changing the mentioned state of affairs. Partially because of their work and that of others with interest in Jewish biblical theology, the consensus began to include a second element: a substantial shift is taking place in the present, and as a result Jewish biblical theology is finally flourishing or beginning to flourish.[9] Thus, the consensus includes not only a characterization of the past, at least in the main, as devoid of Jewish biblical theol-

---

5. M. Z. Brettler, "Biblical History and Jewish Biblical Theology," *JR* 77 (1997) 563–83, esp. p. 563.

6. M. A. Sweeney, "Why Jews Should Be Interested in Biblical Theology," *CCAR Journal* 44 (1997) 67–75.

7. T. Frymer-Kensky, "The Emergence of Jewish Biblical Theologies," in *Jews, Christians, and the Theology of the Hebrew Scriptures* (ed. A. O. Bellis and J. S. Kaminsky; Symposium 8; Atlanta: Society of Biblical Literature, 2000) 109–12 (quoting p. 109).

8. M. A. Sweeney, "The Emerging Field of Jewish Biblical Theology," in *Academic Approaches to Teaching Jewish Studies* (ed. Z. Garber; Landham, MD: University Press of America, 2000) 83–105, esp. p. 83.

9. See Brettler, "Biblical History," 565–66, and his comment that "a revision of Levenson's article in a decade's time might have to be called "Why Jews *Were* Not Interested in Biblical Theology" (p. 565; emphasis original). Note the title of Frymer-Kensky's essay cited in n. 7 above and her reference to "one time, not too long ago" (p. 109). Cf. the title of an essay by M. A. Sweeney published the same year, namely, "The Emerging Field of Jewish Biblical Theology" (n. 8 above), and the last quotation in the series of statements that opens this chapter. There is substantial evidence for much interest in Jewish biblical theology in recent years, as the very publication of this volume suggests. There are numerous articles published by Jews on matters of biblical theology/ies in recent years. See also I. Kalimi, "Religionsgeschichte Israels oder Theologie des Alten Testaments? Das Jüdische Interesse an der Biblischen Theologie," *Jahrbuch für Biblische Theologie* 10 (1995) 45–68; and recently in idem, *Early Jewish Exegesis and Theological Controversy*, 107–34; Bellis and Kaminsky, eds., *Jews, Christians, and the Theology of the Hebrew Scriptures* (Symposium 8; Atlanta: Society of Biblical Literature, 2000). Incidentally, one may notice also that the Theology of the Hebrew Scriptures section of the Society of Biblical Literature is presently co-chaired by S. Tamar Kamionkowski, who is a major figure in teh Reconstructionist Rabbinical College (Kamionkowski remains in the steering committee of the section; its present co-chairs are Esther J. Hamori and Julia M. O'Brien). Paraphrasing Brettler, one may say that studies to be published in the second half of this decade will probably bear titles such as "The Flourishing of Jewish Biblical Theology" or introductory sentences such as "Numerous studies in Jewish Biblical Theology have been published recently," or "The recent explosion in interest on Jewish Biblical Theology," or the like. (This essay was completed in early 2007. Since then, even more works on Jewish Bibli-

ogy but also a sense of an ongoing and substantial shift that is currently developing and has no precedent. An important observation concerning this consensus: all the citations cover a relatively short period of time. It seems that the question whether or not Jews were active in biblical theology had no important hold, if any, within the discourse of Jewish biblical scholars in, for instance, the three previous decades (that is, from the early 50s to the early 80s).

This essay focuses not on Jewish biblical theology / biblical Jewish theology but on the social phenomenon of the creation of the mentioned consensus within a short period of time, on now-common social memories about Jewish biblical theology / biblical Jewish theology.[10] The development of any widespread agreement among a circle of scholars is always worth exploring, at least from the perspective of intellectual historians. The fact that the consensus opinion developed quickly within little more than a decade is in itself remarkable. However, this is not the only "odd" feature that draws attention. As all of us are well aware, consensus among "biblicists" is a very rare commodity. Moreover, in this case, it is achieved in a particular subdiscipline, namely, biblical theology. Given that there is a general lack of consensus among most scholars working in this field about its very nature,[11] the mentioned consensus is not only remarkable

cal Theology have been published. To mention just one, Marvin A. Sweeney, *Reading the Hebrew Bible after the Shoah: Engaging Holocaust Theology* [Minneapolis, MN: Augsburg / Fortress, 2008].)

10. I have to admit that, contrary to the development I mentioned, I am not interested in biblical theology per se, unless it is understood as a disciplinary area that deals with the ancient world views reflected in and shaped by the books that eventually became included in the Hebrew Bible. These matters are part and parcel of the study of the (intellectual) history of ancient Israel. Being a historian, however, I cannot but have some interest in constructions of the past and social memories beyond those of that period and that society. Thus, the constructions of the past and social memories that shaped and are reflected in the mentioned consensus draw my attention and, hence, have given rise to this essay.

11. To illustrate, there is no general consensus on questions as central as:

1. Does "Old Testament" theology involve the critical study of ancient world views reflected in the Hebrew Bible, or does it involve the study of what the text means (or should mean) in the present time for any particular group (which at times is defined in opposition to other ideologically construed groups, for example, "oppressors" vs. "oppressed") or for a group ideologically and rhetorically construed as (representing/embodying) "all humanity"?

2. Must/may its practitioners consciously (and emphatically?) bring to bear, in a substantive way, their faith or existential/ideological assumptions or must/may they not?

3. Should/may biblical theology consciously involve the type of "engaged scholarship" that sets aims outside those ever contemplated by the biblical text in its original setting or not? (Some would claim that such use is really an abuse of the text; others would counter that this sort of use of the text is required for its "liberating" powers to effect change in society.)

but perhaps even somewhat astonishing. Thus, this chapter explores how and why a diverse group of Jewish "biblicists" reached the mentioned widespread agreement, and, in particular, I would focus on the ways in which the construction of the past (and the social memory that it creates) shaped and reflected in this consensus is related to particular social and ideological contingencies.

To begin with, as in almost any other case of a general agreement among a group of academics, this is based on sets of data or information. However, as in any construction of the past or present, data by themselves carry no significance. To be significant, they must be placed in the context of an interpretive framework(s) or (meta)narrative(s).[12] Of course, these explanatory frameworks/(meta)narratives, by necessity, tend to emphasize certain data and deemphasize or "erase" (that is, ignore or downplay) other

---

4. Should/may the term *theology* in "biblical theology" be understood as pointing to concepts about the deity or address matters of general world views or ideologies, which may or may not include references to the deity? And if the former is preferred, which concept/s of "deity" should be operative? Whose concepts of deity should/would be adopted, those of the original readership or those of the biblical theologians and their readers?

5. Must Christian Old Testament theologies deal with the text of the Hebrew Bible as if the New Testament does not exist, and Jewish biblical theologies as if the rabbinic tradition of interpretation never existed? Are references to traditional interpretations by the Church Fathers, Luther, or Calvin, on the one hand, and to traditional Jewish commentators (e.g., Saadia Gaon, Rashi, ibn Ezra, Radak, Ramban) not kosher for these endeavors?

6. Should/may one speak of (Christian/Jewish/ancient Israelite) biblical theology or of biblical theologies?

These examples can be easily multiplied. One may mention, in addition, there exists, at least on the theoretical level, the question which text should be used for developing a biblical theology. To be sure, there is a clear tendency to use the MT as the base text, even if one may understand why some Christian scholars would consider using the LXX. I am not aware, however, of recent attempts by Catholic scholars to use the Vulgate as their base text or of Jewish scholars to use the Targum for similar purposes, despite the obvious historical importance that these versions had as the conveyers of the meaning of the Bible and, accordingly, as the operative text of the Bible for many ancient audiences (note, further, b. Ber. 8a, and later relevant *halacha*). But what about texts reconstructed by text critics, source critics, or redactional critics? Should/may they serve as the base text for Christian/Jewish biblical theologies? Needless to say, particular scholars may have advanced normative responses to many or most of these questions, but as any overview of the field would show, these responses have not been greeted with uniform acceptance.

12. Similar processes are at work in the writing of history, both contemporary and ancient. See, for instance, L. Hölscher, "The New Annalistic: A Sketch of a Theory of History," *History and Theory* 36 (1997) 317–35; R. Martin, "Progress in Historical Studies"; and my "Malleability and Its Limits: Sennacherib's Campaign Against Judah as a Case Study," in *"Bird in a Cage": The Invasion of Sennacherib in 701 BCE* (ed. L. L. Grabbe; JSOTSup 363; European Seminar in Historical Methodology 4; Sheffield: Sheffield Academic Press and Continuum, 2003) 73–105.

data.[13] The consensus discussed here is based on data on which scholars agree. These data are certainly not devoid of (historical/external) referentiality. For instance, at the very outset of his essay "Why Jews Are Not Interested in Biblical Theology," Levenson refers to his failure to find a Jewish equivalent of "Walter Eichrodt's *Theology of the Old Testament* or Gerhard von Rad's *Old Testament Theology*."[14] He was undoubtedly correct that there is no Jewish equivalent to these volumes. Not surprisingly, references to this observation of Levenson appear in later works.[15] In fact, though there is no need to stop at these two classic works of the genre, one might argue that there is no real Jewish equivalent to any of the full-length volumes entitled *Old Testament Theology* that are known among academic "biblicists."[16]

This observation, however, raises a number of substantial issues. To begin with, Levenson tells us that he realized the relevant gap in biblical research conducted by Jews after a Christian colleague asked his help in

13. That the latter process has taken place here is not only expected but in fact quite conspicuous, because statements such as that Jews are/were not, until recently, interested in biblical theology or theology in general, as is often the case, raise some difficulties not only concerning the far-away past (for example, medieval times) but also the chronologically closer past (for example, the large corpus of works that deal with matters of biblical theology written by liberal Jews or from liberal Judaic approaches in the second half of the 19th century and the first decades of the 20th). See Kalimi, *Early Jewish Exegesis and Theological Controversy*, 107–34, esp. pp. 118–23. Moreover, depending on one's definition of "biblical theology," one may consider also the relevance of matters such as the centrality of the Bible in Israeli secular religion till recently and still for many (see, for instance, A. Shapira, "The Bible and Israeli Identity," *AJSRev* 28 [2004] 11–42 and bibliography) and its impact in national education in Israel, or theological reflections on the Bible from orthodox Jewish groups such as those involved in the series דעת מקרא (Mosad Harav Kook) and Artscroll. On these matters, see pp. 41– 50 below. It is worth stressing that both Goshen-Gottstein and Levenson (in the articles mentioned above) are well aware of the difficulties that claims such as these raise and attempt to address at least some of them, through arguments that either minimize their value or reject their relevance to the matter under discussion, by means of particular definitions of biblical theology; cf. Frymer-Kensky, "Emergence of Jewish Biblical Theologies," 109. Possible reasons for these processes are discussed toward the end of this chapter.

14. Levenson, *Hebrew Bible*, 33. He is referring, of course, to W. Eichrodt, *Theology of the Old Testament* (2 vols.; Philadephia: Westminster, 1967; originally published in German: *Theologie des Alten Testaments* [3 vols.; Leipzig: Hinrichs, 1933–39]); and G. von Rad, *Old Testament Theology* (2 vols.; London: SCM, 1975; originally published in German: *Theologie des Alten Testaments* [Munich: Walter Kaiser, 1957, 1960]).

15. Brettler, "Biblical History and Jewish Biblical Theology," 564.

16. E.g., W. Brueggemann, *Theology of the Old Testament: Testimony, Dispute, Advocacy* (Minneapolis: Fortress, 1997); R. E. Clements, *Old Testament Theology: A Fresh Approach* (London: Marshall, Morgan & Scott, 1978); J. L. McKenzie, *A Theology of the Old Testament* (Garden City, NY: Doubleday, 1976); H. D. Preuss, *Old Testament Theology* (Louisville, KY: Westminster John Knox, 1995); C. Westerman, *Elements of Old Testament Theology* (Atlanta: John Knox, 1982; first German edition: *Theologie des Alten Testaments in Grundzügen* [Göttingen: Vandenhoeck & Ruprecht, 1978]); W. Zimmerli, *Old Testament Theology in Outline* (Atlanta: John Knox, 1978; first German edition: *Grundriß der alttestamentlichen Theologie* [Stuttgart: Kohlhammer] 1972). A possible exception concerns D. Neumark, *Philosophy of the Bible* (Cincinnati: Ark, 1918).

creating a more evenhanded bibliography for an elementary "introduction to the Old Testament theology" course for both divinity school and liberal arts students. This colleague, in turn, was drawn to the necessity of balancing the bibliography at the request of a Jew in that course.[17] In other words, the question's origin and the impetus to address it were deeply involved in Jewish-Christian interaction both at the level of introductory liberal arts and divinity school students and at the level of scholars. Levenson's awareness of the lack of Jewish research in the area was not a necessary corollary of Levenson's previous research, which is a contribution to biblical theology,[18] nor was it in his mind when he was first asked to suggest a volume to add to his colleague's bibliography. Significantly, when asked to suggest a volume, Levenson framed the question in terms of a book written by a Jew that could be equivalent to Eichrodt's or von Rad's volume. In other words, he framed the question in terms of not only Christian theologies of the Old Testament but of very particular theologies and of a particular scholarly genre, namely, the full-length, comprehensive "theology of the Old Testament."[19] Significantly, as he recognizes the lack of Jewish biblical theologies of this type, he begins to ask himself why this is the case. His explanation involves a number of different matters. For the present, it is worth stressing that, on the one hand, it clearly expresses anger about the unfair way in which Judaism was construed in some Christian biblical theologies,[20] but on the other it is clearly influenced by central elements of inner discourse among Christian biblical theologians.[21] This example, which significantly relates to one of the prominent practitioners of Jewish biblical theology today, suggests that the entire question whether or not Jewish biblical theology exists or existed is a result of interaction between Christian scholars (and institutions) involved with Old Testament theology and Jewish biblical scholars. The negative response he gave to that question was contingent on the way in which the subject was framed, that is, in terms of a particular set of Christian biblical theologies assumed to be

---

17. Levenson, *Hebrew Bible*, 33. See also the additional anecdote he shares in pp. 33–34.

18. Levenson's contributions to biblical theology include: *The Book of Job in Its Time and in the Twentieth Century* (Cambridge: Harvard University Press, 1972); *Theology of the Program of Restoration of Ezekiel 40–48* (Harvard Semitic Monographs 10; Missoula, MT: Scholars Press, 1976); *Sinai and Zion: An Entry into the Jewish Bible* (Minneapolis: Winston, 1985); *Creation and the Persistence of Evil: The Jewish Drama of Divine Omnipotence* (2nd ed.; Princeton: Princeton University Press, 1994).

19. For a sharp critique of Levenson's views, see Kalimi, *Early Jewish Exegesis and Theological Controversy*, 118–26.

20. Levenson generalizes as he moves from particular Christian biblical theologies in the past to references to Christian biblical theology.

21. A point stressed in J. Barr, *The Concept of Biblical Theology: An Old Testament Perspective* (Minneapolis: Fortress, 1999) 291–302.

representative of "Christian biblical theology" and of the scholarly literary genres in which this sort of scholarship may be communicated.[22]

Among other scholars whose statements are cited at the beginning of this essay, one finds Tsevat, whose article originated in a lecture given in a conference held under the auspices of the theological department in Bern. Its very setting was Christian-initiated involvement with Jewish perspectives on biblical theology.[23]

One may note that Sweeney opens his essay "Why Jews Should Be Interested in Biblical Theology" with an explicit reference to "the appointment of Jewish Bible scholars to full-time, tenured, or tenurable faculty positions in Christian theological schools," to the "marked change in Christian higher education" that these appointments indicate, and then asserts:

> The turn to Jews as a source for instruction reflects a fundamental shift in Christian attitudes towards Jews and indeed toward the theological interpretation of their own scriptures. This obviously indicates that Jews are now in a position to play a major role in the definition of Christian biblical theology. But it also has implications for Jews who are engaged in such teaching and research, and indeed for the Jewish community at large. In essence, it demonstrates the need for Jews to be concerned with biblical theology, both in terms of defining their relationship to Christianity and in terms of defining their theological identity for themselves (p. 67).

Notwithstanding all the differences between Sweeney and Levenson on matters of Jewish biblical theology, here too and most explicitly, the need

---

22. Obviously, references to the lack of Jewish works comparable to the full-length, comprehensive volumes on "Old Testament theology" such as those of von Rad or Eichrodt raise matters of genre. It is worth stressing that the majority of the Christian scholars involved in Old Testament theology did not produce such comprehensive volumes, nor are these volumes necessarily the most common way to advance and disseminate knowledge in this academic area. In fact, leaving aside projects titled "outline" or "elements," one may argue that the first major work that qualifies as comparable to Eichrodt's and von Rad's volumes within the German-speaking world appeared only a generation later, namely, Horst Dietrich Preuss, *Theologie des Alten Testaments* (2 vols.; Stuttgart: Kohlhammer, 1991–92). Even within the English speaking world, the number of "biblical theologies" published from the 70s until the late 80s is not formidable, despite the large number of "biblicists" with academic education and Christian theological background. The very small number of Hebrew Bible Jewish scholars in the past, the places in which most of them worked—certainly not departments of theology or religion or seminaries—the emphasis on Jewish education—including communal/religious education—that was common in the past, and their own education (mainly in philological or rabbinic matters) did not make them the best candidates to produce books in this particular scholarly genre. On these matters see already Kalimi, *Early Jewish Exegesis and Theological Controversy*, 123–24; and see also below.

23. The English version of Tsevat's paper was presented orally in a meeting of the Society of Biblical Literature and was followed by a response by Bernhard W. Anderson. The mentioned interaction is reflected in the published version of the paper in *HBT* ("Theology of the Old Testament"), in which Anderson's comments follow those of Tsevat.

for awareness among Jews in the academic world of the need for Jewish theology/ies is directly related to the interaction between Christian and Jewish scholars, their students, and their traditions. Here, the impetus for working in this field is not only new and unparalleled but also directly associated with a marked shift in Christian theologies and institutional policies in North America. Significantly, according to Sweeney, this shift, among others, now allows Jewish concerns to influence the field of Christian biblical theology, and this sort of opportunity (and responsibility) is to be taken.[24]

Brettler[25] raises another issue. He is interested in the question of how the lack of historicity in biblical texts may affect biblical theology. He discusses possible approaches for Jewish biblical theologians[26] but raises the question of whether "there needs to be fundamental differences between Jewish and non-Jewish biblical theology." His examples suggest that this is not necessary the case, for he finds that, when confronting the matter that is the theme of his essay, namely, the lack of historicity and the "gain in meaning," as well as in a few other issues, there are no uniquely Jewish positions.[27]

24. "Jewish biblical theology provides a means to assert that Judaism is not simply a prelude to the advent of Christianity that will ultimately be absorbed as Jews come to recognize Jesus as God's messiah, but that Judaism constitutes a distinctive, continuing, and legitimate theological reality that must be accepted and engaged as such in Christian theology;" Sweeney, "Emerging Field," 85–86. One may compare in some ways the basic gist of Sweeney's position—including his references to instances of Christian misunderstandings and misappropriations of Judaism or Jewish texts—with that of Reform Jews in late 19th-century Germany who, against a background of theological hostility—unlike what exists today—tried to convince Jews and non-Jews alike that Judaism is not a wooden or dead leftover to be eventually removed by history but a legitimate theological reality, which reflected (in their opinion), even better than Christianity, the prophetic spirit of Scripture and the ethical monotheism that they considered to be at its core. Moreover, some of them attempted to influence Christian (biblical) theology not only through their readings of the Tanak but also by constructing a very Jewish Jesus. Their efforts to remove common Christian misunderstandings and misappropriations of Judaism(s) in their time were, however, not successful, at least for the most part. This is easily explainable given the discursive and theological context within which they lived. Their efforts to create new forms of Jewish self-identity, nevertheless, were successful, even if not to the extent they expected, and led to the development of Reform Judaism. On Geiger's Jesus and its role in his defense of Judaism against common mischaracterization in his day, see S. Heschel, *Abraham Geiger and the Jewish Jesus* (Chicago: University of Chicago Press, 1998).

25. See Brettler, "Biblical History and Jewish Biblical Theology."

26. This includes using traditional/rabbinic approaches in untraditional/unrabbinic ways, which raises the issue of the relationship between traditional Jewish and contemporary critical approaches to the Hebrew Bible. Compare and contrast this with Tsevat's "judaizing" or "positive" theological approach, which is one of the two he advances in "Theology of the Old Testament."

27. Incidentally, I think that at times his construction of "the other" is based on a misunderstanding of the positions of some of the people referred to in the article. For instance,

To be sure, any survey of the field of (biblical) theology would suggest that there are large areas in which no (substantially) unique Jewish positions exist. For instance, biblical scholars/theologians who approach the biblical text from a perspective informed not only by their Jewish or Christian commitments but also by their ideological or existential commitment to gender issues or a particular set of gender issues may find much common ground. In these cases, far more often than not, the main dividing line is not between Jewish and non-Jewish biblical scholars/theologians but among biblical scholars/theologians with different world views.[28] Similar considerations hold for scholars/theologians with ideological or existential commitments to social, political, or environmental positions. In all these cases, there is not only a strong sense of interaction between Christian and Jewish scholars but also a sense of commonality within the field of biblical theology.

The preceding observations suggest that the recent developments in the field of Jewish biblical theology that include an awareness of a perceived lack in that area among Jews in academic biblical studies cannot be explained only by internal developments within Judaism or Jewish scholarship.[29] Sociological, institutional, and ideological shifts developed quickly within the last decades, even if they reflected a long process of change in Christian views about Judaism. These shifts have led to the spread of new forms of scholarly interaction between Christian and Jewish "biblicists." This interaction has posed some challenges and opportunities for Jewish scholars interested in theological matters. These challenges and opportunities have contributed to the development of interest and of different approaches to the question of Jewish biblical theology/ies among many Jewish biblical scholars.[30] Some of them adopted approaches that either have led, or are conducive to the development of areas within the field that are not exclusively Jewish or Christian but shared. In other cases, recent efforts have led to the development of a hyper-area of biblical theological

---

see his reference to Davies and Thompson as writers who work within the mode of "a time for tearing down, and a time for tearing down." In fact, both are good examples of "historicity lost is compensated for by meaning gained—a time for tearing down and a time for building up." See Brettler, "Biblical History," 582. If this is taken into account, his argument would reinforce the already-existing tendency to show that there are no uniquely Jewish positions in these matters.

28. E.g., those at times labeled "progressive," "socially conservative," or the like.

29. Of course, the substantial increase of tenured and tenurable positions held by Jews in Hebrew Bible/Old Testament played a role in the development (see Kalimi, *Early Jewish Exegesis and Theological Controversy*, 134), but it is more a consequence of the general change than its originator.

30. One must keep in mind that there are also many Jewish scholars of the Hebrew Bible who do not have much or any interest in theology, just like their many non-Jewish (mainly Christian and secular-humanistic) counterparts.

discourse in which Christian and Jewish biblical theologies enter into dialogue and shed light on each other. In general, Jews who were involved in these developments—most likely in a way unbeknownst to them—responded as one may expect from a minority group that interacts with challenges posed by new approaches, ideas, and interpretive frameworks held by a majority group: they appropriated some of these approaches, ideas, and frameworks and adapted them to their own ideological discourses.[31] They used these hybrid forms not only to interact with the majority and their discourses but also to express their own constructions of self-identity and boundaries, within the inner group and vis à vis others.[32]

The mentioned developments in biblical theology had additional, important implications, as noted by Sweeney. Because of their status among religious communities, biblical texts as interpreted by these communities have traditionally served to assign legitimacy to particular world views (social influence and power to those who uphold them) and, in today's world of multiple communities for whom the Bible may "state" many different things, to negotiate legitimacy, social influence, and power among contending, contemporary world views and their adherents. The development of the "hybrid" cultural forms mentioned above, along with their constructions of self-identity and boundaries by necessity play a role in this process of negotiation.

Needless to say, there is absolutely nothing sinister about this set of processes involving "hybrid" forms. Quite the opposite: it represents a set of social and cultural processes (that is, hybridity) that very often led to enrichment of Jewish life and thought[33] and that enriched the lives of Jews

31. One of the most obvious and poignant cases concerns the subject study in this field, namely, a "Hebrew Bible/Tanak," that is, a comprehensive, well-structured text that begins with Genesis and ends with Chronicles. According to many practitioners of Jewish biblical theology, this comprehensive text is supposed to be approached, at least to a very large extent, as a work by itself, without much or any (?) interference of later, rabbinic sources or late Second Temple texts for that matter. But significantly, the work is in itself a product of the early rabbinic or at the very earliest the late Second Temple period and, if one takes into account the order of the Writings, even later. In other words, the proposed conceptualization of a meaningfully and Jewish-structured "Hebrew Bible" to be studied as a text by itself does not reflect historical concerns or traditional Jewish/rabbinic theological concerns. It is a rather a contemporary Jewish response and counter-balance to the concept of the Protestant Old Testament. As such, it is an excellent case of hybridity at work. For works on the Judaic character of the story from Genesis to Chronicles, see M. A. Sweeney, "Tanak *versus* Old Testament: Concerning the Foundation for a Jewish Theology of the Bible," in *Problems in Biblical Theology: Essays in Honor of Rolf Knierim* (ed. H. T. C. Sun et al.; Grand Rapids: Eerdmans, 1997) 353–72; idem, "Emerging Field."

32. See ibid., 85–86.

33. One may note, among many other examples, the influence of Arabic philosophy in Medieval Jewish thought and of Hellenistic cultural patterns in the development of rabbinic thought. Turning to biblical matters, the many results of interactions such as these include

and members of the majority group through cross-fertilization and shared work.

The novelty of the situation facing many Jewish biblical scholars and its contingent character—including the association of present Jewish biblical theology with the mentioned interactions with contemporary Christian biblical scholars—has contributed much to the shaping of the mentioned consensus among many of them. Certainly, the element of newness, perceived at both the ideological and existential/personal level, played a role in the formation of a sharp sense of dramatic change and discontinuity, namely, before there was neither "Jewish biblical theology" (or, as often stated, not even Jewish "theology") nor even an awareness that there was such a thing, but now the situation is vastly different as Jewish biblical theology / biblical Jewish theology flourishes. Moreover, because the circumstances that initiated and nourished this process did not obtain before, the (new) Jewish biblical theology / biblical Jewish theology that has been developing now could not have existed in earlier times. This (often-implied) way of thinking contributed much to the construction of the mentioned social memory that emphasizes discontinuity that shapes and is reflected in the consensus.

Although the considerations advanced above contributed much to the construction of a social memory in which there was no Jewish biblical theology before the present,[34] other important factors were also at play. As it will be shown below, the social memory reflected in the consensus deemphasizes or "erases" (that is, ignores or downplays) a relatively large corpus of data. This process can take place only if the community that bears this consensus is able to consider the relevant data "erasable." Why would this be the case? And which of the data were turned invisible, as it were?

Surely, there were and are Jewish theologies. Certainly, Jewish theologians and their systems of thought (that is, theologies) existed in medieval times.[35] Perhaps more important in terms of direct relevance to the consensus, it is a well-established historical fact that engagement with matters of Jewish theology/ies flourished during the first half of the 20th

---

matters as diverse as the development of the vocalized Masoretic Text and the transformation of a national deity into a universal one who is the king of the kings. It may be noted that, from an overtly Jewish theological perspective, M. M. Kaplan wrote, "[n]o policy could be more detrimental to Jewish survival than one which would reject a true idea, a beautiful form or a just law on the ground that it did not originate among Jews" (M. M. Kaplan, *The Meaning of God in Modern Jewish Religion* [New York: Reconstructionist Press, 1962; first published, 1937] 351).

34. Or not even now, according to a few. The matter is one of definition rather than of presence or absence of relevant works.

35. Thus, for example, Saadia, Maimonides, and Yehuda Halevi; see in detail Kalimi, *Early Jewish Exegesis and Theological Controversy*, 119–21.

century.[36] Further, it cannot be maintained that Jews in America—most of the bearers of the mentioned consensus are Americans—refused to use the term *theology*,[37] despite the recent widespread agreement about the absence of its use among Jews. When Frymer-Kensky writes that "it was a truism that Jews don't do theology" and "theology was narrowly understood as the study of God, and writing about God was not considered a Jewish activity,"[38] she correctly identifies a "fact" agreed on by many Jews today, but, as she knows and insinuates, this is a "fact" that defies a massive number of data.[39] As such, this counter-historical "agreed fact" represents a primary example of a social memory in which some data are marginalized or erased. In many ways, the case of the consensus about the lack of Jewish theology provides a good parallel for the consensus about the lack of Jewish biblical theology / biblical Jewish theology.

There is no dispute that there exists a very long history of texts that address theological issues raised by texts in the Hebrew Bible.[40] The process of developing texts such as these began already within the corpus of texts that eventually became the Hebrew Bible (for example, Chronicles[41] Jonah, which provides keys for interpreting prophetic literature), and, at times, it takes place within the same book (for example, Isaiah). This pro-

36. Names such as Hermann Cohen, Martin Buber, Franz Rosenzweig, Emil G. Hirsch, Kaufmann Kohler, Mordecai M. Kaplan, and Abraham J. Heschel immediately come to mind.

37. Note the name "Jewish Theological Seminary." See, for instance, Kaufmann Kohler, *Jewish Theology Systematically and Historically Considered* (New York: Ktav, 1968; first published in 1918); and multiple references to "Jewish theology," in the *Jewish Encyclopaedia* (1901–6). See also S. Schechter, *Aspects of Rabbinic Theology* (New York: Schocken, 1961; first published as *Some Aspects of Rabbinic Theology*, [New York: Macmillan, 1909]). From later periods, note the title in J. Neusner's *Understanding Jewish Theology: From Talmudic to Modern Times* (New York: Ktav, 1973) or Jacob B. Agus's *Jewish Quest: Essays on Basic Concepts of Jewish Theology* (New York: Ktav, 1983). One may note that M. M. Kaplan, despite his attacks on those who equated Judaism with theology (or religion), never had problems using the term *theology* or its derivates. Of course, the term was used also outside America, for instance by Louis Jacobs, *A Jewish Theology* (London: Darton, Longman, & Todd, 1973).

38. Frymer-Kenskyi, "Emergence," 109.

39. It is also not true that Jews did not write about concepts of the deity. See, for instance, the explicit title of M. M. Kaplan's book *The Meaning of God in Modern Jewish Religion* and his characterization of God; Heschel's well-known discussions of the character and pathos of God; and Harold M. Schulweis, *Evil and the Morality of God* (Cincinnati: Hebrew Union College Press, 1984), which is a study about the attributes of God.

40. For a summary of many of its highlights see the relevant essays in A. Berlin and M. Z. Brettler, eds., *The Jewish Study Bible* (New York: Oxford University Press, 2004).

41. For this point, see Kalimi, *Early Jewish Exegesis and Theological Controversy*, 120. Also see idem, *An Ancient Israelite Historian: Studies in the Chronicler, His Time, Place and Writing* (Studia Semitica Neerlandica 46; Assen: Van Gorcum, 2005) 19–39, esp. pp. 27–39. Kalimi claims that, although the book of Chronicles contains some theological elements, the book *as a whole* is not a theology but mainly a historiography. From my viewpoint, the Chronicler is both at the same time. The Chronicler would have probably not understood a strong dichotomy between "historian" and "theologian."

cess continued, though in different ways, through the late Second Temple period (in Hebrew, Aramaic and Greek), and beyond. It is certainly present in the New Testament (which may be considered a repository of "sectarian" Jewish texts), and at an even later time involved midrashic, rabbinic literature and Targumic texts. It was certainly present during the medieval period[42] and clearly continued into the post-medieval period. There is no doubt that Spinoza addressed biblical theological matters, and so did Mendelssohn and the "biurists" (that is, the "exegetes/commentators") who adopted his interpretive principles.

To be sure, it may be argued that all these instances do not involve critical studies of the text, and as such they should not be included under definitions of (academic/critical) Jewish biblical theology.[43] On similar grounds, or because of their dependence on traditional Jewish texts other than the Tanak, one may argue for the exclusion from the field of (academic/critical) Jewish biblical theology of works dealing with theological issues in the Tanak written by either rabbis in *haredi* communities[44] or by many Jewish orthodox thinkers.[45] One may also argue that the use of the Tanak as the "Holy Scriptures of Zionism" in Israeli life (until recently) and the methods of biblical interpretation that made this use possible should be excluded from consideration within this field, because they deal with texts and ideology rather than concepts of the deity and, perhaps, because

---

42. Significantly, in the medieval period there were debates over whether a reading of the Torah may contradict actual *halacha* and whether the text should be studied on its own. See, for instance, the (implied) position of Rashbam on these issues,

ידעו ורבינו יודעי שכל כי לא באתי לפרש הלכות אעפ"י שהם העיקר . . . ואני לפרש פשוטן של
מקראות באתי

(Rashbam, note on Exod 21:1)

which may be translated as "those with wisdom should know and understand that I did not come to explain halakot, even if they are of primary importance . . . instead I came to explain Scriptures within their own internal context [פשוטן של מקראות]"

כי לא אאריך אלא במקומות שיש לפרש פשוטי מקראות

(Rashbam, note on Lev 1:1)

This may be translated as "I will not expand [because Rashi, his grandfather, already did so] except in places that Scriptures need to be explained within their own internal context."

43. It is worth noting that the case against including Spinoza on these grounds is weak. To be sure, others may exclude either Spinoza or Spinoza's work on the grounds that he/it is not fully Jewish, but this is a different matter altogether, which, needless to say, raises the question of boundaries of/in Jewishness.

44. For example, the commentaries in the Artscroll series. The term *haredi* is at times translated in English as "ultra-orthodox." This translation is problematic because it ignores — and, to some extent, rejects — the self-understanding of the group.

45. For example, the works of Nechama Leibowitz, with a more American perspective; see in particular the many relevant contributions and books reviewed in *Tradition* (e.g., E. Shkop, "Rivka: The Enigma Behind the Veil," *Tradition* 36/3 [2002] 46–59).

they are more *derash* than *peshat*.[46] On the same grounds, one may argue
for the exclusion of theological reflections that develop in a form akin to
modern midrash of biblical texts.[47] On similar grounds (and perhaps also
on the basis that their authors are not academic "biblicists" working within
the historical mode), one may claim for the exclusion of the type of works
gathered in the volume *Congregation*.[48] All these potential arguments belong to the discursive domain of decisions about boundaries and so involve
questions such as which studies qualify for the scholarly/ideological domain of Jewish biblical theology/ies?[49] Why? Who is enforcing the boundaries and what is at stake on these disciplinary boundaries? These questions
deserve an in-depth discussion that cannot be carried out in this essay. For
the argument advanced here, it suffices to state that the mentioned consensus involves a very large and diversified corpus of works dealing with the
biblical texts and their meanings and significance for Jewish communities
as outside the realm of Jewish biblical theology. Significantly, all these decisions are comparable and, in fact, parallel to those taken by most practitioners in the academic field of Christian biblical theology. The latter scholars
would normally exclude comparable works from the academic field. Given
that the field of Jewish biblical theology is deeply intertwined from the
outset with that of Christian biblical theology, the presence of comparable
disciplinary boundaries is only to be expected. But this being so, exceptions are particularly noteworthy and demand explanation.

Perhaps the most salient of these exceptions involves works by lib-
eral/reform Jews—both in the 19th and 20th centuries in Germany and in
America—who dealt with critical texts to the best of their understanding and as their theological messages would allow.[50] It is obvious that the

---

46. On these matters, see U. Simon, "The Bible in Israeli Life," in *The Jewish Study Bible*
(ed. A. Berlin and M. Z. Brettler; New York: Oxford University Press, 2004) 1990–2000.

47. Including, but not restricted to, recent feminist retelling or counter-telling of biblical narratives. Of course, some of these new midrashim have brought about much debate and
criticism from other Jewish theologians; see, for example, J. D. Levenson, "Abusing Abraham:
Traditions, Religious Histories, and Modern Misinterpretations," *Judaism* 47 (1998) 259–77. It
is worth stressing that there are often Jewish interpreters on both sides of these debates. See
Levenson on Abraham: "The Conversion of Abraham to Judaism, Christianity and Islam,"
in *The Idea of Biblical Interpretation: Essays in Honor of James L. Kugel* (ed. H. Najman and J. H.
Newman; Supplements to the Journal of the Study of Judaism 83; Leiden: Brill, 2004) 3–40.

48. See *Congregation: Contemporary Writers Read the Jewish Bible* (New York: Harcourt
Brace Jovanovich, 1987).

49. Of course, questions such as these often raise additional questions. For instance,
should the work of nonhistorically oriented/trained "biblicists" be included from or excluded
of the field? Is there a difference between biblical Jewish theologies and Jewish biblical theologies?

50. This survey does not include cases in which biblical texts were used as a kind of (mar-
ginal) proof-text for a particular Jewish theology, as is in the case, for instance, in Hermann
Cohen, *Religion of Reason out of the Sources of Judaism* (New York: Ungar, 1972; first published as
Religion der Vernunft aus den Quellen des Judentums [Leipzig: Fock, 1919]).

consensus opinion and the consensus memory of the discipline of Jewish biblical theology do not include these works. In fact, they claim that only now are Jews dealing or beginning to deal with biblical theology.[51]

A complete discussion of these works is well beyond the scope of this essay. A brief survey pointing to a variety of illustrative works written at different times, for different addresses, against diverse circumstances and in various genres suffices to make the point. Comparable to those in use in Christian biblical theology, A. Geiger would have been considered a biblical theologian.[52] He certainly dealt with the text critically and advanced theological positions on the basis of his understanding of the text.[53] These positions included, among other things, a lionization of "ethical monotheism," a lionization of the prophets, a negative approach to cult and ritual including the sacrificial system (which was considered transitory and not permanent), the claim that the Jews as a people shaped Judaism (including the Bible),[54] and the emphasis on the national religious genius of the Jewish people. It is the latter stance that led him to stress his contention that the Jews, because of that genius, were able to develop ethical monotheism, out of nothing, as it were.[55]

51. It is worth stressing that dealing with biblical theology does not require the publications of full-length, comprehensive volumes on the theology of the Bible. The first refers to work in a particular field of studies; the other refers to a particular scholarly (and literary) genre.

52. Of course, A. Geiger would not have been considered *only* a biblical theologian but *also* a biblical theologian. If Wellhausen was a biblical theologian, among other things, then Geiger was also a biblical theologian, among other things.

53. He did so in interaction with Protestant biblical theology and Protestant theologies of his time. This interaction involved Geiger's acceptance of many of its main thrusts and rejection of negative constructions of Judaism and often of Jews that were common among these theologies and theologians (for example, J. G. Eichorn, J. D. Michaelis).

54. "Nor does Judaism claim to be the work of single individuals, but that of the whole people. It does not speak of the God of Moses or of the God of the Prophets, but of the God of Abraham, Isaac and Jacob, of the God of the whole race, of the patriarchs who were equally gifted with that endowment, with that prophetic vision; it is the Revelation which lay dormant in the whole people, and was concentrated in individuals. . . . A thornbush produces no wine, a neglected people produces no prophets, such as the people of Judah gave to the world. It is true that the Historical books of the Bible mostly inveigh against the morals, the depravity of the people at the time of the Kings; they intend to prepare us for the devastation that came upon them as a punishment for their sinfulness. Yet that people must have possessed noble powers in great abundance; it must have had a native endowment, considering that it could produce, that it could rear such men" (A. Geiger, *Judaism and Its History* [New York: Thalmessinger & Cahn, 1866] 60–61; this text is free and available for download at: http://books.google.com. This translation is based on an early version of A. Geiger, *Das Judentum und seine Geschichte*, which in itself went through three editions. The most common printing of this book is the one published in Breslau, 1910 by Jacobson, which is also available for free online at http://www.archive.org/details/dasjudentumundse00geiguoft.

55. Cf. the conception of the beginning of monotheism in Israel developed later by Y. Kaufmann. Many of A. Geiger's works are collected in his *Nachgelassene schriften* (ed.

The *Jewish Encyclopaedia* was published in the U.S.A. from 1901 to
1906. E. G. Hirsch and K. Kohler were among the main authors on biblical texts. Although the Encyclopaedia attempted to be as scientific and
objective as possible, there is no doubt that it conveyed strong theological
messages in many of its entries[56] and that these messages fit very well with
the biblical theologies of reform Judaism of the time, which in turn were
grounded in their own perspective on the known results of biblical "higher
criticism" of the time.[57] These entries attest to the existence of a relatively
widespread interest and strongly held positions on biblical theological matters among (intellectual) reform Jews at the time. D. Neumark's *Philosophy
of the Bible*[58] represents a "high-end" academic expression of some of the
biblical-theological discourses among reform Jews at the time.

L. Geiger; 5 vols.; Berlin: Gerschel, 1875–78). His *Judaism and Its History* was published in three
editions in German and three in English.

56. See, for instance, "the facts now [at the time of "written prophecy"] first practi-
cally realized, that God's government and interests were not merely national, but universal,
that righteousness was not merely tribal or personal or racial, but international and worldwide. Neither before nor since have the ideas of God's immediate rule and the urgency of His
claims been so deeply felt by any body or class of men as in the centuries which witnessed the
struggle waged by the prophets of Israel for the supremacy of Yhwh and the rule of justice
and righteousness which was His will. The truth then uttered are contained in the writings
of the Latter Prophets, They were not abstractions, but principles of the divine government
and of the right, human, national life"; see E. G. Hirsch, J. F. McCurdy, and J. Jacobs, "Prophets and Prophecy," *The Jewish Encyclopaedia. A Descriptive Record of the History, Religion, Literature, and Customs of the Jewish People from the Earliest Times to the Present Day* (12 vols., New
York: Funk & Wagnalls, 1901–6) 10:213–19, citation from p. 214a, under the subentry "Written
Prophecy" written by J. F. McCurdy.

57. "The Pentateuch is not the work of one period. Pentateuchal legislation also is the
slow accretion of centuries. The original content of Judaism does not consist in the Law and
its institutions, but in the ethical monotheism of the prophets. Legalism is, according to this
view, originally foreign to Judaism. It is an adaptation of observances found in all religions,
and which therefore are not originally or specifically Jewish. The legalism of Ezra had the
intention and the effect of separating Israel from the world" (K. Kohler, E. G. Hirsch, and
D. Philipson, "Reform Judaism from the Point of View of the Reform Jews," *Jewish Encyclopaedia* (New York: Funk & Wagnalls, 1901–6) 10:347–59, citation from p. 350a, under subentry
"Influence of Higher Criticism," written by E. G. Hirsch. It is worth noting that the opposition of S. Schechter and others to "higher criticism" was in fact to "higher criticism" of the
Torah, and it was deeply related to the weight they attached to the Pentateuch in their version
of Judaism, which was far more traditional than that of their contemporary reform Jewish
thinkers and rabbis. Cf. D. J. Fine, "Salomon Schechter and the Ambivalence of Jewish Wissenschaft," *Judaism* 46 (1997) 3–24.

58. David Neumark was the chair of Jewish philosophy at the Hebrew Union College for
many years. His approach to biblical theology is also evident and explicitly advanced in his
discussion of the principles of Judaism; see D. Neumark, "The Principles of Judaism in Historical Outline," *Essays in Jewish Philosophy* (ed. S. S. Cohon; Amsterdam: Philo, 1971) 101–44,
esp. pp. 105–24, which serve as a kind of compendium of his Jewish biblical theology. The
latter, as expected, was fully grounded in the "accepted" results of historical-critical studies
of the Bible in his day. The same, of course, holds true for his work in *Philosophy of the Bible*.

According to a yardstick comparable to the one in use among most Christian practitioners of biblical theology, it is difficult not to characterize A. J. Heschel as a person involved in biblical theology.[59] The same holds true for M. M. Kaplan. After all, he strongly maintained that Judaism/Jews should not continue to ascribe meanings to biblical texts that could not have been contemplated by their authors (a process he calls "transvaluation") but rather that they "must enter imaginatively into the thought-world of its authors, and try to grasp what it meant to them in the light of their experience and world-outlook."[60] Then, and only then, they should reevaluate the significance of these religious ideas for their own lives and adapt them in ways that are consistent with an "authentic" concept of the deity and so contribute to salvation.[61]

Jumping in time to 1962, S. D. Schwartzman and J. D. Spiro published an important volume, namely, *The Living Bible: A Topical Approach to the Jewish Scriptures*.[62] The goal of the book was to provide (reform) Jewish educators and students with an accessible compendium of what *Jewish Scriptures* means. Of course, it was written at a "popular level." The book includes the expected chapters "Who Wrote the Bible?" and "How the Bible Was Completed?" but also, and mainly, chapters that directly address theological issues entitled, such as "Who Is God?" "Does God Have a Favorite People?" "Are We Really Free?" "Why Is There Evil in the World?" and "Is Death the End?" The book expounds these topics in terms of a historically-critically understood Bible and with concern toward the significance of these biblical ideas for contemporary Jews. The text is a Jewish theology of the Hebrew Bible written at a "popular" level. It reflects and attests to a (then-)relatively widespread discourse on biblical Jewish theology among intellectuals in American reform Judaism; one that the authors and the Union of American Hebrew Congregations thought should be communicated to a larger readership. It also attests to the centrality of Jewish education and, indirectly, to the tendency toward works aimed at Jewish education in biblical studies conducted by Jews.[63]

---

59. One may note that some have argued that Heschel's theological approach to the Bible is, in part, a response to Spinoza's. See S. D. Breslauer, "Spinoza's *Theologico-Political Treatise* and A. J. Heschel's Theology of Biblical Language," *CCAR Journal* 24 (1977) 19–17. Note also the reference in the title of this work, published in 1977, to Heschel's "theology of biblical language."

60. Quotation from Kaplan, *Meaning of God*, 7.

61. On Kaplan's own work with biblical texts, see M. M. Kaplan, "Isaiah 6:1–11," *JBL* 45 (1926) 251–59.

62. S. D. Schwartzman and J. D. Spiro, *The Living Bible: A Topical Approach to the Jewish Scriptures* (New York: Union of American Hebrew Congregations, 1962). The "reading committee" that approved the text for publication included Harry M. Orlinsky.

63. To be sure, this is in part due to the lack of enough academic positions open to Jews but also in part due to the importance given to Jewish education among Jewish intellectuals

In sum, a large corpus of works that deal with biblical theology was written by liberal Jews or from liberal Judaic approaches for well over a century, and significantly, much of it was written and communicated in America, where the consensus about the lack of interest in Jewish biblical theology before very recent times has chiefly developed. These works are either not mentioned or, if mentioned, marginalized in the mentioned construction of the history/memory of past Jewish biblical theology.[64] There cannot be any doubt that the existence of this corpus of works is not reflected in the consensus image about the emergence of biblical Jewish theology as something new and as something Jews did not do in the past. In fact, there is even a kind of "fact" agreed on among contemporary Jews that Jews did not deal with theology in the past. How can the "erasable" character of this corpus be explained?

To be sure, the mentioned constructions of the past, along with the drastic change that they imply or explicitly state regarding the last years, reflect the social and ideological changes that took place and play a role in this erasure, as mentioned above. In addition, matters of definition (and of the related boundaries they create) may be at work,[65] but the positions of Jewish biblical theologians tended as whole to reflect and adapt (contemporary) common boundaries of "biblical theology" and "theology" accepted in Christian discourses, which would not have precluded the inclusion of the mentioned corpora in the history of works on biblical-theological matters in the history of Jewish biblical theology that is implicitly communicated by the present consensus.

There seem to be several crucial factors that fed this process of memory shaping (and erasing), including: (a) implicit constructions of what is Judaic, (b) self- and/or community-produced lines of continuity and identification between present scholars and their ancestors/predecessors, and (c) sociological differences.

It is not unreasonable to assume that many present-day Jewish biblical theologians may harbor some reservations about the Judaic character of "classical" Reform Judaism. For instance, some of these biblical theologians might feel that a strong criticism of the cult and priests is a bit "un-Judaic," or they might harbor concerns about the Judaic quality of a Judaism in which the "Law" is seen as peripheral at best, in which prophets and ethi-

---

of the first half of the 20th century and the decades that closely followed. Hirsch, Heschel, Kaplan, Leo Horn, and the like were, above all, Jewish educators.

64. Levenson is among the few who mention some of these works, but he excludes them from the field of "Jewish biblical theology" on a set of grounds that, if consistently applied, would exclude almost every Jewish work, from that field. See Levenson, "Why Jews Are Not Interested in Biblical Theology." By the same standards, Wellhausen's work would have failed to qualify as relevant to or as an expression of biblical theology.

65. This is particularly true in the case of Levenson; see n. 63 above.

cal monotheism are at the center and fully Jewish, whereas the Pentateuch shows "foreign" influences.

This type of consideration does not apply only "classical" Reform thought. For similar reasons, many of today's Jewish biblical theologians might harbor reservations about the Judaic component of the secular (partially atheistic) Zionist religion/ideology that played a central role in the discourses of the Jewish civil society Israel till recently and that served as a/the main impetus for the development of biblical studies and archaeology there, as well as for the strong emphasis placed at that time on biblical literacy among Jewish educators and their students.[66]

It seems reasonable also to assume that at an existential level many of today's Jewish biblical theologians do not see themselves as standing in direct continuity with liberal Jewish scholars and thinkers of generations ago.[67] Because they do not identify themselves with these liberal predecessors, they see discontinuity in relation to the past.[68] The newness of their endeavor, as they perceive it, is in part due to the lack of personal and communal identification with these scholars. The former are not the latter, nor are their Jewish congregations/synagogues like those of the liberal rabbis of the past, and therefore memories of these past rabbis are not part of, or at least play no major role at an existential level in, contemporary theologians' own (main) set of memories. Thus, they tend to be absent from the histories they construct.

This sense of lack of identification is secondarily strengthened by sociological and institutional differences. The social and ideological world in which Geiger, Hirsch, and Schechter grew up was vastly different from

---

66. On these matters, see U. Simon, "The Bible in Israeli Life." An area that deserves further work is that of the ideological overlap between "biblical theologies" among reform Jews and several aspects of the ideological understanding of the Bible in secular Zionism in Israel. For instance, both emphasized "ethical monotheism," and both tended strongly to support "socialist" positions, which they thought to be grounded in the biblical text, if properly understood. The matter stands, of course, beyond the scope of this paper. It is worth noting that the mentioned approach to the Bible and its world view was not the only approach present in Israel even at those times. On the one hand, there were always *haredi* interpreters; on the other, there were attempts to bring some elements of Christian biblical interpretation to bear on the development of a Jewish (Israeli) understanding of the world views present in the Tanak. See Z. Adar (ed.), השקפת העולם של התנ״ך ("*The World View of the Tanak*"; Tel Aviv: Massadah, 1965).

67. In fact, for better or worse, similar feelings are present among some reform rabbis today. These days, it is more likely that a reform rabbi would quote a Hasidic rabbi than Hirsch or Geiger in a sermon, and some neotraditionalist reform rabbis sharply criticize "classical" Reform Judaism. Needless to say, they do not feel a sense of transgenerational identity with Spinoza. Some secular philosophers in Israel, however, do.

68. These Jewish biblical theologians also do not identify with the secular Zionists in Israel—they certainly do not see themselves as disciples of Ben Gurion—or with *haredi* thinkers, for that matter.

that of present days, particularly in terms of the appraisal of Judaism and Jews among Christian theologians. In addition, most Jewish biblical theologians today live in a world in which the basic concepts about Judaism and the ways in which Judaism may continue to exist and flourish are not a heightened matter of debate among American Jews themselves.[69] A sense of precariousness of existence is certainly not a pervasive component of today's Jewish theological discourse, biblical or otherwise. Institutionally, many of the scholars involved in Jewish biblical theology hold teaching and research positions at departments of religious studies or Jewish studies at universities and colleges—some of them private, Christian universities— and a few at Christian seminaries. Their scholarly location, along with the literary genres in which they are able to write, given their occupation,[70] are not necessarily those of the majority of liberal Jewish thinkers of the past, many of whom were rabbis or saw themselves as Jewish educators working at Jewish institutions, who taught mainly or even only to Jews, to foster their Judaism. In other words, there is a drastic gap between the world of the previous generations of Jewish biblical theologians and the present generation and, accordingly, also between their discourses. This gap contributes to the latter generation's sense of estrangement from the former.

The erasure of liberal/reform Jewish biblical theological undertakings in the construction of the past discussed here is an excellent case of history writing (or social memory construction) in the making. It is worth exploring whether the considerations advanced here may apply to other cases of marginalization or partial (or full) erasure of groups and ideas, whether momentary or long-lasting, in the construction of Jewish histories and in the development of the socially accepted memories of the past. This issue, however, is beyond the scope of this contribution.

69. This is implicitly or explicitly assumed in the works of K. Kohler and M. M. Kaplan.

70. Matters of genre appear in references to the lack of Jewish works comparable to the full-length, comprehensive volumes on "Old Testament theology" such as those of von Rad and Eichrodt.

Part 2

Case Studies

4

Fighting Forms of Idolatry: The Meaning of an Image of Moses in Jewish Theology

Asa Kasher

To interpret a verse or a chapter is to embed its text in a broader meaning framework. Interpretations can differ from each other in the breadth of the related meaning frameworks. One can embed a chapter in a meaning framework of a book, a school of thought, or a tradition. The purpose of this essay is to embed an image of Moses that arises from a certain Jewish tradition within the broadest possible Jewish meaning framework, one that interprets Jewish texts and practices in terms of a comprehensive, deeply entrenched, strictly observed opposition to all possible forms of idolatry.[1] A proper understanding of an image of Moses that emerges from a certain Jewish tradition is a gate to an understanding of Jewish texts and practices in a unified way. The merits of the proposed way of understanding will be discussed in the latter part of the present chapter.

AN IMAGE OF MOSES: OBSERVATIONS

Our starting point is a series of observations about an image of Moses that appears in some verses of the Bible and in a variety of midrash stories. Before I present that series of puzzling observations, I should clarify one aspect of my approach. The observations I am going to make are related to texts of different periods. They were created by different authors, under different circumstances, probably for different purposes. However, I will disregard the historical circumstances under which a certain image of Moses was evoked, in particular the purposes for which it was done, and focus on the image itself. On the firm assumption that all our sources are generally accepted as legitimate parts of Jewish tradition, a method of abstraction such as this seems to be useful to the extent that the emerging image of Moses is not trivial.

---

1. A similar study could have been devoted to an image of Abraham. The image of Moses seems to me to be more interesting.

This section will be devoted to observations about an attitude toward Moses or certain aspects of his story that can be made from traditional Jewish sources.

Our first source is the biblical story of Moses, particularly its earlier parts in Exodus. The first verse that refers to Moses does not mention proper names in the ordinary biblical manner. "And there went a man of the house of Levi, and took to wife a daughter of Levi. The woman conceived and bare a son. And when she saw him that he was a goodly child, she hid him three months" (Exod 2:1–2).[2] We are told about the birth of a child, but neither his name nor those of his parents are mentioned. This is an odd presentation of the facts. Recall the presentation of the birth of Reuben and Simeon, for example: "And Leah conceived, and bare a son, and she called his name Reuben. . . . And she conceived again, and bare a son . . . and she called his name Simeon" (Gen 29:32–33). The differences are quite startling. Moses is a biblical figure of much more significance than either Reuben or Simeon.[3] Why, then, start his story without mentioning the names of his parents as well as the name his father or his mother called him? Moreover, eventually we are going to be told who those people were: "And Amram took him Jochebed his father's sister to wife, and she bare him Aaron and Moses" (Exod 6:20). What could be the reason for starting the story of Moses by mentioning neither his own name nor his parents', when the three names are revealed soon afterward?

To be sure, the question has already been raised. The discussion of those verses in the *Zohar* includes the question about the father: "For what reason, his name was not mentioned?" and then there is an answer that ascribes much significance to the phrase "and there *went* a man," based on a story about a wrong decision made by the leader to divorce his wife, as a measure against Pharaoh's decree to kill all the sons. Amram's act was eventually considered so gravely mistaken, even by Amram himself, that he remarried Jochebed. According to that midrash, the nature of the mistake justifies blurring the identity of the culprit. Illuminating as a midrash such as this may be considered, it does not answer our major question: the three persons involved in the story are soon identified; why postpone identifying them fully?

Nahmanides' commentary of the same verses addresses the issue but answers it in a different way: the names of the man and his wife were not mentioned, "because if they had been mentioned, the names of their fathers and their grandfathers would also have to be mentioned, until Levi, but now it had to be brief until the birth of the savior." Nahmanides' answer does not fare better than the previous one. If the text is in a hurry to

---

2. All English biblical quotations will be from the King James Version.
3. Cf. the introduction of Korah (Num 16:1).

pronounce "the birth of the savior," why isn't his name mentioned in the text? Moreover, would the specification of the lineage "until Levi" be a real obstacle on the way toward "the birth of the savior"? Instead of "the man of the house of Levi," we would have had "Amram son of Kohath son of Levi." In Hebrew, it would mean five words rather than three—not reasonably a problem on the way to the end of the next verse.

Our next problem is the name *Moses*, given to him by the daughter of Pharaoh rather than by his parents. A medieval midrash, *The History of Moses* (*Divrey HaYamim LeMoshe*), includes a long list of names given to Moses by various people, according to a variety of midrash sources, for example, by his father (Hever), by his mother (Yequtiel), by his sister Miriam (Yered), by his brother Aaron (Avi Zanoah). The story of each name is illuminating, but I opine that every assertion that Moses had another, Hebrew name casts a shadow on the use of the name *Moses*, even though it ubiquitously appears in the Pentateuch, in all portions but one, from the first parts of Exodus to the last verses of Deuteronomy.

Not only has the *use* of the name *Moses* been marked as problematic but also the name *Moses* itself. Several times in the midrash literature, such as in *Midrash HaHefetz*, the question was posed, "Why is the name 'Moshe' written in the Bible without the letter Vav," as it should have been written according the Biblical Hebrew morphology?

The answer is intriguing. Resting on the numerical value of the letter *waw* which is six, the midrash says that the letter *waw* is missing from Moses' name because "he missed six prescriptions (*halachoth*)." Indeed, according to the Bible itself or exegetical discussions thereof (for example, *b. Zebahim* 101a), on six separate occasions, Moses was unable to issue the proper prescription, either because he had become angry (for example, *Sifri, Matoth* 157) or for some similar reason (*Midrash Mishley* 25). Accordingly, the name "Moses" is written in a way that marks a rare though recurrent weakness of Moses.

The next issue emerges with respect to the story of Moses killing an Egyptian during an attempt to defend a Hebrew. A medieval midrash, *Moses' Dying* (*Petirath Moshe*), includes a dialogue between God and Moses that takes place after Moses was told he would not be allowed to cross the Jordan into the promised land:

> Moses: "You have already written about me: 'My servant Moses . . . who is faithful in all mine house." (Num 12:7)
> God: "Did I tell you to kill the Egyptian?"
> Moses: "You killed all the firstborn Egyptians and will I die because of a single Egyptian?"
> God: "Are you similar to me, 'killeth and maketh alive' [1 Sam 2:6], can you make alive as I can?"

Most of the exegetical literature of the story of that incident involves attempts to exonerate Moses. A typical expression is what *Midrash Exodus Rabbah* says about the verse "he slew the Egyptian" (Exod 2:12): "because he was worthy to die (*ben maveth*)," because he had committed some grave crime against the Hebrew he was hitting when Moses intervened. However, the midrash I have just quoted manifests an utterly different attitude toward the same incident.

The next midrash I would like to quote is related to Moses' encounter with the daughters of the priest of Midian. When they return home, they tell their father Reuel: "An Egyptian delivered us out of the hands of the sheperds" (Exod 2:19). Again, some of the commentators on the verse interpret its depiction of Moses as an Egyptian most simply: "Was he an Egyptian? His clothes were Egyptians," not himself (for example, *Midrash Exodus Rabbah* 39). However, other midrashim understand it differently and even critically: "It means that Moses estranged and hid himself from being a Hebrew" (*Tanhuma Yashan* MS, quoted in *Tora Shlema* on that verse). Moreover, adds the same midrash, "and this is why he did not enter the land of Israel." The same idea is elaborated in *Midrash Deuteronomy Rabbah*, where Moses asks God to enter the promised land, if not alive then at least the way the late Joseph was about to enter it. The request is denied: "God told Moses: Whoever admits that he is from his land is buried in it and whoever does not admit it, is not buried in it. Joseph admitted that he was from his land and he will be buried in Shechem. You, who did not admit it, won't be buried in your land." Evidence that Joseph did not hide his origin is the way he was depicted by the chief butler of Pharaoh: "And there was there with us a young man, a Hebrew" (Gen 41:12). The evidence against Moses is that Reuel's daughters depicted him as an Egyptian.[4]

Finally, I would like to mention a related, well-known fact, namely, that Moses is hardly mentioned at all in the traditional text of the Passover *Haggadah*. Actually, Moses is mentioned just once, in passing, when verses are quoted that use the words "finger" and "hand" in the context of what God did in Egypt (Exod 8:15 and 14:31, respectively).

The second expression appears in a verse that mentions Moses, but the passage of the *Haggadah* does not put that fact to any use, being interested just in the number of plagues as related to the divine "finger" and "hand." Accordingly, some manuscripts of the *Haggadah* omit from it the part of the verse that mentions Moses.

This is, indeed, an oddity in the context of a ceremony the expressed major point of which is "our duty to tell the story of the deliverance from Egypt," and that "whoever dwells on the departure from Egypt is praisewor-

---

4. It seems that an interpretation is possible that would view Moses' fate as ethical reaction rather than legal punishment, but we cannot dwell on it presently.

thy." The striking absence of Moses from the text that describes a biblical process in which he played a major role is in obvious want of explanation.[5]

AN IMAGE OF MOSES: INTERPRETATION

We move now from the observations made in the previous section to a reasonable interpretation of all of them. I will do it in three steps. First, I will put forward a general attitude toward Moses. Second, I will justify this attitude on commonly held Jewish religious ground. Finally, I will show how this justified attitude explains each of the observations I made in the previous section.

First, then, is a general attitude toward Moses. It consists of two parts. One of them, the more prevalent in the literature of the Jewish tradition, rests on a highly positive portrayal of Moses as a person of extraordinary virtues and achievements. One example will suffice: the last verses of the book of Proverbs are devoted to the "virtuous woman." One of its praises of her is that "many daughters have done virtuously, but thou excels them all" (31:29). Common understanding of the praises of the virtuous woman takes it to refer, under appropriate circumstances, to a certain virtuous woman. However, several interpretations of a different nature have also appeared in the same tradition. A medieval midrash that I have already mentioned poses a question that presupposes the praises of the "virtuous woman" are all allegorical: "[The phrase] 'thou excellest them all,' whom was it used by Solomon [its alleged author] to refer to?" (*Moses' Dying*). The answer is that "he refered to nobody but Moses." The midrash goes on describing God as "comparing each of the sages to Moses and he fared better than all of them." The author then explains that Moses is greater than Adam, Noah, and, more significantly, Abraham, Isaac, Jacob, and Joseph. According to these portrayals of Moses, he was the most appropriate person for the duty of obtaining the commandments from God and delivering them to the children of Israel.

The first part of the general attitude toward Moses is, then, extraordinary praise, respect, and admiration. "There arose not a prophet since in Israel like unto Moses whom the lord knew face to face" (Deut 34:10), which is the conclusion of the Pentateuch. However, the second part seems to be just the opposite. Moses is a human being who is not beyond weakness, whose record is not free of sin and error. Moses is "not eloquent . . . slow of speech and of a slow tongue" (Exod 4:10). He did not behave perfectly. Moses committed a grave sin, for which he was severely punished: "Because ye trespassed against me among the children of Israel . . . because ye sanctified me not in the midst of the children of Israel, yet you shall see the land before thee, but thou shalt not go thither unto the land which I

---

5. Some kibbutzim, non-Orthodox *Haggadoth*, do mention Moses in their texts.

give to the children of Israel" (Deut 32:51–52). Moses did not have a strictly impeccable record as leader of the children of Israel. Moses was not a flawless person.

Now, what justifies a conspicuous portrayal of Moses as both superb and imperfect, within the framework of the Scripture? This may seem an odd question to pose let alone answer, so its presuppositions should be clarified before any attempt is made to tackle the difficulty it points out. We take it for granted that the holy writings of a religion constitute a pure expression of its basic values, whatever literary form they take. Every book, chapter, and verse of these writings is thus assumed to be directly related to some basic value of the related religion. Hence, there is room for an elaboration of the role played by a given element of Scripture in terms of what religious message it conveys. When a religion is taken to rest on certain values, a natural question with respect to each element of its holy writings would be how the latter manifest the former. Accordingly, our question about the portrayal of Moses within the framework of the Pentateuch concerns the religious significance of Moses' image as both superb and imperfect, and if one takes the Jewish religion to manifest in all its practices a certain set of religious values our question is how those are values expressed in the image of Moses that emerges from the Pentateuch.

The starting point of our answer is one of the Ten Commandments: "You shall not make unto thee any graven image, or any likeness of any thing that is in heaven above, or that is in the earth beneath, or that is in the water under the earth. You shall not bow down yourself to them, nor serve them" (Exod 20:4–5). These famous words express the basic religious value of absolute opposition to idol worship. Within the framework of the commandments, the prohibition of idolatry is justified on grounds of the distinction between God and "other gods," which are all false and the service of which is always idolatrous (Exod 20:3, 5). However, we use the opposition to idolatry as our starting point thus circumventing many theological difficulties.

The absolute nature of the biblical opposition to idolatry should be stressed. The commandment I mentioned does not specify certain idols to avoid serving. Actually, it does not mention any single idol, though it could have mentioned well-known idols, those of the neighboring peoples and countries. It does not mention any idol in particular because it is interested in all forms of idolatry, whether extant or merely possible. It is not very difficult to create a new form of idolatry. "They invent idols every day," says *Midrash Mekilta of Rashbi* (Exod 20:3, on "other gods"). The conclusion that one naturally draws from observations of this sort about idolatry is that everything on earth can under some circumstances become an idol. Moreover, the more admirable something is, the more natural, imminent, and significant is the danger that may be rendered an idol. A perfect person would be extremely admirable and thereby also naturally worshiped. Because the portrayal of Moses includes his superb qualities, the possibility exists of his being worshiped. Thus, on the one hand, the biblical portrayal of Moses risks Moses' being served by the children of Israel and their descendants as an idol.

Here is where the other elements of the image of Moses enter the picture. On the one hand, he is superb, but on the other hand, he is a human being of ordinary faults. If a person of superb qualities seems a natural candidate for idol worship, when his shortcomings are revealed, his candidacy for idol worship diminishes. The religious point of all the negative elements of the image of Moses, whether in the Bible or in midrash, is that, though Moses is an extraordinary human being, he should not be served as an idol, a false divinity. The mixed nature of the image of Moses, first in the Bible and then in midrashim, is justified.

Now, we return to the observations I made in the first section of this essay and briefly consider the significance of each of them. Generally speaking, they all contribute, in different ways, to the religiously crucial precautionary measure against the possibility of Moses' being worshiped as an idol.

Our first observation was related to the first appearance of Moses in Exodus, where neither his name nor his parents' are mentioned. The significance of this oddity is now clear. It plays down the appearance of Moses, by omitting from its presentation details that, on the one hand, are major but, on the other hand, are not crucial at the very beginning of the story. The names of the parents are mentioned in passing at a later point, while the name *Moses* is described as being conferred on the child by an Egyptian princess, whose name is not specified. On the assumption that, when a person is worshiped, all major details are regarded as significant, including his first name and the identity of his parents, the anonymity of the three persons in the beginning of the story seems to be naturally understood as a measure taken against the religious danger of Moses' eventually becoming the object of worship.

Now, consider the midrash that draws attention to the odd biblical spelling of the name *Moses*. The very fact that one's name is unique in some clear respect can facilitate an attitude of admiration and then worship; therefore, relating this oddity to occasions when Moses was wrong is again an attempt to play down his image or, more accurately, to prevent Moses' being treated as an idol. Whenever one faces the name *Moses*, one encounters his weakness too, the fact that Moses was not a perfect person. These reminders of his weakness and imperfection indeed recalls the absolute prohibition against worshiping Moses.

The midrash made another observation that compared self-portrayals of Joseph and of Moses, as implied by details included in the story of Joseph in jail and in the story of Moses on the well. One may assume that, on numerous occasions, biblical heroes acted wrongly because it left viewers with some negative impressions. The question arises as to why the midrash was interested in pointing out an incident in which Moses was involved, one that could have easily been consigned to silence. My answer is that what seems insignificant when it is ascribed to an ordinary person is highly significant when it is ascribed to an extraordinary person such as Moses, whose otherwise superb virtues render him an object of possible idolatry.

Similarly, the extremely marginal role played by Moses in the text of the Passover *Haggadah* is best explained as a precautionary step. Because the traditional text has been shaped within the framework of deep tensions between Jews and Christians, the precautionary silence can be naturally explained by those tensions, as suspicion of any presentation of the relationship between God and Moses, "his servant" (Exod 14:31), that is similar to Christian presentations of the relationship between God and Jesus, "his son." Be this as it may, it is clear that the silence of the *Haggadah* can be explained as an attempt to avoid any possibility of exaggerated admiration of Moses that could eventually confuse him with divinity.

Finally, let us add an observation that will lend itself naturally to a parallel explanation. Toward the end of the Pentateuch, the story of Moses comes to its sad end: "So Moses the servant of the Lord died there in the land of Moab . . . but no man knows of his sepulcher unto this day" (Deut 34:5–6). The reason for the sepulcher of Moses remaining unknown "unto this day" becomes apparent when the last verses of Deuteronomy are read on the background of our interpretation: "And there arose not a prophet since in Israel like unto Moses, whom the Lord knew face to face, in all the signs and wonders, which the Lord sent him to do in the land of Egypt to Pharaoh, and to all his servants, and to all his land, and in all that mighty hand, and in all the great terror which Moses showed in the sight of all Israel" (Deut 34:10–12).

Looking at the end of Moses' life, a person encounters a formidable hero, a prophet, the only one God "knew face to face," enabling him to show "terror . . . in the sight of all Israel." However, the higher the praises are, the higher is the awe, and the more religiously significant is the danger of possible idolatry. Against the background of popular worship of a golden calf, it is only natural to expect even more egregious worship of a "golden tomb" marking Moses' grave. The golden calf was eliminated after it had been created. The "golden tomb" should be eliminated before it is created. Hence, naturally, from the related religious point of view, "no man knoweth of [Moses'] sepulchre unto this day."

Notice that the concluding verses of the Pentateuch involve yet another object that could have easily become a focus of idolatry. It has been natural for Bible commentators to pose a question about the very last expression of the Pentateuch, which ascribes to Moses an act of showing great terror; namely, they ask, what was that act? Many commentators have answered it in terms of what happened at the top of Mount Sinai, when Moses was given the commandment tablets. This was the view of Ibn Ezra, Naḥmanides, Sforno, and others. However, the most interesting answer has been given by Rashi: "that he had the courage to break the tablets facing all of Israel." Facing people who have just witnessed the wondrous events of Mount Sinai dancing around a golden calf, saying "These be thy gods, O Israel, which brought thee up out of the land of Egypt" (Exod 32:4), Moses immediately realized that the tablets in his hands, created during an encounter with divinity, are prone to become objects of idolatry. They had to be broken, so he understood, not only as a precautionary measure directly related to the tablets themselves but also as an example of what should, from the religious point of view, be the right attitude toward any object of idolatry. The commentary of Rashi is thus deeper and more insightful than the alternatives. While many people seem to regard highly the "first Rashi," the very beginning of his commentary of the Pentateuch, we are much more impressed by the "last Rashi," the very end of the same commentary.

CONCLUSION

I have devoted much attention to a family of observations related to a certain image of Moses in the Pentateuch and midrashim. I have put forward an interpretation related to a deeply entrenched cause of religious concern, namely, the possibility of Moses being worshiped for his superb virtues and extraordinary achievements.

In conclusion, it ought to be pointed out that the case of Moses is just an example of how verses of the Bible and passages of midrashim can and, we dare say, should be interpreted as conveying one of the deepest principles of the Jewish religion, namely, the practical commitment of fighting idolatry, whatever form it takes.

Much of the Jewish tradition can be thus interpreted.[6] Maimonides tried to carry out this sort of programme of interpretation in parts of his *Guide of the Perplexed*. I am interested in the same programme, but for a philosophically different purpose.[7] I am interested in an interpretation of Jewish religious tradition that bears these three marks: First, it is acceptable from an internal religious point of view, being compatible with

6. For a full-fledged presentation, see my recent *Judaism and Idolatry* (Tel Aviv: Miśrad ha-biṭaḥon, 2004 [Hebrew]).

7. In modern times, *via Negativa* appeared in *Meshech Hochma* of Rabbi Meir Simha Hacohen of Dwinsk and in the writings of Yeshaiahu Leibowitz. Our version is more radical and systematic.

common conceptions of the principles of that tradition. Second, it is comprehensible from an external point of view as well, being couched in terms that can be used, analysed and understood both inside and outside of a religious tradition. Third, it is not a trivial observation about that tradition.

These three conditions apply the interpretations of many verses of the Scriptures, passages of midrash and observed practices that manifest a practical commitment to fighting all forms of idolatry. First, the idea of the Jewish religious tradition being commited to fighting idolatry is indeed compatible with all common conceptions of that tradition from its internal points of view. Second, the idea of opposing idolatry, in the sense of worshiping an aspect of one's world, is comprehensible, from internal as well as external points of view. Third, the idea that a war on idolatry is the meaning of much of what one encounters within the Jewish religious tradition is not trivial at all.

The fact that those three conditions obtain is interesting in an additional respect. Fighting idolatry can serve as a cultural common denominator for people who hold different attitudes toward the Jewish religious tradition or, in other words, for people who view it from both an internal point of view and an external point of view. Here, then, is a value that can be shared by both kinds of people, thus serving as a cultural common denominator.

5

◇◇◇◇◇◇◇◇◇◇◇◇◇◇◇◇◇

Jewish Conceptions of the Human Factor in Biblical Prophecy

Moshe Greenberg

Modern critical study of Hebrew Scriptures by Jews has seldom been conducted in the light of any theological principle.[1] Its proponents have either ignored the tenets of traditional religion in philological-historical inquiries that avoid engagement with theology or existential issues or have focused on different objects of inquiry, such as poetics, in which the historical factor is muted.[2] By orthodoxy, biblical criticism is generally regarded as incompatible with the foundations of Jewish belief.[3]

This situation differs from that obtaining in Christianity. Both Protestant and Roman Catholic Christians have accommodated themselves to the practice and main findings of criticism: theological seminaries today are the academic berths of most biblical critics. This was not accomplished without overcoming opposition, but the battles fought in churches in the 19th and 20th centuries and the conceptual refinement and clarification

Author's note: This chapter is slightly revised and updated by the editor, I. Kalimi, from M. Greenberg, *Studies in the Bible and Jewish Thought* (Philadelphia: Jewish Publication Society, 1995) 405–19. My thanks go to the editor and to the Jewish Publication Society for permission to republish this essay.

1. For rare exceptions see the prefaces of S. D. Luzzatto to his commentaries on the Pentateuch (1829) and Isaiah (1855), available in S. D. Luzzatto, *Selected Writings* (ed. M. E. Artom; Jerusalem: Bialik Institute, 1976) 2:97–134, 206–16. Also consult Franz Rosenzweig's letter to J. Rosenheim in F. Rosenzweig and M. Buber, *Die Schrift und ihre Verdeutschung* (Berlin: Schocken, 1936) 46–54, disproportionately famous owing to the scarcity of theological deliberation by Jewish scholars with critical sophistication.

2. Examples of the first category: Y. Kaufmann, H. L. Ginsberg, H. M. Orlinsky, E. A. Speiser; of the second: U. Cassuto, M. Weiss. For brief surveys of modern Jewish critical exegesis, see M. Waxman, *A History of Jewish Literature* (New York: Bloch, 1947) 4:633–70; *Encyclopaedia Judica* (Jerusalem: Keter, 1971) 4:899–903.

3. See S. Shaw, "Orthodox Reactions to the Challenge of Biblical Criticism," *Tradition* 10 (1969) 61–85 (with bibliography); S. Rosenberg, "Biblical Criticism in Modern Jewish Religious Thought," in U. Simon (ed.), *We and the Bible* (Tel Aviv: Dvir, 1979) 86–110 (extensive bibliographic survey [Hebrew]. A good exposition of theological reactions to criticism is R. J. Z. Werblowsky, "Biblical Criticism as a Religious Problem," *Molad* 18 (1960) 162–68 [Hebrew].

resulting from them have had no counterparts in the synagogue.[4] This essay seeks to contribute to the assessment of the relation of critical principles to Judaism and to the practice of Jewish exegetes. It focuses on one aspect of the critical stance: the supposition that, in the formulation of prophetic writings (and most of Scripture is ascribed by Jews to prophets), a human factor was present to such an extent that no account of them can overlook the personal circumstances and particular situation of their human authors.[5]

That this supposition is not in itself a denial of divine inspiration or revelation has been affirmed vigorously by modern Christian critics. Canon S. R. Driver stated in the preface to the eighth edition of his *Introduction to the Literature of the Old Testament*:

> It is not the case that critical conclusions, such as those expressed in the present volume, are in conflict either with the Christian creeds or with the articles of the Christian faith. Those conclusions affect not the *fact* of revelation, but only its *form*. . . . That both the religion of Israel itself, and the record of its history embodied in the Old Testament, are the work of men whose hearts have been touched and

---

4. The distinction certain rabbis made between allowed and prohibited criticism (*Hirschensohn*) or the metaphysical accommodation of it to faith (*Kook*) described by Rosenberg (see n. 3 above) remained private musings for all practical purposes. Decades later, M. Kapustin ("Biblical Criticism: A Traditionalist View," *Tradition* 3 [1960] 25–33) could still crudely characterize and reject "Biblical criticism [for which] the Torah is not word for word and letter for letter direct divine revelation. Neither are the writings of the *Nevi'im* (Prophets) or the *Ketuvim* (Hagiographa) divinely inspired, products of the *ruach ha-koiesh* (holy spirit). For the critics [they are] the works of certain individual personalities representing the 'Hebraic genius.'" Contrast the position of S. R. Driver—an eminent British critic—adduced below in the body of this chapter.

5. The question is this: when the prophet says, "Thus said Yʜᴡʜ," and proceeds to deliver a speech, what is the relation of his speech to what God said to him? I shall not deal with the question how the prophet receives revelation or what form the divine communication to him takes but only with the question of the immediate origin of the speech issuing from the prophet and that he commonly prefaces by the formula, "Thus said Yʜᴡʜ" or the like. How precise is "thus"?

The views presented in this essay are chiefly those arising from explication of scriptural data, whether by exegetes or others. They are not as such primarily grounded in a theology, in which extrascriptural (often extra-Jewish) systematic thinking is determinative. (Even the citation of the theologian Joseph Albo (below, p. 72 n. 24) bases itself on scriptural phenomena.) I seek to document the acknowledgment of literary facts, particularly those that resist easy accommodation to dogma. It is notable that, when Abarbanel writes as a philosophic critic, his position is more doctrinaire than when he writes as an exegete; see p. 74 n. 26.

For the following selection of sources, I have drawn heavily on the monumental collection of A. J. Heschel (*Torah from Heaven in the Perspective of the Ages* [London: Soncino, 1965] 2:123–298 and on the treatise on "the order in which the Torah was written," in *Torah Shelemah* (ed. M. Kasher; New York: American Biblical Encyclopedia, 1959) 19:328–79. Selection, arrangement, and interpretation are my own.

minds illumined, in different degree, by the Spirit of God, is manifest: but the recognition of this truth does not decide the question of the author by whom, or the date at which, particular parts of the Old Testament were committed to writing. . . . There is a human factor in the Bible, which, though quickened and sustained by the informing Spirit, is never wholly absorbed or neutralized by it; and the limits of its operation cannot be ascertained by an arbitrary a *priori* determination of the methods of inspiration; the only means by which they can be ascertained is by an assiduous and comprehensive study of the facts presented by the Old Testament itself.[6]

Such a latitudinarian approach to Scripture would seem to have no place in Judaism. Certainly Maimonides' formulation of the 8th of his 13 principles of faith (a byword among orthodox Jews) leaves little room for it:

[The] Torah from Heaven. To wit: we believe that the whole of this Torah that we have today is the selfsame that was given to Moses; and all of it is from the Power [הגבורה, i.e., God]; that is, it came to him, all of it did, from God—a coming called metaphorically speech, but whose manner is unknown to all but him (peace be to him) to whom it came; and that he was in the capacity [lit. degree] of a scribe to whom one dictates, and he wrote it all down—dates, stories, and commandments.[7]

This rigorous formulation is directed against Muslim attacks on the integrity of the Torah and the charge or the suspicion that Moses, independently of God, invented it.[8] A glance at talmudic antecedents shows that Maimonides chose the language of the most uncompromising of several views found in that treasury of classical (and wellspring of all subsequent) Jewish thought.

6. S. R. Driver, *Introduction to the Literature of the Old Testament* (Edinburgh: T. & T. Clark, 1909) viii, ix, xi.

7. Maimonides, Commentary to Mishnah *Sanhedrin* 10.1; see J. Kafah (ed.), *Mishnah ʿim Perush Rabbenu Moshe ben Miimon, Seder Neziqin* (Jerusalem: Mossad Harav Kook, 1964) 214.

8. See, for example, M. Perlmann, "Samauʾal al-Maghribi: Iftiam al-Yahud" ("Silencing the Jews") *PAAJR* 31 (1964) 53–57. K. P. Bland ("Moses and the Law according to Maimonides," in *Mystics, Philosophers, and Politicians* [ed. D. Swetschinski; Durham: Duke University, 1982] 49–66) argues that Maimonides "does not believe that Moses ever received the particulars of his law in revelation," but rather "considered Moses to have been the direct author of the Law" (p. 63)—despite "the obvious efforts [in the 13 principles] to find language that emphasizes the divine origin of the Law while minimizing the creative role of Moses in its promulgation" (p. 65). Bland's argument has cogency for Maimonides' esoteric doctrine; however, any reading of the 8th principle will yield not a "minimizing" of Moses' "creative role" but a forceful denial of it: Moses is figured as a scribe taking dictation. That is how believers through the ages have understood the principle, and Maimonides' choice of language and figure indicates that is how he intended to be understood by the masses. I am grateful to Alfred Ivri for calling my attention to Bland's stimulating article.

It was a jealously guarded dogma of early Judaism that "[the] Torah was from Heaven," meaning that not a word of the Pentateuch was—as charged by anti-Jewish writers of Hellenistic-Roman times[9]—an invention of Moses:

> And these have no portion in the world to come: Whoever says [the] Torah is not from Heaven. (Mishnah, *Sanhedrin* 10.1)

Another Tannaitic dictum:

> "Because he has spurned the world of the Lord" (Num 15:31)—this refers to whoever says, "[the] Torah is not from Heaven"; and even if he said, "The whole Torah is from Heaven excepting a given verse, which the Holy One—blessed be He—did not utter, but Moses, on his own [lit. from his own mouth]," he is one who "has spurned the word of the Lord. (Babylonian Talmud, *Sanhedrin* 99a)

This dogma had to be adjusted to evidence contrary to several scriptural passages. For example, the final verses of the Pentateuch tell of Moses' death and burial.

> There died Moses, the servant of the Lord" (Deut 34:5), is it possible that Moses wrote "There died Moses" while he was still alive? Rather, up to that verse Moses wrote, but from that verse onward Joshua wrote; so Rabbi Judah. . . . Rabbi Simeon retorted: Is it possible that the Torah scroll [that Moses delivered into the custody of the Levite-priests] was missing even a letter? Yet it is written, "Take this Torah scroll" (Deut 31:26, the account of the delivery)! Rather, up to that verse ["There died Moses"] the Holy One—blessed be He—was speaking and Moses was writing; from that verse on, the Holy One—blessed be He—was speaking and Moses was writing with tears, as it is written [of a similar procedure], "Baruch said to them, 'He [Jeremiah] recited aloud [lit. from his mouth] to me all these things while I wrote in a scroll with ink.'" (Babylonian Talmud, *Menahot* 30a)[10]

Other difficulties arise, perhaps the foremost being the style of Deuteronomy in which Moses speaks in the first person and appears to gloss freely, on his own, quotations of God's utterances (for example, the insert, "as the Lord your God commanded you," in the Sabbath commandment of the Decalogue, 5:12). The rabbis described the difference between the curses at the end of Leviticus (26:14–39.) and the curses at the end of Deuteronomy (28:15–68) as follows:

---

9. See M. Stern, *Greek and Latin Authors on Jews and Judaism* (3 vols.; Jerusalem: Israel Academy of Sciences and Humanities, 1984), 3:137, indexes s.v. Moses: Legislator of Jews.
10. Compare Babylonian Talmud, *Baba Batra* 15a (Isaac Kalimi).

Those [of Leviticus] are couched in the plural and Moses said them from the mouth of the Power, while these [of Deuteronomy] are couched in the singular and Moses said them on his own [lit., from his own mouth]. (Babylonian Talmud, *Megillah* 31b)[11]

This blatant contravention of the Sanhedrin passages troubled commentators. The Tosafists took the edge off the *Megillah* statement by qualifying "Moses said on his own" with the explanation "and by the Holy Spirit [of prophecy]," which at least derives Moses' speech from divine inspiration. Abarbanel made a distinction:

> Moses . . . said these things and expounded the commandments mentioned here to Israel under the necessity of his taking leave of them, and the Holy One wished that after he finished saying them . . . all should be written down in the Torah scroll just as Moses said it. . . . Hence, while the saying of these things to Israel was of Moses . . . the writing of it in the Torah scroll was not . . . for how could he write down anything on his own in God's Torah? . . . So this book is included among the divine books just like the others. Whoever says that Moses wrote down any given verse of them on his own—he is one who has "spurned the word of the Lord. . . ." That is why they said in *Megillah*, "The curses in Deuteronomy . . . Moses said them on his own"—said them, not wrote them . . . Similarly Moses prayed on behalf of the people at the incident of the Golden Calf on his own, for he was not commanded to do so by God—indeed to the contrary, he demanded that Moses desist from him . . . But the writing down of all such in the Torah was from the mouth of the Power . . . and whoever says . . . about the writing of the Torah that he [Moses] wrote anything that God did not say [dictate] to him, he is one who has "spurned the word of the Lord."[12]

The pietistic commentator Hayyim ben Atar did not hesitate to emphasize the Mosaic provenience of Deuteronomy in his comment to the book's first verse:

> "These are the words"—these and not the preceding ones—"that Moses spoke"—these are his own words, for the whole book is Moses' warning and admonition directed against any who would transgress

11. "'Moses said these [of Leviticus] from the mouth of the Power'—having been commissioned by Him to say . . . 'I shall set [such a curse], I shall visit [you with such a bane], I shall let loose [such a scourge]'—He who has the ability to do speaks so. But in Deuteronomy . . . Moses speaks on his own, 'He will visit [you with such a bane]'" (Rashi). Rashi's comment to Deut 28:23: "[Moses] mitigated his curses compared with those of God [in Leviticus]."

12. See Isaac Abarbanel, *Commentary on the Torah*, in his introduction to the book of Deuteronomy.

God's words. . . . Even when he resumed God's words in order to explain them it was not because he was ordered to do so but on his own.

Ben Atar calls the reference to the Egyptian bondage in Deuteronomy's version of the Sabbath commandment of the Decalogue (it is missing from Exodus) "the words of Moses" (at 5:15). He regards the speech beginning in 8:1 as displaying Moses' psychological insight.[13]

Such attributions to Moses do not deprive Deuteronomy of divine sanction (or even dictation); that is a dogmatic necessity no medieval believer would have challenged. What is notable is the latitude permitted within the scope of the dogma for human creativity. The literary (stylistic) facts point to Moses as the author of most of the book of Deuteronomy; the book's authority derived from the dogma that Moses' language was adopted by God and dictated back to him at the time the book was written down.

Quite surprising is the latitude shown in the interpretation of the prophetic message-formula, כה אמר יהוה "thus said the Lord," used by Moses in the narrative of Exodus. In Exod 32:27, Moses cites a divine command to slay the worshipers of the calf; but where is that command? The *Mechilta*[14] finds it in Exod 22:19, "Whoever sacrifices to a god other than the Lord alone shall be proscribed." A midrash puts it this way:

> Where did the Holy One—blessed be He—tell him to slay his fellows? He intimated to him at Sinai that anyone who worshiped an alien deity is subject to the death penalty; as it is said, "Whoever sacrifices to a god, etc." When he descended and found them worshiping an alien deity . . . he thought, "These are subject to the death penalty."[15]

It is clearly implied that the message-formula need not always be taken literally; a prophet's inference from an earlier utterance of God may be couched in the language of a direct citation, when in fact the prophet tailored it for the occasion.[16]

13. See E. Touito, *Rabbi Hayyim ben Atar and his Commentary to the Torah "Or ha-hayyim"* (Jerusalem: Ministry of Education, 1982) 33–34 [Hebrew].

14. *Massechet de-Pisha, parasha* 12; restored from early quotations: see H. S. Horovitz and I. A. Rabin, *Mechilta deRabbi Ishmael* (Jerusalem: Bamberger & Wahrman, 1960) 40, lines 9–10.

15. L. Ginzberg, *Genizah Studies in Memory of Solomon Schechter* (New York: The Jewish Theological Seminary, 1928) literature vol., 74–75 (reference from Heschel, *Torah from Heaven*, 145).

16. Or even invented it deliberately; see the following midrash aggadah from *Seder Eliahu Rabba* (ed. M. Friedmann; Vienna: Verlag der israelitisch theologischen Lehranstalt, 1900) 17:

> I call heaven and earth to witness that the Holy One—blessed be he—never said to Moses to stand in the gate of the camp and say, "Who is for the Lord—to me!" (Exod 32:26), or to say, "Thus said the Lord . . . 'Each of you . . . slay brother, neighbor, and kin'" (v. 27). Rather, righteous Moses reasoned: "If I say to the Israelites, 'Each of you slay his brother, etc.,' they will say, 'Did you not teach us that a court that condemns to death

An obscure passage in Sifre to Num 30:2 was understood by later interpreters to refer to this latitude:

> "This is the word that the Lord spoke" (Num 30:2). This tells that just as Moses prophesied with [the formula] "Thus said [the Lord]" so the other prophets prophesied with "Thus said"; but Moses exceeded them in that of him it is said, "This is the word, etc."[17]

The 15th-century philologist Profiat Duran[18] interpreted this passage in the course of explaining the Hebrew particle כה, which he called "a term of comparison":

> "Thus shall you say to my lord (= Esau; Gen 32:5)" means "the likes of these words," for Jacob did not care about the wording, only that they kept to the purport. I take similarly every "thus said the Lord" found in the sayings of the prophets. They mean by it the purport of God's speech to them, what is to be understood by his words. They do not scruple to make some verbal changes in it so long as the purport is kept unchanged. Hence "thus said the Lord" means "the likes of these words said the Lord." Now, when the sages said [that Moses used this common prophetic formula, yet exceeded the other prophets in using "This is the word"] they meant that what Moses relates [after the preface, "this is the word"] is the very speech that God uttered, without any verbal change. By saying, "This" it is not enough to retain the purport—the general idea—as did the other prophets. That much may be inferred from the sense of *koh*. But a better case can be made from the substance of the matter: Since the other prophets were foretellers only, not having been sent to give commandments but to admonish and warn concerning the observance of the Torah, while Moses alone (peace be to him) was sent to give commandments and Torah, therefore they said that "all the prophets prophesied with 'Thus said'—referring to the foretelling and the admonitions; but Moses our teacher (peace be to him) . . . exceeded them in that he gave commandments and Torah, and that is what is conveyed by 'This is the word that the Lord commanded.'"[19]

As lawgiver, Moses had to be precise in communicating the divine statutes.

---

one person in a sabbatical cycle is called murderous' [*Mishnah, Makkot* 1.10]? How come you put three thousand to death in one day (v. 28)?'" So he ascribed [the order] to the Heavenly Glory, as it is said, "Thus said the Lord, etc." What follows? "The Levites did [as Moses had bidden]" (v. 28).

17. *Seder Mattot, pisqa* 153: *Sifre D'be Rab* (ed. H. S. Horovitz; Lipsiae: Fock, 1917) 198.

18. Profiat Duran, named in Hebrew: Isaac ben Moshe Halevi (also known as the "Efodi"), was born in the second half of the 14th century, probably in Catalonia (Northern Spain), and died ca. 1415.; see I. Kalimi, *The Retelling of Chronicles in Jewish Tradition and Literature: A Historical Journey* (Winona Lake, IN: Eisenbrauns, 2009), 279–82.

19. *Maase Efod* (ed. J. Friedlaender and J. Kohn; Vienna: Holzwarth, 1865) 170.

Rashi, at Num 30:2, cites the enigmatic midrash without explanation; a supercommentary to Rashi fills the lack, offering a variation of Duran's view:

> "Thus" refers to the purport of some verbal matter while "this" refers to the matter itself. Since all the prophets prophesied through an "unclear mirror," being incapable of receiving more than the purport of the matter communicated to them, they had to use the formula, "thus said the Lord." . . . But since the prophecy of our teacher Moses (peace be to him) was through a "clear mirror," and he was capable of receiving what was communicated to him just as it was, in his case "this is the word" was used, meaning this very matter, without any alteration. But because at the start of his mission our teacher Moses (peace be to him) had not yet attained to the degree that he enjoyed at its end, he had also to use to formula "thus said the Lord" on several occasions . . . namely, at the start of his career.[20]

The application to Moses of varying degrees of prophecy[21] recurs in another way in Abarbanel's comment to Moses' Song at the Sea (Exodus 15). How is it that the song is attributed to Moses (and, similarly, Deborah's Song to her and Barak, and Solomon's Song to him)? Because, Abarbanel answers, what is called song (שירה) is produced by a human whose ability has been heightened by the Holy Spirit:

> The Holy Spirit is not [like a full-fledged prophecy], for it does not produce visions of forms and parables, and its appearance is not marked by deep sleep and loss of senses. Rather the prophet voluntarily chooses to speak wise sayings, or hymns, or admonitions, etc. And because the divine spirit joins itself to him and helps him shape his speech, his degree is called the Holy Spirit. . . . For just as a prophet does not prophesy continuously, but starts and stops, so he may prophesy at one time in the form of the highest degree and at another in a lower degree, or through the Holy Spirit. . . . Every song found among the sayings of the prophets is an utterance they themselves formulated through the Holy Spirit. . . . When they are not prophesying they can speak through the Holy Spirit in beautiful figures and in high style. . . . Jeremiah wrote his book and the book of Kings through prophecy, which is why they are included in the second division of Scripture, the Prophets; Lamentations he composed through the Holy Spirit, which is why it is in the Hagiographa. And because songs are produced and

---

20. Eliyahu Mizraḥi printed in *ʾArbaʿa Perushim ʿal Rashi* (Jerusalem: Divre Hakamim, 1958) part 4 (Numbers) 54b. On "(un)clear mirror," see I. Gruenwald, *Apocalyptic and Merkabah Mysticism* (Leiden: Brill, 1980) 135.

21. See Maimonides, *The Guide of the Perplexed*, II:45; in the translation of S. Pines (Chicago: University of Chicago Press, 1963) 395ff.

formulated by the prophet . . . they are always attributed to the one who made them. . . . To be sure, all those songs were written down in the Torah and the Prophets because they were approved by God and ordered by him to be written there. . . . Thus the formulation of the Song at the Sea was by our teacher Moses, but its having been written down in the Torah was from the mouth of the Power. [22]

In summary, the prevailing dogma was that every word in the Torah was dictated by God. This dogma was the necessary support of a hermeneutic that ascribed significance not only to the contextual sense but to subcontextual units—clauses, phrases, even individual words torn out of context. Extreme hermeneutical freedom had to be counterbalanced by absolute assurance that the ground-text was perfect and supercharged with significance—in other words, that it was divine through and through. This formal ascription of the final form of the text to divine dictation did not blind exegetes to the varied styles of the Torah and the exigencies that indicated a human (Mosaic) origin for many passages. Room was left for a natural attribution to humans, even of prophetic speech introduced by the formula, "thus said the Lord."

In dealing with the rest of the prophets, tradition readily conceded the presence of a human factor, in accord with the literary evidence. The fundamental observation was made by a late 3rd-century Talmudic sage:

> Rabbi Isaac said: The same communication (*signon*, from Latin *signum* "watchword") occurs to several prophets, yet no two prophets prophesy the same communication. [The prophet] Obadiah said, "Your arrogant heart has seduced you" (1:3), while Jeremiah said, "Your horrible nature has seduced you, your arrogant heart" (49:16). (Babylonian Talmud, *Sanhedrin* 89a)

Meiri glossed this as follows: "Prophets do not prophesy in the same language even when their prophecy is the same communication. For example: Obadiah and Jeremiah [have identical communications] in their prophecies against Edom, yet the language differs." [23] By this criterion, the Talmud discovers the sign by which King Jehoshaphat of Judah judged the four hundred prophets of the Israelite king false: they all predicted victory at Ramoth Gilead in identical language (1 Kgs 22:6).

How did Jewish thinkers explain this diversity in unity? By variations in the vehicles of prophecy. Here are excerpts from the account given by Joseph Albo, a 15th-century theologian:

22. Isaac Abarbanel, *Commentary on the Torah* (Jerusalem: Bne Arb'el, 1964) 2:124–25.

23. Menahem Meiri, *Sefer Bet Ha-beḥira 'al Sanhedrin* (ed. A. Sofer [Schreiber]; Frankfurt: Hermon [no date]) 323.

Since prophecy springs from a single active cause—God, may He be
blessed, and its end is forever the same—to lead mankind to happiness, why do the words of the prophets differ from one another even
when they treat of the same topic? . . . Our sages suggest an explanation in *Bereshit Rabbah* (4.4): A Cuthean [Gentile] once asked Rabbi
Meir, "Is it possible that he of whom it is said, "Do I not fill heaven
and earth" (Jer 23:24), should have spoken to Moses from between
the staves of the Ark' (cf. Exod 25:22)? He replied, "Bring me a large
[magnifying] mirror"; and he brought it. He said, "Look at your reflection"; he looked and saw it large. Then he said, "Bring me a small [re-
ducing] mirror"; and he brought it. He said, "Look at your reflection";
he looked and saw it small. Then he said to him: "If you, mere flesh
and blood, can change yourself into several forms at will, how much
more so he who spoke and the world came into being!" Apparently the
Cuthean meant to deny that prophecy was an emanation from God.
He thought that it was rather a mere work of the imagination, as is
the opinion of the philosophers and their followers . . . because it is
impossible that he, being one, should be seen by prophets under so
many different forms. For that conduces to thinking that if it comes
from the deity, the divine active cause must be plural and changing in
nature. . . . Rabbi Meir confuted this notion through the analogy of
mirrors. As an object appears in different forms . . . according to the
shape of the mirror in which it is reflected . . . though the object is
unchanging, so God, be He blessed, appears to the prophets in many
forms according to the clarity and purity of the media [e.g., the imaginative faculty], though he . . . is neither plural nor changing. . . . In the
same manner, the object seen changes in accord with change in the
seers: if the seer . . . has clear vision he will see the reflection one way,
but if he is weak-visioned he will see it in another. . . . (*Ikkarim* 3.9)[24]

As Albo himself summarizes at the start of the discussion, "Different effects may arise from the same agent, depending on the nature of the recipients." This medieval theory states abstractly the assumption of a Talmudic
comparison of the throne visions of Isaiah (chap. 6) and Ezekiel (chap. 1):

> Rava said: All that Ezekiel saw Isaiah saw [only he did not go into
> detail]. To whom may Ezekiel be likened? To a country bumpkin who
> saw the king. To whom may Isaiah be likened? To a dweller in the
> [capital-] city who saw the king [and does not trouble to tell about it].
> (Babylonian Talmud, *Hagigah* 13b)

Thus, the human factor is regarded as decisive in explaining divergences
between prophetic descriptions of one and the same object of vision.

---

24. For the full text, see Joseph Albo, *Book of Principles* (ed. and trans. I. Husik; Philadelphia: Jewish Publication Society, 1946) 3:76–84.

The most developed conception of human conditioning of prophecy is found in Abarbanel's commentary. We have already noted how he ascribed "songs" to prophets freely composing under the Holy Spirit, and how near contemporaries—Duran and Mizrahi—affirmed that the prophetic formula "Thus said the Lord" introduces the gist of a divine communication whose wording belongs to the prophet. Evidently, the humanism of Christian Europe, with its renewed emphasis on the individual and self-expression, affected Jewish conceptions of prophecy. Here is how Abarbanel elaborated the Talmudic observation of prophetic diversity in unity in accounting for the similar eschatological visions of the Temple Mount in Isaiah 2 and Micah 4:

> [Rabbi Isaac asserted] that it is possible that the matter perceived by [two prophets] will be identical but the wording divergent. When I saw that Isaiah and Micah both prophesied the same communication, I thought: Isaiah prophesied this first, wherefore it is said here, "The word that Isaiah visioned," since he indeed was the one who had the vision. When Micah perceived the same general matter in the course of his prophesying he couched it in Isaiah's very words. That is to say: Micah received from God . . . the matter of the prophecy, while the wording of the communication he took from Isaiah. Hence [the vision] is not introduced in Micah with the formula, "Thus said the Lord" or "The word of the Lord that came to Micah," like other prophecies of his. For this speech came from God first to Isaiah, not to Micah who took it from Isaiah's words and inserted into it some explanatory additions.
>
> Likewise . . . our lord Moses himself said in the *Ha'azinu* song (Deut 32:36), "For the Lord will vindicate His people, and get satisfaction for His servants," and David repeated this very verse in Psalm 135[:14]. . . . Surely David did not prophesy the very same communication as did [Moses] . . . rather, he took that verse from the words of his teacher. . . . Frequently we find . . . that one prophet says what another prophet already said in the very same words. (Comment to Isa 2:1)

Abarbanel reverts to the subject in his comment to Jer 49:16, further developing his understanding of Rabbi Isaac's dictum:

> The prophets [other than Moses] perceived the general purport of the matter communicated to them by the Holy One—blessed be he—and then related and wrote it down in their own language. Hence when they perceived similar matters, they sometimes couched them in the very words that they saw in the prophecies of other prophets, with which they were familiar. . . . Isaiah said, "For my strength and my song is Yah, the Lord; and he has been my deliverance,"[25]—a line derived

25. See Isa 12:2.

from [Moses'] Song at the Sea (Exod 15:2). . . . Not that prophecies came to [later prophets] in the same wording as to Moses our teacher and in his degree; rather they perceived matters [in a general sense] and on their own couched them in the language of verses with which they were familiar. So [is the case of] this prophecy of Jeremiah, which he couched in the language of Obadiah.[26]

Abarbanel has virtually anticipated the modern notion of the literary education of prophets, and on the same ground: evidence within the oracles of familiarity with antecedent Israelite traditions.

Albo ascribed the differences among the prophets to divergences in their faculties; his younger contemporary Abarbanel applied this general principle to specific cases — for example, in this comparison of Jeremiah with Isaiah:

> I am of the opinion that Jeremiah was not very expert either at composition or rhetoric, as was Isaiah or other prophets. Hence you find in his speeches many verses . . . missing a word or two . . . very, very frequent use of *ʿal* [properly, "on"] for *ʾel* [properly, "to"], masculine for feminine . . . singular for plural and vice versa, past for future and vice versa, and shifts of second to third person in a single sentence. Moreover, there is chronological disorder in his speeches.
>
> I believe that the cause of this was the youth of Jeremiah when he was called to prophesy. . . . Indeed he protested, "I do not know how to speak, for I am but a youth" (1:6). Isaiah, of royal blood and raised in the court of the king, spoke with eloquence; the other prophets were called after they attained to maturity in worldly matters and gained experience in dealing with people; so they knew how to arrange their sermons. Jeremiah, on the other hand, was of the priests of Anathoth [a class apart and a villager to boot]; while still young, being called to prophesy . . . he was constrained to proclaim what the Lord commanded in language he was accustomed to.[27]

Abarbanel thus assigns to the human factor a predominant role in the verbal formulation and arrangement of a prophetic collection of oracles. He holds the modern hermeneutical principle that the language of prophecy is conditioned by the personal circumstances and talent of the prophet—his biography, his experience, and his education.[28]

---

26. Abarbanel identifies Prophet Obadiah with the official of King Ahab (ca. mid 9th century B.C.E.; 1 Kgs 18:3–16), as already identified by the rabbis in Babylonian Talmud, *Sanhedrin* 39b. For this phenomenon in biblical and postbiblical literature, see I. Kalimi, "The Story about the Murder of the Prophet Zechariah in the Gospels and Its Relation to Chronicles," *Revue Biblique* 116 (2009) 246–61.

27. See Abarbanel in his introduction to the Jeremiah commentary.

28. These citations from Abarbanel's commentary to the Prophets give much more scope to the human element in the formulation of prophecy than appears in his *Commentary*

Jewish exegesis of late antiquity and medieval times thus recognized that the prophet had a hand in the shaping of his prophecy. Did it also recognize an effect of the audience on prophecy? The one area in which early Jewish thinkers delved into the reception factor in prophecy was anthropomorphism and related theological scandals such as the sacrificial cult. The exigency of adjusting naive biblical conceptions to sensibilities arising from theological reflection resulted in tacit criticism of aspects of biblical language about God. Rudimentary in talmudic literature, this criticism reaches full expression under the influence of Islamic polemics. In defense, Jewish exegesis seized on a talmudic dictum, "The Torah spoke in the language of humankind," originally meaning that biblical language is to be interpreted according to ordinary usage, and gave it the new sense, "biblical speech about God employs language drawn from human experience." By this adroit hermeneutical move, all the vivid imagery of scriptural speech about God became metaphoric. The reason offered by Jewish thinkers and exegetes for the Bible's use of such scandalous language was the ignorant and brutish state of the Israelites who received the Torah: they had to be spoken to in the gross terms suitable to their understanding. The wise, however, realize the necessity of translating the picturesque God-language of the Bible into appropriate philosophic conceptions.

This vast topic—in theological terms, "the condescendence of God"—has been systematically treated by every major medieval Jewish thinker and so will not be further discussed here. But to forestall misunderstanding, the following important caution is cited from a recent survey: unlike the idea that the prophetic message was conditioned by human factors, on which premoderns and moderns agree, the idea of divine condescendence differs in a crucial point from its apparent modern counterpart:

> We are not dealing here with an evolutionary mentality, which sees Jewish history as moving from a primitive state (in need of such condescendence on the part of the divine) to a more perfect one. Such a view was virtually unknown in antiquity. . . . We are dealing here with a synchronic view; at all times there are both learned and simple people, but God places himself within reach of the simple. [29]

---

to Maimonides' *Guide of the Perplexed*—as the latter's position is summarized in A. J. Reines, *Maimonides and Abrabanel on Prophecy* (Cincinnati: Hebrew Union College, 1970); see, e.g., Reines's summary statement (p. ixxv): "prophecy is miraculously communicated as a finished creation from God to the prophet, who is merely a passive recipient and produces nothing of the prophecy he apprehends."

    29. F. Dreyfus, "Divine Condescendence (synkatabasis) as a Hermeneutic Principle of the Old Testament in Jewish and Christian Tradition," *Immanuel* 19 (1984–85) 74–86, esp. p. 83. The original French version of this article appears in *Congress Volume, Salamanca 1983* (ed. J. A. Emerton; VTSuppl. 36; Leiden: Brill, 1985) 96–107. A more extensive treatment is S. D. Benin, "The 'Cunning of God' and Divine Accommodation," *Journal of the History of Ideas* 45 (1984) 179–91. On page 189, Benin cites Yehuda HaLevi's *Kuzari* (1:98; Hirschfeld translation, 67) to

In summary, from the Talmud to the Renaissance, classical Jewish thought and exegesis invests the prophetic writings with divine authority: all were inspired by the Holy Spirit—in the case of the Torah (the prophecy of Moses), the text was ultimately dictated by God. This formal, dogmatic predication of divine inspiration and authorship does not hinder acknowledgment of the literary evidence of human shaping of the text. The Torah even contains extensive tracts formulated by Moses; their inclusion in the Torah means that they were ultimately sanctioned (dictated) by God, but the personal touch of Moses is there "to this day." Apart from the Torah, it is freely posited that prophecy is conditioned by the personality and the capacity of the prophet: his age, his spiritual level, his education—all affect his message. This alone accounts for the variety of styles and formulations that distinguish the prophets from one another, even when—and particularly when—they communicate similar messages. Hence, the introductory prophetic formula "thus said the Lord" signifies no more than "this is the substance of the Lord's communication to me, couched in my own language." It also happens that one prophet adopts the wording of his predecessor, with which he was familiar by education, when that wording seemed to him a suitable vehicle for the word of God that came to him. The personal factor may be so dominant that the inexperience and lack of learnedness of a prophet result in faulty language and a disordered text.

Classical Jewish exegetes acknowledged these literary facts in the face of the great temptation to absolutize the authority of Scripture and silence the incessant challenges to its integrity and validity by categorically asserting that all is simply divine dictation. To modern Jewish critics, they are a model of reverence toward the source of religion that does not entail blindness to the complexity of that source or the adoption of a far-fetched cloaking of that complexity. The tradition of honest and sober reasoning, accommodating articles of faith to (literary) facts, stands the critics in good stead as they confront a wave of simplistic dogmatic piety that seeks to

---

the effect that even if all persons at the time of Israel's beginnings had been philosophers, "discoursing on the unity and government of God, they would have been unable to dispense with images, aid would have taught the masses that a divine influence hovered over this image, which was distinguished by some miraculous feature" (*Kuzari*, 1:98). This seems to conflict with Dreyfus' rejection of an evolutionary view. And yet it may be harmonized with Dreyfus as follows: The masses do gradually move from crude to more refined ideas, through divine pedagogy and condescendence, so one may speak of an evolution of refinement among masses. Philosophers (like Moses and the prophets) knew better from the first. HaLevi's assertion that even the philosophers of antiquity would have been unable to dispense with images is connected with what they "would have taught the masses"—suggesting that their teaching was an accommodation to a level of understanding lower than their own. I am grateful to Mr. Benin for calling my attention to his illuminating article.

impose itself on the entire community, stifling curiosity and independence of judgment.[30]

30. On the disinclination of modern Jewish Bible scholars to theologize, see J. D. Levenson, "Why Jews Are Not Interested in Biblical Theology," in J. Neusner, B. A. Levine, and E. S. Frerichs, eds., *Judaic Perspectives on Ancient Israel* (Philadelphia: Fortress, 1987) 281–307; and the response by I. Kalimi, "History of Israelite Religion or Hebrew Bible / Old Testament Theology? Jewish Interest in Biblical Theology," *Early Jewish Exegesis and Theological Controversy: Studies in Scriptures in the Shadow of Internal and External Controversies* (Jewish and Christian Heritage 2; Assen: Van Gorcum, 2002) 107–34 esp. pp. 118–34.

6

◇◇◇◇◇◇◇◇◇◇◇◇◇◇◇◇◇◇◇

Biblical Destinies: Conditional Promises

URIEL SIMON

The blessing recited after the prophetic reading (*Haftarah*) in synagogue during the Shabbat morning service conveys our belief that the biblical destinies of ultimate redemption, of days in which "the land shall be filled with devotion to the Lord as water covers the sea," will be achieved in their entirety: "You are faithful, O Lord our God, and Your words are faithful, and not one of Your words shall come back unfulfilled, for You are a faithful (and merciful) God and King. Blessed are You, O Lord, the God Who is faithful in all His Words." We must surely ask whether the realization of these destinies has already begun, whether the return to Zion and establishment of the State of Israel are the first stages of the *ultimate* redemption, that is, of the End of Days? Or should our return and revival be more rightly seen in the perspective of the two previous redemptions— from Egyptian bondage and from Babylonian exile? The late Chief Rabbi Shlomo Goren, in an address at the "Merkaz ha-Rav" yeshiva, was absolutely confident: "Everything is proceeding in accordance with the heavenly plan, and we have no reason to fear any man. We must be confident that we are destined to realize the third redemption, and in our time Judah shall be delivered and Israel shall dwell secure" (*Ha-Tzofeh*, January 27, 1974). The rabbi's reference to "the third redemption" was based on a midrash according to which the third redemption will be the last: "'The third shall be left in it' [Zech 13:8]: That is to say, only in the third redemption shall they settle in their land [the words 'shall be left in it' are interpreted in the sense of 'shall stay in the land forever']; the first redemption is the redemption from Egypt, the second is the redemption of Ezra, and *the third will never end*" (*Tanḥuma*, Shofetim 9).

It is generally agreed that our actions may influence the acceleration or frustration of the process, but differences arise when one asks whether the process itself is unidirectional, irreversible, and final. Most religious Zionists believe that we are currently in the early stages of our ultimate redemption—indeed, an attractive, exciting, and inspiring belief, but wishful thinking should not be an adequate reason to adopt it on the narrow basis of the midrash I have just quoted and a few others like it. We must clarify the ideas underlying this belief and its moral implications and, in addition, determine to what extent it indeed agrees with the overall message of the Hebrew Bible.

In the Bible, the divine promise is not a unilateral, isolated action, supposed to be fulfilled to the letter under any circumstances; rather, it is part of a complex "educational" process directed by God's plan for the recipient of the promise, dependent on the recipient's responsiveness and obedience,[1] and considerate of its implications for a third party on whom it impinges.

The divine promises have a formative impact on the life of the patriarch Abraham. By virtue of the crucial fact that Abraham was not born in Canaan, his bond with that land was not natural (as it would be for a native); neither was the bond normal (as it would be for an emigrant), because Abraham did not come to it for reasons of subsistence or quality of life, as his father Terah had indeed intended (as related in Gen 11:31). His bond with the land of Canaan was destiny-oriented, based as it was on an intertwined command and promise: "The Lord said to Abram, 'Go forth from your land and your birthplace and your father's house to the land I will show you [that is, that I have chosen for you]'" (12:1). However, Abraham's heroic obedience to the command did not yield the expected, immediate fulfillment of the divine promise: during the ritual of the "covenant between the pieces," he was informed that the promise would come true only 400 years later, when the Israelites would be released from Egyptian bondage (15:13).

To the astounding delay in fulfillment of the promise of the land was added the even more perplexing delay in fulfillment of the complementary promise, to create a nation: Isaac was born only after Sarah had been barren for many long years, after Abraham had almost given up hope.[2] This seems to mean that our very existence as a nation resulted not from natural,

---

1. See Deut 8:1, 19–20; 11:16–21. What Jeremiah says of God's decrees is equally true, a fortiori, of His promises: "At one moment I may decree that a nation or a kingdom shall be uprooted and pulled down and destroyed; but if that nation against which I made the decree turns back from its wickedness, I change My mind concerning the punishment I planned to bring on it. At another moment I may decree that a nation or a kingdom shall be built and planted; but if it does what is displeasing to Me and does not obey Me, then I change My mind concerning the good I planned to bestow upon it" (Jer 18:7–10).

2. Abraham indeed obeys God fully and with marvelous alacrity: He leaves Haran "as the Lord had spoken to him" (Gen 12:4); circumcises himself, his son, and all male members of his household on the very day he was commanded to do so; rises early both to expel Ishmael and to sacrifice Isaac; and runs to greet the three wayfarers and offer them his hospitality. God, however, does not immediately keep His promises, and Abraham's faith is put to an unbearable test, namely, the need to reconcile himself to the ongoing, endless delay and wait passively. Abraham's ability to live under the tremendous tension between activism and passivism, between quasi-Zionist activity and quasi-*ḥaredi* hopeful waiting, is perhaps his greatest

normal increase but from the miraculous intervention of a God who kept the promise "I will make of you a great nation" (12:2). Moreover, Abraham lived in the promised land with the status of a "resident alien" (23:4); his wells were stopped up by the Philistines, and only when he had to bury his dead wife did he finally secure a real foothold and buy a small burial plot.

These basic facts imply the distinction between the *natural* bond with a land—any land—and the *supernatural* or *destiny-oriented* bond with the land of Israel. A natural bond is that of a nation living in its own land, and it is this presence that gives it possession; most nations of the world indeed see their attachment to their country in that light. They consider national possession of land to be a "natural right," the result of a significant historical development: native birth, emigration, conquest, long-lasting presence, creation of a distinctive local culture, and so on. In their national consciousness, the natural bond is seen as a basic element: a nation may be required to defend its land and its independence, but it is not generally in danger of being uprooted from that land. The danger of exile is not perceived as a real threat, nor does it impinge on their consciousness.

The destiny-oriented bond, on the other hand, implies that the right to the land is defined as based on a divine promise, which takes precedence (in time and, in particular, in principle) over any real presence and is not conditional on this presence. The divine promise is like a pact or covenant, the conditions of which must be fulfilled if presence in the land is to be guaranteed; violation of those conditions is punished by being uprooted from the land and sent back (for a shorter or longer time) into exile.

Each kind of bond has its advantages and disadvantages: The natural connection of a nation with its land is continuous but generally finite, because when the nation ceases to exist as a distinct entity (as indeed happened to most ancient peoples), that presence comes to an end. Israel's destiny-oriented bond with its land is intermittent but nevertheless eternal.

This distinction between the temporary nature of our domination of the land and the eternity of our existence as a nation is taught in the Torah and repeated in the prophetic books of the Bible. Thus, on the eve of our entry into the land, Moses informed us in the book of Deuteronomy of God's admonishment and promise:

> When you have begotten children and children's children and are long established in the land, should you act wickedly and make for yourselves a sculptured image in any likeness, causing the Lord your God displeasure and vexation, I call heaven and earth this day to witness against you that you shall soon perish from the land that you are

achievement. Indeed, how could we pick ourselves up after 2,000 years of exile, were it not for the Abrahamic heritage combining the two opposites: immediate obedience to a command and boundless patience in the face of tardy salvation?

crossing the Jordan to possess; you shall not long endure in it, but shall
be utterly wiped out. The Lord will scatter you among the peoples, and
only a scant few of you shall be left among the nations to which the
Lord will drive you. . . . But when you search there for the Lord your
God, you will find Him, if only you seek Him with all your heart and
soul—when you are in distress because all these things have befallen
you and, in the end, return to the Lord your God and obey Him. For
the Lord your God is a compassionate God: He will not fail you nor
will He let you perish; He will not forget the covenant which He made
on oath with your fathers. (Deut 4:25–31; see also Lev 26:38–45; Deut
30:1–5)

The prophet Amos delivered a similar message to the complacent, self-
confident Northern Kingdom of Israel, about one generation before the
destruction of Samaria (722/21 B.C.E.):

Behold, the Lord God has His eye upon the sinful kingdom: I will wipe
it off the face of the earth! But I will not wholly wipe out the House
of Jacob—declares the Lord. For I will give the order and shake the
House of Israel—through all the nations—as one shakes [sand] in a
sieve, and not a pebble falls to the ground. All the sinners of My people
shall perish by the sword, who boast, "Never shall the evil overtake us
or come near us." In that day, I will set up again the fallen booth of
David: I will mend its breaches and set up its ruins anew. I will build it
firm as in the days of old. (Amos 9:8–11; see also Jer 29:10–14)

Now, as then, our settlement in this land is the result of obeying the commandment "Go forth!" (whether as a religious imperative or a Zionist
commitment), and this abnormal bond of our nation with its land is most
sublimely expressed in the Law of Return (enacted by the Knesset in 1950),
which guarantees all Jews, anywhere, the right to observe that commandment, automatically grants them full citizenship on arrival in the country,
and exempts them from all the demands made on any person going through
the usual citizenship procedures.

The delay in fulfillment of the divine promises to the patriarchs may
be viewed in two ways: one metaphysical, the other educational. The metaphysical aspect concerns the supernatural character of the chosen people
and of its attachment to the chosen land, whereas the educational aspect
concerns the obligation of those to whom the promises were made to pass
difficult tests in order to be worthy of their future fulfillment. The stories
of the patriarchs indeed bring out the difficulty of these tests. Abraham
has his doubts: "How shall I know that I am to possess it?" (Gen 15:8), and
"O that Ishmael might live by Your favor!" (17:18). Sarah, too, can hardly
believe the tidings: "Sarah laughed to herself" (18:12). Steadfast faith is a
prerequisite for realization of the promises to Abraham: "He trusted in

the Lord, and He reckoned it to his merit" (15:6), "Walk in My ways and be blameless, and I will establish My covenant between Me and you, and I will multiply you very greatly. . . . And I will give unto you and your seed after you the land in which you sojourn, the whole land of Canaan, as an everlasting holding, and I will be their God" (17:1–2, 8).

Because the destiny-oriented bond with the land is supernatural, it has a purpose, as defined in God's comment to the angels about the election of Abraham: "For I have singled him out so that he will charge his sons and his posterity to keep the way of the Lord, to do righteousness and justice, so that the Lord may bring upon Abraham what He has promised him" (18:19). This formative verse enunciates two basic principles: (a) The election is not an independent goal; it serves a well-defined religious and moral purpose. (b) Fulfillment of the promises is conditional on Israel "keeping the way of the Lord." This means that the realization of the destiny-oriented bond between Israel and its land is conditional on the nation's doing "righteousness and justice," and this condition serves as insurance, first, against the danger that a nation under divine protection might relapse into improper behavior and, second, against the danger that a nation, chosen from among all other nations, might become arrogant and self-centered. The universal scope of divine morality is indeed underlined in the Torah by the grim announcement that Abraham's descendants' possession of the land will be postponed by several hundred years and that they will have to await their destiny in the Egyptian "house of bondage": "And they shall return here in the fourth generation, for the iniquity of the Amorites is not yet complete" (15:16). In other words, the right of Abraham and his offspring to possess the land will not come to fruition as long as the "seven nations" are still possessing it rightfully. That is, Israel's destiny-oriented right does not automatically cancel out the natural right of others,[3] just as the Canaanites' natural right does not cancel out Israel's destiny-oriented right.[4]

3. Rashi emphasizes this in his commentary to Gen 13:7, relying on a midrash that I quote in full: "'And there was strife between the herdsmen of Abram's flocks and the herdsmen of Lot's flocks' [Gen 13:7]—Rabbi Berechiah said in the name of R. Judah: Abraham's flocks would go out muzzled, Lot's went unmuzzled. Abraham's herdsmen said to [Lot's herdsmen]: Is robbery permitted?! Lot's herdsmen said to them: Thus said the Lord to Abraham: 'I will give this land to your offspring' [12:7]; Abraham is a barren mule and does not beget offspring, so Lot will inherit him, and [the flocks] are eating their own property. The Holy One, blessed be He, said to them: Thus I told him: 'I have given this land to *your offspring*' [Gen 15:18]. When? When the seven nations are uprooted from its midst. 'The Canaanites and Perizzites were then dwelling in the land etc.' [the continuation of the verse on which the midrash is expounding]—until now they possess rights in the land" (*Gen. Rab.* 41:5).

4. Over-interpretation of Gen 12:3 (which expands "I will bless those who bless you and those who damn you I will curse," originally a promise of protection and assistance, into an utterly amoral theological principle), coupled with total disregard for Gen 15:16 (which clearly indicates that the Canaanites' sins are quite independent of their behavior toward the Israelites, then sojourning in Egypt) enable Rolf Knierim to draw the exaggerated conclusion that

As it turns out, what made Abraham's territorial generosity toward Lot possible was the (implicit) distinction between destiny-oriented and temporary bonds. In fact, the land had been promised to Abraham and his offspring (12:7), not to his orphaned nephew Lot, who had joined his household (11:28, 31). When the dispute over pasture broke out between Abraham's and Lot's herdsmen, the patriarch had every legal right to banish Lot and order him to return to Haran. Instead, however, he appealed to him, "Pray, let there be no strife between you and me, between my herdsmen and yours, for we are kinsmen. Is not the whole land before you? Pray, let us separate: if you go north, I will go south; and if you go south, I will go north" (13:8–9). Abraham was convinced that making peace with his kinsman had priority (in time and importance) over realizing his exclusive right to the land; indeed, to preserve the peace, he even gave Lot first choice in choosing a holding in the land that had actually been promised to him. Lot took full advantage of this extreme generosity and unhesitatingly chose the best part available—the well-watered plain of Jordan, "like the garden of the Lord (!), like the land of Egypt" (v. 10). We may well ask whether this "territorial compromise" was considered an act of righteousness on Abraham's part. One need only read on to learn that the answer is very definitely in the affirmative. Immediately after Lot's departure, God repeats his promise to Abraham: "Raise your eyes and look out from the place where you are, to the north and the south, to the east and the west [four directions, as opposed to the two mentioned in Abraham's appeal to Lot], for *all the land* that you see I will give to you and your seed forever" (vv. 14–15). Not only will Abraham's temporary concession not detract from his eternal right, but what ultimately happened was that, because Lot threw in his lot with the sinful people of Sodom, his choice territory was laid waste when God destroyed the cities of the plain, and Lot and his descendants finally settled in the lands of Moab and Ammon to the east of the Jordan (19:37–38).

It follows, then, that the fulfillment of the promise "to give them the heritage of nations" (Ps 111:6) is not an inevitable outcome of the arbitrary will of the Sovereign of the Universe;[5] Israel will inherit the land only when

---

"the exclusionary election theology represents an insurmountable crisis for the Old Testament's claim to Y.'s universal justice" (R. P. Knierim, *The Task of Old Testament Theology* [Grand Rapids: Eerdmans, 1995] 451). See the well-reasoned response of Isaac Kalimi, *Early Jewish Exegesis and Theological Controversy* (Jewish and Christian Heritage 2; Assen: Van Gorcum, 2002) 150–54. The theological implications of this biblical issue are dealt with by Gary A. Anderson, "How to Think about Zionism," *First Things* (April 2005) 30–36.

5. As seems to follow from Rashi's commentary on the first verse of the Torah, which is regularly cited as the ultimate proof of our exclusive right to the land, above morality insofar as it is of divine origin: "Said R. Isaac: The Torah should have begun only from the verse 'This month shall be for you . . .' [Exod 12:2], which is the first commandment given to Israel. Why, then, did it begin with 'In the beginning'? Because 'He revealed to His people His powerful

worthy of it and when the other nations, for their part, forfeit their right to it.[6]

Moreover, lest we become arrogant and haughty, the Torah admonishes us not to think that the wonders that God performs for us attest to our religious or moral superiority:

> And when the Lord your God has thrust them from your path, say not to yourselves, "The Lord has enabled us to possess this land because of our virtues"; it is rather because of the wickedness of those nations that the Lord is dispossessing them before you. It is not because of your virtues and your rectitude that you will be able to possess their country; but it is because of their wickedness that the Lord your God is dispossessing those nations before you, and in order to fulfill the oath that the Lord made to your fathers. . . . For you are a stiff-necked people. Remember, never forget, how you provoked the Lord your God to anger in the wilderness: from the day that you left the land of Egypt until you reached this place, you have continued defiant toward the Lord. (Deut 9:4–7)

In itself, fulfillment of the promises is no evidence that the generation in question is righteous. The conquering Israelites entering Canaan were the "rod of God's anger" (Isa 10:5), whose task was to carry out his judgment on the Canaanites. What is more, if they followed the Canaanite example,

---

works, in giving them the heritage of nations' [Ps 111:6], so that, if the nations of the world tell Israel, You are bandits, having conquered the lands of the seven nations!—they will answer, All the land belongs to the Holy One, blessed be He, he created it and gave it *to whomever he pleased, at his will* he gave it to them *and at his will* he took it from them and gave it to us."

    6. As Naḥmanides explains in an alternative interpretation of the first verse of the Torah: "If so, it were proper that when a nation continues to sin, it should lose its place and another nation come to inherit its land, for such is God's law in the land [phrase taken from 2 Kgs 17:26] from antiquity [as demonstrated by the expulsion from the Garden of Eden, the destruction of the flood generation, and the dispersal of the builders of the Tower of Babel, which Naḥmanides had referred to previously]. All the more so when it is reported in Scripture that Canaan is under a curse and sold as a permanent slave [Gen 9:25] and so is not worthy of inheriting the best inhabited territories. Rather, he will be dispossessed by the servants of the Lord, seed of His friend [cf. Isa 41:8], as it is written: 'He gave them the lands of nations; they inherited the wealth of peoples, that they might keep His laws and observe His teachings' [Ps 105:44–45]. That is to say, He expelled those who rebelled against Him from there and settled his servants there, *so that they should know that by worshiping Him they would inherit it, but if they sinned against Him the land would spew them out, as it spewed out the nation that came before them.*" Naḥmanides concludes his long argument by quoting a midrash from *Gen. Rab.* 1:2, which is actually a slightly different version of the midrash quoted by Rashi, except that Israel do not rely on God's arbitrary will but on his judicial decision in reaction to the actions of human beings: "And Israel will answer: But you yourself have plundered [the land], for 'the Caphtorim, who came from Crete, wiped them out and settled in their place' [Deut 2:23]! The whole world belongs to the Holy One, blessed be He; when He decided, He gave it to you [as a punishment for your predecessors' deeds], when He decides, He will take it from you and give it to us."

they would suffer a similar fate, as warned at the end of the chapter prohibiting illicit sexual relations: "But you must keep My laws and My rules, and you must not do any of those abhorrent things. . . . So let not the land spew you out for defiling it, as it spewed out the nation that came before you" (Lev 18:26–28). In principle, the meaning of this condition is that Israel's possession of the land will not become permanent until the messianic era; for otherwise its destiny would, as it were, backfire (shielding the people even if they emulated the Canaanites). On that basis, we must say that God's promise of the land to Abraham "as an everlasting holding" (Gen 17:8) refers not to actual, uninterrupted possession but to an everlasting, destiny-oriented right.

The serious danger inherent in the transformation of the conditional promise into an absolute promise is aptly demonstrated in the prophecy of Jeremiah 7. The Judahites believed that the Temple would protect Jerusalem from occupation and destruction, for it was inconceivable that God would allow his Temple to be plundered by idolaters. Thus, the sanctity of the Temple was seen as a protective shield over the sinning city, and so the Temple, instead of purifying and cleansing Israel, became an obstacle and a stumbling block. Hence, the prophet's demand, "Do not put your trust in illusions and say, 'The Temple of the Lord, the Temple of the Lord, the Temple of the Lord are these [buildings]'" (Jer 7:4), is followed by the admonition, "Do you consider this House, which bears My name, to be a cave [that is, shelter] of thieves?" (v. 11) and the warning, "therefore I will do to the House which bears My name, on which you rely, and to the place which I gave you and your fathers, just what I did to Shiloh" (v. 14). Indeed, the destruction of Shiloh (and eventually also of Jerusalem) provides conclusive proof that even the sublime sanctity of the sanctuary is not immune to the destructive power of sin; and the same is true of the divine promise.

Natural possession of the land endows its people with confidence and a feeling of stability. But it is equally capable of deadening their hearts and leading them to sin, whereas the destiny-oriented bond with the land implies faith and arouses the heart to heed God's commands. Thus, the pendulum of exile and redemption, so characteristic of our long history from its beginnings to this very day, has not necessarily come to a rest. It may, heaven forfend, begin to swing again.

I believe that we are living in a period of fulfillment of divine promises, of God's assistance to his people, of the realization of some of the destinies foreordained in the Torah and the prophetic books of the Bible. This faith should imbue us with patience, mental and spiritual confidence, and readiness to endure sacrifices; above all, it should encourage us to devote all our strength and energy to the appropriate achievement of those destinies. At the same time, we must beware of the danger of "false messianism," of historical shortcuts that willfully ignore the distinction between an era subject to prevailing conditions and the messianic era of universal, everlasting peace and good will. A "short circuit" of this kind is created when we convince ourselves that our return to the land is indeed final, by virtue of the divine promise. This sort of false confidence may well cause us, heaven forbid, to miss the great opportunity that has been given us. On the contrary, our possession of the land will deepen, provided we remember that it is conditional on the nature of our actions. These actions must also include the realization of social justice and the quest for political peace. Just as having concern for the welfare of the weak, safeguarding the rights of aliens and foreigners, immigrating to the land, settling it, and rebuilding it are religious duties that must be observed in our time, the task of making peace with our neighbors should be considered a religious and moral imperative here and now and not postponed to the messianic era.

Our destiny-oriented right to the land will be more fully realized to the degree that we take our neighbors' natural right to the same land seriously (just as Abraham did Lot's right). The Torah reiterates, time and time again, that our presence in the Holy Land is *conditional* on the sanctity of our camp: "Justice, justice shall you pursue, that you may thrive and occupy the land that the Lord your God is giving you" (Deut 16:20).

God and Human Rights in a Secular Society: A Biblical-Talmudic Perspective

David Novak

God, Human Rights, and Democracy

The concept of human rights is endemic to democracy. Indeed, its acceptance is what distinguishes a democracy from "ordered brutality," to borrow the words of a leading democratic legal philosopher.[1] To be sure, some democratic theorists have argued that there is an overemphasis on human rights, but that is only when human rights are reduced to individual claims on society at the expense of individual responsibilities to society.[2] Nevertheless, it is hard to find any conservative critic of the overemphasis of human rights who would argue in principle for the value of societal system that affirmed no human rights at all and only enforced duties to itself. And, as it turns out in fact, human rights seem to be affirmed only in democratic societies. Nondemocratic societies, such as those run according to fascist, communist, or clericalist (wrongly called "theocratic") ideologies, are notorious for their denial of any human right that could challenge the absolute authority presumed by those who have power in these nondemocratic societies.[3] So, these other forms of society are not

---

1. Ronald Dworkin, *Taking Rights Seriously* (Cambridge: Harvard University Press, 1978) 205.

2. See Mary Ann Glendon, *Rights Talk* (New York: Free Press, 1991) 47–89.

3. The term *theocracy* (literally, "the rule of God") was coined, it seems, by the 1st century C.E. Jewish historian Josephus, who said it means "placing all sovereignty [*archē*] and authority in the hands of God" (*Against Apion* 2.167 [trans. H. St. John Thackeray; LCL; Cambridge: Harvard University Press, 1926] 1:358–59). Josephus is referring to a Jewish society ruled according to the revealed law of God. Yet, even in this sort of society, one can recognize the two features of democracy most of us hold dear, namely, popularly chosen government and human rights. Moreover, as I shall argue later, even secular societies such as the United States and Canada, which are not governed by divinely revealed law, might be considered "theocracies" inasmuch as they recognize in their founding documents that all rights, including the right popularly chosen government, are from God. Unfortunately, though, the term *theocracy* is now frequently used to designate anti-democratic states such as Iran and Saudi Arabia, which are clerically dominated dictatorships.

only nondemocratic in principle, but they are almost always antidemo-cratic in practice as evidenced by their contempt for human rights, even their contempt for the concept of human rights.

Religious people who affirm the value, even the necessity, of demo-cratic society should be prepared to show how human rights are affirmed by their respective traditions. Religious people should also be prepared to show people from other traditions how their own tradition can provide guidance to these "others" in their concern with human rights and how the reception of this guidance by no means requires acceptance of the govern-ing authority of one's own tradition. In other words, one needs to argue in a truly universal way and thus not use insights from one's own tradition to proselytize or even engage in any kind of apologetics. One must walk a fine line between triumphalism and obsequiousness. In this context, then, I do not speak *for* the Jewish tradition but, instead, as a philsopher thinking *out of* the Jewish tradition, that is, not as a theologian let alone as a religious jurist (*ba'al halakhah*).

There is a great difference, though, between religious members of a democracy and its secularist members, especially in the ways they affirm human rights and even in the way they determine what some of these rights are. Also, even when religious people and secularists agree about a certain human right in practice, they frequently differ as to who are the actual subjects of this right. By "religious members" of a democracy, I mean those who publicly affirm their relationship with a god (most often, *the God*) and who assert that their relationship with God has bearing on their political commitments, especially their commitment to human rights. By "secular-ist members," I mean those who deny that anyone's relationship with a god should have political significance. (These secularists are not necessar-ily atheists in their private lives, but it seems that most of them whom I know have no god even in their private lives.) The religious members of a democratic society assume that public affirmation of human rights entails an affirmation of God. (But, as we shall see, this "need" is philosophical, not political.) Secularist members of a democratic society deny that this sort of affirmation of God is necessary, let alone desirable.

Religious members of a democratic society should be prepared to ar-gue publicly why their affirmation of human rights requires a prior affirma-tion of God and suggest why this need is not just theirs. Nevertheless, they should do this without requiring any sort of prior affirmation of God from those who do not believe in God as the price for admission to philosophical discourse with believers, especially discourse about human rights in secu-lar society. Indeed, to require any prior religious affirmation for admission to political discourse in civil society would be most undemocratic in any democracy that also affirms religious liberty, which is the liberty to affirm some religion or to deny any religion at all. Moreover, in debates about the foundations of human rights, religious members of a democratic society need only show why their religious affirmation of human rights provides a stronger foundation for these rights than do the various secularist alternatives, not that these secularist alternatives have no plausibility at all. Secularists, on the other hand, should know why they do not regard a religious affirmation of human rights to be inherently antidemocratic (as some of them certainly have done), and their logic should also lead them toward outlawing religion in public. But that would be as antidemocratic as requiring citizens in a democracy to have one particular religion or even any religion at all.

Because I am a religious member of a democratic society (actually, two: the United States and Canada), I can only make a religious case for human rights in good faith. Secularists should make their own arguments by themselves, and I am prepared to listen to them carefully because I want to live in peace and understanding with them in civil society. Nevertheless, secularists should be able to do so without denying me the right to connect my religious belief to my political advocacy, just as I should be able to do so without denying them their right to connect their nonbelief to their political advocacy. This type of reciprocal tolerance clearly recognizes that no one comes to political advocacy from nowhere, that all of us, believers and nonbelievers alike, come to our respective political positions from prepolitical commitments.[4] For most people, at least in the democracies of the United States and Canada, their prepolitical commitment is religious. Yet there are people whose prepolitical commitment lies elsewhere. It is important for this secularist minority to locate for the rest of us more explicitly just where they are coming from. Religious people, on the other hand, should realize that no human coercion, whether legal or moral, should ever be employed to make secularists affirm any sort of religious commitment. Thus, I do not deny anyone's right to argue his or her affirmation of human rights in public, even when I think the original reasons for this affirmation are wrong or insufficient. I ask that the same right be affirmed by those who think my original reasons are wrong or insufficient.

BIBLICAL PRECEDENTS

Let us now tentatively define human rights as justified claims a human individual makes on the human collective among whom he or she lives, that is, his or her own society. And, in a society where the moral authority of God is recognized, all these claims are clearly justifiable because they refer to God's moral authority, exercised on behalf of God's unique human

---

4. See my *The Jewish Social Contract: An Essay in Political Theology* (Princeton: Princeton University Press, 2005).

creatures. By "God's moral authority," I mean God as the original source of moral law and God as the judge who ultimately enforces that moral law. As a Jew, let me cite the Hebrew Bible and bring in some talmudic comments for a few illustrations of how God's authority operates in both grounding human rights and enforcing them.[5] But, as I shall argue later, none of these biblical illustrations is limited to the context of a particular covenanted community: that is, one does not have to be Jewish or adhere to Jewish faith or to any particular faith in order to invoke these illustrations in his or her moral reasoning. Thus, they can be cogently invoked in a secular society, which turns out to be for almost all of us *the* secular society, the only kind of society we either live in or want to live in.

By "secular society," I mean a society that does not look to any particular historical revelation to justify its political existence and its legal authority. Thus, a secular reason is one that does not look to any revelation as its moral source; but that does not mean God cannot be cogently invoked when making a moral or political argument in a secular context. Accordingly, one need not be a secularist to speak and act secularly. One can very well be a religious advocate of secularity, in fact, I think, a better advocate of secularity.

The first illustration of the relation of human rights to God is the statement of an actual biblical norm. "Any widow or orphan you shall not oppress. If you do wrong them, when one of them does complain [*tsaʿoq yitsʿaq*] to me, I shall listen to his complaint. My anger shall burn and I shall kill you by the sword; thus your wives will become widows and your sons orphans" (Exod 22:22–24). Now this clearly refers to an individual who has a legitimate claim on his or her society. The language of Scripture indicates that the victim is an individual person: *a* widow (*almanah*) or *an* orphan (*yatom*). The use of the plural *you* and *your* indicates that it is a collective that is victimizing these individuals who are, no doubt, taken to be the most obvious examples of a larger class of those who are socially and economically vulnerable and who are usually without powerful advocates on their behalf.[6] The presentation of this norm in the sequence of the biblical narrative, however, seems to assume that the reader is already familiar with the way injustice and its rectification have been described earlier in that narrative.

The language in Exodus is very reminiscent of two previous instances of rights violations and their rectification by God in Genesis. Indeed, it is God whose original rights have been violated in the person of those cre-

5. Unless otherwise noted, all biblical quotations in English are my own translations from the traditional Massoretic texts: *Biblia Hebraica* (ed. R. Kittel et al.; 7th ed.; Stuttgart: Württernbergische Bibelanstalt, 1951).

6. *Mechilta de-Rabbi Ishmael*, vol. 3: *Neziqin* (trans. J. Z. Lauterbach; Philadelphia: Jewish Publication Society, 1935) 141 on Exod 22:21.

ated in his image, and it is God who will ultimately vindicate the "brother's blood crying [*tsoʿaqim*] to me from the ground" (Gen 4:10).[7]

In the Cain and Abel story, Abel has a claim on Cain: Do not kill me! Why? It is because God takes personal interest in every human person who has been created in the divine image. In fact, that is very likely what it means to say that all humankind is made to "resemble [*bi-demut*] God" (Gen 5:1), namely, God and humans are interested in each other insofar as they share some commonality, a commonality not found in God's relations with the rest of creation. "And the Lord God said that humans are like one of us [*k'ehad mimmennu*], experiencing good and bad" (Gen 3:22).[8] As such, an assault on any other human being is taken to be an assault on God himself; in fact, one's ultimate reason for assaulting another human being might be because this is the closest one can come to assaulting God. Let it be remembered that Cain was still very angry with God for having rejected his sacrifice (Gen 4:4–7) just before we read that "when they were in the field, Cain rose up against Abel his brother, and he killed him" (Gen 4:8). Killing his brother Abel, whom God had favored, might well have been his attempt to take revenge on God for God's rejection of him.

Yet the very fact that it is Cain who initiates religion by being the first to offer "a gift to the Lord" (Gen 4:3) shows that Cain himself surely believed that God takes a personal interest in him and his brother, who joined him in this act of worship (the two of them at that point in history constitute humankind). One brings a gift only when one has an intuition that it will be accepted, even expected, by the one to whom it is being given. Cain is surely familiar with God when God asks him, "Where is Abel your brother?" (Gen 4:9). It is assumed that God takes a personal interest in every human person created in his image, so we can thereby infer that God prohibits one human from harming another and that God will not allow one who harms somebody else to escape retribution for his or her crime. Because of that personal interest, both in the experience of the victim and in the act of the victimizer, God will not allow any crime between human persons to go unnoticed without proper response to the moral situation of both persons so involved, whether victim or assailant.

The proscription of injustice against the vulnerable and the promise of divine retribution in Exodus, which was brought as the normative example of God's involvement in human rights, are primarily addressed to the victimizer rather than to the victim. In both the Cain and Abel story in Genesis and the normative passage from Exodus, the rights of a vulnerable

---

7. I translate the first sentence in the vocative rather than in the interrogative mood (as in most of the English translations), following Martin Buber and Franz Rosenzweig's German translation, *Die Fünf Bücher der Weisung* (Cologne: Hegner, 1954) 18: "Was hast du getan!"

8. See my *Halakhah in a Theological Dimension* (Chico, CA: Scholars Press, 1985) 96–101; also, my *Natural Law in Judaism* (Cambridge: Cambridge University Press, 1998) 167–73.

human being are being violated, whether that victim be one's younger (and presumably weaker) brother or a widow or an orphan. But, whereas in the Cain and Abel story we have only two individuals–there being no organized society until Cain "builds a city" (Gen 4:17)–in the Exodus passage there is an organized society. It is the society of the Israelites who have just accepted God's offer to be "a holy nation" (*goi qadosh*, Exod 19:6), which means they were already a nation that was now to become a holy nation especially covenanted with God. The fact that they were already a nation even before being covenanted with God is evidenced by their already having a system of laws by which cases of injustice were being adjudicated. Even before the revelation of the Torah (beginning with the Ten Commandments) at Mount Sinai, a court system was already in place (Exod 18:20–24).[9] The purpose of that court system was to protect the human rights of those who had been wronged by others.[10]

Because there was no society at the time of Cain and Abel, Abel can only appeal to God for justice. There is no one else to avenge his death. In the Exodus account, however, there are two possibilities. First, a victim of crime can appeal to the social collective to enforce his or her God-given right not to be harmed; or second, a victim can appeal directly to God to enforce that same God-given human right.

It seems that a victim would appeal to his or her society for justice when he or she could be harmed or when he or she has already been harmed by another individual member of that same society. It also seems that an appeal to society of this sort would be made in a society that considers its prime duty to be the protection of the human rights of its members, first and foremost, their rights to be protected from injustice and to have injustices committed against them by fellow members of that society avenged. A society that recognizes that the rights it is enforcing are inalienable divine endowments rather than its own revocable entitlements will be able to perform its social duty with maximum cogency because it has earned the rightful trust of its members. As such, that society can in good faith call on its members to "rightly pursue justice" (Deut 16:20). According to one rabbinic opinion, it is wrong for a victim to appeal directly to God for justice when there is just human authority already present in his or her society.[11] In this sort of case, God has delegated the immediate enforcement of justice to the authorities in society, who are to act *in loci Dei* because they understand that "justice is God's" (Deut 1:17). Nevertheless, those hav-

---

9. See *Babylonian Talmud: Zevahim* 116a (the view of Rabbi Joshua).

10. See *Babylonian Talmud: Baba Kama* 99b–100a on Exod 18:20, where the practice of equity is prescribed in cases where following the strict sense of the positive statute would lead to great injustice in fact. See, e.g., *Babylonian Talmud: Baba Metsia* 83a on Prov 2:20.

11. *Babylonian Talmud: Baba Kama* 93a on Gen 16:5 and *Tosafot*, s.v. *d'eeka*; also, Naḥmanides, *Commentary on the Torah*, Exod 22:22.

ing political power may not assume that, because of their collective status, they are thereby exempt from the moral obligation to do justice to others, which is what God had already required of individual persons. No person, not even an official of society having collective authority, is above God's law or above God's judgment.

It is unlikely that a victim would appeal to his or her society for justice if the injustice is being committed by the society itself through its positive laws and public policies. To be sure, if that society is devoted to the enforcement of human rights as being mandated by divine law, then it is possible that the social injustice being committed can be shown to contradict the fundamental norms of the political-legal system itself. Here, internal rectification of the system itself is still possible, at least in principle. Nevertheless, what if those having political and legal power are in fact unwilling to rectify their own unjust victimization of the innocent and the vulnerable? In that case, the cries of the victims of social injustice will fall on deaf ears, the same deaf ears on which Abel's cry to Cain for justice (before his being murdered by Cain) no doubt fell.[12] One's only recourse, then, is to seek justice from God. Indeed, a victim of injustice at the hands of society ought to complain to God as true Sovereign about what has been done to him or her wrongfully rather than sink into political despair.

Belief in the God of justice (*mishpat*), the God who is "the Judge [*shofet*] of the whole earth" (Gen 18:25), gives the victims of injustice the assurance that in the ultimate scheme of things, they do not have to "settle" for the injustice done to them or to anybody else, that all injustice will be rectified when God "will rightly [*be-tsedeq*] judge the world" (Ps 96:13). And it also means that the victims of injustice may not themselves violate the rights of others by cynically assuming that the harm done to them proves that there is no injustice ever, for if so, what difference does it make whether one harms someone else or not? Either the victims assume the idea of justice itself is an illusion, or they assume justice is an ideal having no consequences in any real world.[13] In fact, very often the experience of injustice leads its victims to imitate their victimizers by finding their own victims: "Those to whom evil is done, do evil in return," in the memorable words of the poet W. H. Auden.[14]

---

12. In *Midrash ha-Gadol: Genesis* (ed. M. Margulies; Jerusalem: Mosad Harav Kook, 1947) 119, it is Cain who, during a fight with his brother, pleads for his life from Abel, but when Abel releases him, he then treacherously turns on Abel and kills him on the spot. The implication here is that Abel would also have pleaded with Cain for his life if Cain had given him the chance to do so. Cf. Louis Ginzberg, *The Legends of the Jews*, vol. 1: *Bible Times and Characters from the Creation to Jacob* (Philadelphia: Jewish Publication Society, 1909) 109.

13. See my *Jewish Social Ethics* (New York: Oxford University Press, 1992) 163–65.

14. "September 1, 1939," in *Seven Centuries of Verse: English and American* (ed. A. J. M. Smith; 2nd ed.; New York: Scribners, 1957) 686.

One can see true opposition to this type of moral or political cynicism in the instruction, "A sojourner [*ger*] you shall oppress," the reason being given: "because you know what the life of the sojourner [*ha*-ger] is, since you were sojourners [*gerim*] in the land of Egypt" (Exod 23:9). The noun "sojourner" or "resident-alien" is used three times here and has three different referents: (1) an individual Gentile living in Israel; (2) the state of being a resident-alien in general; (3) the people of Israel who had been resident-aliens in Egypt (even before Pharaoh enslaved them). It is the concept of "resident-alienhood" (*gerut*) in general that enables the Israelites to identify with those living under their own rule. So, instead of concluding that one may do the evil done to oneself to somebody else, Scripture concludes that from the negative we derive the positive.[15] That is, from the injustice the Egyptians did to the Israelites when they were sojourners, we learn the justice the Israelites are to do for the sojourner who lives in their land. "There shall be one justice [*mishpat ʾehad*] for the sojourner and the native-born" (Lev 24:22). Neither justice nor the God of justice died in Egypt, or even in Auschwitz.

Both the Egyptians and the Israelites are expected to know already what are the human rights of sojourners in their respective societies. The Israelites are to respect the rights of sojourners. "What is hateful to you, do not do to somebody else," which the Talmud assumes is the most basic moral precept common to both Jews and Gentiles.[16] Respect for the right not to be harmed and to be protected by society and the corresponding duty not to harm but protect the rights of others are not just a civil right and a civil duty but, rather, a human right and a human duty. Neither the right nor the duty is to be violated anywhere by anyone, whether that individual is functioning individually or collectively.

The situation of human rights is even worse in a society where basic injustice is built into the very political and legal institutions of the society itself. This comes out in the biblical account of the destruction of the cities of Sodom and Gomorrah, whose citizens are described as being "exceedingly wicked and sinful toward the Lord" (Gen 13:13). Their evil and sinfulness comes to a head when God announces to Abraham that he plans to investigate "the cry [*zaʿaqat*] of Sodom and Gomorrah because it is excessive" (Gen 18:20). According to rabbinic interpretation, the "cry" of the two evil cities is not the cry of the citizenry protesting their innocence before the divine Judge. It seems that their society had already determined not only that "there is no law" (*din*), meaning no just legal system but that there is also "no judge" (*dayyan*), which is the rabbinic term for practical

---

15. See *Babylonian Talmud: Nedarim* 11a and parallels.
16. *Babylonian Talmud: Shabbat* 31a.

atheism.[17] The citizens themselves, being beyond any sense of social guilt, would not have known how to protest their innocence. Instead, the cry is the cry of the innocent people who have been persecuted by that very citizenry of Sodom and Gomorrah, a persecution that had been sanctioned by the political and legal institutions of those cities.[18]

The injustice here is more than the work of individual criminals. Were that the case, the officials of that society could be called on to punish properly those individuals who have violated the laws of that society. Indeed, the injustice here is more than the work of officeholders who have abused their office. Were that the case, one could call attention to the fact that these officeholders themselves are in violation of the laws of that society, even though, in that situation, there is often no one more powerful than these officeholders to call them to task. That is why, in ancient Israel, it took a prophet to remind kings of their violation of God's law that protected the rights of weaker members of the society. One sees this in the prophet Nathan's rebuke of King David for violating the rights of Uriah (2 Sam 12:7–10) and in the prophet Elijah's rebuke of King Ahab for violating the rights of Naboth (1 Kgs 21:17–22). Both Nathan's rebuke and Elijah's rebuke were taken seriously because David and even Ahab were rulers of Israelites societies that still recognized God law and God's judgment.[19] One can even assume that is why the Israelite prophet Jonah was able to call the people of the Gentile city of Nineveh to repentance by commanding them to turn away from "the violence [*he-hamas*] in their hands" (Jonah 3:8). This was possible because "the people of Nineveh believed in the God of justice [*'elohim*]" (Jonah 3:5). Thus, one sees that, for the Bible, the seriousness with which the moral admonition of prophets was taken is not something confined to Israel. Israel is not the only nation that considers itself answerable to God's law and God's judgment. Furthermore, prophetic moral admonition itself is not confined to Israel. It does not seem that the people of Nineveh listened to Jonah because he was an Israelite prophet telling them to follow the law of Israel; rather, they listened to him because he reminded them to follow God's law as they knew it from their own cultural experience.[20]

Nineveh could be saved from its own sins, especially its collective sins, because the people there still recognized God's law within their own

17. This fundamental denial is put in the mouth of Cain by the rabbis. See *Targum Yerushalmi*, Gen 4:8; also, *Palestinian Talmud: Kiddushin* 4.1/65b.

18. See *Babylonian Talmud: Sanhedrin* 109a–b; also, Ginzberg, *The Legends of the Jews*, 1:245–50.

19. See *Palestinian Talmud: Sanhedrin* 2.3:20a on Ps 17:2.

20. See *Babylonian Talmud: Taanit* 16a on Jonah 3:8; also, Ginzberg, *The Legends of the Jews*, 4:250–53.

tradition. But Sodom and Gomorrah were beyond this salvation because their own tradition had already lost any recognition of a divine law and divine Lawgiver who instituted human rights and specified them. In addition, they had already lost any recognition of divine judgment. In talmudic language, they had forgotten collectively both the moral admonition (*azharah*) and the penalty for violating the admonition (*'onesh*).[21] Sending a prophet to admonish them would have been futile. Thus, when Lot, the nephew of the prophet Abraham, admonishes the men of Sodom not to violate the strangers who have taken shelter in his house as sojourners, they revile him by reminding him that he himself is "this one who has come to sojourn [and who] is now acting as a judge!" (Gen 19:9).[22]

Sodom and Gomorrah become, in the Bible, the epitome of social and political depravity that deserves the most severe divine punishment.[23] Their being "exceedingly wicked and sinful toward the Lord" (Gen 13:13) is primarily their violation of basic human rights: a fundamental breach of divinely mandated morality. If so, why is their sin referred to God? The answer seems to be that "one who reviles the poor despises his Maker" (Prov 17:5).[24] Though one is not to abuse any of God's creatures, it seems that this verse refers to God as the maker of every human, whether male or female, rich or poor, "in his image" (Gen 1:27, 5:1–2, 9:6). In the case of Sodom and Gomorrah, the violation of human rights is so endemic to the social system itself that there is no longer any recourse to either uncorrupted public officials or the traditions of the society itself. Thus there is only recourse to God himself to destroy the cities that have so fundamentally violated his moral law, the law that irrevocably entitles human beings to dwell in safety anywhere on earth, which God "has created to be a dwelling" (Isa 45:18).

THEOLOGICAL-POLITICAL ARGUMENTATION IN A SECULAR SOCIETY

I submit that everything represented above, which is only a small sample of biblical-talmudic discussions of God's connection to human rights, is germane to the great debates now being conducted in the secular societies of the United States, Canada, and elsewhere. The founding document of the American republic, the Declaration of Independence of 1776, asserts that all humans "are endowed by their creator with certain inalienable rights." The Canadian Charter of Rights and Responsibilities of 1982 asserts, "Canada is founded on principles that recognize the supremacy of

21. See *Babylonian Talmud: Sanhedrin* 54a.
22. Cf. Exod 2:14.
23. See, e.g., Deut 29:22–23; Isa 1:9.
24. Tosefta, *Sanhedrin* 13.8.

God and the rule of law." And my interpretation of "the supremacy of God and the rule of law" is not as two separate assertions but, rather, that they are two terms in apposition. That is, *the supremacy of God is the rule of God's law*. That is what "supremacy of God" means as distinct from the more-vague "existence of God."

The separation of church and state asserted in the bills of rights of both nation-states only means that there is to be no official national religion and that there are to be no religious requirements for citizenship or the holding of public office. It also implies that one cannot make a public argument, intended to bring others into agreement with oneself, whose basic premise is "because the Bible says so." Therefore, in public discussions of matters of law and right, one may not make an argument that presupposes acceptance of the authority of any particular historical revelation and its written record, such as the Torah from Sinai, the Sermon on the Mount, or the word of the Qur'an. But one can certainly quote Scripture to illustrate and clarify moral truths that can be argued for rationally rather than just authoritatively. Accordingly, one can definitely make an argument from a divine law that one can show is understandable by human reason and affirmed in many different traditions, both religious and secular (for example, in English Common Law, which can still be invoked as precedent in American and Canadian courts). Religious people who understand this fundamental distinction will be able to make very cogent arguments in secular society for human rights, rights that are originally *from* God and finally vindicated *by* God. By so doing, they can "find grace and good favor in the yes of God and man" (Prov 3:4).

8

The Biblical Attitude toward Human Toil

Amos Frisch

Point of Departure: Engnell's Assessment

The Swedish scholar Ivan Engnell wrote a short essay on the biblical attitude toward human toil. He divides the Bible into six subcorpora ("D-work": Genesis to Numbers; "P-work": Deuteronomy through 2 Kings; "K-work": Ezra, Nehemiah, and Chronicles; the psalm literature; the prophetic literature; and the wisdom literature) and investigates the attitude toward work in each of them. His conclusion is that all six evince a negative attitude toward physical toil. In the prophetic literature, though, work is taken for granted, and this is the most positive assessment of work to be found in the Bible.[1]

The Biblical Data: A Study of Three Texts

Let us look at the Bible to see whether the texts support Engnell's conclusion. Because we cannot discuss all of his six corpora here, we will limit ourselves to a consideration of three representative texts. After that, we will expand our view and consider other texts.

The Creation and Garden of Eden Pericopes (Genesis 1–3)

The story of the garden of Eden in Genesis 2–3 is a crucial text for understanding the biblical view of work. In the words of one scholar: "Genesis 2:4b–3:24 is a *unified narrative,* in which work . . . is *a,* if not *the,* essential theme."[2]

Author's note: The translation of biblical passages in this essay is mostly the RSV, but where linguistic precision or differences in interpretation require it, the NJPSV or some other version has been silently incorporated. Similarly, passages from the Talmud and *Genesis Rabbah* are the Soncino translations, modified as deemed necessary.

　　1. See I. Engnell, "The Biblical Attitude to Work: 1. Work in the Old Testament," *Svensk Exegetisk Årsbok* 26 (1961) 5–12.

　　2. G. Agrell, *Work, Toil and Sustenance: An Examination of the View of Work in the New Testament Taking into Consideration Views Found in the Old Testament, Intertestamental, and Early*

If we think about the attitude toward work in the Eden narrative, the first thing we remember is the sentence passed on Adam: "By the sweat of your brow shall you get bread to eat" (Gen 3:19). The person who disobeyed the divine injunction by eating the forbidden fruit is punished by expulsion from paradise, where all the fruits of the garden have been available to him. After his sin, though, Adam will have to work strenuously until his food is ready for him to eat. Cassuto, based on his understanding of Gen 3:23, puts it this way: "Furthermore, the task of tilling the earth, as we are subsequently informed, was not imposed upon man till after his banishment from the Garden of Eden."[3]

But this view is astonishing. Even before Adam sinned, the narrator tells us, "The Lord God . . . put him in the garden of Eden to work it and serve it (*lĕʿovdāh ulšomrāh*)" (Gen 2:15).[4] Thus, the idea that Adam would work preceded his sin; physical labor was to be his lot even in his ideal, pretransgression condition. One answer to this difficulty is that the work mentioned there is not physical toil but service of the Almighty. This idea is found in various homilies of the talmudic sages, such as "'to work it and serve it' is an allusion to the sacrifices: thus it is written, 'you shall serve [*taʿabdûn*] God upon this mountain' (Ex. 3:12); and, 'you shall take heed [*tišmĕrû*] to offer to me in its due season' (Num. 28:2)" (*Gen. Rab.* 16:5).

We hear this explanation not only from the homilist, but also from the exegete and scholar. Cassuto would understand this talmudic reading not as homiletic (*derash*) but as the plain meaning (*peshat*) of Scripture. He argues that understanding the phrase "to work it and serve it" as a reference to the sacrificial ritual "corresponds to an ancient tradition of the Orient often mentioned in Mesopotamian inscriptions, according to which Man was created for the express purpose of *serving God*."[5] He rejects the common interpretation that "to work it and serve it" means tilling the soil. Instead, he opts for a variant text, which he says is found in some books, that omits the dot (*mappiq*) in the final *hê* that represents the accusative pronoun; this turns *lĕʿovdāh ulšomrāh* into verbal nouns ("for worship and service"), like *lĕʾoklāh* ("for food": Gen 1:29–30). A non-Jewish scholar who probably was not influenced by the talmudic sages also explains *lĕʿovdāh* in this way. Engnell, mentioned at the start of this article, states that Adam was not placed in Eden to till the soil and was in fact exempt from physical labor. What he

---

    3. U. Cassuto, *A Commentary on the Book of Genesis* (trans. I. Abrahams; Jerusalem: Magnes, 1961) 1:122.

    4. The discussion that follows will be easier to understand if readers bear in mind that the semantic field of *ʿbd* begins from "work/serve" in the physical sense and then extends to "wor(k)ship/sacrificial-ritual duty," while *šmr* proceeds from "watch/guard/keep" to "observe/preserve" in their various connotations.

    5. Ibid.

was enjoined to perform was a ritual task. His condition changed only after his transgression, when he changed from being the servant of the Lord to a slave of the earth (compare the reference to Cain as a tiller of the soil (*ʿoved ʾădāmâ*: Gen 4:2).[6]

Now let us turn to consider these two ideas, raised by critics who view this as a negative attitude toward physical toil. After that, we shall take up two other arguments that go back to the creation narrative in Genesis 1.

Man's Task: lĕʿovdāh ulšomrāh

The verse cited above appears at the very beginning of the story of the garden of Eden: "The Lord God took the man and put him in the garden of Eden to work it and serve it" (2:15), with the dot in the *hê* of the two verbs, implying a reference to a feminine antecedent. The commentators have offered two main identifications of this antecedent: first, that it is the closest previous noun, *garden*; although *gan* is normally masculine, here, they say, it is irregularly thought of as feminine; second, that this antecedent is the noun *ʾădāmâ*, "soil" or "ground" (v. 9), despite its somewhat remote location. In either case, the meaning is that Adam was to tend the garden or till the soil even before he sinned, so that there is absolutely nothing negative about the activity.[7]

Adam's labor, as defined here, consists of two parts: an active part, some form of agricultural effort, "to work it"; and a passive part, protecting what exists—"to [pre]serve it." Perhaps we should see this division as paralleling the Creator's activity in the creation story in Genesis 1: "to work it" corresponds to the six days of Creation, "to [ob]serve it" to the Sabbath day (as suggested by another homily in *Genesis Rabbah*).[8] We should remember

---

6. Engnell, "The Biblical Attitude," 6–7. Wenham, too, thinks that *ʿbd* and *šmr* have a religious meaning here; see G. J. Wenham, *Genesis 1–15* (WBC; Waco, TX: Word, 1987) 67. He also connects the story with the symbolism of the Temple, referring explicitly to the midrash; see idem, "Sanctuary Symbolism in the Garden of Eden Story," *Proceedings of the Ninth World Congress of Jewish Studies, Division A* (Jerusalem: World Union of Jewish Studies, 1986) 19 and 21. We should note, however, that Wenham, in opposition to Cassuto, states explicitly that Adam was meant to work even before he sinned (*Genesis*, 67).

7. Westerman makes a significant statement about the importance of work when he begins by rejecting Budde's statement, in his 1883 commentary, that *lĕʿovdāh ulšomrāh* is a later addition to the text, because, in Budde's words, "man is in Paradise for blessed enjoyment, not to work and keep." Westerman vigorously disputes this idea and shows that it is based on a distorted conception of the garden of Eden. As he notes: "Work is regarded as an essential part of man's state not only in the Creation narrative but in the whole of the Old Testament. A life without work could not be a complete life" (C. Westerman, *Creation* [trans. John J. Scullion; Philadelphia: Fortress, 1974]) 80–81.

8. "*Wayyanniḥēhu* ('and he put him') means that He gave him the precept of the Sabbath, as you read, 'And rested (*wayyānaḥ*) on the seventh day' (Exod 20:11). *lĕʿovdāh* ('to till it'): as you read, 'Six days you shall labor—*taʿăvod*' (v. 9). *Ulšomrāh* ('and to keep it'): 'Keep (*šāmôr*) the

that the contrasting pair *ʿbd-šmr*, in the context of the workweek and Sabbath rest, is highlighted in the phrasing of the fourth commandment in Deuteronomy: "Observe (*šāmôr*) the Sabbath day, to keep it holy. . . . Six days you shall labor (*taʿăvod*), and do all your work; but the seventh day . . ." (Deut 5:12–14).

As a counterweight to the homilies that remove *lěʿovdāh ulšomrāh* from the realm of human activity we should mention another saying of the sages, in which they infer from this verse the priority of work even to eating. I am referring to the statement by the tanna R. Simeon b. Elazar:

> R. Simeon b. Elazar says, "Even the first Man tasted nothing before he had performed work. For it is said, 'And he put him into the Garden of Eden to tend it and to keep it; of every tree of the garden you may freely eat [having worked] (Gen 2:15–16).'" (*Avot R. Nat.* version A, ch. 11)[9]

I am not persuaded by Cassuto's application to *peshat* of homilies that attach a spiritual meaning to *lěʿovdāh ulšomrāh*. A spiritual acceptation of these activities, which transfers them to the domain of divine worship, is appropriate to the homiletic approach. By introducing sacrifices (as well as observance of the precepts, according to another homily) into the narrative, it makes Adam's life in the Garden of Eden a prefiguration of the lives of Torah-observant Jews. But what satisfies the criteria of homily is not necessarily suitable for a *peshat* interpretation, which relies on the context to determine the meaning of the words and refrains from adding "outside" information. *Peshat* interpretation should lead us to a totally different conclusion.

It is not just that there is no basis for the textual variant mentioned by Cassuto, and the two verbs do have an embedded pronominal object, whose antecedent is either the soil or the garden. In addition, even the reading without the *mappiq* does not require his explanation, because working and serving have a perfectly good nonritual and workaday sense. Cassuto's partial Mesopotamian parallel is insufficient to remove the plain meaning of the verse—all the more so because the verb *ʿbd* appears in our story several verses earlier, where it unambiguously refers to the soil: "there was no man to till (*laʿăvod*) the ground" (Gen 2:5). In addition, Engnell's contrast between the servant of the Lord and the slave of the earth has no foothold in the text, not only because the latter refers to Cain in distinc-

---

Sabbath day' (Deut 5:12). Another interpretation: *lěʿovdāh ulšomrāh* ('to till it and to keep it') is an allusion to sacrifices: thus it is written, 'You shall serve (*taʿăvdûn*) God upon this mountain' (Exod 3:12); and, 'You shall take heed (*tišměrû*) to offer to Me' (Num 28:2)" (*Gen. Rab.* 16:5).

9. *The Fathers according to Rabbi Nathan: An Analytical Translation and Explanation* (ed. and trans. J. Neusner; Atlanta: Scholars Press, 1986) 83. On this issue, see W. Bienert, *Die Arbeit nach der Lehre der Bibel: Eine Grundlegung Evangelischer Sozialethik* (Stuttgart: Evangelisches Verlagswerk, 1954) 50–51.

tion to Abel the shepherd (Gen 4:2) but chiefly because there the term is actually *ʿōved ʾădāmâ* ("a *worker/tiller* of the soil," not servant/slave); on the other hand, Adam himself is never called the servant of the Lord. Nor does *lĕʿovdāh* have anything to do with servitude.[10] The reading that associates it with religious ritual interpretation is a lovely homily, but it cannot be defended as the plain meaning of the text.

Adam's Punishment

If, as we have seen, Adam was meant to labor even before he sinned, we can no longer understand physical toil as a punishment. In addition, a comparison of Adam's punishment with Eve's leads to the same conclusion. The talmudic sages compared their punishments (Gen 3:16–17): "R. Jo-hanan said: 'Man's sustenance involves twice as much suffering as [that of] a woman in childbirth. For of a woman in childbirth it is written, "in pain" (*bĕʿeṣev*) [you shall bear children], whereas of sustenance it is written, "in toil" (*bĕʿiṣṣāvôn*) [shall you eat of it]' " (*b. Pesaḥ.* 118a and passim). Here, "in toil," found in Adam's punishment, is interpreted homiletically as express-ing greater difficulty than "in pain," found in Eve's punishment. But if we stick to the plain meaning, we should note that the word *ʿṣbwn* also appears in Eve's punishment ("I will greatly multiply your *pain* in childbearing"). Hence, I believe that a *peshat* commentator can adopt the comparison made in the homily, but not the greater severity of Adam's punishment. The common word in fact highlights the similarity between the two pun-ishments. What precisely is Eve's punishment? Evidently, it is not the fact of pregnancy but the pain of childbirth: "I will greatly multiply your *pain* in childbearing; in *pain* you shall bring forth children" (Gen 3:16). Thus, by analogy to Eve, it is not having to perform physical labor that is Adam's punishment—he was to labor even before he sinned—but the pains that will henceforth be associated with it.

In his commentary on v. 23—"the Lord God sent him forth . . . to till the ground from which he was taken," David Kimḥi notes that what is new is the exertion associated with the labor, not the labor itself: "Because he re-jected the easy work when he was in the Garden and could eat the fruits of the trees without toil, but violated the commandment, he had to leave the Garden and perform hard labor to till the soil." Outside the garden of Eden, Adam will continue to till the soil as he had been doing, to some extent, in the garden; but now he will have to work in much more difficult conditions.

The Imperative of Human Endeavor: "And Subdue It"

An important source for any assessment of human endeavor can be found in the creation story: "And God blessed them, and God said to them,

---

10. For criticism of Engnell, see also Agrell, *Work*, 10.

'Be fruitful and multiply, and fill the earth and subdue it'" (Gen 1:28). The blessing "be fruitful and multiply" first appears on the fifth day: "And God blessed them, saying, 'Be fruitful and multiply and fill the waters in the seas, and let birds multiply on the earth'" (Gen 1:22). Several commentators have noted the difference in the phrasing of the two verses. For the sea creatures and birds, it is merely a blessing, whereas when addressed to the man ("God blessed them and God said to them") it can be understood as connoting a command and not only a blessing.[11]

For our purposes, the important word in this verse is the verb *subdue*, through which God confides to human beings their control over the earthly realm; or, as Naḥmanides puts it: "He gave them power and dominion over the earth to do as they wish . . . and to build and *to pluck up that which is planted*, and from its hills to dig copper, and other similar things. This is included in what He said *and over all the earth.*"[12]

A contemporary scholar reaches a similar conclusion while advancing a different significance for the verb *subdue*, drawing on its senses in talmudic Hebrew (improvement, proliferation, and addition): "Drawing on the sense of improvement and increase in the verb *kbš* we arrive at a suitable interpretation of this verse. The injunction 'and subdue it' assigned human beings the mission of improving the earth and making it bloom."[13]

As part of their vocation, assigned to them when created, human beings were also charged with the task of subduing the earth, whether in the sense of mastering it or of improving it. This is stated not offhand or in aside but in a verse that scholars see as a theological underpinning of human history in Genesis 1–11.[14]

God as Maker and Doer

God created the entire universe with a word—that is, through his spirit. Yet in the creation narrative in Genesis 1, we also find him linked to a number of verbs that seem to be extremely physical: *create* (vv. 1 and 21

---

11. See, for example, Gersonides' commentary *Rabbinic Pentateuch with Commentary on the Torah by R. Levi ben Gershon: Genesis* (ed. B. Braner and E. Freiman; Maʿaleh Adumim: Maʿaliyot, 1993) 66–67, 74–77. See also the commentaries of Abarbanel and David Zvi Hoffman. On the other hand, see Rashi on 9:7.

12. Ramban (Naḥmanides), *Commentary on the Torah: Genesis* (trans. C. B. Chavel; New York: Shilo, 1971) 55.

13. N. M. Brunswick, "From the Language of the Sages to the Language of the Mishnah," *Beit Miqra* 29 (1984) 39 [Hebrew].

14. See L. A. Turner, *Announcements of Plot in Genesis* (JSOTSup 96; Sheffield: JSOT Press, 1990) 21 n. 11. Turner develops this attitude at length (pp. 21–47). But he also maintains that, as a practical matter, the curse on the earth (3:14–19) revoked the injunction to subdue it (pp. 40–41). I disagree with him (see my *Bible's View of Labor* [Tel Aviv: Hakibbutz Hameuchad, 1999] 25–26 n. 50 [Hebrew]). Even if he is right, though, the original plan, before Adam sinned, was that he subdue the land.

and three times in v. 27), *make/do* (vv. 7, 16, 25, 26, and 31), *separate* (vv. 4 and 7), and *set* (v. 17). Quite surprisingly, physical associations with the creation are most conspicuous in the seventh section, devoted to the Sabbath (Gen 2:1–3). Here we find the noun *work* three times as well as the verb *make/do* three times. The importance of this passage to the creation story is emphasized by its location at its very end.

What is the point of this corporealization and anthropomorphization in the creation story? The *Mekhilta* offers a fitting explanation in a homily on the precept of Sabbath observance in the Ten Commandments:

> Now if the One who is not affected by fatigue had it written concerning himself that he created the world in six days and rested on the seventh, how much the more so should a human being, concerning whom it is written, "but man is born to trouble" (Job 5:7) [also rest on Sabbath]? (*Mek. Rab. Ishm., Baḥodesh* VII)[15]

Even if the anthropomorphism of work and rest is intended to reinforce and encourage observance of the Sabbath, it also conveys a positive attitude about human toil, given that human beings are following the example of the creator when they work, just as when they rest.[16]

God is also active in the Eden story, which ascribes to Him physical actions in various context: the creation of the flora—*planted* (Gen 2:8), *made to grow* (v. 9); the creation of the fauna—*formed* (v. 19); the creation of man—*formed, breathed* (v. 7), *formed* (v. 8); supervising and caring for the man—*put* (v. 8), *took, put* (v. 15), *brought them to the man* (v. 19), *cast a deep sleep, took, closed up* (v. 21), *fashioned, taken, brought* (v. 22). The Lord is described as taking action after Adam and Eve sin, too: "And the Lord God made for Adam and for his wife garments of skins, and clothed them" (Gen 3:21), which evidently means that, before expelling the human couple from Eden, God equipped them with better clothing than the loincloths they had made themselves from fig leaves immediately after their transgression (Gen 3:7).[17]

To sum up our investigation thus far, in contrast to the view presented at the outset that physical toil was a punishment meted out to Adam after he sinned, we now see that labor was always part of the divine plan for him

---

15. *Mekhilta attributed to R. Ishmael: An Analytical Translation* (trans. Jacob Neusner; Atlanta: Scholars Press, 1988) 2:81.

16. Richardson tries to demonstrate a development from an anthropomorphic outlook that has God working with His hands to a transcendent view that He creates with His word. Nevertheless, he emphasizes, this evolution stems not from a negative evaluation of physical toil but rather from a desire to eliminate anthropomorphisms from descriptions of divine activity (A. Richardson, *The Biblical Doctrine of Work* [London: Camelot, 1952] 14–16).

17. This is in contrast to the view of A. B. Ehrlich (*Mikrâ ki-Pheschutô* [Berlin, 1899; repr., Jerusalem: Ktav, 1969] 13) and Cassuto (*Genesis*, 171), that the meaning is that God instigated Adam and Eve to make themselves clothes, not that he made them himself.

and part of his vocation in this world. The consequence of the sin was that labor became an arduous task and burden, not its mere existence. Human labor is a form of *imitatio dei*, in that the activities of the Creator are presented in the creation and Eden stories in a somewhat anthropomorphic fashion. Thus, human beings are following in His path both when they work for six days and when they rest on the seventh. What we have found in these two paradigmatic stories expresses a fundamental biblical outlook that labor is part of the human life as originally intended by the Creator.[18]

Psalm 127

Engnell assesses the attitude of the Psalm 127[19] literature to labor as "entirely negative." In his discussion he infers two points from the psalm: "All work is in vain if God withholds his blessing; God even gives his 'friends' all they need without any effort on their part, 'while they sleep' (127.1ff.)."[20] Let us read Psalm 127 closely and endeavor to extract its true attitude toward human labor.

The first part of the psalm (vv. 1–2) dismisses human toil as useless when it is not accompanied by a heavenly blessing. This is illustrated by two tasks: "Unless the Lord builds the house, those who build it labor in vain. Unless the Lord watches over the city, the watchman stays awake in vain" (v. 1). Neither the dynamic and creative activity of building nor the static activity of guarding can succeed without divine assistance. The vanity of human activity is highlighted by the threefold repetition of the word *vain* in vv. 1 and 2. The third occurrence—made more emphatic by its position at the start of the verse—casts an ironic light on the efforts of human beings who imagine that the success of their enterprises depend only on the number of hours they devote to them: "It is in vain that you rise up early and go late to rest, eating the bread of anxious toil" (v. 2a). The two verbs used for human activity in v. 1, *labor* and *stay awake*, highlight the intensive nature of human effort. They are supplemented in v. 2 by a reference to the long workday of laborers ("rise up early and go late to rest"), unlike the situation described elsewhere in Psalms: "Man goes forth to his work and to his labor until the evening" (Ps 104:23), where the work day is limited to the daylight hours. Here, the meal these laborers eat after their long and strenuous work day is referred to as "bread of anxious toil" (that is,

---

18. We should note two observations by Richardson that are relevant here: "Unlike the Greeks, who thought that working for one's living was beneath the dignity of a gentleman, the Hebrews looked upon daily work as a normal part of the divine ordering of the world, and no man was exempt from it. . . . The basic assumption of the biblical viewpoint is that work is a divine *ordinance* for the life of man" (*Biblical Doctrine*, 22–23).

19. The discussion of Psalm 127 precedes that of Isaiah 40–66, even though the latter is in the Prophets, which in the Hebrew Bible precedes the Hagiographa (which includes Psalms), because I believe that Psalm 127 antedates those chapters of Isaiah.

20. Engnell, "The Biblical Attitude," 9.

bread prepared painfully, in a process of exhausting physical labor). These workers are contrasted with those whom God loves, to whom (according to the most common understanding of the verse, equating *šn'* with *šnh*) "He gives . . . sleep" (v. 2).

But is the reward granted to those whom God loves exemption from all labor, or merely a reduction in their working hours so that they can get a good night's sleep? The answer to this question is tied up with understanding the underlying intention of the Psalm and identifying the object of its criticism.

Is the psalmist expressing here a fundamental rejection of the value of physical labor? The medieval commentator Menaḥem Hameiri (1249–1316) thought otherwise:

> None of this is intended to prevent exertion, for no wise man condemns exertion and praises sloth. Rather, it means only that one should not put his full trust in labor and believe that, when he attains some goal, he has done so through his own efforts. Instead, it is the Lord who showed him favor in this. [21]

We can supplement Hameiri's general argument with exegetical considerations that can be inferred from a close reading of the psalm and that lead to the same conclusion: (1) In v. 1 the activities of building and watching are associated with the Lord, so that he too performs them, as it were (alongside the human laborers). (2) "Those who build it labor in vain" and "the watchman stays awake in vain" (vv. 1 and 2) are not absolute statements—a total rejection of all human exertion—but the apodosis of the condition "unless the Lord." (3) The criticism in v. 2 is directed at working overtime, beyond due measure, and not at work itself. (4) In v. 5, as we shall see, blessed and successful guarding is described.

In his detailed discussion of the second half of v. 2, Emerton rejects the interpretation that *šn'* means sleep and offers a new rendering of the verse (based on linguistic parallels in Syriac, Arabic, Ethiopic, and Ugaritic): "Surely He gives *high estate/honor* to whom He loves."[22] This reading does not affect our conclusions about the attitude toward labor expressed here. The first part of the psalm rejects the idea that human exertion per se is a guarantee of success. Human endeavor is an important and necessary condition but by no means a sufficient condition. For work to produce results, a divine blessing is also essential.[23]

21. Cf. J. A. Emerton's view: "It may be doubted whether the idea that God blesses men when they do nothing would have been congenial to the ethos of Israelite wisdom literature, to which this passage belongs" ("The Meaning of Šēna' in Psalm CXXVII 2," *VT* 24 [1974] 20).

22. Ibid., 15–31.

23. Cf. A. Weiser, *The Psalms: A Commentary* (trans. H. Hartwell; OTL; London: SCM, 1962) 765–66.

The second half of the psalm (vv. 3–5) turns to a new theme—sons as a heavenly blessing. The conclusion—"They shall not be put to shame when they contend [*or* speak] with the enemy in the gate" (v. 5)—stands in contrast to its opening: sons, "a heritage from the Lord," will successfully defend the city,[24] even though "the watchman stays awake in vain." This contrast makes it plain that what is rejected is not the action of guarding itself but only guarding that is not blessed by heaven. The word *sons*, which appears twice (vv. 3 and 4, as well as the rhetorical "fruit of the womb" in v. 3), is conspicuous in this half of the psalm. A homophonic root is prominent in the first half of the psalm—*bnh* (*yivneh, vônāw*; v. 1). The sons (*bānîm*) whom the Lord gives to those who fear Him succeed where the builders (*bônîm*) fail.

The juxtaposition of the two halves of the psalm creates a parallel between a man's toil and the progress of his family. This correspondence, which emphasizes the importance of work in a man's life by making it parallel to the birth of his children, can already be found in the punishment of Adam and Eve: the first human couple was punished in that its major tasks were made more onerous—labor pains for Eve, the pain of labor for Adam. Psalm 127 adds that success in both the public and family domains depends on a divine blessing. First it presents the dark side of toil and exertion, when the labor is not blessed by heaven: "Unless the Lord" (twice). Only at the end of the first half is there a reference to its bright side: "he gives sleep [or honor] to whom he loves." The second half of the psalm presents only the happy side of expanding the family: "sons are a heritage from the Lord, the fruit of the womb a reward."

The allusion to the story of the Garden of Eden is found not only on the thematic level, in the parallel between labor and labor, but also on the linguistic plane. In the language that describes the workers who are exhausted by their work—"*eating* the *bread* of anxious *toil*" (v. 2)—we may hear an echo of Adam's punishment: "in *toil* you shall *eat* of it. . . . By the sweat of your brow you shall *eat bread*" (Gen 3:17–19).[25] Amos Ḥakham explains the meaning of this allusion as follows: "It is possible that the Psalmist is seeking to hint here that the God-fearing man who places his trust in God is free from the curses imposed on Adam and eats his bread in serenity and

24. For the various ways of reading the parts of the verse, in a military or judicial sense, see D. J. Estes, "Like Arrows in the Hand of a Warrior (Psalms CXXVII)," *VT* 41 (1991) 308–9. I prefer the military reading, for several reasons: the advantage contributed by young people is their physical strength, rather than legal skills and experience; "arrows in the hand of a warrior" tends to the military sense; and the emphasis on quantity—"who has his quiver full of them" is important in warfare but not in legal proceedings.

25. See Sforno ad loc.; Amos Ḥakham, *Sefer Yeshaʿyahu* (Jerusalem: Mossad Harav Kook, 1984) 468 n. 3; P. D. Miller, *Interpreting the Psalms* (Philadelphia: Fortress, 1986) 133–34.

not in sorrow."[26] That is, the person loved by the Lord can work in moderation; he is exempt from the pains of physical toil, but not from work itself.

Isaiah 40–66

In his article about the biblical attitude toward work, Engnell has this to say about the prophetic literature:

> An examination of the role and evaluation of work in the prophetic literature gives the same result, although it is perfectly obvious that work as such plays a more prominent role at the advanced stage of the history of Israel where the prophets belong.[27]

In these general remarks, Engnell does not take account of differences within the prophetic literature. I believe, however, that the chapters of consolation in Isaiah (40–66)[28] present a unique attitude toward work, one that seems to be unfavorable. Yet Engnell, who was always on the *qui vive* for such a negative evaluation, failed to note it.

A critical position vis-à-vis work is implied by the fact that liberation from toil is presented as a blessing. This blessing is expressed clearly, with relationship to specific types of labor, in two different passages in the prophecies of consolation: (1) "Foreigners shall build up your walls, and their kings shall minister to you. . . . For the nation and kingdom that will not serve you shall perish" (Isa 60:10–12). God decrees that foreigners, including their kings, will serve Zion, in particular to rebuild the walls of Jerusalem. (2) "Aliens shall stand and feed your flocks, foreigners shall be your plowmen and vinedressers; but you shall be called the priests of the Lord, men shall speak of you as the ministers of our God; you shall eat the wealth of the nations, and in their riches you shall glory" (Isa 61:5–6). Here the people are exempt from labor in the fields and vineyards and from tending the sheep—tasks that will be performed for them by foreigners.

In more general terms, and without referring to any particular form of labor, the same blessing is found in two other passages: "Kings shall be your foster fathers, and their queens your nursing mothers" (Isa 49:23) and "Thus says the Lord: 'The wealth of Egypt and the merchandise of Ethiopia, and the Sabeans, men of stature, shall come over to you and be yours, they shall follow you; they shall come over in chains and bow down to you. They will make supplication to you'" (Isa 45:14).

---

26. A. Ḥakham, *Psalms with the Jerusalem Commentary* (trans. and ed. Israel V. Berman; Jerusalem: Mosad Harav Kook, 2003) 3:323.

27. Engnell, "The Biblical Attitude," 9.

28. The two most salient passages are in chaps. 60 and 61, attributed by some modern scholars to "Trito-Isaiah." Other scholars assign Isaiah 40–66 to a single author ("Deutero-Isaiah"). I have not found any significant difference in the attitude toward work in the chapters putatively assigned to two different prophets (pp. 40–55 and 56–66).

What underlies this vision of a time when Israel will no longer have to work and its labor will be performed by the Gentiles? Does it constitute a deprecation of physical labor?

The passage quoted above—"aliens shall stand and feed your flocks"— served as a proof text for the radical stance that work is an encumbrance that interferes with Torah study and that right conduct can free the Jews from this burden. I have in mind a homily by the tanna R. Simeon bar Yoḥai:

> If a man ploughs in the ploughing season, and sows in the sowing season, and reaps in the reaping season, and threshes in the threshing season, and winnows in the season of wind, what is to become of the Torah? No; but when Israel perform the will of the Omnipresent, their work is performed by others, as it says, "And strangers shall stand and feed your flocks, etc." But when Israel do not perform the will of the Omnipresent their work is carried out by themselves, as it says, "you shall gather in your grain" (Deut 11:14). Nor is this all, but the work of others also is done by them, as it says, "you shall serve your enemies." (Deut 28:48). (*b. Ber.* 35b)

Despite its extreme phrasing, this homily seems to understand the verse in its literal meaning; namely, that Israel is blessed when foreigners do its work for it. It is true that the verse does not explicitly refer to Torah study as an ideal that is incompatible with work; but the statement in the next verse that "you shall be called the priests of the Lord" offers an analogous justification for the exemption from labor: because in the future Israel will serve as the priests of all humanity and engage in spiritual guidance, it is appropriate that they be exempt from physical toil.[29] This amounts to a rejection of work in favor of a higher calling—serving as the Lord's priests in the world. Are we to infer that the prophet looks down on and totally rejects work?

I do not believe so. Rather, these verses highlight the future glory and splendor of Israel, which are embodied in a reversal of the current status of Zion and her children. The prophet is fond of this future reversal and mentions it several times. He notes it at the end of the first verse in the first passage quoted above—"for in my wrath I smote you, but in my favor I have had mercy on you" (Isa 60:10b)—and restates it more explicitly later: "The sons of those who oppressed you shall come bending low to you; and all who despised you shall bow down at your feet. . . . Whereas you have been forsaken and hated, with no one passing through, I will make you majestic for ever, a joy from age to age" (vv. 14–15). In the second passage the reversal is more salient (and exemplified by an inversion in the order of

---

29. Joseph Kara goes further in his commentary on the verse: "You should not do any work, but will be called priests of the Lord."

letters—פאר will replace אפר): "to grant to those who mourn in Zion—to give them a garland instead of ashes, the oil of gladness instead of mourning, the mantle of praise instead of a faint spirit" (Isa 61:3); "Instead of your shame you shall have a double portion, instead of dishonor you shall rejoice in your lot" (v. 7).

Having observed the centrality of the idea of a reversal in the status of Israel we can understand that the good tidings presented in these prophecies is not the liberation from physical toil but the exchange of roles: those who enslave Israel in its exile will henceforth be subservient to Israel and perform various labors for it.

But there is another side as well. In adjacent prophecies the prophet speaks innocently of work performed by Israel, too: the two opposing facets seem to be juxtaposed most prominently in Isa 61:5–6 ("Aliens shall stand and feed your flocks"). On the one hand, these verses free Israel of having to do agricultural labor and add a sort of justification for this exemption, in the form of their vocation as priests of the Lord. On the other hand, the previous verse mentions their involvement in construction: "They shall build up the ancient ruins, they shall raise up the former devastations; they shall repair the ruined cities, the devastations of many generations" (v. 4). Other verses, too, make explicit reference to physical activity by Israel: "And your ancient ruins shall be rebuilt; you shall raise up the foundations of many generations; you shall be called the repairer of the breach, the restorer of streets to dwell in" (58:12).[30] "But those who garner it shall eat it and praise the Lord, and those who gather it shall drink it in the courts of my sanctuary" (62:9). "They shall build houses and inhabit them; they shall plant vineyards and eat their fruit. . . . They shall not labor in vain, or bear children for calamity" (65:21–23).[31] In three more passages, work by Israel, called "your sons," though not explicit, is implied: "For as a

---

30. This verse should be juxtaposed with Amos 9:11:

Isaiah	*Amos*
And your *ancient* ruins shall be *rebuilt*;	In that day I will *raise up* the booth of David that is fallen
you shall *raise up* the foundations of many generations;	and *repair* its *breaches*,
you shall be called the *repairer* of the *breach*,	and *raise up* its ruins,
the restorer of streets to dwell in.	and *rebuild* it as in *ancient* days.

The common elements bring the strong contrast into fuller relief: Amos attributes these actions to the Lord, whereas Isaiah assigns them to the people.

31. This is another juxtaposition of work with childbirth. Sommer noted the similarity of these verses to Jer 29:4–6 and demonstrated that our prophecy inverts that passage in a positive sense. See B. D. Sommer, *A Prophet Reads Scripture: Allusion in Isaiah 40–66* (Stanford: Stanford University Press, 1998) 42–43.

young man marries a virgin, so shall your sons marry you" (62:5).[32] "Swiftly your children[33] are coming; those who ravaged and ruined you shall leave you" (49:17). "Great shall be the prosperity of your sons" (54:13).[34] In these last two verses, *bānayik*, "your sons," evidently has a double meaning and also connotes *bônayik*, "your builders."[35]

We might further note that various prophecies in Isaiah 40–66 describe work performed by the Lord, sometimes anthropomorphically. With regard to the Creation we find: "I made the earth, and created man upon it; it was my hands that stretched out the heavens, and I commanded all their host" (45:12); "My hand laid the foundation of the earth, and my right hand spread out the heavens" (48:13). With regard to His providential protection of Israel, we find: "Your people . . . the shoot of my planting, the work of my hands, that I might be glorified" (60:21); "the planting of the Lord, that he may be glorified" (61:3).

In light of all this, it is hard to see any consistently negative attitude toward the idea of Israel doing physical labor; indeed, we may question whether so many diverse statements can indeed be reconciled in a single comprehensive outlook. We cannot eliminate the contradiction by distinguishing among types of work, because labor in the vineyards is ascribed both to foreigners ("your vinedressers") and to Israelites ("they shall plant vineyards and eat their fruit"); construction, too, is associated with both foreigners ("foreigners shall build up your walls") and Israelites ("they shall build up the ancient ruins"). Nor will the claim of distinct sources for the conflicting statements help, because some of them appear in adjacent passages and the most prominent of them, as we have seen, contrasts 61:4 with 61:5–6. Some sort of stylistic exegetical method that blunts the sting of sharp statements might do the trick: Kaufmann[36] refers to an extreme bent in the description of the future wealth of Zion and its people as compared to other, more realistic prophecies; that is, in his description of the

32. See Ḥakham, *Isaiah*, 654 and n. 28. He sees this as a reference to tilling the soil.

33. The reading of 1QIsaiah is *bwnyk*. This is also attested by other source texts and adopted by some moderns (e.g., RSV). It was also adopted, but exegetically, by Saadia Gaon and Samuel b. Hofni Gaon; see M. Goshen-Gottstein, with the assistance of M. Peretz, *R. Judah Ibn Balaam's Commentary on Isaiah* (Ramat Gan: Bar-Ilan University Press, 1992) 200 [Arabic and Hebrew]. Nevertheless, there is logic in Gesenius's argument, quoted by Luzzatto: "After this he says, 'they all gather, they come to you' [v. 18], and then 'who has borne me these?' [v. 21], so the reference is to the sons, not to the builders" (*S. D. Luzzatto's Commentary to the Book of Jesaiah* [Tel Aviv: Dvir, 1970] 344).

34. 1Q Isaiah: *bwnyky* (with suspended *waw*); compare the homily of R. Ḥanina: "Do not read *bānayik*, but *bônayik*" (*b. Ber.* 64a and passim).

35. In Isa 49:17, *bānayik/bônayik* (see above, n. 33) is contrasted with "those who ravaged and ruined you," whereas in 54:13 it is paralleled by "you shall be established through righteousness" in the following verse. See Ḥakham, *Isaiah*, 585 n. 6b.

36. Y. Kaufmann, *History of the Religion of Israel*, vol. 4: *From the Babylonian Captivity to the End of Prophecy* (New York: Ktav, 1977) 154.

future prosperity, the prophet sometimes used extreme and bold images, but he never meant to imply that Israel would not have to work. Amos Hakham writes, in his commentary on Isa 61:5–6: "But it seems likely that the prophecy does not mean that Israel will not engage in tilling the soil and that all of their labor will be performed by the Gentiles; rather, the meaning of the prophecy seems to be that when the Gentiles come to learn Torah from Israel they will help them do their work, as remuneration for the Torah that they learn from Israel."[37] Hakham's explanation, even though it refers to a single verse only, has significant weight for a final summing up, because that verse is the only one of those discussed that presents an explicit contrast between work by the Gentiles and work by Israel: "Aliens shall stand . . . but you. . . ." If we can explain this verse as meaning that the aliens help Israel get its work done, and not that they perform it instead of Israel, a similar reading is certainly possible in the other verses, where there is no such contrast between Israel and the nations. A solution such as this, following Kaufmann and Hakham, belongs to the species of argument that is simple to advance but difficult to prove. Still, anyone who wants to ascribe some overall stand to the prophet must adopt a solution of this sort.

Whatever solution we accept, and even if we do not manage to solidify a single viewpoint for Isaiah 40–66 on this matter, we now see that we cannot accept the idea that it totally rejects work. At the same time, a certain deprecation of its value cannot be ignored.

OTHER PASSAGES AND CONCLUSIONS

We have traced the biblical attitude toward work as reflected in three texts that represent three different corpora and genres—the narrative of Genesis, the psalms, and the prophecy of Isaiah 40–66. In all three, we began with and scrutinized the view that this attitude is unfavorable. In the first two cases, we refuted this view. In the third case, we concluded that, although the attitude is not totally negative, work is not accorded a particularly high value.

Nevertheless, to complete an account of the biblical attitude toward labor, we must briefly consider three other biblical corpora. In the legal corpus of the Pentateuch, labor is presented as a natural reality, and there seem to be no reservations about it (unlike the limitations imposed on chattel slavery). It includes social laws that display a concern for the rights of workers, who are weaker than their employers (for example, the ban on withholding wages [Lev 19:13 and Deut 24:14–15] and the social aspect of the Sabbath [esp. Exod 23:12 and Deut 8:14).

37. Hakham, *Isaiah*, 650 n. 13.

The Deuteronomistic History seems to evince a positive attitude toward work and presents exemplary figures as laborers (for example, the only righteous man in the city of Gibeah [Judg 19:16]; Saul at the beginning of his career [1 Sam 11:5]; David before his election [1 Sam 17:15, 28, 34–35). Josh 24:13, where Joshua reminds the Israelites that they have received a ready-made patrimony, with no need to work for it, deserves attention; but, in contrast to Engnell's view,[38] I do not believe that this verse can be seen as reflecting a fundamental disapproval of work.

In the Wisdom literature, Proverbs contains maxims that certainly praise hard work and condemn sloth. Ecclesiastes, though, mixes skepticism about the utility of work with others praising it. These seem to be contradictory, but the tension may be resolved by distinguishing between essential work in moderation, which is accompanied by happiness and pleasure, and unnecessary and excessive labor, which merely exhausts a person.[39]

THE DIFFERENTIAL VALUE OF DIFFERENT OCCUPATIONS

Does the Bible express a differential evaluation of various occupations? Are some forms of work preferable from a theological perspective?

The two basic occupations of herding and tilling the soil have been in conflict in many cultures since the dawn of history. In the Bible, too, we sometimes find them juxtaposed. The most conspicuous confrontation can be found in the story of the very first internecine quarrel, that of Cain and Abel in Genesis 4. The beginning of that narrative (Gen 4:1) introduces Abel as a shepherd and Cain as a tiller of the soil. Many see this clash of occupations as a value judgment that deprecates the farmer, who is a murderer. I believe, however, that the role played by the brothers' contrasting occupations is not that large; it is certainly not the axis on which the plot turns.[40]

Aberbach believes that the Bible prefers the shepherd to the farmer. He points to the story of Cain and Abel (as mentioned above), the casting of major biblical heroes as shepherds (Moses, David), the description of the Lord as a shepherd (notably Ps 23:1), and Jeremiah's praise of the Rehabites, who neither sowed nor planted (Jeremiah 35).[41]

I doubt whether the biblical scale of values is so unambiguous. "Fill the earth and subdue it" (Gen 1:28) is an explicit divine injunction, to be imple-

38. Engnell, "The Biblical Attitude," 8.

39. For a more detailed discussion of the legal corpus, see my *Bible's View*, 61–88. For a more detailed discussion of the topic in the wisdom literature (Proverbs and Ecclesiastes), see ibid., 115–30.

40. Ibid., 34–38.

41. M. Aberbach, *Labor, Crafts and Commerce in Ancient Israel* (Jerusalem: Magnes, 1994) 1–4.

mented, first and foremost, by tilling the soil, as we mentioned above. The Lord's original plan for Adam was that he "work it and serve it" (Gen 2:15)— again referring to tilling the soil. Various prominent biblical characters are described as involved with farming, including Isaac when he lived in Gerar (Gen 26:12) and King Uzziah of Judah (2 Chr 26:10). Again, as mentioned above, the only righteous man in the town of Gibeah (Judg 19:16) and Saul at the beginning of his career (1 Sam 11:5) are described as farmers. The role of the farmer is prominent in the prophetic visions of the future, such as the end of the book of Amos ("when the plowman shall overtake the reaper and the treader of grapes him who sows the seed" (Amos 9:13)[42] and the vision of the end of days shared by Isaiah (2:4) and Micah (4:3).

Perhaps farming was seen as having both greater risks and greater prospects, but that is no reason to define it as essential inferior to herding. We should not forget that shepherds, too, are described as failing in their duty and harming their flocks (see especially Ezekiel 34).

CHANGES IN THE ATTITUDE TOWARD HUMAN TOIL
IN JEWISH THOUGHT OVER THE YEARS

In his essay on labor, Avraham Shapira discerns a positive attitude toward work in both the Bible and the talmudic literature.[43] Ayali, who offers a more detailed discussion of the sages' attitude toward work than Shapira does,[44] analyzes many statements in praise of labor and avoids drawing excessively far-reaching conclusions. He maintains that passages from which we might infer reservations about labor derive not from a devaluation of work but from a preference for Torah study over physical labor. In any case, he argues, "the statements and stories in praise of physical labor outweigh the other opinions in both quantity and intensity."[45] Shapira identifies disdain for work only in the literature of the exilic period, when the Jews no longer engaged in physical labor, especially agriculture, and even this only after the 13th century.

42. For a comprehensive discussion of this prophecy, see M. Weiss, *Scriptures in Their Own Light: Collected Essays* (Jerusalem: Bialik Institute, 1987) 88–98 [Hebrew]. Through a comparison with the promise of fertility in Lev 26:5, Weiss shows that the crux of this prophecy is the emphasis on constant labor as a result of the great productivity. He concludes: "Their promise is not that in the future human beings will eat and be sated because of the perpetual bounty, but that they will labor without letup. . . . There will be no end to the blessed toil of human beings. . . . Adam's state before the decree that, on account of him, 'cursed be the ground' and 'horns and thistles it shall bring forth for you' (Gen 3:17–18), will be restored and endure" (98).

43. A. Shapira, "Work (עבודה)," in *Contemporary Jewish Religious Thought* (ed. A. A. Cohen and P. Mendes-Flohr; New York: Free Press, 1988) 1055–67.

44. See M. Ayali, "Labor as a Value in the Talmudic and Midrashic Literature," *Jerusalem Studies in Jewish Thought* 1/4 (1982) 7–59 [Hebrew].

45. Ibid., 12.

In his expanded Hebrew survey of the topic,[46] Shapira devotes major attention to the hasidic doctrine, propagated by Israel Ba'al Shem Tov and his followers, of *avodah be-gashmiyut*; namely, that any physical exertion may be a form of divine service. In other words, every human endeavor has the potential to elevate and redeem the *nitzotzot* ("sparks"); everything a person does can have great significance in the higher spheres. This exaltation of physical labor also raises the stature of the working masses who engage in "less than respectable" occupations. Later, Zionism, too, placed physical labor on a pedestal, as he notes: "Labor was seen as the Zionist destiny and the essence of the Zionist vision."[47]

A. D. Gordon (1856–1922), the ideologue of the Second Aliya, laid special emphasis on manual labor. Gordon, who borrowed elements from the long Jewish written tradition, including quite a bit from kabbalah and hasidism, revered labor and attached importance to even the tiniest everyday activity.

Shapira concludes his essay by noting that physical labor lost its shine in Jewish Israeli society after the Six-Day War, when the number of foreign workers began to increase. He is right about the new scorn for work, though the extent to which this is linked to the Six-Day War and its aftermath requires further study. A more balanced picture would take account of the harbingers of a return to "Hebrew labor," especially among the Jews living in Judea and Samaria. In this context, we even find Jews returning to occupations such as shepherding and construction. In any case, contemporary Israeli society, which sees itself as implementing the Zionist idea, should investigate the current status of work among its members and attempt to bring wider circles closer to the idea of labor.

46. A. Shapira, "עבודה [Work]," in *Contemporary Jewish Religious Thought* (ed. A. Shapira; Tel Aviv: Am Oved, 1993) 362–78 (quoting pp. 367–69) [Hebrew].
47. Shapira, "Work (עבודה)," 1060.

9

New Testament and Rabbinic Views of Election

Joel Kaminsky

The concept of election, that is, God's mysterious choice of a particular group as his special people, is a central concern within much of the Hebrew Bible. In several recent articles, I have explored the importance of election and the ways in which modern biblical scholarship has at times misunderstood and thereby mistreated this concept.[1] However, election is not only a major concern within the Hebrew Bible. Both rabbinic Judaism and early Christianity have adopted and adapted this notion in unique yet comparable ways. Thus, to articulate the meaning of election for Jews and Christians fully, it is necessary to explore how this idea fits into the theological grammar of each religion. Though conducting a comprehensive study of election within these two complex, multifaceted traditions is well beyond the reach of a single essay, one can sketch out, even if rather briefly, some of the distinctive ways each tradition uniquely appropriated, highlighted, or downplayed various aspects of this rich biblical concept.

Before proceeding with this comparison, it is important to make clear that election is a central idea not only within Judaism but also for Christianity. This point needs emphasis because there is a popular tendency to assume that election and the particularism and exclusivism it entails are Old Testament / Jewish ideas that were transcended by the New Testament and

Author's note: I wish to thank Jon Levenson, Mark Reasoner, Greg Spinner, and my student Anne Stewart, for reading various drafts of this essay and for giving me many valuable suggestions on improving it. I also am grateful to the Mellon Foundation and my provost, Susan Bourque, who supported this project by funding a course release in the spring of 2004 that allowed me to bring this essay into publishable form. The reader should note that this essay was slated to appear before the publication of my book *Yet I Loved Jacob: Reclaiming the Biblical Concept of Election* (Nashville: Abingdon, 2007), where much of this material appears in chaps. 9 and 11.

1. "Election Theology and the Problem of Universalism," *HBT* 33 (2011) 34–44; "Loving One's Israelite Neighbor: Election and Commandment in Leviticus 19," *Int* 62 (2008): 123–32; "Reclaiming a Theology of Election: Favoritism and the Joseph Story," *PRS* 31 (2004) 135–52; "Did Election Imply the Mistreatment of Non-Israelites?" *HTR* 96 (2003) 397–425; and "The Concept of Election and Second Isaiah: Recent Literature," *BTB* 31 (2001) 135–44.

Christianity.[2] A brief example from Arnold Toynbee, a very widely read author, exhibits this propensity. "They [the Jews] persuaded themselves that Israel's discovery of the One True God had revealed Israel itself to be God's Chosen People."[3] An explicitly Christian attempt to disown the idea of election can be found in the following excerpt from a 1937 *Christian Century* editorial that blames the Jews for inventing and sustaining Nazi anti-Semitism: "it is just this obsession with the doctrine of a covenant race that now menaces the whole world. . . . [the Jewish] idea of an . . . exclusive culture, hallowed and kept unified by a racial religion, is itself the prototype of nazism."[4] This viewpoint is still in vogue today, albeit in more covert forms. Thus, E. P. Sanders states that "Christian scholars habitually discuss the question [of Jewish pride in separatism] under the implied heading 'What was wrong with Judaism that Christianity corrected?'"[5]

While major streams of New Testament thinking broadened the elect group to include Gentiles who came to believe in Jesus as the Christ, this does not mean that Christianity rejected the biblical concept of election and its implied exclusivism.[6] The following passage from Romans 4 illustrates that early Christians saw themselves not as universalists who accepted everyone because of their common descent from Adam, but rather as particularists who found a new way to link believing Gentiles to Abraham and through him to God's elect people.

> For this reason it depends on faith, in order that the promise may rest on grace and be guaranteed to all his descendants, not only to the adherents of the law but also to those who share the faith of Abraham (for he is the father of all of us, as it is written, "I have made you the father of many nations")—in the presence of the God in whom he believed, who gives life to the dead and calls into existence the things that do not exist. Hoping against hope, he believed that he would become "the father of many nations," according to what was said, "So

---

2. It is important to point out that there are Christians, particularly those with strong Lutheran and Calvinist roots or others influenced by Barth, who recognize how central the concept of election is to the Christian tradition. But the fact remains that on the popular level many contemporary Western Christians see election as an exclusivistic Jewish idea that a universal Christianity transcended.

3. Arnold Toynbee, *A Study of History* (abridged vols. 1–6; New York: Oxford University Press, 1947) 310.

4. From an editorial entitled "Jewry and Democracy," *The Christian Century* (June 9, 1937) 734–36, here at p. 736.

5. E. P. Sanders, "Jewish Association with Gentiles and Galatians 2:11–14," in *The Conversation Continues: Studies in Paul and John* (ed. Robert Fortna and Beverly Gaventa; Nashville: Abingdon, 1990) 170–88, here at p. 181.

6. Thus, Sanders in "Jewish Association," p. 181, goes on to state that Christians would "follow the same range of behavior as Jews. They would hesitate to marry pagans, Jews, and even Christians who belonged to the wrong party."

numerous shall your descendants be." . . . Therefore his faith "was reckoned to him as righteousness." Now the words, "it was reckoned to him," were written not for his sake alone, but for ours also. (Rom 4:16–18, 22–24)

Christians, like their Jewish counterparts, believed that one joined the people of God by relinquishing their fallen adamic state.

Yet death exercised dominion from Adam to Moses, even over those whose sins were not like the transgression of Adam, who is a type of the one who was to come. But the free gift is not like the trespass. For if the many died through the one man's trespass, much more surely have the grace of God and the free gift in the grace of the one man, Jesus Christ, abounded for the many. (Rom 5:14–15)

The argument between Judaism and Christianity was over who held the proper key to repair the fractured relationship between humans and God. Was this accomplished through the giving of the Torah to the Jews at Sinai (and the dynamics of repentance and reconciliation inherent in Torah observance) or through the death and resurrection of Christ at Golgotha (with its alternative schema of divine-human reconciliation)?[7] While various New Testament authors may have changed the particular way one joined the people of God, Christianity clearly appropriated the concept of chosenness.

But you are a chosen race, a royal priesthood, a holy nation, God's own people, in order that you may proclaim the mighty acts of him who called you out of darkness into his marvelous light. Once you were not a people, but now you are God's people; once you had not received mercy, but now you have received mercy. (1 Pet 2:9–10)

Here, 1 Peter reapplies to the early church language found in Exod 19:6, a passage that is central to ancient Israel's understanding of her own election. Thus, the nascent Christian community not only took over the concept of election, but at times it even utilized the Hebrew Bible's terminology for election.

Clearly, the New Testament authors maintained the fundamentals of the Hebrew Bible's particularistic notion of election. Nevertheless, there are substantial differences between the New Testament's ideas of election and those found in rabbinic Judaism. The two traditions diverge on a number of central theological issues including the issue of missionary outreach,

7. For those who would object to the notion that Judaism has any sense of a fall, or for deeper discussion of the parallels between how Judaism and Christianity each heal the rift caused by human disobedience to God, see my "Paradise Regained: Rabbinic Reflections on Israel at Sinai," in *Jews, Christians, and the Theology of the Hebrew Scriptures* (ed. Alice Bellis and Joel Kaminsky; SBL Symposium Series 8; Atlanta: Society of Biblical Literature, 2000) 15–43.

the fate of those not elected, the role played by God's actions and human actions respectively, and the acceptability of God's arbitrariness.

Of course, any attempt to draw hard and fast distinctions between two traditions as vast and ancient as Judaism and Christianity is difficult. After all, the two traditions grew out of a common matrix and thus share much in common. More importantly, even when most texts in one tradition diverge in substantial ways from the dominant strain of thinking in the other faith, there are subcurrents in each tradition, which sometimes seem more at home in the sister religion than in the textual corpus in which they occur. Thus, none of the arguments below should be taken as evidence of the univocality of the two traditions. Rather, they are useful observations about the ideas to which each tradition gives greatest weight and emphasis.

THE QUESTION OF MISSION AND THE FATE OF THOSE NOT ELECTED

Judaism and Christianity diverge in the manner and extent that each tradition absorbs or accepts outsiders into the community as well as in the way that each community views those who are not part of the elect. These issues are interrelated because each religion's stance on the place of those not elected informs its view of how outsiders are integrated and whether one actively seeks to missionize them. It is important to avoid the common propensity of labeling the contemporary minority religion, Judaism in this case, as close-minded and intolerant, while falsely portraying Christianity as tolerant and universalistic in its stance toward others. The truth is that there is a rather complex relationship between each tradition's view of the nonelect and the question of tolerance toward others. While Judaism is much more tolerant of those not elected in that its general propensity is to assume that one can remain nonelect and still be in right relationship to God, this fact likely contributed to Judaism's lack of an active mission to convert the Gentiles. On the other hand, although Christianity, most especially its Pauline elements, is committed to evangelizing outsiders, it is important to see that this is not a sign of its great tolerance for the Other as Other. Rather, Christianity's strong impulse to convert those outside the faith seems at least partially driven by the realization that without faith in Christ these individuals are damned. In other words, dominant streams of Christian tradition[8] have reduced the three biblical categories of the

---

8. There are some significant Christian thinkers over the centuries (Origen and Barth among them) who have argued, on the basis of texts such as Rom 5:18–19, for the idea that all souls will ultimately be saved. Nevertheless, major streams of both New Testament and later Christian tradition make salvation contingent on one's confession of belief in Christ as lord and savior (Rom 10:9–13, John 3:16). For a recent endorsement of universal salvation, see Richard John Neuhaus, *Death on a Friday Afternoon* (New York: Basic Books, 2000) 35–70.

elect, the anti-elect (that is, those few groups like the Canaanites of the Hebrew Bible doomed for destruction), and the nonelect (that is, all other non-Israelites) down to the two categories of the saved and the damned. This sort of binary categorization led Christians to missionize those who without conversion would have been lost to God.[9] This is far from what a modern liberal would consider tolerant.[10] While the question of mission and the fate of those not chosen are intertwined issues, for the sake of clarity I will briefly discuss each independently.

MISSION

A number of New Testament texts charge Christians with the task of actively spreading the faith (Matt 28:19, Mark 16:15–16, Luke 24:44, 49). While there may be some evidence that Jesus originally intended his message only to reach other Jews (Matt 10:5–15), by the time of Paul's death it was widely accepted that the gospel was to be preached to the whole world. Although some scholars have argued that Judaism exhibited certain missionary tendencies for a time, the growing consensus is that Judaism never developed into a truly missionary faith. Even a scholar such as Scot McKnight, who finds wide evidence of Jewish proselytization of Gentiles in antiquity, draws the following conclusions:

> [A] positive attitude toward, and an acceptance of, proselytes is to be methodologically distinguished from aggressive missionary activity among the Gentiles. In other words, although Jews clearly admitted proselytes, and although they clearly encouraged Gentiles to convert,

---

Neuhaus makes clear that this position has been marginalized for much of Christian history and even though he thinks it deserves renewed attention, he is aware that Origen's teachings on this and other subjects were condemned by the Council of Constantinople in 553. Whether this sort of universalism reaches back to Paul himself is a matter of debate. Scholars such as E. P. Sanders think that Paul had two strains in his work that were never fully reconciled, one of them being the notion of universal salvation, the other Christological exclusivism. See, for example, his short chapter entitled "Paul," in *Early Christian Thought in Its Jewish Context* (ed. John Barclay and John Sweet; Cambridge: Cambridge University Press, 1996) 112–29. For a fuller exploration of exactly this idea and its implications for theology today, see Sven Hillert, *Limited and Universal Salvation: A Text-Oriented and Hermeneutical Study of Two Perspectives in Paul* (ConBNT 31; Stockholm: Almqvist & Wiksell, 1999). Nevertheless, when one sets Paul's thought into its religiocultural milieu, it is difficult to see how one can maintain that he ultimately advocated universal salvation. Thus, Stendahl brilliantly shows how even passages that have been read as holding out hope for the repentance of one's enemies are really about leaving retaliation to God. Krister Stendahl, "Hate, Non-Retaliation, and Love: 1QS x, 17–20 and Rom 12:19–21," *HTR* 55 (1962) 343–55.

9. I have explored the import of these three categories in greater depth in my article "Did Election."

10. Henry Chadwick, "Christian and Roman Universalism in the Fourth Century," *Christian Faith and Greek Philosophy in Late Antiquity* (ed. L. Wickham and C. Bammel; Leiden: Brill, 1993) 26–42.

and although they anticipated that Day when hordes of Gentiles would convert, there is almost no evidence that Jews were involved in evangelizing Gentiles aggressively and drawing them into their religion. [11]

While some rabbinic texts praise converts, "there is no evidence whatever from late antiquity that rabbinic leaders in any Jewish community anywhere ever set up an organized program to attract gentiles to Judaism." [12] Interestingly enough, Judaism's resistance to missionizing and Christianity's forceful call to engage in it have been used by not a few Christians to justify a supersessionist displacement theology in which the church as the new Israel has replaced those obstinate Jews who refused to share the word of God with others. Thus, no less an authority than H. H. Rowley sees election as ultimately requiring Israel "to mediate to all men the law of her God, and to spread the heritage of her faith through all the world." [13] Inasmuch as the historic people of Israel failed to missionize the Gentile nations of the world, Rowley believes that they forfeited their elect status to the church who engaged in such active missionizing. [14]

> Through the Church Gentiles from every corner under heaven. . . . have learned the law of God. The Jewish Bible has been translated into innumerable languages and has become the cherished Scripture of multitudes who would never have heard of it through Jews alone. These are objective facts. It is not merely that the church believed she was commissioned to take over the task of Israel. She did in fact take over from an Israel that was less willing to undertake it; and she has indisputably fulfilled that task in a great, though still insufficient, measure. [15]

11. Scot McKnight, *A Light among the Gentiles: Jewish Missionary Activity in the Second Temple Period* (Minneapolis: Fortress, 1991) 48. For a much more skeptical view toward the whole notion of Jewish proselytization, see Martin Goodman, *Mission and Conversion: Proselytizing in the Religious History of the Roman Empire* (Oxford: Clarendon, 1994).

12. Robert Goldenberg, *The Nations That Know Thee Not: Ancient Jewish Attitudes towards Other Religions* (New York: New York University Press, 1998) 94.

13. H. H. Rowley, *The Biblical Doctrine of Election* (London: Lutterworth, 1950) 165.

14. It needs to be stressed that Rowley is not alone in his view and that similar assertions occur regularly in more recent scholarship. The contemporary, widely read New Testament scholar N. T. Wright endorses this same idea: "Paul argues that ethnic Israel has failed in the purpose for which she was called into being. . . . Israel rejected the call of Jesus and now rejects the apostolic message *about* Jesus because it challenges . . . her relentless pursuit of national, ethnic and territorial identity" (N. T. Wright, *What Saint Paul Really Said* [Grand Rapids: Eerdmans, 1997] 84, emphasis his). For a critique of Wright's position, see Douglas Harink, *Paul among the Postliberals: Pauline Theology beyond Christendom and Modernity* (Grand Rapids: Brazos, 2003) 153–68. Views of this sort are widespread among more evangelical Christians as evidenced by articles such as Gerald Bray's "The Promises Made to Abraham and the Destiny of Israel," *The Scottish Bulletin of Evangelical Theology* 7 (Autumn 1989) 69–87, esp. p. 77.

15. Rowley, *Election*, 165.

Rowley's position is itself based on the assumption that the Hebrew Bible did, at least eventually, come to endorse the notion of an active mission to the Gentiles. In fairness, Rowley is much more cautious than Walter Kaiser, who claims that the idea of an active mission to the Gentiles is widespread in the Hebrew Bible: "The Bible actually begins with the theme of missions in the book of Genesis and maintains that driving passion throughout the entire Old Testament and on into the New Testament."[16] Rowley, a more judicious scholar, thinks that any call for outright mission only reaches clarity in certain late prophetic texts such as Second Isaiah. The question is, does the Hebrew Bible in fact support Kaiser's position or even the more limited claims made by Rowley?

A number of other recent scholars have been much more circumspect in their assessment of the Hebrew Bible's endorsement of an active mission to the Gentiles. Donald Senior and Carroll Stuhlmueller see an inherent biblical tension between the particularity required by God's election of Israel and God's plan for universal salvation. They argue that the possible resolution to this tension is first introduced by the prophecies of Second Isaiah. Although they do not believe this prophet ever explicitly articulated the notion of universal salvation, they see him as the first to link Israel's unique call to the fate of the other nations of the world. In fact, these two scholars see Paul building on Second Isaiah's work and achieving a new theological synthesis. They go on to suggest that the suffering servant passages show that this prophet's universalistic vision was rejected by his coreligionists, just as Paul's Jewish contemporaries would do when he attempted to reckon uncircumcised and nonobservant Gentiles as members of Israel. Speaking of Isa 49:6, "I will give you as a light to the nations," they claim the following:

> This verse not only captured and expressed the intuitions and signals of Second Isaiah's early preaching, but also enabled him to endure the suffering of being rejected by his own people. . . . It extended Israel's election to the world, and so fulfilled the mission of Israel's being chosen in the first place.[17]

While one appreciates the greater nuance in the positions of Rowley and of Senior and Stuhlmueller, their understandings of the notion of election as well as of the texts in Second Isaiah remain problematic. The Hebrew Bible resists reducing the meaning of Israel's special election down to a matter of divine service (Deut 9:4–7, Jer 31:1–20). More seriously, it is highly dubious to argue that these eschatologically charged texts found in

16. Walter C. Kaiser, *Mission in the Old Testament: Israel as a Light to the Nations* (Grand Rapids: Baker, 2000) 7.

17. Donald Senior and Carroll Stuhlmueller, *The Biblical Foundations for Mission* (Maryknoll, NY: Orbis, 1989) 105.

Second Isaiah and other late biblical passages ever conceived of extending Israel's elect status to the other nations of the world. Discussion of the Hebrew Bible's view of Gentile inclusion is complicated by the host of texts that touch on it: Isa 2:2–4 and its close analogue Mic 4:1–5; Isa 14:1–2; 19:18–25; 24:14–16; 25:6–7; Jer 3:17; 12:14–17; 16:19; Zeph 3:8–10 ; Zech 2:11–12; 8:20–23; 14:16–19; Mal 1:11, 14; the entire book of Jonah; a number of psalms (e.g., 2, 46, 48, 87, 96, 98, 117); and many passages in Second and Third Isaiah (e.g., Isa 42:1–7; 44:1–5; 45:14, 20–25; 49; 51:4–6; 56; 60; and 66:18–21). These passages contain a plethora of images, some of which are in tension or even in contradiction with each other. Certain texts such as Isaiah 2 speak in rather irenic terms, whereas others, such as Isaiah 66, portray matters in violent and aggressive terms. Some speak of the nations serving Israel (Isaiah 60), others of Israel or God instructing the nations during a universal pilgrimage to God's Temple in Jerusalem (Isaiah 2; Zech 8:20–23), or of the nations worshiping God and observing Succot (the fall harvest festival) in Jerusalem, God's holy city (Zechariah 14). A number of these passages may have been written in hyperbolic terms, and thus one must not assume that they are describing what will happen literally so much as describing God's greatness. Does Psalm 117 really mean that all the nations will praise God, or is it the psalmist's call to awaken the congregation to praise God as loudly as possible? It is quite likely that many of the passages that speak of God's collecting adherents from around the world are more focused on God's intention to gather the dispersed Judean exiles and bolster their depressed spirits (Isa 42:1–7), than on the conversion of the nations to YHWHism. [18]

What generalizations, if any, can one make about the notion of mission in the Hebrew Bible from this wide array of differing texts? First, many of these passages contain a universalistic thrust, and quite a few reveal a belief in the idea that God's relationship to Israel was part of a larger salvific plan involving the whole world. Second, although many of these texts articulate a kind of universalism in which Israel plays a central role in God's larger salvific plan, there is little evidence to support the case that any of these texts advocated the notion of mission as it is typically understood within early Christianity or in contemporary discourse. Normally, the idea of mission is used in the strong sense of actively proselytizing others to bring them around to one's own faith. Rather, it seems that, in these texts,

> The encounter of the heathen and YHWH, effected by the agency of the Chosen People gathered together in Jerusalem, depends upon the divine initiative alone. It is grounded not in any independent interven-

---

18. Similarly, a careful reading of the Pentecost incident in Acts 2 makes clear that the people from many nations were in fact pious Jews from around the world (Acts 2:5).

tion by Israel but in a YHWH theophany. . . . Finally, Israel has no other mission than to be the Chosen People.[19]

In other words, one cannot claim that the Hebrew Bible endorses an active mission to the Gentiles, although it does conceive of the special relationship between God and Israel as being central to God's larger plan for the world. Thus, it appears that the stance of Second Temple and later rabbinic Judaism is in fact more consonant with most, if not all, streams of the Hebrew Bible's theological speculation on this topic. In turn, Christianity's propensity toward mission must be seen as a new thing that grew out of earlier biblical statements that portray the elect as attracting the attention of the Gentile nations in a magnetic way, rather than actively missionizing them. If this is true, Christians in the past and those living today who claim that Israel lost her elect status by refusing to missionize the Gentiles as the prophets supposedly proclaimed will need to rethink their theological presuppositions. They will need to acknowledge that Jews in fact are hewing more closely to the text of the Hebrew Bible, whereas Christians are reading these texts through a new lens of Christ as risen savior. This type of theological reading of the Hebrew Bible is not at all a plain-sense, contextual understanding of these texts but rather a highly innovative supernaturalist reading. As I will argue below, a similar acknowledgement must be made about the Jewish and Christian understandings of the place of the nonelect.

THE FATE OF THOSE NOT ELECTED

As briefly indicated above, the Hebrew Bible generally conceived of three categories of people: The elect who are called the people of Israel, the anti-elect who are beyond divine mercy and thus doomed for destruction, and the nonelect who are the vast majority of those not chosen but by no means condemned. This latter group plays an important role in the divine economy, and Israel works out her destiny in relation to these other peoples even while remaining separate from them. In a few late apocalyptic texts within the Hebrew Bible, one begins to see a breakdown of these three groups into two, the righteous chosen against the wicked doomed for total destruction (Isaiah 65 is a possible example of such a text). For the most part, however, almost all of the relevant texts within the Hebrew Bible still imagine the existence of other nonchosen nations. Generally, such nations come to recognize God, or become subservient to God and his people Israel, yet they continue to exist as separate nonelect peoples (Isaiah 49, 60, 66; Zechariah 14; and Daniel 7). Even a radical passage such

---

19. Robert Martin-Achard, *A Light to the Nations: A Study of the Old Testament Conception of Israel's Mission to the World* (Edinburgh: Oliver & Boyd, 1962) 75.

as Isaiah 66, which imagines some priests being chosen from Gentile nations, does not go so far as to imagine there are no other nations in the post-eschatological era. In fact, Isa 19:19–25 imagines that Assyria and Egypt might also become elect while maintaining their unique national identities. Thus, these powerful eschatological and occasionally apocalyptic images are only at the beginning of a process that will eventually give rise to the New Testament's full-blown polarization of the saved and those lost to God.[20] Furthermore, even where certain texts begin the process of collapsing the Hebrew Bible's categories of the nonelect and anti-elect into each other, it must be remembered that within the context of the Hebrew Bible as a whole, these ideas do not displace the older, predominant notion that election leaves room for the nonelect peoples of the world in the divine economy.

Major streams of rabbinic Judaism continued to maintain the idea of the nonelect and affirmed that righteous non-Jews can attain the rewards of the righteous as illustrated in the following exchange from t. Sanh. 13.2. Initially, Rabbi Eliezer argues that none of the Gentiles have a portion in the world to come on the basis of Ps 9:18[17], which states, "the wicked shall depart to Sheol, all the nations that forget God." However, Rabbi Joshua has the best of this argument, noting that, because the verse says "all the nations that forget God," it "indicates that there are also righteous people among the nations of the world, who do have a place in the world to come."[21] Rabbinic Judaism developed the idea that Gentiles could indeed

20. This should not be taken to mean that early Christianity was the only Jewish sectarian group of its time to make such a theological move. The overheated apocalypticism of various Essene texts (especially the *War Scroll*, the *Damascus Document*, and the *Rule of the Community*) found among the Dead Sea Scrolls reveals a similar propensity to collapse the three biblical categories of election into the saved and the damned. "For the sectarians, the renewed covenant was the indication of their particular relation with God—what made them the true Israel and disqualified the rest of the Jewish people. In this respect, some affinity does exist between the Qumran 'new covenant' and that of the early Christians." Cited from Lawrence Schiffman, "The Concept of Covenant in the Qumran Scrolls and Rabbinic Literature," in *The Idea of Biblical Interpretation: Essays in Honor of James L. Kugel* (ed. Hindy Najman and Judith Newman; Leiden: Brill, 2004) 257–78, here at p. 276.

21. *The Tosefta, Neziqin* (trans. Jacob Neusner; New York: Ktav, 1981) 238. Rabbi Joshua understands the implication of the verse as only those from among the nations who forget God will end up in Sheol. See the similar statement attributed to Rabbi Joshua in *Midr. Prov* 19:1: "Anyone who lives blamelessly before his Creator in this world will be saved from the torment of Gehenna in the coming future." *The Midrash on Proverbs: Translated from the Hebrew with an Introduction and Annotations by Burton Visotzky* (Yale Judaica Series; New Haven, CT: Yale University Press, 1992) 87. For a deeper introduction to this subject, see the following works: Benjamin Helfgott, *The Doctrine of Election in Tannaitic Literature* (New York: King's Crown Press, 1954); David Novak, *The Image of the Non-Jew in Judaism: An Historical and Constructive Study of the Noahide Laws* (Toronto Studies in Theology 14; New York: Edwin Mellen, 1983), and Gary Porton, *Goyim: Gentiles and Israelites in Mishnah-Tosefta* (BJS 155; Atlanta: Scholars, 1988). It is important to note that while the Rabbis in theory accorded a place for

attain salvation through observing the seven Noahide commandments, and thus they need not convert, a stance affirmed by contemporary Judaism. In fact, such conversions are discouraged unless someone is persistent. While some rabbis, like their Christian counterparts, speculated that in the messianic era everyone would eventually acknowledge Judaism and the truth of Torah, many rabbinic texts leave room for righteous Gentiles to attain salvation during the premessianic era through observance of the Noahide commandments alone.[22]

Another interesting rabbinic maneuver is that there are a number of attempts to dissolve the concept of the anti-elect. Thus, the *Sifre* on Deut 20:18 argues that this verse implies that, if the Canaanites repent, they are not to be slain.[23] A more elaborate tradition is found in *b. Sotah* 35b, which informs us that the Canaanite nations were indeed given full notice because they could read the stones that Joshua erected in the Jordan and be moved to repent. A similar midrashic idea about Amalek, another arch foe included among the anti-elect, is expressed in *b. Sanh.* 96b, which reports that the descendants of Haman, a character linked to the king of the doomed Amalekites in Esth 3:1, studied Torah in the academies of Bnei Braq.

On the other hand, New Testament and early Christian thinkers make clear that there is no salvation outside of faith in Jesus as the risen Christ (John 14:6, Acts 4:12, Gal 2:15–16). While this creates not only an openness to converts but also a drive to convert as many people as possible, it is important to recognize that this missionary impulse is not a sign of respect for the nonelect. Missionary activity is often bound up in imperialism and intolerance because at root it assumes the inadequacy of the religion of those being missionized. In the Christian case, those who refuse to join the missionary group are damned and cannot possibly be righteous before God. In fact, believers are warned in 2 Cor 6:14–7:1 against close social interaction with nonbelievers. Christians are indeed more open to converts but this is a double-edged sword. It led to the impulse to missionize non-Christians because it was not possible to attain salvation or be in right relationship with God unless one became a believing Christian.

---

righteous Gentiles, in their experience they were often skeptical that Gentiles could actually keep the seven Noahide laws required of the righteous Gentile, as one can see from *b. 'Abod. Zar.* 2–3. For other examples of negative portrayals of the Gentiles, see Sacha Stern, *Jewish Identity in early Rabbinic Writings* (Leiden: Brill, 1994).

22. Marc Hirshman, *Torah for the Entire World* (Tel Aviv: Hakkibbutz Hameuchad, 1999) [Hebrew], has cogently argued that there is an alternative rabbinic position on Gentile salvation that did not survive the talmudic period in which Gentiles can keep the Torah without converting to Judaism rather than observing only the seven Noahide commandments.

23. For the text, see Louis Finkelstein, ed., *Sifre on Deuteronomy* (New York: Jewish Theological Society, 1993) 238 (*Piska* 202). The standard English translation is *Sifre: A Tannaitic Commentary on the Book of Deuteronomy* (trans. Reuven Hammer; Yale Judaica Series 24; New Haven, CT: Yale University Press, 1986) §202, p. 218.

Judaism is inevitably less interested in active missionary work because the nonelect peoples of the world are accorded greater respect as long as they adhere to the seven Noahide commandments. In this particular case, it seems likely that rabbinic Judaism is more in tune with the dominant streams of the Hebrew Bible's concept of election, which often portray the nonelect in neutral or positive terms except when they act in an utterly reprehensible fashion (Genesis 19). Furthermore, though the Hebrew Bible generally sees the elect as playing a key role in God's salvific plan, it does not call on the chosen to missionize the nonelect. This is not to say that the Christian stance on election is not grounded in the Hebrew Scriptures, for surely it is. But the tendency to conceive of election as a binary opposition between the saved and the damned is a notion that only begins to develop in a few late apocalyptic biblical texts rather than in broad swaths of the Hebrew canon. Furthermore, the allied impulse to missionize the Other grows out of a particular theological reading of certain biblical passages that in context point to a more passive role on Israel's part. Of course, such ideas gained wider currency in certain extra biblical texts from the Hellenistic era, but the point is that they have only the most tenuous support within the Hebrew Scriptures.

GRACE AND WORKS IN JUDAISM AND CHRISTIANITY

Another important area of divergence between Judaism and Christianity centers on the emphasis that each tradition places on the roles played by divine and human initiative in the redemptive process. This distinction is often spoken of by employing the Christian terms *grace* versus *works*, and unfortunately discussions of this sort commonly reach simplistic conclusions that are derogatory to Judaism. Typically, Judaism is characterized as a religion that focuses on works, and Christianity is portrayed as a higher religion centered on faith. But this false generalization is belied by a closer look at a wider range of texts in each tradition. While one finds the statement quoted below in Paul's letter to the Romans, one need only look at the second passage listed below from James to gather that the radical emphasis on faith alone was not a view held by all early Christians.[24] In fact, the parable of the sheep and goats in Matt 25:31ff. appears to endorse the position of James, not that of Paul.

---

24. This is not to imply that Paul had no interest in works or that James is directly attacking Paul's theology. Paul clearly thought one could not be a member of the Christian community and engage in immoral behavior (1 Corinthians 5). And James is likely attacking people who lived long after Paul who had employed Paul's theology in an unacceptable way. But the fact that James puts down his opponents by emphasizing Abraham's works does suggest he was unhappy with Paul's heavy emphasis on salvation being based on faith alone apart from any works at all.

Is this blessedness, then, pronounced only on the circumcised, or also on the uncircumcised? We say, "Faith was reckoned to Abraham as righteousness." How then was it reckoned to him? Was it before or after he had been circumcised? It was not after, but before he was circumcised. He received the sign of circumcision as a seal of the righteousness that he had by faith while he was still uncircumcised. The purpose was to make him the ancestor of all who believe without being circumcised and who thus have righteousness reckoned to them, and likewise the ancestor of the circumcised who are not only circumcised but who also follow the example of the faith that our ancestor Abraham had before he was circumcised. For the promise that he would inherit the world did not come to Abraham or to his descendants through the law but through the righteousness of faith. If it is the adherents of the law who are to be the heirs, faith is null and the promise is void. (Rom 4:9–14)

What good is it, my brothers and sisters, if you say you have faith but do not have works? Can faith save you? If a brother or sister is naked and lacks daily food, and one of you says to them, "Go in peace; keep warm and eat your fill," and yet you do not supply their bodily needs, what is the good of that? So faith by itself, if it has no works, is dead. But someone will say, "You have faith and I have works." Show me your faith apart from your works, and I by my works will show you my faith. You believe that God is one; you do well. Even the demons believe—and shudder. Do you want to be shown, you senseless person, that faith apart from works is barren? Was not our ancestor Abraham justified by works when he offered his son Isaac on the altar? You see that faith was active along with his works, and faith was brought to completion by the works. Thus the scripture was fulfilled that says, "Abraham believed God, and it was reckoned to him as righteousness," and he was called the friend of God. You see that a person is justified by works and not by faith alone. (Jas 2:14–24)

Similarly, while much of rabbinic literature, continuing a movement already begun within the Pentateuch itself, places ever greater emphasis on the revelation of the *mitzvot*, (the commandments) given at Sinai, one can still find rabbinic passages that emphasize the salvific power of faith over works. Take, for example, the following comment from a 2nd-century tannaitic collection of halakhic (legal) midrashim, *The Mechilta de Rabbi Ishmael*, which sounds strikingly Pauline in its conclusion that salvation and redemption were gained by faith alone.

And so you also find that our father Abraham inherited both this world and the world beyond only as a reward for the faith with which he believed, as it is said: *And he believed in the Lord*, etc. (Gen 15:6).

And so you also find that Israel was redeemed from Egypt only as
a reward for the faith with which they believed, as it is said, *And the
people believed.* (Exod 4:31)[25]

Clearly, it is wrong to label Judaism as a religion that gives no attention to
one's faith in God's gracious actions or Christianity as a religion that always
disconnects salvation from human actions. Furthermore, it is important to
point out that the dichotomy between grace (or faith) and works (or law)
is itself part of a Christian paradigm that inherently does an injustice to
any attempt to understand Judaism in its own terms. While it is fair to say
that Judaism thinks that the human/divine relationship reaches its highest
consummation when the people of Israel fulfill the obligations of the Sinai covenant, Israel's failure to live up to these obligations does not nullify
God's gracious actions toward his people (Lev 26:40–45, Deut 30:1–5, Jer
31:1–20). It must be remembered that in the Jewish paradigm, the giving
of the commandments is itself the greatest manifestation of God's grace
toward the human community. The commandments are not opposed to
grace, God's giving of them is an act of grace in that observing them heals
the rift that developed between humans and the divine.

Bearing in mind the nuances that I have brought to the fore, it still
seems fair to say that on the whole Christianity places greater weight on
the notion of faith, and major streams of Christian thinking tend to deni-
grate human actions as a way to attain salvation. Much of the Pauline corpus is occupied with arguing this position at length, and it seems more than
self-evident that Paul has occupied a much larger place in the Christian
imagination than has James. Similarly, while one can find occasional rabbinic texts stressing the virtue of faith apart from any observance of the
commandments, one would be overwhelmed if one attempted to collect
every rabbinic text that praised the commandments or noted their salvific
power.

One can gain a greater appreciation of how each tradition grapples
with this somewhat intractable theological tension by seeing that the ancient rabbis and Paul are forced to deal with the opposite sides of the same
problem. Paul, wishing to make faith in Christ central and to demote the
place of Sinai, faced two interpretive issues: (1) How does one explain Abraham's act of circumcision, which appears to imply that Abraham engaged
in works as well as having faith? (2) Why did God give the law to Israel if
it is ultimately irrelevant to one's salvation? Paul addresses each of these
problems several times. Thus, in Galatians he argues that the law that came
430 years later cannot annul the unconditional Abrahamic covenant (Gal
3:17), while in Romans 4 (cited above), he argues that, even if Abraham

---

25. *The Mechilta de Rabbi Ishmael* (trans. J. Z. Lauterbach; Philadelphia: Jewish Publication Society, 1976) 1.253 (ז בשלח).

himself was circumcised in Genesis 17, it occurred after he had received the unconditional divine promise back in Genesis 15. In terms of demoting Sinai, in Gal 3:19–20 he claims the law was revealed not by God but by the angels. In Romans, he shifts the inadequacy of the law to human sinfulness (Rom 7:7–25).

The rabbis who wish to emphasize the place of the law do not have to explain why it has been displaced, as Paul does, but they do have to explain why, if it is so important, God failed to reveal it to the Patriarchs. These venerable ancestors appear to be in right relationship to God with knowledge of only a few commandments such as circumcision and an assumed knowledge of other more general prohibitions such as those against murder and theft, which we as well as the ancients think of as a type of natural law.[26] Through various midrashim like the two cited below, some rabbis claim that the various Patriarchs knew the whole of the law before it was revealed to Israel at Sinai.

> We thus find that Our Father Abraham had practiced the whole Torah in its entirety before it had been given, as it is said, *inasmuch as Abraham obeyed me and kept my charge: my commandments, my laws, and my teachings.* (Gen 26:5)[27]

> How did our father Jacob come in this world to merit a life with no distress, with no evil inclination—a life something like the life that God bestows upon the righteous only in the time to come? Because from his youth to his old age he frequented the house of study, familiarizing himself with Scripture, Mishnah, and Midrash of Halakot as well as Aggadot, as is said, *Jacob was an ideal man—he sat in tents [of study]*. (Gen 25:27)[28]

26. This problem is one that came to the fore long before the rabbinic period. For some of the various strategies employed by differing groups in the Second Temple period, see Gary Anderson, "The Status of the Torah before Sinai: The retelling of the Bible in the Damascus Covenant and the Book of Jubilees," *DSD* 1 (1994) 1–29. In fact, there was even an ancient Jewish propensity to import the revelation at Sinai back into Eden as indicated by texts such as Sir 17:11–13. For a more in-depth discussion of this issue, see John J. Collins, "Wisdom, Apocalypticism and the Dead Sea Scrolls," in *Jedes Ding Hat seine Zeit . . .* (ed. Anja Diesel et al.; Berlin: de Gruyter, 1996) 19–32, esp. pp. 21–26.

27. *m. Qidd.* 4:14, trans. Jon D. Levenson, "The Conversion of Abraham to Judaism, Christianity, and Islam," in *The Idea of Biblical Interpretation: Essays in Honor of James L. Kugel* (ed. Hindy Najman and Judith Newman; Leiden: Brill, 2004) 3–40, here at p. 22. This essay contains many thoughtful reflections on the variant protrayals of Abraham's observance of the law in ancient Jewish and Chrisian sources.

28. *Eliyyahu Rabbah* 5; *Tanna Debe Eliyyahu* (trans. W. G. Braude and I. J. Kapstein; Philadelphia: Jewish Publication Society, 1981) 67. The rabbis are here building on the notion that Jacob studied in the academy of Shem and Eber, an idea facilitated by the word *tents* used in Gen 9:27 and 25:27.

This brief survey reveals that both Judaism and Christianity chose to emphasize differing parts of a partially shared, although not identical, biblical heritage.[29] Both traditions are faced with the fact that the Hebrew Bible itself contains internal tensions concerning the question of how much of a role God and humans each play in the divine economy. These biblical tensions can be seen in a variety of loci. Perhaps they are most clearly in view when one examines the variety of covenants found in the Hebrew Bible. Not only does one find tension between more and less conditional covenants but one also discovers that a single covenant can be alternatively framed as conditional or unconditional.[30] The existence of the various covenants and tensions within individual streams of covenantal theology makes it difficult to determine how precisely divine grant and human responsibility relate to each other. Even more interesting is that similar tensions also occur in other major streams of biblical thought, such as in questions surrounding how election occurs. Is election by divine fiat, or is it due to human action, or is it finally some mysterious interaction that includes both a divine and a human component? Because these tensions are already embedded in the biblical text, each tradition's theological trajectory will inevitably show signs of struggle with the other parts of the biblical heritage that it lowered to secondary status. Thus, the seeds that ultimately grew into Judaism and Christianity were planted within the Hebrew Bible itself. Once they blossomed, it was likely that the two traditions would become vociferous rivals over who was the true heir of the biblical tradition. In this recent era of rapprochement between these two rival traditions, it is important to see that each tradition has much to learn from the other about those pieces of the biblical heritage it chose to deemphasize.

God's Elective Arbitrariness in Pauline Christianity and Rabbinic Judaism

One of the starkest contrasts between Judaism and Christianity is found in the way each tradition understands the place of human action in relation to election. On the whole, Christianity has chosen to elevate the motifs of God's mysterious and arbitrary actions. On the other hand, Judaism has tended to soften these arbitrary edges by midrashically filling in the biblical story in ways that explain why those chosen by God deserved this status or how those not chosen had forfeited their election.

29. It is important to note that the Christian Old Testament and the Jewish Tanakh are ordered differently. Furthermore, the church drew on the Septuagint, which at times contains a substantially different text from the Masoretic Tanakh.

30. For fuller treatment of this issue, see Jon D. Levenson, *Sinai and Zion: An Entry into the Jewish Bible* (Minneapolis: Winston, 1985).

On the Christian side, the following Pauline text is an excellent example of the movement to further emphasize God's mysterious, free, and arbitrary actions.

> It is not as though the word of God had failed. For not all Israelites truly belong to Israel, and not all of Abraham's children are his true descendants; but "It is through Isaac that descendants shall be named for you." This means that it is not the children of the flesh who are the children of God, but the children of the promise are counted as descendants. For this is what the promise said, "About this time I will return and Sarah shall have a son." Nor is that all; something similar happened to Rebecca when she had conceived children by one husband, our ancestor Isaac. Even before they had been born or had done anything good or bad (so that God's purpose of election might continue, not by works but by his call) she was told, "The elder shall serve the younger." As it is written, "I have loved Jacob, but I have hated Esau." What then are we to say? Is there injustice on God's part? By no means! For he says to Moses, "I will have mercy on whom I have mercy, and I will have compassion on whom I have compassion." So it depends not on human will or exertion, but on God who shows mercy. (Rom 9:6–16)

In this text, Paul pictures God's elective choice as completely unwarranted by any human action whatsoever. While one might object that this text only reflects Pauline concerns but does not apply to other parts of the New Testament, it seems quite likely that the New Testament's central story, which tells a tale of human failures that are only remedied by God's resurrecting of Jesus, indicates that God's unwarranted actions are emphasized throughout this textual corpus.[31] Further evidence might be found in the dualistic language employed by the Fourth Gospel. Some might argue that the Gospel of John is just using persuasive rhetoric when it speaks in dualistic terms of light and darkness (3:17–21), those who belong to either God or Satan (8:42–44). But this kind of language has close affinities to gnostic notions that one's fate has been fully determined before one's birth, leaving little room for human initiative (John 6:29, 8:47).

On the other hand, the rabbis, while not eliminating the notion of God's free and mysterious action, clearly are troubled by the idea that God acts in totally arbitrary ways. There are many instances in which the ancient rabbis demonstrate that God's actions may at times seem utterly mysterious in the cryptic language of the Bible, but on a deeper midrashic level, once the gaps in our knowledge are filled in, God's behavior becomes

---

31. For full argumentation to support this contention, see Michael David Goldberg, *Jews and Christians, Getting Our Stories Straight* (2nd ed.; Philadelphia: Trinity Press International, 1991) 135–210.

morally and rationally understandable. In these rabbinic midrashim, God elects certain individuals because they were in fact deserving human beings. An obvious example of this is the series of midrashic tales that describe Abraham as someone who reasons his way to monotheism through a variety of personal circumstances and is only then chosen by God as the founder of Judaism.

> Terah was a manufacturer of idols. He once went away somewhere and left Abraham to sell them in his place. . . . [Once] a woman came with a plateful of flour and requested of him, "Take this and offer it to them." So he took a stick, broke them, and put the stick in the hand of the largest. When his father returned he demanded, "What have you done to them?" "I cannot conceal it from you," he rejoined. "A woman came with a plateful of fine meal and requested me to offer it to them. One claimed, 'I must eat first,' while another claimed, 'I must eat first.' Thereupon the largest arose, took the stick, and broke them." "Why do you make sport of me," he [Terah] cried out; "have they then any knowledge!" "Should not your ears listen to what your mouth is saying," he [Abraham] retorted.[32]

One finds analogous midrashim that deal with perhaps the most central Jewish idea, the gift of the Torah to Israel. While it is important not to overstate things by implying that midrashic texts speak with a unified voice that always diminishes God's arbitrariness while enhancing the human role in warranting election,[33] there is a major stream of rabbinic thinking that rationalizes God's election of Israel by enhancing Israel's deservedness. One can see this quite clearly in the following midrash that claims that other nations were offered the Torah and found undeserving, while Israel unreservedly accepted it.

> And it was for the following reason that the nations of the world were asked to accept the Torah: In order that they should have no excuse for saying: Had we been asked we would have accepted it. For, behold, they were asked and refused to accept it, for it is said: *And he said: The Lord came from Sinai*, etc. (Deut 33:2). He appeared to the children of

32. *Gen. Rab.* 38:13. *Midrash Rabbah, Genesis* (trans. H. Freedman; 3rd ed., vol. 1; London: Soncino, 1983) 310–11.

33. Clearly, there are rabbinic texts that enhance God's arbitrariness while diminishing Israel's role in God's plan. For example, note the following text from *b. Shabb.* 88a, which comments on the fact that the text in Exodus 19 says Israel stood "at the foot of" or literally "under" the mountain: "*And they stood under the mount* (Exod 19:17). R. Abdimi b. Hama b. Hasa said: This teaches us that the Holy One, blessed be He, overturned the mountain upon them like an (inverted) cask, and said to them, 'If ye accept the Torah, 'tis well: if not, there shall be your burial.' This is not a portrait of a willing and deserving Israel and God's arbitrariness is here heightened." Translation from *The Babylonian Talmud, Seder Moed* (trans. I. Epstein; vol. 1; London: Soncino, 1938) 417.

Esau the wicked and said to them: Will you accept the Torah? They said to Him: What is written in it? He said to them: *Thou shalt not murder* (ibid., 5:17). They then said to him: The very heritage which you left us was: *And by thy sword shalt thou live* (Gen 27:40). He then appeared to the children of Amon (sic) and Moab. He said to them: Will you accept the Torah? They said to Him: What is written in it? He said to them: *Thou shalt not commit adultery* (Deut 5:17). They, however said to Him that they were all of them children of adulterers, as it is said: *Thus were both daughters of Lot with child by their father* (Gen 19:36). Then he appeared to the children of Ishmael. He said to them: Will you accept the Torah? They said to Him: What is written in it? He said to them: *Thou shalt not steal* (Deut 5:17). They then said to him: The very blessing that has been pronounced upon our father was: *And he shall be a wild ass of a man: his hand shall be upon everything* (Gen 16:12). . . . But when he came to the Israelites and: *At his right hand was a fiery law unto them* (Deut 33:2), they all opened their mouths and said: *All that the Lord hath spoken we will do and obey* (Exod 24:7).[34]

While at first glance these midrashim appear far removed from the portrayal of the God of the Bible, it is quite likely that the rabbinic tendency to rationalize God's actions is something that began to occur in the biblical text itself. Thus, one finds passages such as Gen 22:15–18, in which Abraham's election is grounded in and only finalized by his positive response to God.[35] Similarly, Exod 2:11–22 portrays Moses as someone who early on exhibited a deep sense of righteous indignation when other weaker parties were maltreated, indicating that God's selection of Moses to lead the Israelites was warranted on the basis of Moses' previous behavior. Of course, the rabbis deepen the evidence of Moses' earlier righteous behavior beyond what one finds in the biblical text just as they do with Abraham (see *Exod. Rab.* 2:2). But the process of linking the special status of Abraham and Moses to their behavior, rather than just viewing their selection as an utterly arbitrary choice by God, was something that is already underway in the biblical period itself. Although in this instance Pauline Christianity's emphasis on God's mysterious and arbitrary actions may be more attuned to the characterization of God as found in most narratives in the Hebrew Bible, the rabbinic drive to explain that God did not act arbitrarily is built on earlier biblical rationalizations.

Whether the rabbinic attempts to rationalize further Israel's election by portraying Israel and her progenitors as deserving of God's favor are part of a natural unfolding of earlier theological ideas or, alternatively, primarily driven by a need to defend the Jewish notion of election from

---

34. Lauterbach, *The Mechilta*, 2.234–35 (דבחודש ה).
35. R. W. L. Moberly, "The Earliest Commentary on the *Akedah*," *VT* 38 (1988) 302–23.

Christian attacks remains an open question.[36] The difficulty in ascertaining the background behind these midrashic innovations is due not only to the editorial practices of the rabbis that obscure the original social location of each pericope but also to the fragmentary nature of the historical evidence that makes it difficult to determine the extent of interreligious interchange at this time. On occasion, as I will argue below about a particular set of midrashim, a strong case can be made that a certain exegetical move was generated by an interreligious polemic. However, some scholars have reached beyond the meager evidence and claimed that a vast array of exegeses are best seen as polemical.[37] Arguments of this sort often fail to consider that many of these exegetical developments might be better explained by looking at internal Jewish considerations.[38] It is also quite possible that these midrashic developments are due to a complex interaction between a variety of internal theological factors and certain external social and religious pressures and that any attempt to posit a single causal explanation may obscure the truth of the matter. In the case of the two longer midrashim considered above, it is important to be aware that, while it is possible that interreligious polemic might be driving these ideas, they may be attributable simply to continuing Jewish reflection on Abraham's

36. Thus, Irving Mandelbaum ("Tannaitic Exegesis of the Golden Calf Episode," in *A Tribute to Geza Vermes* [ed. Philip Davies and Richard White; JSOTSup 100; Sheffield: JSOT Press, 1990] 207–23) finds substantial differences between the tannatic discussions of the golden calf episode and those attributed to amoraic sources. In particular, he sees the tannaitic sources as much more critical of Israel's idolatrous behavior while the amoraic midrashim introduce a variety of mitigating explanations that function in an apologetic manner. This may indicate that the rabbis softened their approach to this material in reaction to early Christian claims that the golden calf story demonstrated that the relationship between God and Israel had been totally abrogated.

37. Examples of those who see many midrashim as direct responses to Christian charges include L. Smolar and M. Aberbach, "The Golden Calf Episode in Postbiblical Jewish Literature," *HUCA* 39 (1968) 91–116; and A. Marmorstein, "Judaism and Christianity in the Middle of the Third Century," in *Studies in Jewish Theology* (ed. J. Rabbinowitz and M. S. Lew; London: Oxford University Press, 1950) 179–224.

38. One scholar who deserves praise for her careful analysis is Judith Baskin, *Pharaoh's Counsellors: Job, Jethro and Balaam in Rabbinic and Patristric Tradition* (BJS 47; Chico, CA: Scholars Press, 1983). Note her clear statement "that in certain times and places, most especially Palestine of the third, fourth and fifth centuries of our era, some rabbis were aware of and combatted through their exegeses various claims of the Christian Church which were seen as threatening to Judaism. Ultimately, however, the differences between rabbinic and patristic biblical interpretations are far greater than their points of contact. The contrasting principles and aims that inform these two bodies of commentary account for the vast differences in the interpretations of Job, Jethro and Balaam" (p. 121). For a careful comparison of Jewish and Christian interpretive techniques and an investigation into the question of the ways in which interreligious polemics might have shaped certain interpretations, see Marc Hirshman, *A Rivalry of Genius: Jewish and Christian Biblical Interpretation in Late Antiquity* (trans. Batya Stein; Albany: State University of New York Press, 1996).

election as well as on the meaning of Israel's subsequent reception of the Torah.

THE USE OF RIVALRY STORIES TO
DELEGITIMATE SISTER TRADITIONS

As the above arguments demonstrate, Judaism and Christianity each appropriated the Hebrew Bible's notion of election in distinct but related ways. However, sometimes each community's assertion of its unique identity over and against the other community reveals not a divergence but rather a type of mirroring. Oddly enough, as explored at length in Jon Levenson's masterful study on the biblical trope of the death and resurrection of the beloved son, Christianity is perhaps most Jewish when it uses the various stories of brotherly struggle in Genesis to substantiate its supersessionist theology.[39] Although these biblical tales from Genesis often present election in much more nuanced and ambiguous terms,[40] the fact is that both rabbinic Judaism and New Testament Christianity reinterpret and deploy these stories to secure their own legitimacy as the true people of God while delegitimizing other rival claimants.

A paradigmatic Christian example of this maneuver can be found in the following text from Paul's letter to the Galatians:

> For it is written that Abraham had two sons, one by a slave woman and the other by a free woman. One, the child of the slave, was born according to the flesh; the other, the child of the free woman, was born through the promise. Now this is an allegory: these women are two covenants. One woman, in fact, is Hagar, from Mount Sinai, bearing children for slavery. Now Hagar is Mount Sinai in Arabia and corresponds to the present Jerusalem, for she is in slavery with her children. But the other woman corresponds to the Jerusalem above; she is free, and she is our mother. For it is written, "Rejoice, you childless one, you who bear no children, burst into song and shout, you who endure no birth pangs; for the children of the desolate woman are more numerous than the children of the one who is married." Now you, my friends, are children of the promise, like Isaac. But just as at that time the child who was born according to the flesh persecuted the child who was born according to the Spirit, so it is now also. But what does the scripture say? "Drive out the slave and her child; for the child of the slave will not share the inheritance with the child of the free woman." So then, friends, we are children, not of the slave but of the

39. Jon D. Levenson, *The Death and Resurrection of the Beloved Son* (New Haven, CT: Yale University Press, 1993) 200–232.

40. R. Christopher Heard, *Dynamics of Diselection: Ambiguity in Genesis 12–36* and Ethnic Boundaries in Post-Exilic Judah (Semeia Studies 39; Atlanta: Society of Biblical Literature, 2001).

free woman. For freedom Christ has set us free. Stand firm, therefore, and do not submit again to a yoke of slavery. (Gal 4:22–5:1)

In this text, Paul utilizes an early biblical tale that originally legitimated ancient Israel's claim to be the chosen people and reinterprets it in a rather radical fashion to claim that the emerging church rather than the Jewish people are the true people of God.[41] He does this by associating the newer religion (what will eventually come to be called Christianity) with the younger sibling in the story, that is, Isaac, while linking Judaism, the older religion, with the eldest and ultimately nonchosen sibling, Ishmael. There are a number of unusual details in this Genesis text that facilitate Paul's attempt to read this story counterintuitively. For example, the fact that Hagar came from Egypt and that later she and Ishmael are placed in the Wilderness of Paran (Gen 21:21), a location in the Sinai Peninsula, allows him to read the story in Genesis as a negative allegory for the Israelites, who at a later date came out of Egypt and received the law at Sinai. Paul also manages to explain the Jewish reaction against the nascent Church of his time by midrashically exegeting the cryptic ending of Gen 21:9. The Masoretic Text reads "When Sarah saw the son that Hagar the Egyptian had borne for Abraham playing" (מְצַחֵק). In this reading, either Ishmael is simply playing in a frivolous manner, or perhaps "Ishmael was acting like Isaac, claiming Isaac's spot."[42] However, the Septuagint contains the words "with Isaac her son," which certainly helps clarify the text, although it still leaves it ambiguous enough to sustain a variety of interpretations. The easiest option would be to assume possibly that Ishmael was playing with Isaac, but the text can support more sinister readings such as mocking, persecuting, or even molesting Isaac.[43] Paul, working from the Septuagint,[44]

---

41. Here I disagree with the argument of J. Louis Martyn ("The Covenants of Hagar and Sarah," in *Faith and History: Essays in Honor of Paul W. Meyer* [ed. John Carroll and Charles Cosgrove; Atlanta: Scholars Press, 1990] 160–92), who argues that Hagar here is a reference not to Judaism but to a Law-observant mission to the Gentiles. Martyn's arguments in this essay are held by a number of other prominent New Perspective scholars such as John Gager in his *Reinventing Paul* (Oxford: Oxford University Press, 2000) and Lloyd Gaston in his *Paul and the Torah* (Vancouver: University of British Columbia Press, 1987). In any case, even if Martyn, Gaston, and Gager were correct on this point, within a century of Paul's time the Church understood this passage as an endorsement of the idea that the Church superseded the old Israel, as argued at length in Jeffrey S. Siker, *Disinheriting the Jews: Abraham in Early Christian Controversy* (Louisville, KY: Westminster/John Knox Press, 1991).

42. George W. Coats, "Strife without Reconciliation: A Narrative Theme in the Jacob Traditions," in *Werden und Wirken des Alten Testaments* (ed. Rainer Albertz et al.; Göttingen: Vandenhoeck & Ruprecht, 1980) 97.

43. "Behaving wantonly with someone," as suggested in Gerhard von Rad, *Genesis* (OTL; Philadelphia: Westminster, 1973) 232.

44. J. Ross Wagner (*Heralds of the Good News: Isaiah and Paul "in Concert" in the Letter to the Romans* [NovTSup 101; Leiden: Brill, 2002] 344–45) makes the following comments on the use of Isaiah in Romans:

reads the text as describing Ishmael persecuting Isaac, and furthermore he hints that the persecution represented Ishmael's attempt to claim Isaac's elect status for himself.[45] This would then support Paul's construal of his contemporary situation as one in which the elder displaced sibling, that is, the historic Jewish community, is persecuting the younger chosen sibling, that is, the church.

Interestingly enough, in Genesis Ishmael appears much less nefarious, and in fact he may be a rather young child at this time as indicated by the description of him possibly being placed on Hagar's shoulders (Gen 21:14), as well as that he appears to be a crying infant or small boy when Hagar abandons him under the bush (Gen 21:15).[46] The truth is that the real rivalry in this story is between Sarah and Hagar, not between Ishmael and Isaac, who rarely interact directly with each other. While the biblical text ultimately excluded Ishmael from the covenant (Gen 17:15–22), he appears to be a beneficiary of many of the promises God made to Abraham. He becomes the father of 12 tribes (Gen 25:12–18), receives a divine blessing of great fertility (Gen 17:20), and is even circumcised (Gen 17:25). Although the text of Genesis is both more subtle and less excluding in its treatment of the nonchosen brother in the various sibling rivalry stories in Genesis, Paul's reading removes much of the Hebrew Bible's ambiguity in order to

My own close examination of the wording of Paul's quotations and allusions to Isaiah in Romans supports the consensus view that Paul cites a Greek text (or texts) of this prophetic book. In most cases, Paul's *Vorlage* seems to have been nearly identical with the Septuagint version of Isaiah; at times, Paul's interpretation of a verse clearly depends on the form of the text distinctive to LXX Isaiah. In some cases, however, it appears that Paul has drawn his citation from a Greek text that reflects efforts to revise LXX Isaiah toward a Hebrew exemplar. Although I have given full consideration to the textual evidence provided by MT, the Qumran finds (biblical MSS, pesharim, and quotations in other documents), the Targum, and the Peshitta, at no point has it been found necessary to suppose that Paul has relied on a Hebrew or Aramaic text of Isaiah. This does not prove that Paul could not read these languages, nor does it show that he knew the book of Isaiah only in Greek. It does suggest, however, that Paul was intimately acquainted with a Greek version of Isaiah much like the LXX and that he apparently did not hunt down and exploit textual variants in other languages as he interpreted the book.

Because Isaiah is the most quoted Scripture in Paul's letters, Wagner's statement is indicative of a general pattern for Paul's use of his Scriptures.

45. One finds a similar idea expressed in *Gen. Rab.* 53:11 in which Rabbis Simeon b. Yoḥai commenting on the word מצחק in Gen 21:9 says the following: "But I say: This term sport [mockery] refers to inheritance. For when our father Isaac was born all rejoiced, whereupon Ishmael said to them, 'You are fools, for I am the firstborn and I receive a double portion.'" Cited from *Midrash Rabbah, Genesis*, 3rd ed., vol. 1 (trans. H. Freedman; London: Soncino, 1983) 470, compare *t. Sotah* 6:6. For a fuller analysis of the character of Ishmael in various rabbinic sources see Carol Bakhos, *Ishmael on the Border: Rabbinic Portrayals of the First Arab* (Albany, NY: State University of New York Press, 2006).

46. For an insightful reading of the ambiguous language of Gen 21:14, see Larry Lyke, "Where Does 'the Boy' Belong?: Compositional Strategy in Genesis 21:14," *CBQ 56* (1994) 637–48.

heighten the election of the elect as well as the rejection of the nonchosen sibling. Elsewhere in the New Testament, the rejected community is actually demonized (John 8:44).

However, this kind of thinking is far from unique to Paul. Rabbinic interpretations at times move along lines strikingly similar. Thus, one finds midrashim such as the following one, in which the rabbis undercut the Bible's ambiguity toward the nonchosen siblings in order to marginalize and delegitimize them completely. This is surely done to secure Jewish claims to God's election against rivals who might argue that they are God's special people because of their relationship to Abraham. As a quick glance at the following midrash makes clear, the rabbis link election to Jacob in order to nullify assertions by others, likely including Christian others, that they are the true chosen people on the basis of their relationship to Abraham.

> *For the portion of the Lord is His people* (Deut 32:9): A parable. A king had a field which he leased to tenants. When the tenants began to steal from it, he took it away from them and leased it to their children. When the children began to act worse than their fathers, he took it away from them and gave it to (the original tenants') grandchildren. When these too became worse than their predecessors, a son was born to him. He said to the grandchildren, "Leave my property. You may not remain therein. Give me back my portion, so that I may repossess it." Thus also, when our father Abraham came into the world, unworthy (descendants) issued from him, Ishmael and all of Keturah's children. When Isaac came into the world, unworthy (descendants) issued from him, Esau and all the princes of Edom, and they became worse than their predecessors. When Jacob came into the world, he did not produce unworthy (descendants), rather all his children were worthy, as it said, *And Jacob was a perfect man dwelling in tents* (Gen 25:27). When did God repossess His portion? Beginning with Jacob as it said, *For the portion of the Lord is His people, Jacob the lot of His inheritance* (Deut 32:9), and, *For the Lord hath chosen Jacob for Himself* (Ps 135:4). [47]

While it can never be known for certain if this midrash is in fact aimed at delegitimizing Christianity in the same way that many commentators have seen Paul's midrash on Hagar and Sarah as a directed attack on the Judaism of his day, at least one scholar has made a cogent case that certain nuances of this midrash are best explained as a point-by-point refutation of common Christian polemics against Judaism. [48] Additional support might be

---

47. *Sifre: A Tannaitic Commentary on the Book of Deuteronomy* (trans. Reuven Hammer; Yale Judaica Series 24; New Haven, CT: Yale University Press, 1986) *Piska* 312, p. 318.

48. Eugene Mihaly, "A Rabbinic Defense of the Election of Israel," *HUCA* 35 (1964) 103–43.

drawn from the fact that this midrash has an uncanny resemblance to the parable of the wicked tenants (Matt 21:33–46; Luke 20:9–19), another text that in its current form appears to attack Judaism's claim of God's permanent and irrevocable election of the Jewish people.

That both Jews and Christians read themselves back into the sibling stories in Genesis certainly makes clear how central these stories and the notion of election are to both traditions. It is only natural and even expected that the rabbinic Jewish and early Christian communities, religious groups that imbibed their theological world view from the Hebrew Bible, would both identify themselves with God's chosen people. The very act of claiming the Hebrew Bible as one's sacred text would have led each group to envision themselves as the people of God. However, the historical rivalry that arose between the leaders of the nascent Church and their rabbinic counterparts may explain why both traditions mirror each other in their propensity to read the biblical rivalry tales against the grain, emphasizing the rejectedness of the nonchosen sibling or group. It is important to remember that, although Paul portrays Judaism as the older sibling, implying that Christianity grew out of some form of preexisting Judaism, a portrait such as this ignores the reality that rabbinic Judaism, the religion we know today as Judaism, and Christianity "were born at the same time and nurtured in the same environment."[49] In the Hebrew Bible, the nonchosen characters are presented in a more nuanced fashion that allows them a greater and frequently positive place in the divine economy. In fact, the destiny of the chosen group is worked out in relation to the nonchosen others, who themselves benefit from the blessings that flow from God through the elect, and in turn, to the world at large.

While both traditions could benefit by emphasizing the elements in their shared scriptural heritage that create greater theological space for the other community, the truth is that Christianity is disproportionately more in need of a scriptural corrective such as this. There are indeed rabbinic midrashim, like the *Sifre* passage discussed above, in which the nonelect are depicted in unfairly harsh terms. Additionally, while the ancient rabbis erect a theoretical framework that affirms Gentiles can attain salvation through observing the seven Noahide laws, at times they characterize the Gentile nations of the world as utterly depraved and thus beyond redemption (*b. 'Abod. Zar.* 2–3). Clearly, the heat of such passages can be tempered by the Hebrew Bible's message that the righteous nonelect are not only not damned but are recipients of God's blessing. But one should not lose sight of the fact that vast swaths of rabbinic Judaism remained quite in tune with the Hebrew Bible's understanding that the nonelect can indeed stand in right relationship to God.

---

49. Alan Segal, *Rebecca's Children* (Cambridge: Harvard University Press, 1986) 1.

For Christians, the possibility of this sort of scriptural correction is complicated because it involves questions about the relationship between the two testaments. Is it possible for the Hebrew Bible, the Church's earliest Scripture, to provide a hermeneutical corrective to the New Testament, the part of the canon given greatest authority within later Christian tradition? Christian thinkers may decide that the New Testament, even when it interprets texts from the Hebrew Bible in ways at odds, or even in direct contradiction with a passage's contextual meaning, is the final authority in the Church's attempt to understand its sacred Scriptures. But one can imagine certain instances, especially places in which the New Testament's language is highly polemical, in which the Church might consider according greater weight to the Hebrew Bible's theological vision. It may be that the New Testament's propensity to view all nonbelievers as members of the anti-elect who must either convert or be damned is in need of a critique such as this. It is a notion with little warrant in the Hebrew Bible and one that may have been overemphasized early on when the apocalyptic fervor was at its highest and the nascent Church felt most threatened by those outside it. An additional point in support of using the Hebrew Bible to reconceptualize Christianity's theological understanding of nonbelievers is that the group that has most suffered from the classical Christian conception is a very unusual party of nonbelievers, the Jewish people (that is, Israel according to the flesh). The Jews are a unique group in Christian eyes, because, unlike Judaism, in which Christians belong to the nonelect Gentiles of the world, within Christianity Jews occupy a special theological category. Christianity's claims are based on God's promises to the people of Israel as recognized by Paul in Romans 9–11. Christian culpability for persecutions of Jews over millennia in combination with the fact that Jews were and even mysteriously remain God's elect people (Rom 9:4, 11:1) may provide both a moral and theological warrant for Christians to rethink some aspects of their theology of election.

The possibility that contemporary Jewish or Christian theologians might consider recalibrating their visions of the nonelect by giving renewed attention to the Hebrew Bible's construal of election theology should not be mistaken for a move to eliminate election's exclusivism. Whether one is speaking of the Hebrew Bible's idea of election or of later Jewish and Christian appropriations of it, election remains a stubbornly particularistic notion. The purpose of any such theological realignment would be to reattune the tradition to the deepest wellsprings of the Bible's election theology, a theology in which any universal horizon is only glimpsed through God's particularistic interaction with his chosen people.

CONCLUDING REFLECTIONS

As the above survey demonstrates, the most central theological claims of Judaism and Christianity are tied to each community's assertion to be

God's chosen people. This should not be surprising because election plays a very large role within the Hebrew Bible, which is not only the Jewish Bible but for a time was the only Scripture that early Christianity knew. Furthermore, Judaism and Christianity become utterly incoherent when they surrender their unique claims to be God's elect. Both Jews and Christians "to the extent that they are true to their foundational literatures, must continue to affirm the essential dichotomy between insiders and outsiders."[50] This places a limit on either tradition's ability to fit into the modern pluralistic context that looks askance at any exclusivise theological claims.

It also means that Jews and Christians, while sharing much, will continue to disagree with each other theologically. Judaism and Christianity each emphasize certain aspects of the Hebrew Bible's election theology while deemphasizing others. Recognition of this fact should lead both communities toward a greater clarity of their own tradition's theological development as well as toward a deeper understanding of the sister tradition. This is not to imply that the two traditions now can be reconciled theologically. While Judaism and Christianity grew in analogous ways out of a common theological and social matrix, the fact remains that each tradition developed an elaborate and distinctive theological system that poses a real critique of the other. However, this does not mean that Jewish/Christian dialogue is ultimately an exercise in futility. Jews and Christians can learn a great deal about their respective traditions by understanding the unique ways each tradition has appropriated the Hebrew Bible. Sometimes an insight from the other tradition may lead to a rethinking of one's own theology or to a recovery of an idea that was present but muted. In any case, such honest and critical dialogue helps each tradition's adherents clarify their own distinctive theological claims while at the same time leading to greater understanding of the other tradition's unique but somewhat analogous claims.

Whether this sort of understanding ultimately yields greater respect for the sister tradition remains an open question. After all, reaching a deeper understanding of each tradition's theological development may lead to a heightening of the differences between them and possibly a sharpening of each tradition's critique of the other tradition.[51] Nevertheless, both traditions have the resources to create a bit more theological space for the other community. This would not be accomplished by downplaying one's own elective claims or attempting to argue that each community is chosen in its own way. Rather, one would look toward the Hebrew Bible's conception of the nonelect. The Bible's election theology implies that election

50. Jon D. Levenson, "The Universal Horizon of Biblical Particularism," in *Ethnicity and the Bible* (ed. Mark Brett; Leiden: Brill, 1996) 143–69, here at p. 166.

51. Leora Batnitzky, "Dialogue as Judgment, Not Mutual Affirmation: A New Look at Franz Rosenzweig's Dialogical Philosophy," *JR* 79 (1999) 523–44; and Jon D. Levenson, "Must We Accept the Others' Self-Understanding?" *JR* 71 (1991) 558–67.

leads to a blessing for the larger world (Gen 12:2–3; 1 Pet 3:8–9), including the nonelect. The nonelect peoples were always considered fully part of the divine economy, and, in a very real sense, Israel was to work out its destiny in relation to them, even if in separation from them. More importantly, at times the Hebrew Bible declares that the special blessing reserved for the elect can only be fully enjoyed if one is reconciled with one's nonelect brethren. Thus, the chosen brother, Jacob, tells Esau "for truly to see your face is like seeing the face of God" (Gen 33:10), as he voluntarily shares the fruits of the blessing he stole from Esau and seeks reconciliation with his nonchosen brother.

Thus, both Jews and Christians would do well to remember God's promise to Abraham that all the peoples of the world will be blessed (or bless themselves) through his descendants, the chosen people (Gen 22:18). Here, one finds the delicate balance between the universal and the particular carefully maintained. Recognizing the universal horizon implicit in the concept of election is not to be confused with a call to jettison the claim to be God's uniquely elected people. The concept of election is itself the deepest articulation of the biblical God's close and merciful relationship toward humanity as a whole in that it is a declaration of the biblical God's profoundly *personal* character. While Jews and Christians must inevitably disagree over who is God's specially elected people and what is it that God demands from them, just as surely, both religious communities must continue to affirm the notion of God's particularistic election. For as the Hebrew Bible makes clear, God's larger plan for the world, a world composed of the elect and the nonelect, is only accomplished by means of God's special relationship to his chosen people.

Amalek and Amalekut:
A Homiletic Lesson

Zev Garber

OVERVIEW

In *mitzvah* numerology, Commandment 604 is a warrant for genocide:

> Remember what Amalek did to these on the way as you came forth out of Egypt: how he met you on the way, and cut off at your rear all who lagged behind you, when you were faint and weary; and he feared not God. Therefore, it shall be, when the Lord your God had given you rest from all your enemies round about, in the land which the Lord your God gives you for an inheritance to possess it, that you shall blot the remembrance of Amalek from under the heaven; you shall not forget. (Deut 25:17–19)

This commandment confronts an observant Jew, who is committed to living within the bounds of *halacha* (Jewish law), a system of divinely inspired biblical commandments as well as rabbinic decrees and derivations, with a textual ambiguity and a *halachic* conflict. That is to say, it asks this Jew to understand the confrontation with Amalek as a *milhemet mitzvah* (obligatory war) and yet show empathy for the Other, including the Enemy, demanded by the repeated biblical injunction: "Remember, you were slaves in the Land of Egypt" (Lev 19:34, and elsewhere). How to reconcile the conflict of an obligatory *mitzvah* to obliterate a people is the focus of this article.

My hermeneutics at this attempt at Jewish biblical theology is construed as a teaching lesson. My essay embraces scriptural *peshat*, rabbinic midrash, *halachic* derivations, and contemporary example. Among my findings are how biblical language molds the Jewish character and how to resolve the enigma of the Amalek without and within (*amalekut*).

THEODICY: EYES TO EARTH, HEART TO HEAVEN[1]

In the theistic theology of Jews and Christians, God is seen as all powerful, all-wise, completely benevolent, all caring, and all love. But evil exists in his world created from nothingness. How do we reconcile the goodness of God with the presence of evil?

Three centuries before the Christian era, the Greek pagan philosopher Epicurus stated the problem of theodicy (from the two Greek words for god and justice): that the gods cannot or will not prevent evil. If the gods cannot prevent evil, they are not omnipotent. If the gods will not prevent evil, then they are not omnibenevolent. And if the gods are not limited in either power or benevolence, why is there evil in the world?

In a popular college text, *Exploring the Philosophy of Religion*, editor David Stewart suggests that there are two types of evil in the world: natural and moral.[2] Natural evil refers to elements of nature that cause pain and suffering to human beings, such as natural disaster, disease, and death. Moral evil is suffering brought about by human perversity, and history testifies that human beings are capable of causing great physical and psychological pain to their fellows, which makes natural evil pale in comparison.

Stewart further points out that these two kinds of evil challenge important theistic teachings on the nature of God's management of the world. Natural evil raises questions about the order of nature, and moral evil raises questions about human nature. In both cases, the question for the Jew and Christian is why God allows a world such as ours to exist.

> Why does the natural order produce human suffering? Could God have created the world in such a way that it would not produce events that cause human suffering? If so, why did God not? The question posed by moral evil is why God allows us to inflict misery and suffering on others. Could God have created free beings who nonetheless, could not produce misery and suffering for their fellow human beings?[3]

The fundamental evil of human nature permeates the novels of Fyodor Dostoevsky (*The Brothers Karamazov*, *Crime and Punishment*, and others), who asks why does God let children suffer? Rabbi Milton Steinberg, in his classic *Basic Judaism*[4] posits, if God is, why is the world not better? Why is it so marred and weighted down with disorder and suffering that it seems at times to be not the handiwork of a God of goodness but the contrivance

---

1. *Yebamot* 105b. The sages rule that proper prayer is offered with eyes below (to Earth) and heart above (toward heaven). Likewise, questions of natural and moral evil are properly addressed with eyes and heart to providence and the world.

2. David Stewart, ed., *Exploring the Philosophy of Religion* (New Jersey: Prentice Hall. 1988) 254–61.

3. Ibid., 246.

4. Milton Steinberg, *Basic Judaism* (New York: Harcourt, Brace, 1947) 53–57.

of a fiend? Also, radical Christian theologian A. Roy Eckardt, sensing the
silence of God during the Sho'ah, questions, if God is alive and not dead,
then how can he live with himself knowing that millions of Jews, including
1.5 million children, were murdered so cruelly in Hitler's inferno?

The attempts to answer the question of theodicy in rabbinic terms,
why the good suffer and the wicked prosper, match the moral and metaphysical nuances of the question itself. In the end, modernist Rabbi Steinberg comments that evil is inscrutable, an enigma beyond unraveling, to
which the answer, if any, is known only to God himself. This is the purport
of the rabbinic epigram: "It is not in our power to explain the tranquility
of the wicked or the suffering of the upright."[5]

The traditionalist Jew, however, goes one epoch backward and thus
one step farther. For the Jew, the question of theodicy is the question of
anthropodicy (evil by man):

> The Rock, his work is perfect.
> For all his ways are justice.
> A God of faithfulness and without iniquity, just and right is he.
> Is corruption his? No, his children's is the blemish;
> A generation crooked and perverse.
> Do you requite the Lord,
> O foolish people and unwise?
> Is he not thy father that has gotten you?
> Has he not made you and established you? (Deut 32:4, 6)

Free will and humans' ability to discern right from wrong are implicit in
the doctrine of anthropodicy. Without this power, humans cannot be responsible for their actions, and the fabric of society will dissolve into chaos
and anarchy.[6]

In Jewish theology, strict traditionalists believe that the dire effects of
anti-Semitism and Sho'ah are caused by Israel's own backsliding:

> And the Lord said to Moses: You are soon to lie with your fathers.
> This people will then go astray after alien gods in their midst, in the
> land which they are about to enter; they will forsake me and break my
> covenant which I made with them. Then my anger will flare up against
> them and I will abandon them and hide my countenance from them.
> They shall be ready prey; and many evils and troubles shall befall them.
> And they shall say on that day, "Surely it is because our God is not in
> our midst that these evils have befallen us." (Deut 31:16–17)

The antidote to "the lure of strange nations and trust in them" (*Targum Onqelos* for "go(ing) astray after alien gods in their midst") is strict

5. Milton Steinberg, *Basic Judaism* (new York: Harcourt Brace Jovanovich, 1947) 55.
6. See Deut 30:15–20, especially vv. 15 and 19.

adherence to the Torah, *teshuvah* (returning to), its teachings, learning and passing on its moral precepts (Deut 31:19). For the righteous who follow the Torah way, the Deuteronomist proclaims:

> The secret things belong to the Lord our God; but the things that are revealed belong to us *and our children* [these words are dotted] forever that we may do all the words of this Torah. (Deut 29:28)

As a suitable hermeneutic for the *puncta extraordinaria*, I suggest: why do the righteous suffer? Do we parse the verse and connect "revealed things" with God, suggesting that he alone knows why mortals suffer? Or are they overt acts, doing Torah, that are not capable of preventing suffering of the righteous? On this verse, biblical exegesis and homiletic eisegesis form a circle—a theodicy circle.

Commandment 604: "Remember Amalek"

The Sabbath before Purim, designated as *Shabbat Zachor*, confronts the traditional Jew with a paradoxical dilemma. On the one hand, as a survivor of a state-sponsored policy of genocide, this Jew is a strong supporter of the United Nations Genocide Convention. Also, moral and ethical concern for other families of humankind is demanded by the repeated biblical injunction: "Remember, you were slaves in the Land of Egypt" (Lev 19:34, and elsewhere).

On the other hand, this same Jew is confronted with an explicit *mitzvah*, the 604th, to commit genocide (Deut 25:17–19). Other tribes have warred against Israel—Edomites, Moabites, Ammonites, Egyptians, and others—but none have been totally rejected or stigmatized by divine decree for eternal genocide and damnation as Amalek has. Could this be because Amalek "feared not God" and could not be like others who, after a period of moral regeneration, are accepted into the household of Israel? Contrast Deut 25:19 with Deut 23:8–9.

In rabbinic literature, Amalek is shown as a paradigm of absolute wickedness and evil, destroyer and rejecter of all that God and humans have wrought.[7] Thus, the *halachic* Jew, if confronted with a bona fide descendant of Amalek, would be duty bound to kill him or her immediately without needing to obtain a mandate from any rabbinical court.

How does one balance Abraham's agonizing plea over the fate of Sodom and Gomorrah, "Shall not the Judge of all the earth do justly?" (Gen 18:25) and the divine injunction of the descendants of Abraham "to do righteousness and justice" (18:19), with this imperative:

---

7. Cf. *Pesikta Rabbati* 12:47; *Pesikta de R. Kahana* 27; *Exod. Rab.* 26:2–3; *Num. Rab.* 13:3; *Sipre Numbers 84*, *Lam. Rab.* 3:64, 66; *Mekilta Amalek*, etc.

Write this for a memorial in the book, and rehearse it in the ears of Joshua: for I will utterly blot out the memory of Amalek from under heaven. And Moses built an altar, and called it *A-nai-nisi*. And he said: "The hand on the throne of the Lord: the Lord will have war with Amalek from generation to generation." (Exod 17:14–16)

Any attempt at understanding this warrant for genocide against the Amalekites and their descendants must start with knowledge of the biblical texts, in conjunction with known historical data.

The Bible records the collective life of the Amalekites from the days of the Exodus (mid-13th century B.C.E.) till the time of King Saul (1020–1005). The tribe inhabited the Sinai peninsula in the region of Kadesh (Gen 14:2) as far to the south as Shur (1 Sam 15:7, 27:18), from which they made raids on the settled population of southern Palestine (Num 13:29; 14:25, 43; 1 Sam 27:8).

The Israelites first met with the Amalekites in the region near Sinai when Amalek naturally tried to prevent the entrance of a new tribe into the region (cf. Exod 17:8–16). The battle that followed left a powerful impression on Moses: "Then the Lord said to Moses, 'Inscribe this in a document as a reminder, and read it aloud to Joshua: I will utterly blot out the memory of Amalek from under the heaven'" (Exod 17:14). Deut 25:17–19 suggests that Amalek made other attacks on Israel, including "from the rear." On the southern border of Palestine, the Amalekites also helped at a later time to prevent Israel's entrance from Kadesh (Num 13:22, 14:25).

During the period of the Judges (1200–1000), Amalekites aided the Moabites in raiding Israel (Judg 3:13), and at a later time they aided the Midianites in doing the same thing (Judg 6:3–33, 7:12). This enmity kept alive the old hostility that continued in the days of Saul (see 1 Samuel 15; the *haftorah* of *parshat Zakhor*, which talks of the command to exterminate all Amalekites) and David (1 Sam 27:8).

We read of the last of the Amalekites in 1 Chr 4:42–43, where there is a strange report that 500 Simeonites attacked and defeated a remnant of the Amalekites in Edom. Finally, Ps 83:8 refers to the Amalekites as aiding Israel's enemies; but this is probably a poetical imitation of ancient conditions.

In summary, the biblical material on Amalek notes: (1) The hatred between the Israelites and the Amalekites is an expression of clan warfare and feudal conflict over territory. (2) Amalek engaged in a war of killing noncombatants and thus has forfeited all hope of receiving mercy ("cut off at your rear all who lagged behind you, when you were faint and weary"; see Deut 25:18). (3) Amalek cooperated with other enemies of the Israelites in battles, against the Jewish people. This is comparable to conventional warfare among belligerents, and when completed, it is normally forgotten and forgiven. However. the Jew is obligated to "remember," to "blot out," and "not to forget," because the unique evil of Amalek is his war against the covenant, against Judaism ("he feared not God"; see Deut 25:18). Clearly, the biblical record sees Amalek as the traditional enemy for primarily political-military-survival reasons. But how does one explain the existential, *theological* input after the disappearance of Amalek as a recognizable entity? Finally, why is there the need to mold the Jewish character by means of genocide? To wit, "The Lord will be at war with Amalek throughout the ages" (Exod 17:16).

THEOLOGIZING AMALEK

The *mitzvah* of genocide cannot be easily dismissed. The book of Esther, which is read twice on Purim day, claims that Haman is a direct descendant of Agag (Esth 3:1), the Amalekite king (1 Sam 15:8), who from his authoritative position as advisor to the emperor of Persia and Media attempted to eliminate all Jews. His protagonist is Mordechai, the Jew, who, according to rabbinic tradition, is a descendant of Kish the Benjaminite (Esth 2:5). Kish is identified as the father of Saul, the first king of Israel. Biblical tradition maintains that Saul's downfall came about as a direct result of his failure to eradicate Amalek as commanded by divine decree through Samuel (1 Samuel 15).

1 Sam 15:33 suggests that the prophet Samuel "hewed Agag (= Amalek) in pieces before the Lord." His action is existentially imitated whenever and wherever Jews celebrate Purim. How so? Each time Haman's name is read in the synagogue on Purim, noisemakers, foot stomping, and jeering utterly "blot out" his name in the observance of the *mitzvah* of "remembering" what Amalek did and not "forgetting."

The biblical record on Amalek defends the genocide commandment by suggesting that this people "cut off at your rear all who lagged behind you, when you were faint and weary; and he feared not God" (Deut 25:18). Thus, Amalek is a pillaging and lawless tribe that attacks a tired and defenseless people and does not accept basic standards of morality and humanity.

Two biblical characters, Agag and Haman, represent the same characteristics. In contradiction to the *mitzvah* "and you shall love the stranger," stressed 36 times in Scripture, and the principle that "every man be put to death for his own sin" (Deut 24:16), Amalek represents evil in potential, if not in actuality. He is to be eradicated in keeping with the often-repeated deuteronomic admonition "And you shall eradicate the evil from the midst of you" (Deuteronomy 13, 17. 19, 22, and 24). So it is written, "the sons of Simeon, 500 men . . . smote the remnants of the Amalekites" (1 Chr 4:42, 43).

Rabbinic texts and commentaries abound with Amalekite references. But do we know how to read texts such as these? In a paper presented before the National Association of Professors of Hebrew meeting in Boston on December 6, 1987, we observed:

> Jews in pre-modern eras did not look backwards with the aim of discovering facts. They sought rather to derive paradigms from the sacred events of the past by which they could then interpret and respond to contemporary events. Paradigmatic and not pragmatic concern was the issue and emphasis. Jews dabbled in historiosophy (a philosophy of history) and not historiography.[8]

Rabbinic allusions to Amalek reflect not historical data but the Bible, and "historical facts" are not interesting as such but only as applications of the biblical texts. Present events for the rabbis and commentators (traditional) get their meaning when placed in the biblical context: God now speaks through texts. Furthermore, biblical Amalekite passages illustrate well the strong hermeneutical concern in the rabbis' comments on Amalek in general. The rabbinic interpretations are colored by the milieu in which they are used and for which they are intended.

For example: Gen 36:8 states that Esau (brother of Jacob) is Edom, and "Timna was concubine to Eliphaz, Esau's son; and she bore to Eliphaz Amalek" (Gen 36:12). Amalek was the illegitimate grandson of Esau. Isaac's blessing to his son Esau is that he will live by the sword (Gen 27:40), and the Torah records, "Esau hated Jacob because of the blessing with which his father blessed him (Gen 27:27–29). And Esau said in his heart: 'Let the days of mourning for my father be at hand; then will I slay my brother Jacob'" (Gen 27:41).

The medieval commentator Nahmanides (1194–1270) understands the fear of Moses and his charge to Joshua to fight with Amalek (Exod 17:9) because the latter lives by the sword. Nahmanides teaches that the first and last wars against Israel come from this people.

First, note the biblical verse "Amalek was the first of the nations" (Num 24:20). Who were the last? The descendants of Edom-Amalek, namely, Rome and Christendom. The latter was particularly meaningful to Nahmanides, because he lived during the height of the medieval Church's absolutist "teaching of contempt" and persecution of the Jewish people. Totalitarian ideology, political and economic anti-semitism, and Christian anti-Judaism combined in the 20th century to help bring about the Great Catastrophe, the Shoah, in the lands of Christendom.

God speaks through texts. In destruction, there is the seed of creation. Edom-Amalek in the classic rabbinic mentality become a synonym for

---

8. Zev Garber, "Interpretation and the Passover Haggadah: An Invitation to Post-biblical Historiosophy," *BHHE* 2/2 (1988) 27. The article is reprinted in Duane L. Christensen, ed., *Experiencing the Exodus from Egypt* (Oakland: Bibal, 1988) 51–60.

treachery, violence, oppression, and injustice, which one day will be obliterated. "But his end should come to destruction" (Num 24:20) is said of biblical Amalek and applied in talmudic midrashic historiosophy to Edom and to Rome. Thus, by associating (Amalek-)Edom with Rome in the rabbinic mind, a hope theology was born that was intended to ease the Jewish catastrophe of the first and second centuries by suggesting that a day of vengeance against the enemy was coming and that the day of victory was at hand.

After the fall of Rome, medieval commentators read into Edom-Amalek their contemporary sources of evil, such as Christendom and the Great Exile. Again, Naḥmanides teaches: Edom and associates would be discomfited and Israel will be saved from exile. "And saviors shall march up to Mount Zion to wreak judgment on Mount Esau [equated with Edom-Amalek]; and dominion shall be the Lord's" (Obad 1:21). Now, whatever Moses and Joshua did with Amalek at first (Exodus 17), Naḥmanides comments, Elijah and Messiah ben Joseph will do with their descendants. This was why Moses strained himself in this matter (Exod 17:9, 12).

The Amalek _zakhor_ commandment is not just academic but a verbal remembrance. It is not only recalled on Shabbat _Zachor_; it is promulgated as obligatory Jewish law (see _Orach Hayim_ 685:7). Its importance is to mold the Jewish character.

Jewish tradition sees Amalek in metaphorical, metahistorical, and metaphysical categories: (1) The Jews are to destroy the descendants of Amalek when those descendants follow in the Edom-Amalekite path of purposeless cruelty. Amalek represents cruelty and criminality for their own sake, and so do daily acts of terrorism, thousands of years later. (2) Amalek "did not fear God" (Deut 25:18). The crime of Amalek was an act of defiance, predicated on the denial of God's existence. His assumptions are that morality is neither universal nor important and that chance and survival for their own sake dominate the universe. Amalek's perversity, therefore, derives from his nihilistic theological posture. And so do Nazism and other current forms of extreme dehumanization, technological or in the name of radical religion and nationalism. (3) Amalek represents unredeemed evil, and rabbinic thought places its onus on the shoulders of humans. The moral imperative of the _zakhor_ commandment is for all individuals to join together to eliminate evil, not by destroying sinners but by eliminating sins. "May sinners disappear from the earth, and the wicked be no more" (Ps 104:35). Read not _hattaim_ (sinners) but _hataim_ (sinful acts).[9]

9. Cited in _b. Ber._ 10a. This passage is applied by a contemporary writer, Rabbi Moshe Amiel, to the verse, "You shall blot out the remembrance of Amalek" (Deut 25:19), "emphasizing that the commandment is to blot out the remembrance of Amalek, that is, the qualities that Amalek embodies, rather than the Amalekites themselves." See Louis H. Feldman ("Re-

This supports the rabbinic *halachic* thought that teaches the rehabilitation of sinners. Condemn drugs and promiscuity, for example, but show compassion to the victim, and certainly support sincere repentance.

In addition, we may add, the "seeds of Amalek," dwell *among* the Jewish people. In the Song of Deborah, we note: "Out of Ephraim came they whose root is in Amalek; after you, Benjamin, among your peoples" (Judg 5:14). So rendered, the phrase can mean (a) some of the Ephramites (that is, Joseph-tribes of Israel) dwelt among the Amalekites; or (b) some of the Amalekites were absorbed into Ephraim. Rashi (1040–1105) and others translate "against" instead of "in," and explain: from Ephraim, the root (namely, Joshua, a scion of the tribe; see Num 13:8) fought against Amalek (Exod 17:10–13), and after him Benjamin (that is, Saul the Benjaminite; see 1 Samuel 15) will also fight against him.

But overinvolvement today with external powers to wage "war against Amalek" because of the Shoah and Arab terrorism is an Amalekite-inspired red herring. This is *amalekut*, which partially paralyzes and deflects the Jew from going about his/her business, that is, the redemption of the Jewish people from the "seeds of Amalek" by doing what is right and nurturing a climate that would encourage others to do the same.

Because the children of Israel strove with Moses and "tried the Lord, saying, 'Is the Lord among us or not?' Then came Amalek and fought" (Exod 17:7b–8a).

Amalek, Amalekut, and "Amalekphobia"

Different forms and intensity of *amalekut* exist among the children of Abraham today. Consider extreme right-wing Zionists and anti-Zionists' traditionalist statements on the current Israeli-Palestinian impasse. However divergent their views, the former speaks of restricted Arab autonomy within Judea and Samaria and the latter insists on dismantling the (secular) Jewish state, and both claim they represent the right way for Jewish survival in the land of Israel. Equally shortsighted is the oft-repeated slogan, "Saddam Hussein is worse than Hitler," given prominence and notoriety by President George Bush during Operation Desert Storm (1991), and President George W. Bush's choice of "American Crusade" (a Christian statement) against the Muslim al-Qaeda terror network following the attack on America on September 11, 2001. More disturbing, however, are accredited Muslim day schools in America that teach children that it is laudable to kill

---

member Amalek!" [Cincinnati: Hebrew Union College Press, 2004] 48), who cites as his source Avi Sagi, "The Punishment of Amalek in Jewish Tradition: Coping with the Moral Problem," *Harvard Theological Review* 87 (1994) 334.

Jews, acceptable to hurt or steal from non-Muslims, and that the State of Israel has no legitimacy.[10]

Arguably, volatile Israeli nationalism that excuses unconscionable acts of violence should be condemned in the strongest terms. In the assassination of Prime Minister Yitzhak Rabin, the Israeli left showed how militant nationalist-clerical groups can usurp the will of the people, hit an enlightened Western democratic state broadside, and cause it to languish in ethnocentric, xenophobic backwater. By referring to Rabin as "traitor," "informer," and "collaborator," a process of defamation and vilification set in that created the dangerous atmosphere of permissive assassination.[11] But the liberated intellectual is not exempt from intolerant talk or behavior. For example, to make light of the revelation that extreme right-wing leader Avishai Raviv was an *agent provocateur* of the General Security Services and, further, to label the right wing as fascist or to suggest that "ultra-Orthodox" settlers are messianic and not pragmatic is not entirely fair. Many religious Zionists are ethical and commanded so by *halacha*, which molds their life. How can we penetrate Israel's perpetual internal dilemma? We suggest vigilant civil discourse that preempts *sin'at chinam* (hatred without reason) and do so by all means necessary.

The ugly language and face of global antisemitism disguised as anti-Zionism is rising hurriedly in the Islamic world. In the aftermath of the greatest attack on American soil in history, multiple sources cited in worldwide media (audio, electronic, print, video) suggested that Israel and world Jewry are the reason and alternately the mastermind behind the attack on the twin towers of the World Trade Center and the Pentagon on September 11, 2001. A glimpse of this type of thinking occurred days before at the world conference in Durban, South Africa, where Arab delegations succeeded in vilifying Israel—and only Israel—in the conference draft. A once-in-a-lifetime opportunity to mount a worldwide campaign against bigotry, hatred, and racism and to speak on behalf of the world oppressed was severely damaged by venomous, overt Israel bashing and covert antisemitism.[12]

I have no illusions about the aims of Hizballah and Palestinian militancy (Popular Front for the Liberation of Palestine [PFLP], Hamas, Is-

---

10. "Where Two Worlds Collide," *Washington Post* (February 25, 2002) A01. Reporters Valerie Strauss and Emily Wax noted that in some Muslim schools students are taught that "the Day of Judgment can't come until Jesus Christ returns to Earth, breaks the cross and converts everyone to Islam, and until Muslims start attacking Jews."

11. For a discussion of the Rabin assassination in a biblical context and discussion of *din rodef* and *din moser*, see Z. Garber and B. Zuckerman, *Double Takes: Thinking and Rethinking Issues of Modern Judaism in Ancient Texts* (Lanham, MD: University Press of America, 2004) 79–104, especially pp. 82–85.

12. Thoughts contained and developed further in my "America Attacked and Zion Blamed—Old-New Antisemitism: *Fatwa* against Israel," *Shofar* 20 (2002) 1–4. For provoca-

lamic Juhad, al-Aqsa Martyrs Brigades) to destroy Israel and to establish an entirely Islamic-Palestinian state in all of mandatory Palestine. Their deeds are marked by suicide bombings and shooting attacks against innocent men, women, children, and infants. They are fueled by false and vile teachings about Jews, Judaism, and Zionism. [13] Nonetheless, it is thoroughly unsound and morally wrong for Jews to view Palestinians as a modern-day Amalek and to think in Christian terms that the Israeli-Palestinian conflict is a prelude to Armageddon (Rev 16:16). Learning the complexity of the historical, religious, cultural, psychological, and political concern of the Palestinian national movement is one giant step forward to assuage these fears.

And Jews must heed the Voice from Sinai: do not contemplate thoughts of hatred, not even against your enemy, or carry out acts of human degradation or rampant destruction, lest innocent people suffer. The story of the rape of Dinah is informative. Dinah, the daughter of the Patriarch Jacob, was kidnapped and raped by Shechem, son of Chamor the Hivite, and her brothers were "grieved and very angry, because he had committed an outrage in Israel" (Gen 34:7). Dinah's brothers, Simeon and Levi, avenged their sister by killing Chamor and Shechem and all males of the city; their justification, "Should our sister be treated like a whore?" (Gen 34:31). But Jacob did not approve, and in his deathbed blessing he tells us why: "Simeon and Levi are bothers; weapons of violence are their swords . . . for in anger they killed men. . . . Cursed be their anger, for it is fierce, and their wrath, for it is cruel" (Gen 49:5–7). Jacob's response predicates Jewish law: if people do not pose an immediate threat, killing them is not allowed unless there are clear indications that they are planning to kill first. The point is that a nation must defend itself. A forceful assault on the enemy may unfortunately involve harming the innocent, and this is reprehensible, but nothing can be done about it, except trying to prevent it *ab initio*. Learn well the words of Prime Minister Golda Meir that Israel can understand and forgive the killing of Israeli soldiers but never for having made the Israeli soldiers into those who are forced to kill.

What do we do with the divine command (Deut 25:19) to wipe out the memory of Amalek? Think of its trajectory, *amalekut*, and how to eliminate it. Circumvent volatile scriptural passages with benign hermeneutics.

---

tive essays on the sustaining power of European and Arab anti-Semitism and anti-Zionism, see R. Rosenbaum, ed., *Those Who Forget the Past: The Question of Anti-Semistim* (New York: Random House, 2004).

13. Noteworthy examples are that IDF soldiers wear helmets inscribes with "born to kill" ; the Saudi daily newspaper, *Al-Riyadh* (March 10, 2002; cited in *Middle East Research Insitiute Special Dispatch Series* 354, March 12, 2002), claims that Jews use Christian and Muslim blood to make special pastries for the holiday of Purim; and Hamas stating that the Quran teaches that the Day of Judgment will not come about until Muslims fight the Jews and kill them.

Accept religious, cultural, ethnic, and national diversity as an integral Jewish, Christian, and Muslim value. Welcome nonviolent resistance. Express zero tolerance for a philosophy that glorifies death and murder in the name of religious martyrdom from anyone, any time, and any place.[14] Finally, the real antidote to present-day *amalekut*, individually and collectively, is respect and understanding of self and other and not speculative historical, military, and political reconstruction.

APPENDIX: THE COMMAND TO OBLITERATE THE
SEVEN NATIONS OF CANAAN[15]

The Hebrew Scriptures narrate a number of incidents of total or near-total obliteration of society by divine fiat. A strong parallel to wiping out Amalek is the command to obliterate the Seven Nations of Canaan (Deut 7:1–5, 20:17, and, with variation, elsewhere in the Bible).

The commandment to annihilate the seven nations (Hittites, Girgashites, Amorites, Canaanites, Peruzites, Hivites, and Jebusites) is intrinsically connected to the biblical injunction of *cherem*, a legal injunction separating contact from a human, animal, or thing either because it is proscribed as an abomination to God (*to 'evah*) or because it is consecrated to Him in a private or communal vow as *qadosh* ("holy"). The status of a private or communal vow is irrevocable. These are normally seen as priestly offerings; and defeated enemies and their towns vowed as *cherem* are utterly destroyed (Lev 27:28; Ezek 44:29; and Num 18:14, 21:1–3). It appears that *cherem* was administered differently to entities outside and inside the preexilic Israelite community. For example, destruction of Jericho, Ai, Hazor, Zephat, and punishment for the people of Jabesh-Gilead and the Benjamanites (Josh 6:17–26; 8:26; 10:39; 11:13; Judg 1:17, 20–21). Exceptionally severe is the divine admonition against Amalek, whom the Lord swore to "utterly blot," and Moses vowed "war with Amalek from generation to generation" (Exod 17:14). There are situations of devastation and dedication where *cherem* is clear-cut, but the terminology is lacking; for example,

---

14. Writing on the terrorist attacks of September 11, 2001, Mohammed Ayoob, professor of international relations at Michigan State University, observed, "Had responsible Muslim leaders in America been vigilant and forceful in condemning such extremism, the connection between terrorism and Islam would not have been so readily fixed in the public's mind. The Muslim community is now paying dearly for this failure" ("How to Define a Muslim American Agenda," in *The New York Times* [December 29, 2001]). Likewise, the progressive author and journalist Dr. Shaker al-Nabuski condemned the growing support for terrorism and extremism in the Arab world and the rejection of moderation and reason. See www.rezgar.com.

15. Adopted from my essay "Terror out of Zion: Making Sense of Scriptural Teaching," in *Confronting Genocide: Judaism, Christianity, Islam* (ed. Steven L. Jacobs; Lanham, MD: Lexington, 2009).

Moses' instruction to the Levites to kill the worshipers of the golden calf and the war against Midian is described as the "Lord's vengeance on Midian" (Exod 32:27, Num 31:3).

The negativity of *cherem* goes back to the hoary origins of Israelite ethnic religion: "You shall have no other gods beside me" and "he that sacrifices unto the gods, save unto the Lord only, shall be utterly destroyed" (Deut 5:7, and Exod 20:3, 22:19). In addition to passages proscribed for idolatry and apostasy, there are religious ground rules for the wars of settlement: invoke the favor of God to guarantee victory on the battlefield. Thus, in desperate times, the land-crazed Israelites enlisted the God of Israel as their standard bearer in the conquest of the Canaanite land, called the promised land, which together with male circumcision represented the virtual Abrahamic covenantal promise of possession (Gen 17:7–8). This is reflected in the narratives of Deuteronomy and Joshua, which speak of the indigenous populations as enemy *cherem* and thus fair game in wars of aggression and attrition. Deuteronomy speaks of extreme conquests in Transjordan, where man, woman, and child are put to death, but the livestock and booty are left intact (Num 21:24; Deut 2:34, 3:6, 10:28–40, 11:10–12). But in the severest type of *cherem*, livestock are killed and burned as an offering to the Lord, and no spoil taken (Joshua 6–7, Judg 21:5–11, 1 Sam 15:1–9).

However, the decree against the seven nations reflects a bilateral legislation. Exodus law speaks of their dispossession and expulsion lest they cause the Israelites to depart from the way of the God of Israel (Exod 23:27–33, 32:2–3, 34:11–17; Num 33:50–56). Deuteronomy adds extermination and regulates it as a religious duty. This is no doubt because these major populations of the promised land threatened the purity of the Israelite faith and nation.[16]

16. Similarly, the Moabite Stone, discovered in 1868 at Dibon, some 13 miles east of the Dead Sea. This sole extrabiblical rite of *cherem* records that Mesha, king of Moab, commanded by Chemosh, the national god of the Moabites, took back lost property: "I slew all: seven thousand men, boys, women, and [girls] and female slaves, for I had consecrated (*hchrmth*) it to Ashtar-Chemosh. And I took from there the vessels of Yahweh and dragged them before Chemosh." See D. W. Thomas, ed., *Documents from Old Testament Times* (New York: Harper & Row, 1958) 197.

II

◇◇◇◇◇◇◇◇◇◇◇◇◇◇◇◇◇◇◇◇◇◇

Foundations for a Jewish Theology of the Hebrew Bible: Prophets in Dialogue

Marvin A. Sweeney

Introduction

The time has come to consider the possibility of a Jewish theology of the Bible.[1] Such a statement might seem somewhat puzzling, given the plethora of Old Testament theologies that have been written since the origins of the field of biblical theology in Johann P. Gabler's 1787 inaugural lecture at the University of Altdorf.[2] But we must recognize that Gabler and the many biblical theologians that have followed him never intended to address the question of Jewish biblical theology. *Rather, they have been interested in the question of a Christian biblical theology, insofar as they are fundamentally concerned with interpreting the Christian Old Testament in relation to the larger concerns of the Christian biblical canon, particularly the New Testament, and Christian systematic theology.* In proposing the possibility of a Jewish biblical

Author's note: This essay is a revised version of the Henry A. Gustafson Lectures presented October 7–8, 2002, at the United Theological Seminary of the Twin Cities, New Brighton, Minnesota. I would like to thank Dean Richard D. Weis and the United faculty for their invitation to present these lectures and for their warm hospitality during my stay in New Brighton.

1. For overviews concerning the field of Jewish biblical theology, see my "Emerging Field of Jewish Biblical Theology," *Academic Approaches to Teaching Jewish Studies* (ed. Z. Garber; Lanham, MD: University Press of America, 2000) 83–105; Gerhard Hasel, *Old Testament Theology: Basic Issues in the Current Debate* (4th ed.; Grand Rapids: Eerdmans, 1991) 34–38; James Barr, *The Concept of Biblical Theology* (Minneapolis: Fortress, 1999) 286–311; Isaac Kalimi, *Early Jewish Exegesis and Theological Controversy: Studies in Scriptures in the Shadow of Internal and External Controversies* (Jewish and Christian Heritage Series 2; Assen: Van Gorcum, 2002) 105–59.

2. Johan P. Gabler, "An Oration on the Proper Distinction between Biblical and Dogmatic Theology and the Specific Objectives of Each," in *The Flowering of Old Testament Theology* (ed. B. C. Ollenburger, E. A. Martens, and G. F. Hasel; Sources for Biblical and Theological Study 1; Winona Lake, IN: Eisenbrauns, 1992) 489–502; on Gabler, see Rolf P. Knierim, *The Task of Old Testament Theology: Substance, Method, and Cases* (Grand Rapids: Eerdmans, 1995) 495–556.

theology, I intend to address the systematic *interpretation of the Jewish form of the Bible, that is, the Tanak, including the Torah, Prophets, and Writings*, as a coherent and self-standing work that constitutes the foundational text of Jewish tradition and thought. With this general agenda in mind, I would like to focus on two primary themes: (a) "The Temple as Holy Center of Canon and Creation," and (b) "Prophets in Dialogue." I intend to demonstrate that the Temple/tabernacle functions as a symbol for an ideal and stable creation within the Torah. I also intend to demonstrate how the Prophets engage in dialogue, with Israel's foundational traditions and with each other, in their efforts to come to grips with the issues posed by the destruction of the Temple and its restoration.

Jewish Biblical Theology and the Uniqueness of the Jewish Bible

Before turning to the primary topic, the Temple as holy center of canon and creation, I would like to address briefly two preliminary issues. The first is the question, "Why should Jews be interested in biblical theology?" Indeed, Jon Levenson has already posed this question and points to the predominantly Christian character of the field together with its frequent expressions of anti-Jewish sentiments as reasons for Jews to approach such an enterprise with caution.[3] However, interpreters must recognize that Judaism has much to gain by developing its own theological approaches to the interpretation of the Bible.[4] The Bible is fundamentally Jewish literature, written by Jews in ancient times to express their understandings of G-d, the nation Israel, the world at large, and so on, that functions as the basis for all Jewish tradition and thought. Christian biblical theology generally addresses its own concerns, such as the relation of the Old Testament to the New Testament, the nature of human sin and the necessity of divine redemption through Christ, and the inclusion of Gentiles in the divine covenant of Israel. Judaism has a very different set of concerns that are rarely addressed in Christian biblical theology. Judaism discourages speculation concerning the nature and character of G-d as attempts to portray or define G-d compromise divine sanctity and promote idolatry. Although Judaism is intimately concerned with G-d, it tends to focus far

---

3. See Jon D. Levenson, "Why Jews Are Not Interested in Biblical Theology," in *The Hebrew Bible, the Old Testament, and Historical Criticism: Jews and Christians in Biblical Studies* (Louisville, KY: Westminster John Knox, 1993) 33–61, 165–70. For a sharp criticism of Levenson's position, see Isaac Kalimi, "History of Israelite Religion or Hebrew Bible / Old Testament Theology: A Jewish Interest in Biblical Theology," *Early Jewish Exegesis and Theological Controversy* (Jewish and Christian Heritage 2; Assen: Van Gorcum, 2002) 105–34, esp. pp. 118–25.

4. See my essays "Why Jews Should Be Interested in Biblical Theology," *CCAR Journal* 44 (1997) 67–75; "Reconceiving the Paradigms of Old Testament Theology in the Post-Shoah World," *Biblical Interpretation* 6 (1998) 142–61.

more intently on the responsibilities of human beings, who are expected to act as partners with G-d to ensure the completion and sanctity of creation at large. Thus, Judaism is concerned with the character and nature of the people of Israel as an ongoing reality in world history, the development of *halachah* (Jewish law or practice), which defines the holy character of Jewish life and ethics, and the role of Judaism in bringing about *Tikkun Olam* ("the repair of the world"), that is, working to eliminate evil in the world.

Jewish biblical theology also has much to contribute to Christian biblical theology. Fundamentally, it asserts that Judaism is not simply a prelude to the advent of Christianity that will ultimately be absorbed as the entire world comes to recognize Christ. Instead, it demonstrates that Judaism constitutes a distinctive, legitimate, and continuing theological reality that must be accepted and engaged as such by Christians. We must recognize that, although Judaism and Christianity develop out of the same roots in the Bible, they are not the same. Whereas Judaism maintains its understanding of the continuity of the Jewish people and its relationship to G-d, Christianity abandoned its originally Jewish roots very early in its history as it looked to the Gentile world for continued growth and theological development. As Christianity absorbed pagan religious systems and ideas, it developed a very distinctive theological view in which human beings were fundamentally incapable of overcoming their sinful nature and required divine intervention in order to achieve salvation. Acceptance of the principle that Judaism and Christianity are not fundamentally the same, despite their common origins in biblical tradition, is essential for the continued future development of both traditions. This sort of recognition has the potential to bring to an end the moral problem of a long tradition of Christian oppression of Jews, and it provides an opportunity for constructive dialogue and interaction between the two traditions.

An important aspect of the recognition of the distinctive characters of Judaism and Christianity leads us to the second preliminary question, the distinctive form and identity of the Jewish Bible when considered in relation to the Christian Bible.[5] Because Judaism and Christianity share biblical tradition, Tanakh / Old Testament, many treat the Tanakh and Old Testament as if they are one and the same document.[6] Although the Tanak and Protestant versions of the Old Testament include the same biblical books, they are arranged in very different sequences that point to the

---

5. See my essay "Tanak versus Old Testament: Concerning the Foundation for a Jewish Theology of the Bible," in *Problems in Biblical Theology: Essays in Honor of Rolf Knierim* (ed. H. T. C. Sun et al.; Grand Rapids: Eerdmans, 1997) 353–72.

6. E.g., Rolf Rendtorff, "Toward a Common Jewish-Christian Reading of the Hebrew Bible," in *Canon and Theology* (OBT; Minneapolis: Fortress, 1993) 31–45; see now his *Theologie des Alten Testaments. Ein kanonischer Entwurf* (2 vols.; Neukirchen-Vluyn: Neukirchener Verlag, 1999, 2001) esp. 1:1–9.

distinctive understanding of the Bible in each tradition. The theological implications of the Christian term *Old Testament* have been long recognized as a reference to the original covenant between G-d and humanity that was established with the people Israel.[7] The "old covenant" of Israel is expressed through the revelation of divine law to Israel through Moses at Mt. Sinai, and the purpose of this revelation was that Israel serve as the means by which G-d would be revealed to the entire world. But Christianity maintains that G-d was compelled to punish Israel by means of the Assyrian, Babylonian, and Roman empires for failing to keep its covenant. This failure points to the need for the "new covenant" or New Testament, which relates the revelation of Jesus as the Christ to the entire world.

The basic division of the Christian Bible into the Old and the New Testaments demonstrates the fundamental principles of Christian theology. But theological tenets such as these also appear in the basic structure of each Testament. Thus, the four-part structure of the New Testament points to the Christian belief that a sinful world has not yet accepted Christ, and that a second coming is necessary. It employs a chronological sequence to portray the historical process of Christian revelation. Hence, the four Gospels relate the earliest revelation of Jesus, his crucifixion, and his resurrection as the foundation of the New Testament tradition. The Acts of the Apostles then relate the subsequent early history of the nascent church as it spread from Jerusalem to Rome. The Epistles address timeless questions of Christian theology and church organization as Christianity prepares for Christ's return. Finally, the Apocalypse of John or the book of Revelation points to the second coming of Christ as the culmination of human history.

The structure of the Christian Old Testament exhibits a similar four-part chronological sequence that traces the relationship between G-d and humanity from creation to the period prior to the revelation of Jesus.[8] This basic sequence applies to the Protestant, Roman Catholic, and Eastern Orthodox Old Testament canons, although the latter two include books identified as the Apocrypha in Protestant Bibles. Like the Gospels, the Pentateuch relates the earliest history of G-d's relationship with Israel and humanity at large, from the creation of the world through the time of Moses when G-d revealed the covenant with Israel at Mt. Sinai. The Historical Books then relate the subsequent history of Israel, from the time of its entry into the promised land under Joshua, through the postexilic period of Jewish life either in the land of Israel or in the Diaspora under Gentile

---

7. See James A. Sanders, "First Testament and Second," *Biblical Theology Bulletin* 17 (1987) 47–50.

8. For discussion of the formation of Old Testament in Christianity, see esp. Roger T. Beckwith, *The Old Testament Canon of the New Testament Church* (Grand Rapids: Eerdmans, 1986).

rule. The Poetical and Wisdom Books take up timeless questions of the means by which human beings relate to G-d and the world in which they live. Finally, the Prophetic Books point to a future beyond the punishment suffered by Israel when G-d will reestablish a new relationship with Israel and the world at large. Within the larger context of the Christian Bible, the Prophets appear immediately prior to the New Testament so that the New Testament functions within the Christian canon as the fulfillment of the Old.[9]

The Jewish Tanakh is organized according to a very different set of principles, which likewise demonstrate Judaism's fundamental theological world view that the Torah serves the basis for G-d's relationship with Israel/ Judaism and the world at large.[10] *Tanakh* is an acronym for the three major parts of the Jewish Bible: Torah ("Instruction"); *Nevi'im* ("Prophets"); and *Ketuvim* ("Writings"). Although Torah is often mistranslated as "law,"[11] it actually means "instruction" or "guidance." The Torah presents the foundational history of Judaism and the world from creation, through the period of the Patriarchs, and finally through the time of Moses. Altogether, the Torah presents an ideal view of the relationship between G-d and Israel as G-d forms Israel into a people, reveals the Torah by which they are to live, and leads them to the land of Israel. The *Nevi'im* or Prophets includes two subdivisions. The *Nevi'm Rishonim* (the Former Prophets) relate an interpretive history of Israel from the entry into the land of Israel under Joshua to the Babylonian Exile. The books attempt to demonstrate that Israel's suffering is the result of its failure to live according to the divine commandments given through Moses. The *Nevi'im Aḥronim* (Latter Prophets) contain the prophetic oracles and narratives about the prophets that present their understandings of the reasons for Israel's suffering and the future restoration of the people once the punishment is complete. Altogether, the Prophets point to the disruption of the ideal relationship between Israel and G-d, but they also point to its restoration. Finally, the *Ketuvim* (Writings) take up the various means by which human beings understand and express themselves in relation to G-d as a prelude to the accounts of the restoration of Jewish life around the Jerusalem Temple and divine Torah. Essentially, the books of the *Ketuvim* are organized to point to the restoration of the ideal relationship portrayed in the Torah and disrupted in the *Nevi'im*.

9. Cf. Isaac Kalimi, "History of Interpretation: The Book of Chronicles in Jewish Tradition. From Daniel to Spinoza," *RB* 105 (1998), 5–41, esp. pp. 24–25.

10. For discussion of the formation of the Tanakh, see esp. Sid Leiman, *The Canonization of Hebrew Scripture: The Talmudic and Midrashic Evidence* (Hamden: Connecticut Academy of Arts and Sciences and Archon, 1976).

11. In fact, this is just an English equivalent of the Greek term in the LXX, *nomos*.

THE TEMPLE AS HOLY CENTER OF CANON AND CREATION

Having treated preliminary questions, I now turn to the Temple as
holy center of creation. Indeed, a proper understanding of Torah as "instruction" is particularly important for considering the role of the Temple
as holy or ideal center of canon and creation, insofar as the Temple, represented in the Pentateuch as the wilderness Tabernacle, serves as the context for the revelation of divine Torah both to Israel/Judaism and the world
at large throughout the Jewish Bible. [12] Indeed, the portrayal in the Torah
of the Tabernacle/Temple at the center of the people of Israel points to
its understanding of the means by which human beings will act to sanctify
and complete creation, insofar as the people Israel serves as the means by
which G-d's sanctity is introduced into creation at large. In order to demonstrate this assertion, I would like to begin by considering the role of the
Tabernacle/Temple within the context of the Pentateuch as a whole.

In reading the Torah or Pentateuch, modern critical scholarship frequently loses sight of the literary significance of the Torah as a whole,
insofar as scholars are heavily influenced by the Wellhausenian paradigm
that identifies four sources or literary strata in the Pentateuch, that is, J,
E, D, and P. [13] Although there is a certain validity to a reading such as this,
insofar as it provides us with a somewhat defensible model concerning the
compositional history of the pentateuchal text, the division of the Torah
into four sources generally prevents us from recognizing that the present
form of the Torah—in its entirety—is indeed a Priestly composition. Frank
Cross and others point to the redactional role that the Priestly tradition
plays in selecting, organizing, and presenting earlier material into its present literary framework that provides narrative coherence for the whole. [14]
We may note the central role that Priestly texts, such as the so-called Sinai
pericope, roughly Exodus 19–Numbers 10, play within the literary structure of the Pentateuch. It is in the Sinai pericope that we read of G-d's
revelation to Israel through Moses of divine Torah, including the essential
instructions concerning the organization and conduct of the people of Israel. These instructions include those pertaining to social life in the land
of Israel, such as laws concerning property, criminal conduct, social expectations; the construction of the wilderness Tabernacle, its implements,
and its associated structures, which provides a temporary, mobile Temple

12. For discussion of the translation of the Hebrew term *tôrâ* as "instruction," rather
than as "law," see "Nomos," *Theological Dictionary of the New Testament* (ed. G. Kittel; Grand
Rapids: Eerdmans, 1967) 1022–85.

13. For an overview of pentateuchal scholarship, see Ernest Nicholson, *The Pentateuch in
the Twentieth Century: The Legacy of Julius Wellhausen* (Oxford: Oxford University Press, 1998).

14. Frank Moore Cross Jr., "The Priestly Work," in *Canaanite Myth and Hebrew Epic:
Essays in the History of the Religion of Israel* (Cambridge, MA: Harvard University Press, 1973)
293–325.

for the people until their settlement in the promised land; the associated instructions concerning the vestments and ordination of the priests; and finally the instructions concerning the performance of ritual action by the people and the priests. Indeed, the entire revelation of Torah at Mt. Sinai is carried out through the agency of Moses, identified in the Torah as both a prophet and a Levitical priest, whose actions in communicating divine Torah to the people provides the paradigmatic model for the role of the priests who will serve in Israel's/Judah's temples.

And yet it is quite clear from a synchronic reading of the Pentateuch that the Sinai pericope does not stand in isolation. Indeed, the accounts of creation, the primeval history, and the ancestral history in Genesis, together with the accounts of the Exodus from Egypt and the wilderness wanderings in Exodus 1–18, provide the initial literary framework, which places G-d's revelation of Torah to Israel at Sinai within the larger context of the history of the world. Likewise, the accounts of the wilderness wanderings in Numbers 11–36 and Moses' last speeches to Israel in Deuteronomy provide the subsequent literary framework that links the pentateuchal narrative to the following account of Israel's/Judah's life in the land of Israel from the time of Joshua through the Babylonian Exile.

Although there are certainly literary tensions within this overarching framework, it is important to recognize that there are also significant literary features that hold the entire narrative together and that signal a central interest in the establishment of the Temple in the land of Israel as a primary concern in this presentation of world history. In this respect, the establishment of the Temple in the land of Israel establishes the holy center of creation at large.[15]

The first is the use of the so-called *tôlĕdôt* formulas, that is, "these are the generations of *PN*," which define the literary structure of the Pentateuch by pointing to stages in the progression of human history, from creation to the establishment of the Temple priesthood through the generations of Moses and Aaron. In this regard, it is important to note that the etymology of the Hebrew word, *tôlĕdôt*, is based on the verb root *yld*, "to give birth," so that the formula points forward to those who are born of or proceed from the entity or person(s) named in the formula. Thus, following the initial account of the creation of the world in Gen 1:1–2:3, Gen 2:4–4:26 recounts the generations of heaven and earth, that is, Adam and Eve and their first children, Cain and Abel; Gen 5:1–6:8 recounts the history of the later descendants of Adam; Gen 6:9–9:29 recounts the history of Noah's descendants; Gen 10:1–11:9 recounts the history of Noah's three sons; Gen 11:10–26 focuses specifically on the descendants of Noah's son, Shem; Gen

15. See esp. Jon D. Levenson, "The Temple and the World," *JR* 64 (1984) 275–98; idem, *Sinai and Zion: An Entry into the Jewish Bible* (Minneapolis: Winston, 1985).

11:27–25:11 recounts the history of Terah's descendants, specifically Abraham; Gen 25:12–18 briefly recounts the history of Ishmael's descendants; Gen 25:19–29 recounts the history of Isaac's descendants, Jacob and Esau; Gen 36:1–8 and 36:9–37:1 recount the history of Esau's descendants; Gen 37:2–Num 2:34 recount the history of the descendants of Jacob, that is, the twelve sons of Jacob who become the twelve tribes of Israel and their experiences of the Exodus and Sinai; and finally, the role of the *tôlĕdôt* formula for Aaron and Moses in Num 3:1 as the culmination of this scheme.[16] Consequently, Num 3:1–Deut 34:12 recount the history of the descendants of Aaron and Moses, that is, the Levitical priesthood that will ultimately serve in the Temple, and their efforts to organize the life of the people and guide them through the wilderness into the promised land. Throughout this sequence, one observes a progressive focus that begins with creation at large, narrows its focus to the ancestors of Israel and then the people of Israel itself, and finally culminates with specific attention to the role of Israel's priests, thereby indicating the significance of Israel, and especially its priesthood, in the larger context of the creation of the world and human history.

In addition to the literary structure of the Pentateuch, based on the *tôlĕdôt* formulas, a variety of other factors must be considered. Many are relatively explicit. Several narratives, for example, portray the ancestors of Israel engaged in worship at sites later recognized as Temple sites in Israel or Judah. Thus, Abraham worships at Shechem (Gen 12:6–7), the site where Moses and later Joshua reiterate the covenant between G-d and Israel, Beth El (Gen 12:8), which later becomes the site of the northern Israelite Temple, at Salem (Gen 14:18–20), later recognized as the site of the Jerusalem Temple, and at Beer Sheba (Gen 21:33), which also functioned periodically as a Temple site. Jacob likewise worships at Beth El (Genesis 28, 35), and his conflict with the presumably angelic figure at Peniel (Gen 32:22–32) results in a limp that serves as an etiological explanation for Israelite sacrificial practice. A statement in the Song of the Sea (Exod 15:17) indicates G-d's intention to bring the people of Israel through the wilderness to the sanctuary of the L-rd, which G-d's hands created. The representation of G-d's presence in the exodus and wilderness traditions as a column of smoke by day and a pillar of fire by night employs the visual imagery of the Temple altar as the priests burn the sacrificial offerings as part of Israel's worship of G-d. Indeed, Exodus 13 explicitly calls on the people of Israel to observe the festival of Passover when they arrive in the land of Israel.

---

16. For discussion of the role of the *tôlĕdôt* in establishing the literary structure of Genesis, see Cross, "The Priestly Work," 301–7. I am indebted to Matthew Thomas, a Ph.D. student in Hebrew Bible at Claremont Graduate University, for his observations concerning the formula in Num 3:1.

Finally, a host of instructions and laws throughout the Pentateuch call for the construction of the Tabernacle/Temple, its associated structures, and its implements; the ordination of its priests; and the inauguration of the various ritual observances that will take place at the Temple to be established once the people arrive in the land.

Others are implicit in that various elements or motifs that appear within Pentateuchal narratives symbolize or anticipate structures, practices, or figures that will be associated with either the Jerusalem Temple or one of the other temples to be established in the land of Israel. First and foremost is the reckoning of the seven days of the week, culminating in the holy Shabbat in Gen 1:1–2:3. This text has long been recognized as a Priestly composition that provides an etiological explanation for the origins of Shabbat observance in the Jerusalem Temple and the reckoning of time by the priesthood. Likewise, the reference to day and night, seasons, and years indicate not only the basic elements of reckoning time but the times for worship in the Temple as well, with daily sacrifice in the morning, afternoon, and evening, the observance of the New Year, and the three primary festivals of the Temple, Pesaḥ (Passover), Shavuot (Weeks), and Sukkot (Tabernacles), which mark the times of harvest at the times of seasonal change, including the beginning of the grain harvest in the spring (Pesaḥ), the conclusion of the grain harvest in the summer (Shavuot), and the conclusion of the fruit harvest in the fall (Sukkot), immediately before the rainy season begins. Other elements, some of which appear in the J and E traditions, must also be considered. The portrayal of the Garden of Eden, for example, with its abundant trees and plants and the cherubim who guard the entrance following the expulsion of Adam and Eve, is particularly noteworthy because 1 Kings 6 indicates that these motifs are incorporated into the decoration of the doors and interior of Solomon's Temple. The cedar walls of the interior were carved with gourds and pomegranates, the Holy of Holies where the ark was kept is guarded by cherubim, and additional carvings of cherubim, palm trees, and pomegranates adorn the inner walls and the doors to both the Holy of Holies and the Temple itself. Indeed, the Holy of Holies or the inner sanctum of the Temple appears to represent the Garden of Eden, which Adam and Eve were barred from reentering by the presence of cherubim.[17] Insofar as only the priests have access to the Temple, and the high priest to the Holy of Holies, it is noteworthy that many later texts from the Second Temple period associate the High Priest with the figure of Adam, who reenters the Temple (or

---

17. For discussion of the correlation of creation and the symbolism of the Temple, see Jon D. Levenson, "The Jerusalem Temple in Devotional and Visionary Experience," in *Jewish Sprituality: From the Bible through the Middle Ages* (ed. A. Green: New York: Crossroad, 1988) 32–61.

Garden of Eden) only on occasions of festival observance.[18] One might note the apparent absence of Eve (and women in general) from the Temple, although the tree of knowledge from which she ate appears to be symbolized by the Temple *mĕnōrôt* or candlabras that stand in the great hall of the Temple. The seven branched *mĕnōrôt*, of course, are designed to resemble the general shape of a tree, and they symbolize once again the seven days of the week. The light that they cast is frequently understood as a metaphor for wisdom or the knowledge of good and evil that Eve gains in the garden. In this respect, it is noteworthy that Rabbinic tradition frequently employs the Aramaic term, *'ôraytā'*, "light," as a synonym for Torah.

Perhaps one of the most telling observations, however, is the correspondence in language between the Genesis creation account, culminating in the holy Shabbat, in Gen 2:1–3, and the accounts of the construction of the wilderness Tabernacle in Exodus 35–40. Indeed, this correspondence points to the role of the wilderness Tabernacle as the holy center of both creation in general and Israel in particular from which the revelation of G-d's Torah proceeds. Insofar as the Tabernacle constitutes the prototype for the Temple, it points to the same role for the Temple once the people are settled in the land. A recent study by Michael Fishbane cites an earlier study by Martin Buber that points to very clear intertextual relationships between the inauguration of Shabbat as the culmination of G-d's acts of creation in Gen 2:1–3 and the construction of the wilderness Tabernacle in Exodus 39–40.[19] Thus, Gen 1:31, "and G-d saw all that He had made, and found it very good," corresponds to Exod 39:43, "and when Moses saw that they had performed all the tasks—as the L-rd had commanded, so they had done—Moses blessed them," through their common use of the verb *wayyar'*, "and he saw," their concern with the completion of work, and their concern with the goodness or blessing of that work. Gen 2:1, "the heaven and the earth were finished, and all their array," corresponds to Exod 39:32, "thus was completed all the work of the Tabernacle of the Tent of Meeting," through their common use of the verb, *kālā*, "to complete," to describe the completion of the work of creation by G-d and the work of the Temple/Tabernacle by the people of Israel. Gen 2:1, "On the seventh day, G-d finished the work that He had been doing," corresponds to Exod 40:33, "when Moses finished the work," through their common use once again of the verb *kālā*, "to complete," and the noun, *mĕlā'kâ*, "work," to describe the completion of G-d's work of creation and Moses' work of the Tabernacle. Gen 2:3, "and G-d blessed the seventh day and declared it holy,"

18. See esp. C. T. R. Hayward, *The Jerusalem Temple: A Non-Biblical Sourcebook* (London: Routledge, 1996).

19. See Michael Fishbane (*Text and Texture: Close Readings of Selected Biblical Texts* [New York: Schocken, 1979] 3–16, 143–44, esp. p. 12), who cites Martin Buber, *Die Schrift und Ihre Verdeutschung* (Berlin: Schocken, 1936) 39ff.

corresponds once again to Exod 39:43, "and when Moses saw that they had performed all the tasks—as the L-rd had commanded, so they had done— Moses blessed them," through their common use of the verb, *wayĕbārēk*, "and he blessed," to describe G-d's blessing of creation and Moses' blessing of the people of Israel for completing the Tabernacle/Temple. Fishbane adds several observations of his own as well. The shift in emphasis from the divine work of creation in Gen 2:1–3 to the human work of Tabernacle construction in Exodus 39–40 is indicated in part by the emphasis on Moses acting as G-d's agent, and by the role played by the rarely mentioned *rûaḥ ʾĕlōqîm*, "wind/sprit of G-d," in the creation of the world (Gen 1:2) and in the inspiration of the artisan, Bezalel, who carried out the tasks of Tabernacle construction (Exod 31:3). Second, the account of creation emphasizes divine rest just as the account of Tabernacle construction emphasizes human rest from labor in Exod 35:2–3 and 31:12–17. Exod 35:2–3 begins the account of Tabernacle construction with the statement "on six days work may be done, but on the seventh day you shall have a Shabbat of complete rest, holy to the L-rd," as a means to set the context in which work on the Tabernacle may be carried out. Likewise, Exod 31:12–17 emphasizes that the Shabbat is a sign of the covenant between G-d and Israel forever, and it concludes with the statement, "for in six days, the L-rd made heaven and earth, and on the seventh day He ceased from work and was refreshed," as a means to emphasize the interrelationship between Shabbat rest and creation at the conclusion of Exodus 25–31, which relate G-d's instructions to build the Tabernacle. Third, the wilderness Tabernacle is built on the first day of the first month of the year (Exod 40:2, 17), which is the same day on which the creation of the world commences in Gen 1:1–2:3.

Indeed, the narrative concerning Moses' completion of the wilderness Tabernacle in Exodus 40 points to the role of the Tabernacle as a model for the construction of the Temple and its role as the locus for the revelation of G-d's Torah within creation. It appears as the concluding and culminating episode of Exodus 35–40, which constitutes an account of Israel's compliance with G-d's instructions to build the Tabernacle complex and its associated furnishings and to prepare the vestments and implements for the priests who will serve within the Tabernacle. Exodus 40 itself comprises three basic segments. The first two segments comprise accounts of G-d's instructions to Moses in vv. 1–15 to prepare the Tabernacle and Moses' compliance with G-d's instructions in vv. 16–33. G-d's instructions draw a clear analogy between the Tabernacle and Solomon's Temple. Moses is to place the Ark of the Covenant in the midst of the Tabernacle, where it is hidden from view by a curtain, to arrange the various fixtures, such as the table, the Menorah, and the gold incense altar before the Ark, to place the altar of the burnt offering and the laver before the Tabernacle, to consecrate the Tabernacle, the altar, and the priests. Of course, each of these features and actions corresponds to the features and activities associated with Solomon's Temple as recounted in 1 Kings 6–8. Indeed, the narrative concerning the consecration of the Temple in 1 Kings 8 makes it clear that the ark of the covenant and other items from the wilderness Tabernacle are placed within the Temple. The third segment of the chapter in vv. 34–38 then depicts the manifestation of G-d's Presence within the Tabernacle with the images of cloud and fire, which corresponds to the images of the cloud that represented the divine presence filling Solomon's Temple at the time of its dedication. Once the Presence of G-d is appropriately depicted in the midst of the Tabernacle, the following statement in Lev 1:1 makes it clear that the balance of G-d's instruction or Torah to Moses and Israel stems from the Tabernacle. This continues until Num 10:11, at which time the divine Presence ascends from the Tabernacle once again in the form of a pillar of smoke and fire to lead the people to the land of Israel, where they will finally construct the Temple and place the Ark and Tabernacle implements therein. Moses' last speech to Israel in Deuteronomy, immediately prior to their crossing into the promised land, likewise emphasizes the central role of the Temple, that is, the place where the L-rd will cause the divine name to dwell, in the midst of Israel and creation. Indeed, the instruction in Deut 31:10–13 to read G-d's Torah to the people from the place that G-d will choose, indicates that the Temple will succeed the Tabernacle as the locus for the revelation of Torah to the people.

Several conclusions emerge from consideration of the overall literary structure of the Torah and the place of the narrative concerning the construction of the wilderness Tabernacle within it? First, it is very clear that the literary structure of the Pentateuch is designed to portray the construction of the Wilderness Tabernacle as the divinely ordained outcome of a larger process that began with creation in Gen 1:1–2:3. Indeed, the construction of the Tabernacle takes place within a narrative framework that begins with consideration of all humanity but which narrows its focus to the people of Israel, who undertake the task of Tabernacle construction. Thus, the pentateuchal narrative portrays the construction of the Tabernacle as an event that takes place not only within the history of the people of Israel but within the history of creation at large. Furthermore, the role of the *tôlĕdôt* formula as structuring devices in the Pentateuchal narrative indicate that the focus of the narrative shifts to the priesthood that will serve in the Tabernacle/Temple once the Tabernacle is completed. In this regard, it is noteworthy that Moses, the primary figure through whom the Tabernacle/Temple is constructed, is identified in the larger Pentateuchal narrative as both prophet and priest.

Second, the pentateuchal narrative itself makes it clear that the wilderness Tabernacle anticipates the construction of a Temple in the land of Israel once the people have completed their journey through the wilderness and settled in the land. Thus, the Tabernacle is only a temporary sanctuary that will be replaced by a permanent sanctuary in the land. Furthermore, the subsequent narrative concerning the construction of Solomon's Temple in 1 Kings 6–8 likewise makes it clear that Solomon's Temple succeeds the Tabernacle as the repository for the ark of the covenant and as the locus for the revelation of divine Torah to the people of Israel. Insofar as the construction of the Tabernacle is tied to creation, Solomon's Temple is also tied to creation, that is, the construction of Solomon's Temple in Jerusalem must also be seen as a culminating event in the history of creation when considered within the framework of the canonical structure of the Tanak.

Third, the Tabernacle and the later Temple therefore serve as tangible symbols of G-d's commitment to the integrity and stability of creation. The Tabernacle/Temple stands as the holy center of creation; it is not somehow antithetical to divine purpose in the world. This, of course, does not entail that G-d alone bears responsibility for the completion and maintenance of creation. The very act of building a Tabernacle/Temple entails that human beings, specifically Israel, bear responsibility for the completion and care of the created world as well by attending to the divine instruction that emanates from that holy center. Of course, this takes up the responsibility of human beings for the completion and maintenance of creation as articulated in Gen 1:24–30. Insofar as Israel is assigned a special role for the care of creation as indicated by the construction of the Tabernacle/Torah in its midst, Israel also has a responsibility to play a major role in enabling humankind to meet that responsibility. In this respect, the establishment of the Tabernacle/Temple in the midst of Israel in particular and creation in general represents the ideal by which creation will be sanctified and completed.

Prophets in Dialogue

The Tabernacle/Temple plays a key role in all three sections of the Tanakh: it serves as the holy center of creation in the Torah; the significance of its destruction and restoration are central concerns in the Prophets; and the Writings focus once again on the Temple as the reconstituted holy center of Israel and creation. Insofar as the Tabernacle/Temple serves as the ideal, holy center of creation in the Tanakh, its destruction by the Babylonians and the question of its restoration must stand as a central concern in the Prophets. The first subsection of the Prophets, that is, the Former Prophets (Joshua, Judges, Samuel, and Kings), presents a history of Israel's/Judah's existence in the land of Israel, from the time of the conquest under Joshua through the time of the Babylonian exile, that reflects theologically on this history by attempting to demonstrate that

the destruction of the Temple resulted from Israel's failure to abide by
G-d's Torah. The second subsection of the Prophets, that is, the Latter
Prophets (Isaiah, Jeremiah, Ezekiel, and the Twelve Prophets), likewise attempts to explain the destruction of the Temple as the result of Israel's/
Judah's failure to abide by G-d's expectations, but it also outlines divine
plans to reestablish both the Temple and Israel/Judah at the center of creation once the period of punishment is over. In this regard, the Prophets
play the central role in the Tanak, insofar as they provide the link between
the ideal portrayal in the Torah of creation with Israel and the Temple at
the center and the reestablishment of that ideal in the Writings following
its disruption.

I intend to examine the central role that the Prophets play within the
structure of the Tanak, insofar as these books examine the questions of
the destruction and the projected restoration of the Temple and articulate
their respective understandings of the significance of these events for Is-
rael/Judah and creation at large. Overall, I attempt to demonstrate that the
Prophets engage in dialogue, both with their respective understandings of
Israelite/Judean tradition and among themselves, in their efforts to make
theological sense out of the crises engendered by the Babylonian destruction of the Temple in 587/6 B.C.E. I begin with the Former Prophets, and
then I consider each of the Latter Prophets, before concluding with a brief
consideration of the means by which the Prophets prepares the reader for
the Writings within the framework of the Tanakh as a whole.

THE FORMER PROPHETS

Jewish tradition considers the books of Joshua, Judges, Samuel, and
Kings as the Former Prophets. Despite their literary form as historical narrative, Jewish tradition identifies them as prophetic books because they
are traditionally believed to have been written by prophetic figures (*b. Bab.
Bat.* 15a). Thus, the Babylonian Talmud identifies Joshua as the author of
the book of Joshua. His identity as a prophet is secured by his designation
as Moses' successor in Num 27:15–23, and Deut 1:38, where it is said that
the divine "spirit" was in him much as it was in the 70 elders who prophesied in the wilderness according to Num 11:16–30 (see *Num. Rab.* 12:9). The
prophet Samuel is the author of the books of Judges and Samuel. Because
he is a prophet, he is able to write about the period following his death
just as Moses was able to complete the book of Deuteronomy. Finally, the
prophet Jeremiah is identified as the author of the book of Kings.

Although the books of the Former Prophets traditionally appear as
four distinct books in the Tanakh, modern scholars recognize them as
components of a relatively unified narrative history of Israel's existence
in the land of Israel from the time of the conquest under Joshua until the

destruction of the Jerusalem Temple and the Babylonian Exile.[20] Because the work has a relatively consistent historiographical outlook in which the major events of history are evaluated according to the requirements of divine Torah as expressed in the book of Deuteronomy, scholars have come to refer to this work as the DtrH. The work emphasizes deuteronomic principles, such as the requirement that worship of G-d take place at only one sanctuary site that will serve all Israel, that the people worship G-d exclusively and reject all foreign deities, that no images of any sort be employed to represent G-d, that the people not intermarry with the Canaanite population of the land because an action such as this would lead to idolatry, that the people act justly in accordance with deuteronomic civil instruction, and so on. Overall, the deuteronomic understanding of the relationship between G-d and Israel envisions a somewhat conditionalized relationship in which Israel will reside peacefully in the land if it abides by G-d's Torah, but it will suffer famine, invasion, and exile if the people fail to abide by divine Torah. Insofar as the DtrH concludes with an account of the Babylonian destruction of Jerusalem and the Temple, it argues that Israel's/Judah's failure to live in accordance with G-d's covenant explains the disaster.

Critical scholarship postulates several redaction-critical hypotheses for reading the DtrH, for example, there is a preexilic edition that supports the claims of the House of David and condemns northern Israel for idolatry and an exilic edition that carries the history through to the Babylonian Exile. Although redaction-critical hypotheses such as this might be correct, they do tend to blind us to the synchronic nature of the narrative in the Former Prophets much as Wellhausenian source analysis has obscured the significance of the present form of the Pentateuch. When the Former Prophets are read as a synchronic whole, two major issues come to the forefront. First, it becomes clear that this is a narrative that wrestles with the nature of the relationship between G-d and Israel/Judah. On the one hand, it posits a conditional view of covenant as articulated in the Mosaic traditions of Deuteronomy, and it reads these traditions in relation to the so-called Zion traditions, which posit an eternal covenant for the protection of Jerusalem Temple and the house of David. Indeed, DtrH ultimately reads the royal covenant in conditional terms, that is, in contrast to the eternal covenant announced by the prophet Nathan to David, Solomon's statements in the book of Kings indicate that the descendants of the house of David will remain on the throne as long as they carry out G-d's will as expressed in divine Torah. The conditional view of the Davidic covenant also

---

20. For overviews of modern critical discussion of the Former Prophets, see Antony F. Campbell, *Joshua to Chronicles: An Introduction* (Louisville, KY: Westminster John Knox, 2004); Richard D. Nelson, *The Historical Books* (IBT; Nashville: Abingdon, 1998).

has implications for the understanding of G-d's presence in and protection of the Temple in Jerusalem. Davidic tradition generally ties the promise to David to the city of Jerusalem as the site of G-d's Temple, and even Deuteronomy privileges the place where G-d will cause the divine name to dwell. But the DtrH presents a much more equivocal view of the matter. Nathan's promise in 2 Samuel 7 makes it clear that G-d neither needs nor desires a permanent house/temple, and certainly, the succession of sanctuaries portrayed in the DtrH, Gilgal, Shechem, Shiloh, Beth El, Dan, Jerusalem, and so on, bears this out. Observations such as these make it clear that the DtrH or Former Prophets are designed in part to present a very different understanding of the Davidic covenant tradition, that is, it challenges the Davidic understanding that G-d promised eternal protection to the house of David and the city of Jerusalem by making that promise conditioned on Israel's/Judah's observance of divine Torah.

Second, a synchronic reading of the Former Prophets also points to the propositional nature of the narrative. Whereas earlier scholarship treats the narrative primarily as historiographical literature, that is, it presents the history of Israel according to its own historiographical viewpoint, historically oriented readings of the DtrH have tended to lose sight of the full theological dimensions of the narrative as they have sought to tie the pro-Davidic and anti-Northern agenda to the interests of King Josiah of Judah and the House of David. But interpreters must observe a more fundamental agenda. The Former Prophets constitute a theodicy, that is, the narrative is designed to defend G-d's righteousness in the face of evil. The DtrH asserts that G-d was not responsible for the fall of Samaria and Jerusalem and the exile of the people; rather, the people were responsible for their own suffering as a result of their rejection of divine Torah.

This is a remarkable contention, especially when viewed in relation to the modern discussion of the theological dimensions of the Shoah or Holocaust.[21] On the one hand, the narrative blames the victims for their suffering, whereas a more pointed question might be "where was G-d in the face of evil?" May the attempt to blame the people for their suffering mask an attempt to avoid the conclusion that G-d was somehow powerless to defend a people that were bound to G-d by an eternal covenant? Might it suggest that G-d is somehow disreputable by failing to maintain fidelity to the covenant when danger approached? Were there not righteous people in Israel or Judah? Certainly, other biblical traditions take these possibili-

21. For overviews concerning modern theological discussion of the *Shoah* respectively in Jewish and Christian traditions, see Zachary Braiterman, *(God) after Auschwitz: Tradition and Change in Post-Holocaust Jewish Thought* (Princeton: Princeton University Press, 1998); Clark M. Williamson, *A Guest in the House of Israel: Post-Holocaust Church Theology* (Louisville, KY: Westminster John Knox, 1993).

ties into account. [22] Job suggests that G-d could be fickle. [23] Esther posits G-d's absence at a time of national threat. [24] Abraham questions G-d when told that all of Sodom and Gomorrah would die, "Far be it from you . . . to bring death upon the guilty as well as the innocent! . . . Shall the judge of all the earth not do justice?" (Gen 18:25). [25] Would this suggest that the righteous suffered along with the purportedly guilty in the destruction of Jerusalem? Indeed, the Former Prophets/DtrH makes a choice to explain the problem of evil in the destruction of Israel and Jerusalem, that is, the people, whether collectively or individually were at fault—G-d is not to blame. Of course, this is a choice, and other options are available as the above examples demonstrate. But it ultimately points to one fundamental fact: the Former Prophets offers its own understanding of the disaster, and, in this respect, it enters an inner-biblical debate concerning the question of Jerusalem's destruction.

THE LATTER PROPHETS

The focus may now turn to the four books of the Latter Prophets— Isaiah, Jeremiah, Ezekiel, and the Book of the Twelve. Although all four books appear together under the general rubric of prophets, each book has a distinctive outlook based in part on the social identity of the prophet portrayed in the respective book. [26] Thus, Isaiah's royalist viewpoint relates to his role as royal advisor; Jeremiah's concern with the application of To-rah stems from his role as a Itamaride priest; and Ezekiel's concern with the reestablishment of the Holy Temple stems from his identity as a Zad-okite priest. Although the Book of the Twelve includes 12 originally dis-crete prophetic compositions, they are now arranged so that they function

---

22. For discussion of post-Shoah biblical interpretation, see Tod Linafelt, *Strange Fire: Reading the Bible after the Holocaust* (New York: New York University Press, 2000); Emil Fackenheim, *The Jewish Bible after the Holocaust: A Rereading* (Bloomington: Indiana University Press, 1990); Rolf Rendtorff, "The Impact of the Holocaust (Shoah) on German Protestant Theology," *Horizons in Biblical Theology* 15 (1993) 154–67; Sweeney, "Reconceiving the Paradigms."

23. Fackenheim, *The Jewish Bible*, 93–99.

24. Marvin A. Sweeney, "Absence of G-d and Human Responsibility in the Book of Esther," in *Reading the Hebrew Bible for a New Millennium: Form, Concept and Theological Perspective* (ed. W. Kim et al.; SAC; Harrisburg: Trinity Press International, 2000) 2:264–75.

25. See my discussion of Abraham at Sodom and Gomorrah in "Isaiah and Theodicy," in *Strange Fire*, 208–19.

26. For an introduction to each of the prophetic books that comprise the Latter Prophets, see Marvin A. Sweeney, *The Prophetic Literature* (IBT; Nashville: Abingdon, forthcoming); see also Joseph Blenkinsopp, *A History of Prophecy in Israel* (Louisville, KY: Westminster John Knox, 1996); David L. Petersen, *The Prophetic Literature: An Introduction* (Louisville, KY: Westminster John Knox, 2002).

as a single composition with a pervasive concern for the city of Jerusalem. Indeed, the differences between the prophets are such that the books of Jeremiah, Ezekiel, and the Twelve frequently cite or allude to Isaiah and express their differences with Isaiah's views. Altogether, the four books of the Latter Prophets each present their respective understandings concerning the significance of the fall of Jerusalem and the projected restoration of the Temple in Jerusalem.

Isaiah generally appears first in the order of the Latter Prophets, and it functions as the most prominent dialogue partner for the other prophetic books. As with the Pentateuch, modern critical scholarship focuses on the identification of the historical layers of the book, which results in reading Isaiah as a three-part composition, that is, Isaiah 1–39, which portrays the 8th-century prophet Isaiah ben Amoz, Isaiah 40–55, which presents the work of an anonymous prophet of the exile known as Deutero-Isaiah, and Isaiah 56–66, which presents the work of an anonymous prophet or prophets identified as Trito-Isaiah. Although various aspects of the paradigm may be disputed, it represents a largely sound model for the reconstruction of Isaiah's compositional history. Nevertheless, an exclusively historical reading of the book impedes a full grasp of its literary and theological coherence.

A synchronic reading of Isaiah points to several fundamental concerns. The book presents itself entirely as the vision of the 8th-century prophet, Isaiah ben Amoz. Isaiah's vision therefore extends forward for some four centuries, from his own period during the times of the Assyrian invasions of Israel and Judah through the Babylonian Exile and the early Persian period, when Jews began to return to the land of Israel to reestablish their life in Jerusalem and Judah around a newly reconstructed Temple. Overall, it contends that both the destruction of Israel and Judah by the Assyrians and Babylonians and the restoration of Jerusalem under Persian rule are acts of G-d that are designed to reveal G-d's sovereignty over all creation and nations. Within this scenario, nations such as Assyria, Babylon, and Persia act as agents of the divine will. Of course, the famous swords into plowshares passage near the beginning of the book in Isa 2:2–4 signals that the nations will come to Jerusalem/Zion, the site of G-d's Temple, to learn divine Torah. Ultimately, the book of Isaiah envisions a future of world peace, in which the Jerusalem Temple stands as the holy center of both Israel and the nations in a new creation.

Nevertheless, there are several very remarkable dimensions to Isaiah's depiction of this ideal scenario, especially when the book is read from a synchronic standpoint. For one, the book is especially concerned with the issue of righteous Davidic kingship. Indeed, many have pointed to the ideological foundations of Isaiah's, Deutero-Isaiah's, and Trito-Isaiah's viewpoints in the royal Zion traditions of the House of David. A diachronic reading of the book points to each prophet's respective viewpoint, that is, Isaiah the royal counselor looks forward to a righteous Davidic king (perhaps Hezekiah), Deutero-Isaiah contends that the Persian monarch Cyrus is G-d's anointed as the Davidic covenant is applied to all Israel, and Trito-Isaiah contends that G-d is the true king, whose Temple in Jerusalem serves as royal throne and footstool in a new heaven and earth. At this level, the three major historical portions of the book are in debate with each other, as each asserts its own respective view of ideal kingship for Israel. But when read synchronically, the three positions collapse into one so that the book of Isaiah ultimately calls for Israel/Judah to submit to Persian rule, that is, the rule of a non-Jewish king, as an expression of G-d's ultimate sovereignty in the newly restored world of creation. Certainly, a contention such as this stands in contrast with the viewpoint of not only Isaiah ben Amoz but the entire Davidic tradition expressed in Samuel, Psalms, and elsewhere, that posited G-d's eternal protection for both Jerusalem and the house of David.

Although Isaiah's perspective finds agreement in the books of Ezra–Nehemiah, which portray the reestablishment of a Temple-based Jewish community in Jerusalem under Persian rule as the fulfillment of the great prophet's vision, Isaiah's prophetic colleagues are hardly so accommodating. Jeremiah is a major case in point. The book of Jeremiah presents him as a prophet and priest like Moses. He lives during the final years of the kingdom of Judah and sees the ultimate decline and destruction of Judah as the Babylonians destroy the city and the Temple and carry the people off to exile. Literary-critical scholarship has wrestled with the question of the interrelationship between the poetic oracles, prose sermons, and prose narratives of the book, generally concluding that the oracles are Jeremian, the sermons are based in Jeremian sermons, and the narratives are the product of another Deuteronomistically influenced author, perhaps Baruch. The issue is complicated by the interrelationship between the Masoretic and Septuagint versions of the book and by complicated questions concerning the redaction-critical reconstruction of the book and the prophet presented therein. In general, however, diachronic critical treatment contends that Jeremiah calls the Temple into question as a source for national security, sharply criticizes the house of David, and says little about the restoration of Jerusalem.

As interpreters begin to consider the synchronic literary dimensions of the book, additional issues come to light. One is the issue of intertextuality, particularly with regard to Jeremiah's relationship with the book of Isaiah.[27] Although interpreters have generally noted Jeremiah's relationship

---

27. See my essay "The Truth in True and False Prophecy," in Christine Helmer and Kristin de Troyer, eds., *Truth: Interdisciplinary Dialogues in a Pluralist Age* (Studies in Philosophical

with the DtrH as part of their efforts to demonstrate Dtr editing of the book, they have paid less attention to its links with Isaiah. Indeed, Jeremiah appears to cite or allude to many passages from the book of Isaiah, most notably in the prophet's portrayal in Jeremiah 5–6 of G-d's plans to bring a far off nation to punish Judah, which draws heavily on Isaiah's similar statements in Isaiah 5 concerning G-d's plans to bring a far off nation to punish Israel. Although Jeremiah appears to agree with his senior colleague about G-d's intention to bring punishment, he disagrees on its ultimate timing and its target. Isaiah announced judgment against northern Israel and Jerusalem/Judah, but he never claimed that Jerusalem would be destroyed. Instead, Isaiah articulates G-d's continuing commitment to Jerusalem as the holy center of creation.

Jeremiah, however, sees things differently. His well-known Temple sermon in Jeremiah 7 presents a striking critique of the people's contention that the presence of the Jerusalem Temple would guarantee the security of the city. The narrative concerning his trial for sedition emphasizes the theme of Jerusalem's destruction when Micah's statement that Jerusalem will be destroyed is cited in defense of Jeremiah. In true Levitical (and deuteronomic) fashion, Jeremiah maintains that security is achieved only insofar as the people abide by divine Torah; without adherence to G-d's Torah, the city and the Temple will be lost just as Shiloh centuries before. Jeremiah's differences with Isaiah are also evident in his confrontation with the prophet Hananiah in Jeremiah 27–28. When Jerusalem falls under Babylonian rule, Hananiah contends that G-d will act to deliver the city within two years. Jeremiah, by contrast, wears a yoke around his neck to symbolize his message that Jerusalem must submit to Babylon in keeping with the will of G-d. During the ensuing confrontation, Hananiah breaks Jeremiah's yoke, but Jeremiah returns with an iron yoke to reiterate his message. With Hananiah's death, he is ultimately identified as a false prophet and Jeremiah's message is confirmed by subsequent events. But we must recognize that Hananiah's position is in fact that of Isaiah, that is, G-d will act to defend the city.

The identification of Hananiah as a false prophet generally obscures an important point to be drawn from this confrontation, that is, Jeremiah considers Isaiah's message of security for the city of Jerusalem to be false prophecy. In Jeremiah's view, Jerusalem would face war, destruction, and 70 years of exile. Although critical scholarship frequently denies passages concerned with restoration to the historical Jeremiah, a synchronic reading of the book indicates that restoration will come after the 70 years of

---

Theology 22; Leuven: Peeters, 2003) 9–26, to be republished in my *Form and Intertextuality in the Study of Prophetic and Apocalyptic Literature* (FAT; Tübingen: Mohr Siebeck, forthcoming), for discussion of Jeremiah's reading of Isaiah.

exile. Jeremiah 30–31 employs the image of the weeping Rachel to portray Israel's return to Jerusalem, but it does so in the context of a new covenant in which Torah is inscribed on the hearts of the people. Whereas the book of Isaiah maintains the continuity of G-d's covenant with David/Jerusalem/Israel as the basis for its portrayal of Jerusalem's restoration, the book of Jeremiah posits a change in covenant that will ultimately result in the restoration of the city and its people. Interpreters might note that Jeremiah's vision of the future does not—like the full form of the book of Isaiah—envision the restoration of a righteous Davidic monarch. Critical scholarship raises questions about the authenticity of the royal oracles in Jer 23:1–8 and 33:12–26, but a synchronic reading of the book necessarily concludes that Jeremiah envisions a restored Jerusalem ruled once again by a righteous member of the house of David. Whereas the book of Isaiah reinterpreted the Davidic covenant to justify submission to Persian rule, Jeremiah envisions a permanent Davidic covenant based in creation as part of the scenario for G-d's new covenant with Israel/Judah.

Ezekiel is an extremely erudite figure, who cites both biblical and ancient Near Eastern mythological tradition as part of his efforts to define the theological significance of the Babylonian Exile and the reconstruction of the Jerusalem Temple. Ezekiel is a Zadokite priest, and his education, practices, and use of Temple-based imagery, such as the use of imagery from the Holy of Holies of the Jerusalem Temple to describe the throne chariot of G-d and the sacrificial destruction of Jerusalem in chaps. 1–11, point to this role.[28]

Again, we must turn to a synchronic reading of the book to gain an understanding of its full theological significance. Critical scholarship has missed the mark in its efforts to separate Priestly and prophetic elements in the book of Ezekiel. Indeed, the attempt to excise the prophet's vision of the restored Temple in Ezekiel 40–48 is fundamentally mistaken.[29] The vision clearly stands as the culmination of the book to express Ezekiel's understanding of divine purpose in which G-d first abandons the Temple so that it and the city might be purged of its impurity and then returns to it so that it might stand once again as the holy center of creation. Ezekiel portrays the destruction of Jerusalem much like the offering of the scapegoat at the Temple on Yom Kippur (see Leviticus 16), that is, the seven men dressed in white linen act as priests in carrying out the sacrificial ritual by marking and recording those to be burnt and by setting the fire much as one ignites the sacrifice on the altar; those left unmarked are killed in

---

28. See my essays "Ezekiel: Zadokite Priest and Visionary Prophet of the Exile," *OPIAC* 41 (2001); and "The Destruction of Jerusalem as Purification in Ezekiel 8–11," both to be published in *Form and Intertextuality*.

29. Cf. Jon D. Levenson, *Theology of the Program of Restoration in Ezekiel 40–48* (HSM 10; Missoula, MT: Scholars Press, 1976).

the destruction of the city; those marked are sent out to the wilderness of exile. Ezekiel is after all a Zadokite priest, and he employs the imagery and conceptual categories for purification and holiness that are characteristic of the Zadokite priesthood.

He shares some characteristics with his prophetic colleagues. Like Isaiah, he envisions the future role of the Temple at the center of a transformed creation and nation Israel. He shares with Isaiah a theological foundation in the Zion tradition, although he focuses on G-d's sanctification of Zion as the permanent site for the Temple in contrast to Isaiah's interest in the House of David. In this regard, he sees some diminishment of the role of the Davidic monarch, but he differs from Isaiah in that he does not dismiss the Davidic king entirely; instead, he clearly places the king under the authority of the Temple and its priesthood. He is able to employ Isaian motifs, such as the portrayal in Ezekiel 31 of Pharaoh as a high, lofty tree that must be brought down, much as Isaiah portrayed the Assyrian king in similar terms in Isaiah 10. Ezekiel likewise shares some concerns with Jeremiah. He employs the proverb "the parents have eaten sour grapes and the children's teeth are set on edge" in Ezekiel 18 to illustrate his contention that people do not suffer for the sins of their parents—rather they suffer for their own wrongdoing—much as Jer 31:27–30 uses the same proverb to make the same point. He might differ from his older contemporary, for example, Ezekiel identifies Jaazniah ben Shaphan as one of those whose idolatrous worship profaned the holy Temple, but it was the Shaphan family that served as Jeremiah's primary supporters in his conflicts with the monarchs throughout his career.[30] Perhaps the Zadokite Ezekiel viewed Levitical supporters with suspicion as potential sources of corruption for the Temple and the people.

But Ezekiel's debate is not primarily with his prophetic colleagues; rather, it is with the tradition in which he has been trained to serve as a priest in the holy center of creation. Ezekiel cites and employs traditions that are well-known in the Torah, but his understanding of that tradition differs to such an extent that Rabbi Hananiah ben Hezekiah later burned 300 barrels of oil working at night to reconcile the differences between Ezekiel and the Torah so that Ezekiel might be accepted as sacred Scripture (b. Shabbat 13b; b. Ḥagigah 13a; b. Menaḥot 45a). For example, his discussion of individual moral responsibility in the above-cited Ezekiel 18 draws extensively on the so-called Holiness Code of Leviticus 17–26 to portray the actions of the righteous and the wicked in terms of the worship of idols, the slaughter and eating of meat, sexual activity, justice to the poor,

---

30. See Jay Wilcoxen, "The Political Background of Jeremiah's Temple Sermon," in *Scripture in History and Theology* (ed. A. L. Merrill and T. W. Overholt; Pittsburgh: Pickwick, 1977) 151–66.

and so on. But he differs markedly from the Torah by stating that an individual alone is responsible for his actions, whereas the Torah indicates that G-d may punish later generations for the wrongdoing of their ancestors. His description of the restored Temple, its sacred precincts, and its altar differs markedly from the requirements of the Torah in many details—to the extent that the altar appears to represent a Babylonian stepped structure. He deliberately eats impure food to illustrate his life as an exile in a land that is not holy. His depiction of G-d's throne chariot draws in part on the imagery of the ark in the Holy of Holies in the Temple, but it also draws on motifs from the depiction of Mesopotamian gods, such as Assur, who flies in his own throne chariot at the head of his armies.

Clearly, Ezekiel employs traditions found in the Torah, but his differences suggest that he is in dialogue with them, insofar as he changes them to meet the needs of a very new situation. He is a Zadokite priest, raised for holy service in the Jerusalem Temple, but he finds himself with a life outside that Temple in a foreign land that can hardly be described as holy by Temple standards. And yet he strives to act as a priest in very different conditions throughout his lifetime, to sanctify that land by demonstrating the reality of the divine presence even in Babylonia. In this respect, he demonstrates that G-d is indeed sovereign of all creation. His portrayal of the restored Temple at the center of a restored Israel and a restored creation supports that contention.

Although Christian Bibles treat the Twelve Prophets as 12 discrete prophetic books, Jewish tradition treats the Twelve as a single book that includes 12 components. Indeed, modern critical scholarship has recently begun to consider both the compositional history and the literary form of the Book of the Twelve.[31] The issue is complicated by the existence of the Septuagint form of the book, which employs its own distinctive hermeneutical perspective to present the Twelve Prophets in a very different sequence from that of the Masoretic Text. Because the present concern is with the Tanak, the following will focus on the MT sequence.

The MT sequence indicates a deliberate concern with Jerusalem and its relationship to G-d and the nations of the world. Thus, Hosea addresses the potential disruption in the relationship between Israel and G-d but envisions resolution when Israel returns to G-d and the house of David in Jerusalem. Joel employs motifs from creation, for example, locust plagues

---

31. See now my commentary, *The Twelve Prophets* (Berit Olam; Collegeville, MN: Liturgical Press, 2000) esp. pp. xv–xlii; see also my "Sequence and Interpretation in the Book of the Twelve," in *Reading and Hearing the Book of the Twelve* (ed. J. D. Nogalski and M. A. Sweeney; SBLSyms 15; Atlanta: Society of Biblical Literature, 2000) 49–64, to be republished in *Form and Intertextuality*. For a review of research on the Book of the Twelve, see Paul L. Redditt, "The Formation of the Book of the Twelve: A Review of Research," in *Thematic Threads in the Book of the Twelve* (ed. P. L. Redditt and A. Schart; BZAW 325; Berlin: de Gruyter, 2003) 1–26.

and images of grain to focus on G-d's defense of Jerusalem from the nations. Amos points to the restoration of Jerusalem and Davidic rule following G-d's punishment of Israel and the nations. Obadiah focuses on G-d's judgment against Edom as a representative of the nations and its submission to Israel at Zion on the Day of the L-rd. Jonah tempers Obadiah's scenario of judgment by raising the question of G-d's mercy to a repentant Nineveh. Micah portrays the rise of a new Davidic monarch in Jerusalem who inaugurates a period of world peace after punishing the nations for their assaults on Israel. Nahum celebrates the downfall of the oppressive Assyrian empire. Habakkuk raises questions concerning divine justice as the Babylonians threaten Judah. Zephaniah calls for a purge of Jerusalem and Judah on the Day of the L-rd that apparently signals for the Babylonian threat against Jerusalem. Haggai calls on the returned people of Jerusalem to rebuild the Temple as the holy center of the nations. Zechariah portrays the process by which the nations will acknowledge G-d at the Jerusalem Temple following a period of worldwide war. Finally, Malachi recaps the initial concerns of Hosea by calling for the observance of divine Torah, thereby rejecting calls for a disruption of the relationship between Israel and G-d.

Of course, the Book of the Twelve includes intertextual relationships with a wide variety of texts from the Bible and elsewhere, but Steck, Bosshard-Nepustil, and others have noted that the MT form of the Book of the Twelve is especially concerned with the book of Isaiah.[32] A primary example is the repeated intertextual use in the Book of the Twelve of the famous "swords into plowshares" passage that appears near the beginning of the book in Isa 2:2–4. Indeed, the passage plays important roles near the beginning, middle, and end of the MT sequence of the Twelve. Thus, Joel employs a reversal of its peaceful imagery in its portrayal of G-d's call to battle against the nations that threaten Jerusalem on the Day of the L-rd.[33] Micah employs a slightly different version of Isaiah's passage in Mic 4:1–5 at the beginning of a sequence that calls for the rise of a new Davidic king, who will confront and subdue the nations that have exiled Israel.[34] Zechariah employs the Isaian oracle in Zech 8:20–23 as a means to express the nations' proposal to seek G-d at Zion, immediately prior to its depiction of world war in Zechariah 9–14 that culminates in the submission of the

32. See Odil Hannes Steck, *The Prophetic Books and Their Theological Witness* (St. Louis: Chalice, 2000); Erich Bosshard-Nepustil, *Rezeption von Jesaja 1–39 im Zwölfprophetenbuch* (OBO 154; Freiburg: Universitätsverlag / Göttingen: Vandenhoeck & Ruprecht, 1997).
33. Marvin A. Sweeney, "The Place and Function of Joel within the Book of the Twelve," in *Thematic Threads in the Book of the Twelve* (ed. P. L. Redditt and A. Schart; BZAW 325; Berlin: de Gruyter, 2003) 133–54, to be republished in *Form and Intertextuality*.
34. See my essay "Micah's Debate with Isaiah," *JSOT* 111–24, to be republished in *Form and Intertexuality*.

nations to G-d at the Jerusalem Temple.[35] Of course, there are many more allusions and citations, both to Isaiah and to other biblical texts, but these examples suffice to demonstrate that the Book of the Twelve takes up concerns very similar to those of Isaiah, that is, Jerusalem's role at the center of the world following a period of judgment. But it differs markedly from Isaiah, which envisions Jerusalem's/Israel's submission to a foreign monarch as part of the divine plan for a restored creation. By contrast, the Book of the Twelve envisions a period of extensive conflict with the nations in which the nations will finally be subdued as they submit to G-d. Although G-d emerges as the ultimate sovereign of creation and Jerusalem serves as the site of G-d's sanctuary, a new Davidic king and restored Judah/Israel play leading roles throughout the Twelve in realizing this goal.

This survey of the books of the Latter Prophets demonstrates that each addresses the problems of exile and restoration in its own distinctive way. Isaiah envisions a restored Jerusalem/Israel that will serve as a source for divine Torah and be ruled by a foreign monarch in the context of G-d's recognition throughout the world. Jeremiah envisions the restoration of Israel to Jerusalem and the restoration of righteous Davidic rule based on divine Torah following the punishment of the nation. Ezekiel envisions the purification of Jerusalem and the world at large as the process by which a new Temple will be built at the center of Israel and all creation. The Book of the Twelve anticipates a period of world conflict in which the nations will recognize G-d at the Jerusalem Temple after their defeat by G-d's Davidic monarch. Indeed, each takes up the problem of Israel's exile as articulated in the Former Prophets by envisioning a restoration of Jerusalem/Israel at the center of a new creation. Each engages in debate, both with the tradition and with their prophetic colleagues, concerning the character of the future restoration.

CONCLUSION

The Prophets play a decisive role within the three-part structure of the Tanakh, that is, the Prophets bridge the gap between the Torah, with its ideal portrayal of Israel assembled around the wilderness Tabernacle at the center of creation, and the Writings, which portray the fundamental concerns of the Israelite/Jewish people centered around its restored Temple in Jerusalem. Insofar as the destruction of the Jerusalem Temple and the Babylonian Exile constitute the major challenge to ancient Israel's/Judaism's sense of identity within the world of creation, the Prophets provide the theological means within the Tanak by which Israel/Judaism constructively

---

35. See my essay "Zechariah's Debate with Isaiah," in *The Changing Face of Form Criticism for the Twenty-First Century* (ed. M. A. Sweeney and E. Ben Zvi; Grand Rapids: Eerdmans, 2003) 315–50, to be republished in *Form and Intertextuality*.

came to grips with fundamental challenges to their existence in a manner that enabled them to rebuild for the future. Indeed, this basic pattern, which calls for the building and rebuilding of the ideal Jewish people and its relationship to the world at large, has continued to inform and sustain Judaism throughout its history.

Psalms and Jewish Biblical Theology

Marc Zvi Brettler

It is difficult to decide what Jewish biblical theology is or might be or even if we should be discussing Jewish biblical theology as something that already exists, something that should be developed, or perhaps something that should be abandoned. In a sense, it is barely a decade old: the first conference on Jewish biblical theology was organized by Michael Fishbane and Tikva Frymer-Kensky at the University of Chicago in May 1996.[1] In comparison to Christian biblical theology, a discipline old enough to be analyzed in a 700-page book,[2] we are "infants and sucklings," to use the language of Psalm 8. Thus, the following remarks are exploratory and tentative. My only hope is that they will advance the status of the question concerning the nature and purpose of Jewish biblical theology.

If one tenet of biblical theology is the engagement of the scholar with the text as a member of a faith community, allowing us to distinguish biblical theology from history of religion,[3] then my earlier article, "Biblical History and Jewish Biblical Theology" might be viewed as addressing the following question: how might the Jewish community simultaneously accept the types of scholarly arguments I advance in *The Creation of History in Ancient Israel*[4] and accept the Bible as Scripture? In that essay, I began to answer this question by developing four points: (1) We should hardly be concerned about the historical veracity of the biblical text, (2) We must not harmonize divergent biblical traditions, (3) We must be more sensitive to the true genres of biblical historical texts, (4) We must understand what stands behind these texts that are framed as depictions of a past.

I will be exploring Psalms in a different manner; I will not be studying it as a Jewish biblical theologian but will be examining the role that Psalms could play in further developing, defining, and refining what Jewish biblical

---

1. My essay "Biblical History and Jewish Biblical Theology," *JR* 77 (1997) 563–83, originated as a presentation at that conference.

2. James Barr, *The Concepts of Biblical Theology: An Old Testament Perspective* (Minneapolis: Fortress, 1999).

3. Barr, *Concepts*, 11.

4. Marc Zvi Brettler, *The Creation of History in Ancient Israel* (London: Routledge, 1995).

theology is. I will focus on two issues. One concerns the second point of my *Journal of Religion* article: "We must not harmonize divergent biblical traditions." The other, with which I will begin, concerns the suggestion that Jewish biblical theology should be explicitly concerned with continuity between the Hebrew Bible and the rabbinic period in just the same way that many scholars believe that Christian biblical theology must deal, on some level, with the OT as part of a larger scripture, which includes the New Testament.[5]

This position concerning the engagement of Jewish biblical theology with the rabbinic tradition may be traced to Matitiahu Tsevat, who discusses "judaizing" the Hebrew Bible by linking it to the talmudic and midrashic tradition, though he is careful to say that he is uncomfortable with the rubric of biblical theology for this venture.[6] This notion is picked up by Barr in *The Concepts of Biblical Theology*, where he suggests that "Jewish biblical theology . . . could be, as Tsevat suggested, a theology of the interlinkage between the Hebrew Bible and the later authoritative sources and interpretations."[7]

My earlier article argued similarly by pointing to rabbinic texts that offer perspectives that resemble my four points about the Bible. For example, in developing the idea that "We should hardly be concerned about the historical veracity of the biblical text," I cite a variety of rabbinic texts that express the attitude of מאי דהוה הוה—"what was was"—that history does not matter *for its own sake*. The same is true of my second observation, that "We must not harmonize divergent biblical traditions." I compare this to the rabbinic דבר אחר, "another matter or interpretation." This is a technical term used especially in midrashic literature to separate alternative, mutually contradictory interpretations.[8] Typically, this term separates these alternatives without explicitly favoring one over the other—none seems to be more correct or authoritative than the other. This phenomenon of adjacent competing textual expositions typifies rabbinic midrashic literature: Jon Levenson has called it "polydoxy," and the scholar of rabbinic and Dead Sea Scroll literature, Stephen Fraade, has called it "polyphony."[9] No matter what term we use, it is a basic characteristic of rabbinic literature,

5. Barr, *Concepts*, 172–88.

6. Matitiahu Tsevat, "Theology of the Old Testament—A Jewish View," *HBT* 8/2 (1986) 33–50.

7. Barr, *Concepts*, 585.

8. Wilhelm Bacher, *Die Exegetische Terminologie der jüdischen Traditionsliteratur* (Hildesheim: Olms, 1965) 2:37.

9. *Polydoxy*: Jon D. Levenson, *The Hebrew Bible, The Old Testament and Historical Criticism: Jews and Christians in Biblical Studies* (Louisville, KY: Westminster John Knox, 1993) esp. pp. 51–56. *Polyphony*: Steven D. Fraade, *From Tradition to Commentary: Torah and Its Interpretation in the Midrash Sifre to Deuteronomy* (Albany, NY: State University of New York Press, 1991) esp. p. 127.

especially of midrashic literature. This concept, however, is not rabbinic in origin—there are cases in Dead Sea Scroll Pesher literature where double interpretations of the same lemma are offered.[10] Here too, there is nothing to suggest which of the pesharim offered is favored. Thus, this phenomenon of polydoxy or polyphony is not an innovation introduced by the early rabbis, whoever they might be,[11] but is clearly earlier.

My core argument is that any Jewish biblical theology needs to be attuned to polydoxy or polyphony, not only because this principle stands at the core of the structure of the rabbinic (and transitional, prerabbinic) world view, but also because it stands at the core of the structure of the book of Psalms. In other words, we need not go to rabbinic midrashic literature or the pesharim, into the early postbiblical world, to see polydoxy or polyphony in a clear manner—we only need to go as far as Psalms. Thus, the book of Psalms, which I believe is a core book of Tanakh,[12] like rabbinic literature, argues strongly for the truth of the principle "We must not harmonize divergent biblical traditions."

This position represents a strong break with classical biblical theology, which expends significant energy on finding the *Mitte* or "center" of biblical theology:[13] Jewish biblical theology, whether it is trying to find continuity with postbiblical Judaism, or whether it is basing itself on models found within the Tanakh itself, should a *Mitte*-less theology. Other Jewish scholars have made similar points, and this may be considered a characteristic of Jewish Bible theology.[14] Jewish biblical theology may thus have a דבר אחר, "an alternative interpretation" rather than *Mitte* perspective at its core.[15]

Two biblical works are most easily examined within this דבר אחר, "an alternative interpretation" theology: תרי עשר—the Book of the Twelve (Minor Prophets), and Psalms. These two works are explicitly *marked* as collections; in contrast, there is no formal superscription at the beginning of Deutero-Isaiah, nor is there the equivalent of a superscription to separate

---

10. H. Gregory Snyder, "Naughts and Crosses: Pesher Manuscripts and Their Significance for Reading Practices at Qumran," *DSD* 7 (2000) 39–40.

11. See Shaye J. D. Cohen, "The Rabbi in Second-Century Jewish Society," *CHJ* 3:922–77.

12. See below, pp. 196–197.

13. See Barr, *Concepts*, 708, index s.v. "Centre for OT Theology."

14. See, for example, Isaac Kalimi, *Early Jewish Exegesis and Theological Controversy: Studies in Scriptures in the Shadow of Internal and External Controversies* (Jewish and Christian Heritage 2; Assen: Van Gorcum, 2002) 113–14; and a similar observation about the rabbinic midrash on Psalms in idem, "Midrash Psalms *Shocher Tov*: Some Theological and Methodological Features and a Case Study—The View of God," in *God's Word for Our World*, vol. 2: *Theological and Cultural Studies in Honor of Simon John De Vries* (ed. J. H. Ellens, D. L. Ellens, R. P. Knierim, and I. Kalimi; JSOTSup 389; London: T. & T. Clark, 2004) 63–76, esp. pp. 67–68. However, this should be seen as neither a sufficient nor a necessary criterion for a work to be considered Jewish biblical theology—see the comments on Gerstenberger on p. 197, below.

15. The importance of the *davar acher* formula is already emphasized by idem, "Midrash Psalms *Shocher Tov*," 69.

J from E from P in the Tetrateuch. The so-called Twelve Minor Prophets were collected together into a single book, even though they are from a wide span of time and reflect different genres.[16] The editing of the Twelve into a single book happened early, before the time of Ben-Sira, which in a Cairo Genizah fragment to 49:10 refers to שְׁנֵים עָשָׂר הנביאים —"the twelve prophets."[17] The Twelve is also found as a collection in the scrolls from Qumran and Wadi Murabaat.[18] It is quite possible that the Twelve became a collection for pragmatic reasons—it was too easy for books like the single-chapter Obadiah to get lost, so the small books were combined together.[19] Superscriptions, often quite detailed[20] divide the book into twelve separate compositions, though it is quite likely that many if not most of these so called "books" are themselves composite, though they are not marked as such.[21] The focus on the Twelve has recently been on what binds it together[22]—it would also be equally worthwhile to highlight the *differences* between the various books that are part of the larger Book of the Twelve, and to view each book as a type of presentation of a דבר אחר, "another interpretation."

Psalms is very clearly marked as a collection in a variety of ways.[23] This is most obvious in the conclusion to Psalm 72 (v. 20): כָּלּוּ תְפִלּוֹת דָּוִד בֶּן־ יִשָׁי, "The prayers of David son of Jesse have ended," and in the editorial division of the Psalter into five books. I will not, however, concentrate on differences between each of the five books. The psalms are also further di-

---

16. At the simplest level, it is possible to distinguish those that reflect apocalyptic tendencies from those that do not and to separate Jonah, which is about a prophet, from the other books, in which prophetic oracles predominate.

17. *The Book of Ben Sira: Text, Concordance and an Analysis of the Vocabulary* (Historical Dictionary of the Hebrew Language; Jerusalem: Academy of the Hebrew Language and the Shrine of the Book, 1973) 62.

18. See P. Benoit et al., *Les Grottes de Murabbat* (2 vols.; DJD 2; Oxford: Clarendon, 1961); and E. Ulrich et al., eds., *Qumran Cave 4, X* (DJD 15; Oxford: Clarendon, 1997).

19. *"Trei ʿasar," Encyclopedia Biblica* (Jerusalem: Bialik Institute, 1982) 8.933 [Hebrew].

20. Many consider these superscriptions to be deuteronomistic, but see Ehud Ben Zvi, "A Deuteronomistic Redaction in/among 'The Twelve'"? A Contribution from the Standpoint of the Books of Micah, Zephaniah and Obadiah," in *Those Elusive Deuteronomists: The Phenomenon of Pan-Deuteronomism* (ed. Linda S. Schearing and Steven L. McKenzie; JSOTSup 268; Sheffield: Sheffield Academic Press, 1999) 250–53.

21. The case for Zechariah comprising at least two separate works, 1–8 and 9–14, is especially clear; see, e.g., David L. Petersen, *Zechariah 9–14 and Malachi* (OTL; Louisville, KY: Westminster John Knox, 1995) 23.

22. See most recently James Nogalski and Marvin Sweeney, eds., *Reading and Hearing the Book of the Twelve* (SBLSymS 15; Atlanta: Society of Biblical Literature, 2000).

23. For an overview, see Klaus Seybold, *Introducing the Psalms* (trans. R. Graeme Dunphy; Edinburgh: T. & T. Clark, 1990) 14–23; in greater detail, see Gerald Henry Wilson, *The Editing of the Hebrew Psalter* (SBLDS 76; Chico, CA: Scholars Press, 1985), and J. Clinton McCann, *The Shape and Shaping of the Psalter* (JSOTSup 159; Sheffield: JSOT Press, 1993).

vided one from the other by the superscriptions. These are of several types, [24] including מזמור לדוד or לדוד מזמור, "A psalm of David," found in 35 psalms, or various other superscriptions such as למנצח, perhaps to be rendered "For the choirmaster," [25] introducing one-third of the psalms, many of which overlap with the previous group, or even שיר המעלות, "A Song of Ascents" [26] introducing 15 psalms, or הללויה, "Halleluyah," typically, though not always, functioning as a marker at the beginning or end of psalms. [27] Stated differently, these formal markers, which are earlier and much more reliable than the chapter headings, [28] separate the psalms into more than 100 compositions. All of these different headings mark the book as a compilation, and as in any compilation, we should not expect to find a unitary perspective.

This expectation of diversity is bolstered by the multiplicity of non-Davidic authors mentioned in the superscriptions: there are 11 Korahite Psalms, 11 Asaphite psalms and 2 psalms לשלמה, "of Solomon" (for example, Psalm 72) and even one למשה, "of Moses" (Psalm 90). [29] Why should these figures, living at different times, have identical perspectives? In fact, even if we were to say that מזמור לדוד, "A Psalm of David" is meant to ascribe Davidic authorship to particular works, [30] the 35 works with this or the inverted superscription need not agree with each other in terms of theology. People's theology changes over time and is often situation specific. Why would we expect the theology of the young David fleeing from Saul, hiding in the Judean Desert (see Ps 63:1) to be identical with that of the mature David confronted by Nathan the prophet in Psalm 51? [31] The rabbinic statement (*Shir Hashirim Rabbah* 1:10) concerning Solomon, that Song of Songs

24. For a more complete list with a discussion, see Hans-Joachim Kraus, *Psalms 1–59* (trans. Hilton C. Oswald; Minneapolis: Augsburg, 1988) 21–32.

25. See *HALOT* 716.

26. There are some variants to this formula as well. For the possible meanings of this superscription, see Loren D. Crow, *The Sons of Ascents (Psalms 120–134): Their Place in Israelite History and Religion* (SBLDS 148; Atlanta: Scholars Press, 1996) 1–27.

27. For more information on many of these, see Christopher Wyckoff, *Poetic and Editorial Closure in the Book of Psalms: A Discourse Analytic Perspective* (Ph.D. diss., Brandeis University, 2005).

28. Indeed, as is well known, the division into 150 psalms is problematic, with several pairs of psalms that are each more correctly a single Psalm (e.g., Psalms 9–10) and joining together several disparate compositions into a single chapter (e.g., Ps 137:1–6, 7–9). In fact, not all Hebrew manuscripts have 150 psalms—see Christian D. Ginsburg, *Introduction to the Massoretico-Critical Edition of the Hebrew Bible* (New York: Ktav, 1966) 725–26.

29. For a list of various collections, see Kraus, *Psalms 1–59*, 17–19.

30. For a discussion of the possible meanings of this term, see Seybold, *Introducing the Psalms*, 34–38.

31. In this observation, I am taking these superscriptions seriously as part of the canonical book of Psalms, though with other scholars, I believe that they are secondary and often late additions to the psalms—see Brevard Childs, "Psalms, Titles, and Midrashic Exegesis," *JSS* 16 (1971) 137–50; Elieser Slomovic, "Toward an Understanding of the Formation of Historical Titles in the Book of Psalms," *ZAW* 91 (1979) 350–80; and Alan M. Cooper, "The Life

represents him at his youth, Proverbs as a mature man, and Ecclesiastes when he was facing death, is suggestive for what I am claiming concerning Davidic psalms: even the same person at different life stages may write and think in very different ways. Thus, the superscriptions, even the Davidic superscriptions, separate psalms into separate compositions, where each may *potentially* reflect a different moment and thus may *potentially* have a different theology or perspective. Thus, the many superscriptions of the psalms encourage us to look for differences between the different compositions.

Psalms, as a book that is explicitly marked as a wide-ranging collection, serves as a particularly good example for developing the idea that a Jewish biblical theology should not have a *Mitte*. It is a better starting point than The Twelve, which may be considered as a single book from a scribal perspective, but is not clearly edited together into a coherent book.[32] Unlike Psalms, it does not have a clear introduction and conclusion, nor is there anything equivalent in the Twelve to how Psalms is secondarily divided into five sections, thus gaining a single book-like status in comparison with the Torah.[33] Thus, in terms of structure, Psalms is the best exemplar of a polydoxic single book. To return to the rabbinic analogy, the מזמור לְ*X*, "A Psalm of *X*" or למנצח, "For the Choirmaster" of Psalms functions in the same way as the rabbinic דבר אחר, "another opinion," leading us to expect, or at the very least, to allow different theological voices.

Even a cursory look through the Psalter brings out these differences. For this reason, books with titles such as *Theology of the Psalms*[34] are fundamentally flawed because it is quite clear that the Psalter is marked by a lack of a common theology.

It would be worthwhile to outline completely the disparities, great and small, related to theology and anthropology, found in the Psalter, but this would be a vast project.[35] Instead, I will here concentrate on three issues that will suffice to illustrate my point concerning the different voices heard in Psalms. The first two issues are theological: Does YHWH always care for

---

and Times of King David according to the Book of Psalms," in *The Poet and the Historian: Essays in Literary and Historical Criticism* (ed. Richard Elliott Friedman; Chico, CA: Scholars Press, 1983) 117–31.

32. See above, p. 190 n. 22.

33. The meaning of Torah in Psalm 1 and its implications vis-à-vis the editing of the Psalter continue to be debated; almost all the essays in McCann, *The Shape and Shaping of the Psalter*, touch on these important issues.

34. Hans-Joachim Kraus, *Theology of the Psalms* (trans. Keith Crim; Minneapolis: Augsburg, 1986).

35. The beginnings of this project are found in the posthumous work of Meir Weiss, *The Ideas and Beliefs in the Book of Psalms* (Jerusalem: Bialik Institute, 2001) esp. pp. 13–30 [Hebrew]. For a different manner of organizing the differences within Psalms, see Erhard S. Gerstenberger, "Theologies in the Book of Psalms" in *The Book of Psalms: Compostion and Reception* (ed. Peter W. Flint et al.; VTSup 99; Leiden: Brill, 2005) 603–25.

the righteous, and does God always hear one's proper and contrite prayer? The final issue, an investigation of the traditions concerning the plagues of Egypt in Psalms, reflects a different type of inconsistency within the Psalter.

What is the Psalmist's opinion about whether or not God cares for the צדיק — the righteous man? Several psalms suggest that God cares for them well and immediately; this is the case, for example, in Psalms 34 and 37, two wisdom psalms[36] that seem unusually concerned with the fate of the wicked. These psalms claim, for example:

רַבּוֹת רָעוֹת צַדִּיק וּמִכֻּלָּם יַצִּילֶנּוּ יְהוָה:

Though the misfortunes of the righteous be many, the LORD will save him from them all. (34:20)

נַעַר הָיִיתִי גַּם־זָקַנְתִּי וְלֹא־רָאִיתִי צַדִּיק נֶעֱזָב וְזַרְעוֹ מְבַקֶּשׁ־לָחֶם:

I have been young and am now old, but I have never seen a righteous man abandoned, or his children seeking bread. (37:25)

וּתְשׁוּעַת צַדִּיקִים מֵיהוָה מָעוּזָם בְּעֵת צָרָה:

The deliverance of the righteous comes from the LORD, their stronghold in time of trouble. (37:39)

This idea is not unique to wisdom psalms; Ps 55:23, for example, reads:

הַשְׁלֵךְ עַל־יְהוָה יְהָבְךָ וְהוּא יְכַלְכְּלֶךָ לֹא־יִתֵּן לְעוֹלָם מוֹט לַצַּדִּיק:

Cast your burden on the LORD and He will sustain you; He will never let the righteous man collapse.

In quite a few places, however, a supplicant in Psalms feels that he is a collapsing righteous person. For example, Ps 7:10 is expressed as a wish:

יִגְמָר־נָא רַע רְשָׁעִים וּתְכוֹנֵן צַדִּיק וּבֹחֵן לִבּוֹת וּכְלָיוֹת אֱלֹהִים צַדִּיק:

Let the evil of the wicked come to an end, but establish the righteous; he who probes the mind and conscience is God the righteous.

This suggests that the righteous do not always prosper, nor are the wicked always punished. This explains the psalm's ending, that only after YHWH acts fairly will the supplicant praise him (7:18):

אוֹדֶה יְהוָה כְּצִדְקוֹ וַאֲזַמְּרָה שֵׁם־יְהוָה עֶלְיוֹן:

I will praise the LORD for His righteousness, and sing a hymn to the name of the LORD Most High.

---

36. On wisdom psalms, see now Avi Hurvitz, *Wisdom Language in Biblical Psalmody* (Jerusalem: Magnes, 1991) [Hebrew].

In looking at psalms such as Psalm 7[37] in the context of psalms such as 34, 37, and 55, what are we to believe? Can the righteous always count on God—is He always "a stronghold in time of trouble," to recall the words of Psalm 37, or should the righteous merely hope for God's deliverance—as in 7:10; "Let the evil of the wicked come to an end, but establish the righteous"? This is a significant difference indeed.

This first theological difference within the Psalter may be connected to a second difference: Does God always hear a proper and contrite prayer? Many psalms, perhaps even the majority of the Psalter, offer an unambiguous yes, suggesting that God is proximate, or קָרוֹב. For example:

קָרוֹב יְהוָה לְנִשְׁבְּרֵי־לֵב וְאֶת־דַּכְּאֵי־רוּחַ יוֹשִׁיעַ:

The LORD is close to the brokenhearted; those crushed in spirit He delivers. (34:19)

קָרוֹב אַתָּה יְהוָה וְכָל־מִצְוֹתֶיךָ אֱמֶת:

You, O LORD, are near, and all Your commandments are true. (119:151)

קָרוֹב יְהוָה לְכָל־קֹרְאָיו לְכֹל אֲשֶׁר יִקְרָאֻהוּ בֶאֱמֶת:

The LORD is near to all who call Him, to all who call Him with sincerity. (145:18)

Other verses in the Psalter suggest a quite different view of when and how God hears prayers. These include psalms that ask God to wake up, such as:

הָעִירָה וְהָקִיצָה לְמִשְׁפָּטִי אֱלֹהַי וַאדֹנָי לְרִיבִי:

Wake, rouse Yourself for my cause, for my claim, O my God and my Lord! (35:23)

עוּרָה לָמָה תִישַׁן אֲדֹנָי הָקִיצָה אַל־תִּזְנַח לָנֶצַח:

Rouse Yourself; why do You sleep, O Lord? Awaken, do not reject us forever! (44:24)[38]

A similar idea is expressed in the stirring Psalm 13, whose theme is divine abandonment,[39] where the psalmist opens with

עַד־אָנָה יְהוָה תִּשְׁכָּחֵנִי נֶצַח עַד־אָנָה תַּסְתִּיר אֶת־פָּנֶיךָ מִמֶּנִּי:

---

37. Psalm 7 may be compared to 92:8, which acknowledges the *temporary* flourishing of the wicked, though they will ultimately "be destroyed forever."

38. There is no reason to take these references to YHWH's sleeping as metaphorical; see Bernard F. Baato, "The Sleeping God: An Ancient Near Eastern Motif of Divine Sovereignty," *Bib* 68 (1987) 153–77.

39. For the meaning of this theme, see Samuel E. Balentine, *The Hidden God: The Hiding of the Face of God in the Old Testament* (Oxford: Oxford University Press, 1983).

How long, O LORD; will You ignore me forever? How long will You hide Your face from me? (13:2)

Thus, is God *always* close to the supplicants, or does he sometimes doze?

The third example is of a different type, illustrating polyphony in the Psalter's recounting of historical traditions. As is well known, two psalms, 78 and 105, recount in significant detail the plagues against the Egyptians.[40] Though each lists seven plagues, the plagues are narrated and ordered differently. In Psalm 78, we have blood, a swarm of frogs, locusts, hail against plants, hail against animals, pestilence, and death of the firstborn, while Psalm 105 describes darkness, blood, frogs, swarms of lice, hail, locusts, death of the firstborn. The differences between these two narrations is not merely in the order of the plagues, for example, whether or not blood is first, but also concerns the plagues themselves; for example, Psalm 78 lacks חֹשֶׁךְ, darkness, the first plague in 105, while 105 lacks דבר, pestilence.

Psalm 105 lacks a superscription, whereas Psalm 78 begins מַשְׂכִּיל לְאָסָף, "A Maskil to Asaph." Because the two are explicitly labeled as coming from different sources or authors, the fact that they tell different stories, or the same story differently, should not be disturbing. It is as if the plot of Psalm 78 is recounted and followed by a דבר אחר, "another opinion," introducing the plot of Psalm 105.

It might seem inappropriate to use Psalms as such a central text for developing Jewish biblical theology. It would seem that Jewish biblical theology should be developed from the Torah instead. Though the Torah is first among equals within rabbinic and especially later Jewish culture, sole or even too much emphasis should not be placed on the Torah. There is a misimpression, for example, that halachic—Jewish legal—decisions are only based on Torah literature. This is simply wrong, and indeed there are various rabbinic dicta that explicitly recognize the force of books in *nevi'im* and *ketuvim*.[41] Rabbinic literature recognizes all of what would later be called the Tanakh[42] as מקרא, "that which is read," or even more significantly, כתבי הקדש, "holy writings"—this status does *not* belong to the Torah only.[43]

---

40. Much of the discussion that follows is based on my essay "The Poet as Historian: The Plague Tradition in Psalm 105," in *Bringing the Hidden to Light: Studies in Honor of Stephen A. Geller* (ed. K. F. Kravitz and D. M. Sharon; Winona Lake, IN: Eisenbrauns, 2007) 19–28. Literature on both Psalms 78 and 105 may be found there.

41. See Brettler, "Biblical History and Jewish Biblical Theology," 576.

42. The term *Tanakh* is medieval and most likely derives from the Aramaic masoretic abbreviation Anakh; see Israel Yeivin, *Introduction to the Tiberian Masorah* (trans. E. J. Revell; SBLMasS 5; Missoula, MT: Scholars Press, 1980) 84.

43. On these and other rabbinic terms for Scripture, see Sid Z. Leiman, *The Canonization of the Hebrew Scripture: The Talmudic and Midrashic Evidence* (Hamden, CT: Archon, 1976) 57.

Internal biblical evidence also suggests the importance of Psalms. Both the opening of *nevi'im* and *ketuvim* contain references to Torah.[44] Josh 1:7–8 reads:

> But you must be very strong and resolute to observe faithfully all the Teaching (התורה) that My servant Moses enjoined upon you. Do not deviate from it to the right or to the left, that you may be successful wherever you go. Let not this Book of the Teaching (ספר התורה) cease from your lips, but recite it day and night, so that you may observe faithfully all that is written in it. Only then will you prosper in your undertakings and only then will you be successful.

Ps 1:2 contains a reference to the righteous individual:

$$\text{כִּי אִם בְּתוֹרַת יְהוָה חֶפְצוֹ וּבְתוֹרָתוֹ יֶהְגֶּה יוֹמָם וָלָיְלָה:}$$

> whose delight is in the Lord's Torah, and he reads or studies that Torah day and night.

It is unlikely that these two references at such key points are accidental, especially since there are good reasons to believe that they are both secondary: Josh 1:7–8 are contextually odd and are framed by a *Wiederaufnahme* or a resumptive repetition, whereas Psalm 1, unlike almost all of the rest of the first book of the Psalter, is what is quaintly called in Hebrew a מזמור יתום, "an orphan psalm," in other words, a psalm without a superscription.[45] These references to Torah were likely put at the beginning of these canonical divisions to create parallels between *nevi'im*, "Prophets," and *ketuvim*, "Writings," and the Torah, as if to say that they are Torah as well. This is a rather potent argument and adds great authority to the canonical divisions that they introduce, as well as to the individual books of Joshua and Psalms.

The Torah-like nature of Psalms is especially compelling due to its division into five Torah-like books with an introduction, Psalm 1, which explicitly mentions Torah. In the words of *Shocher Tov* (1.2), the midrash on Psalms:

משה נתן חמישה חומשי תורה לישראל ודויד נתן חמישה ספרים שבתהלים לישראל

---

44. For what follows, see Alexander Rofé ("The Piety of the Torah-Disciples at the Winding-Up of the Hebrew Bible: Josh 1:8; Ps 1:2; Isa 59:21," in *Bibel in jüdischer und christlicher Tradition: Festschrift für Johann Maier zum 60. Geburtstag* [ed. Helmut Merklein et al.; Frankfurt am Main: Hain, 1993] 78–85), who notes convincingly that the reference in Joshua is secondary and late.

45. Many scholars assume that Psalms 1 and 2 were placed at the beginning of the Psalter as an introduction to it; see McCann, *The Shape and Shaping of the Psalter*. This would explain why these two psalms lack the Davidic superscriptions that characterize those that follow.

Moses gave the five fifths of the Torah to Israel, and David gave the five books of Psalms to Israel.[46]

Finally, in case all of these arguments reflecting on the importance of Psalms in Jewish culture are not sufficiently convincing, it is noteworthy that Psalms is the most oft-quoted book of *ketuvim* in rabbinic literature, and 72 of the 150 psalms have regular liturgical use.[47]

I earlier raised the question of whether having a *Mitte*-less theology is a necessary and/or sufficient condition to consider a biblical theology to be Jewish. An investigation of recent non-Jewish approaches to biblical theology certainly suggests that it is not a sufficient condition. At the Annual Meeting of the Society of Biblical Literature in 2003, the Biblical Theology Group focused on Gerstenberger's *Theologies of the Old Testament*.[48] Several scholars observed then that the word *theology* is in the plural, and Gerstenberger's *Theology* is self-consciously *Mitte*-less.[49] This is an important consideration to bring to bear in relation to Barr's comment concerning nascent Jewish biblical theology: "How far it would agree or disagree with an Old Testament theology written by Christians we cannot yet tell."[50] Thus, we end with a type of irony—Jews have, as Levenson pointed out, shied away from biblical theology,[51] but what I and others believe to be a core element of Jewish biblical theology is not uniquely Jewish, and may indeed reflect the direction in which general biblical theology is moving. Thus, even as Jewish biblical theology begins to emerge as a separate field, it is time to wonder how truly distinct it will remain. I do not mean to imply that Jewish biblical theology will totally lose its identity—after all, its interest in showing continuity with postbiblical *Jewish* tradition (as opposed to NT and early Church traditions) will keep it somewhat distinct, but we should not be surprised if many points of significant overlap between Christian and Jewish biblical theology begin to develop.

46. The translation is my own; the Hebrew text is quoted from Solomon Buber, *Midrash Tehillim: Shocher Tov* (ed. Vilna, 1891; repr. Jerusalem: Hanad, 1977).

47. See the list in Stefan C. Reif, "The Bible in the Liturgy," in *The Jewish Study Bible* (ed. Adele Berlin and Marc Zvi Brettler; New York: Oxford University Press, 2003) 1947–48. Some have suggested that "David," referring to the book of Psalms, may even be a shorthand term for all of *ketuvim* in 4QMMT, but this has recently been disputed by Eugene Ulrich, "The Non-Attestation of a Tripartite Canon in 4QMMT," *CBQ* 65 (2003) 202–14.

48. Erhard S. Gerstenberger, *Theologies in the Old Testament* (trans. John Bowden; vol. 1; Minneapolis: Fortress, 2002).

49. This is emphasized in the "Preliminary Remarks" in Gerstenberger, *Theologies*, 1–3.

50. Barr, *Concepts*, 585.

51. Jon D. Levenson, "Why Jews Are Not Interested in Biblical Theology," in *The Hebrew Bible, The Old Testament, and Historical Criticism: Jews and Christians in Biblical Studies* (Louisville, KY: Westminster John Knox, 1993) 33–61.

13

Psalm 1 and the Canonical Shaping of Jewish Scripture

Benjamin D. Sommer

What sort of religious experience does the book of Psalms reflect and encourage? Given the variety of genres that the book contains, many answers might be given to this question. From among these possible answers, I would like to discuss those given by the redactors of the book and by rabbinic interpreters in order to see how these two sets of answers relate to each other. Doing so will not only open a window on the nature of the book of Psalms; it will also suggest how one can pursue the study of biblical theology in a Jewish context. I have contended elsewhere that it is in the interaction between biblical texts and the work of classical Jewish interpreters that something resembling a Jewish biblical theology can arise.[1] To be sure, strictly speaking, the idea of a "Jewish biblical theology" is an oxymoron, at least if the term *biblical theology* is understood to confine the subject of its analysis to the Bible or to give a privileged place to the Bible. All forms of Jewish theology must base themselves on tradition at least as much as Scripture, and hence they cannot be primarily biblical; conversely, any theology that limits itself to Scripture is by definition Protestant and not Jewish. Nevertheless, there can be such a thing as a Jewish theology that attends to Scripture along with tradition, or perhaps to Scripture as a part of tradition,[2] recovering or renewing biblical voices that are often lost in Jewish thought. We might term this sort of pursuit "Jewish biblical

---

1. See my "Wie kann biblische Theologie möglich werden?" in *Stuttgarter Bibelstudien* (ed. Bernd Janowski; forthcoming); and, more briefly, my "Revelation at Sinai in the Hebrew Bible and Jewish Theology," *JR* 79 (1999) 422–51, esp. 424–25 n. 5.

2. On Scripture as a part of tradition (rather than a wholly distinct category) in rabbinic Judaism, see Abraham Joshua Heschel, *Torah Min Ha-Shamayim B'Aspaqlarya Shel Ha-Dorot* (3 vols.; London: Soncino / New York: Jewish Theological Seminary, 1990) 3:45–47 [Hebrew]; Yochanan Silman, *The Voice Heard at Sinai: Once or Ongoing?* (Jerusalem: Magnes, 1999) 26–27 [Hebrew]; and my own remarks in "Unity and Plurality in Jewish Canons: The Case of the Oral and Written Torah," in *One Scripture or Many? Perspectives Historical, Theological and Philosophical* (ed. Christine Helmer and Christof Landmesser; New York: Oxford University Press, 2004) 108–50, esp. pp. 123–26.

theology," so long as we are mindful of its fundamental differences from Protestant forms of biblical theology. Discovering the interactions between biblical and rabbinic voices should be one of its major concerns. In this essay, I hope to point out one example of this interaction.

Before doing so, it will be useful to sharpen my initial questions by taking note of two attitudes toward religious experience that play prominent roles in Judaism. One of these attitudes emphasizes Torah study and intellectualization over prayer and spontaneous joy; the other adopts the opposite hierarchy of religious values. The tension between these two attitudes is well-known already in classical rabbinic literature, which, with important reservations and exceptions, tends to regard Torah study as the highest religious value. A few passages will suffice to illustrate the relationship between these types of religious experience in classical rabbinic texts.

In *b. Meg.* 26b–27a, both attitudes are suggested, but one is ultimately endorsed over the other. The discussion in these passages presumes a principle stated at the beginning of the fourth chapter of this talmudic tractate (25b–26a), to wit: it is permissible to use the proceeds from the sale of a sacred item to purchase an item of greater sanctity, but it is forbidden to use these proceeds to purchase an item of lesser sanctity. In other words, one can always convert an object (or the proceeds of its sale) upward in holiness but not downward.[3] With this principle in mind, the Talmud records the following debate and its resolution:

> Rav Papi said in the name of Rava, "[It is] permissible [to convert] a house of prayer into a house of study, but [it is] forbidden [to convert] a house of study into a house of prayer." But Rav Papa taught the opposite in the name of Rava. Rav Aḥa held that the method of Rav Papi was more likely, since Rabbi Joshua ben Levi had earlier said, "It is lawful to convert a house of prayer into a house of study."

The implication is clear. Papi, in short, holds that a house of study is of greater sanctity than a house of prayer; Papa holds the opposite; and the tradition accepts the former view, not the latter. This viewpoint is not unique to this passage. The same chapter of the Talmud teaches that a prayer hall ought not be used for certain secular purposes, including funerals (see *b. Meg.* 28a–b). However, an exception is made for "funerals of many" or a "public funeral," which, the gemara goes on to explain (28b, and see Rashi to הספד של רבים ad loc.), means the funeral of a scholar or a member of his family. Thus, the sanctity of a scholar (or even of a member of his family) overrides the sanctity of a prayer hall.

---

3. Incidentally, these rules are of little practical relevance for a community selling its religious objects or properties, because the Talmud explains that these rules do not apply when the items are sold by the seven leading members of the congregation in the presence of the congregation. See Rava's comment in *b. Meg.* 26a and *O.H.* 153:8.

A few texts evince a more ambivalent stance. *Y. Ber.* 1:5 (3b) [4] discusses whether it is permissible to interrupt study in order to pray:

> Rabbi Yoḥanan said in the name of Rabbi Shimon Bar Yoḥai, "People like us, who are involved in the study of Torah [constantly], do not interrupt [their studies] even for the recitation of the Shema prayer [the recitation of which at a set time is required by biblical law, and all the more so not for the recitation of other prayers, whose timing is not required by biblical law, [5] such as the Standing Prayer]." Rabbi Yoḥanan said in his own name, "People like us, who are not [constantly] involved in the study of Torah, do interrupt [their studies] even for the recitation of the Standing Prayer [and all the more so for the Shema prayer]. Each one's ruling is in accordance with his opinions [expressed on other occasions]. For Rabbi Yoḥanan said, "If only one could pray all day long! Why? Because prayer never wanes." Rabbi Shimon bar Yoḥai said, "If I had stood at Mount Sinai when the Torah was given to Israel, I would have requested that the Merciful One make two mouths for human beings, one with which to study the Torah, and one with which to take care of all other concerns."

Each scholar expresses an unrealizable ideal. The highest activity of humanity, which in the best of all worlds would never be interrupted, is either prayer (Yoḥanan) or study (Shimon), and the law takes both views into account. Yoḥanan's legal ruling, which reflects a higher regard for prayer, applies only in cases where exigencies prevent a scholar from studying all the time; whereas Shimon's ruling, which valorizes study over prayer, is applicable only for the purest of scholars. The rabbis cherished both prayer and study, and passages such as these show that their relative ranking was a matter of concern in both the tannaitic and amoraic periods in Israel and Babylon. But where a clear preference is stated, the classical rabbis inclined to give study the highest place of honor. [6]

---

4. Also in *y. Šab.* 1:1 (3a) and, a slightly different version, *b. Šab.* 11a.

5. Cf. Rashi to *b. Šab.* 11a (ד"ה חברים העוסקים בתורה מפסיקים).

6. Many other passages can be cited; in the aggregate, they evince both the tension between these two important values and the greater respect for study, though not without some complexities. See, e.g., *b. Šab.* 10a (concerning which cf. *b. Roš Haš.* 35a); *b. Šab.* 127a; in *b. Ber.* 8a, the teachings of Ḥisda, of Ḥiyya in the name of ʿUlla (note the complexity of his view, which implies that Temple service was greater than study; cf. *m. ʾAbot* 1.2, where the two seem to be of equal value, and see also the attempt to reach a mediating position in *b. Meg.* 3a–b), of Abbaye, and of Ammi and Assi (cf. Abbaye's different perspective in *b. Meg.* 29a, but note that this opinion ought to be attributed not to Abbaye but to Rava according to Rabbeinu Hananel and *Gilyon Hašas*); *b. Ber.* 31a–b. On the paramount value of Torah study over all other religious values (including prayer), see especially the debate involving Rabbi Tarfon, Rabbi Akiva, and the elders in *b. Qidd.* 40b and also the teaching of Rabbi Yosi there, and see further *m. Pesaḥ* 1:1 (= b. Qidd. 40a), and note also the texts collected in *m. ʾAbot*, chapter 6. For a later rabbinic voice valorizing study over prayer, see Maimonides' Code, Laws of Prayer, 8:3 — a passage

The relative weighting of these two religious values remained a question in later Jewish thought as well. The tension between them played a central role in the conflict between Hasidim and Mitnagdim in the 18th century (and to some extent up to the present). The Mitnagdim, centered in the great academies or *yeshivot* of Lithuania (and their successor institutions in Israel, the United States and, to a lesser degree, Britain), represent the apogee of the viewpoint expressed in the Talmud by Simeon bar Yoḥai, Joshua ben Levi, and Papi: they esteem study over prayer. A central element of early Hasidism, on the other hand, was its emphasis on prayer over study.[7] (Indeed, Mordecai Wilensky has argued that the Hasidic devaluation of study was the main reason for the opposition of the great

---

whose higher valorization of study is noteworthy, because it appears in a chapter that emphasizes the great importance of prayer. In light of the consistent tendency of these texts to weigh the relative value of prayer and prophecy, I cannot agree with the claim in Lawrence Hoffman ("Hallels, Midrash, Canon, and Loss: Psalms in Jewish Liturgy," in *Psalms in Community. Jewish and Christian Textual, Liturgical, and Artistic Traditions* [ed. Harold Attridge and Margot Fassler; Atlanta: Society of Biblical Literature, 2003] 33–57) that "the presumed dichotomy between prayer and study exists more in the minds of twentieth- and twenty-first-century critics than it did in the rabbinic imagination" (p. 54). Hoffman is right to point out that, for the rabbis, prayer was not limited to "the current popular notion of prayer as personal conversation with God" but also includes "the midrashic linking of biblical text to the expression of theological realia" (p. 55) so that prayer was itself, in part, a form of sacred and salvific study; the very fact that prayer in rabbinic culture is conceptualized this way itself points to the rabbinic understanding of the religious value of study. For further discussion of the value of Torah study in classical rabbinic literature, see E. E. Urbach, *The Sages: Their Concepts and Beliefs* (trans. Israel Abrahamson; Jerusalem: Magnes, 1975) 612–14; Marc Hirshman, "Torah in Rabbinic Thought: The Theology of Learning" in *The Cambridge History of Judaism*, vol. 4: *The Late Roman-Rabbinic Period* (ed. S. Katz; Cambridge: Cambridge University Press, 2006), 899–924; and Shmuel Safrai, "Oral Torah," in *The Literature of the Sages, Part One* (ed. Shmuel Safrai; CRINT; Philadelphia: Fortress, 1987) 35–119, esp. pp. 102–6.

7. To be sure, Mitnagdim continued to value prayer, and Hasidim eventually began to reemphasize study, a trend evident as early as the development of Chabad. But the pronounced tendencies are clear. For discussions of these differing religious sensibilities, see Norman Lamm, "Study and Prayer: Their Relative Value in Hasidism and Mitnagdism," in *Samuel K. Mirsky Memorial Volume: Studies in Jewish Law, Philosophy, and Literature* (ed. Gerson Appel; New York: Yeshiva University Press, 1970) 37–52; Mordecai Wilensky, *Hasidim Umitnagdim: Letoldot Hapulmus Beyneyhem* (2nd ed.; Jerusalem: Mossad Bialik, 1990) 15–26 [Hebrew]; and Allan Nadler, *The Faith of the Mithnagdim: Rabbinic Responses to Hasidic Rapture* (Baltimore: Johns Hopkins University Press, 1997) 50–77, 151–70. On the tendency of Hasidim to establish new study groups (*ḥavuorot*) for studying Mishna or to infiltrate existing ones in the 19th century, which entailed both a greater emphasis on study within Hasidic communities and also some loss of focus on study in those groups, see Yohanan Petrovsky Shtern, "Hasidism, Havurot, and the Jewish Street," *Jewish Social Studies* 10 (2004) 20–54, esp. pp. 43–44. Attempts at synthesis (albeit sometimes of a limited nature) also occurred among Mitnagdim. For one Mitnadgic attempt to achieve a synthesis, which nonetheless continues to give pride of place to study, see Joseph B. Soloveitchik, "Be-Inyan Birkhat Ha-Torah," in *Shiurim le-Zekher Aba Mari Z"L* (Jerusalem: Solovetsik, 1985) 1–16 [Hebrew].

Lithuanian rabbis to nascent Hasidism.[8]) Consequently, we might use the terms *hasidic* and *mitnagdic* to identify two temperaments within Judaism throughout the ages. For the purpose of this article, "hasidic" will refer to a form of Judaism that emphasizes prayer and spontaneous joy as the highest way of coming to know God, while "mitnagdic" will refer to a form of Judaism that focuses on study and intellectualization as the preeminent path toward the deity. An additional issue that separated (and separates) historical Hasidim and Mitnagdim will also turn out to be relevant to our discussion: this issue involves the style of leadership each group endorses. Many strains of Hasidism (most prominently the Ruzhin/Boyaner groups, as well as the Chabad sect, especially in recent decades) emphasize a royal or at times even messianic model of leadership.[9] The rebbe or tzaddik who leads the group is treated as a monarch (and thus it is quite appropriate that he is succeeded by his son or some other member of his family). Mitnagdim, on the other hand, look toward the scholar as the most important authority for their communities—especially the scholar who holds no official position or holds a decidedly modest one.[10] (While dynasties of scholars exist among the Mitnagdim, most prominent rabbis within that world achieve their positions through intellectual achievement rather than

8. Wilensky, *Hasidim UMitnagdim*, 1:17–19. See further the comments of Nadler, *Faith*, 151, 232–33.

9. To be sure, some scholars (e.g., Martin Buber and Simon Dubnow) argue that early (pre-1800) Hasidism constituted an attempt to do away with messiansim, but others (Ben Zion Dinur, Isaiah Tishby) regard early Hasidism as thoroughly messianic in orientation, and some (Gershom Scholem, Joseph Weiss) take a middle ground, regarding messianism as an accepted doctrine but not an area of intense focus among early Hasidim. For a review of the literature and a defense of the last position, see Gershom Scholem, "The Neutralization of the Messianic Element in Early Hasidism," in *The Messianic Idea in Judaism and Other Essays on Jewish Spirituality* (New York: Schocken, 1971) 176–202, 359–63. For a recent treatment of messianic speculation in the earliest period of Hasidism, see Mor Altshuler, "Messianic Strains in Rabbi Israel Ba'al Shem Tov's 'Holy Epistle,'" *JSQ* 6 (1999) 55–70. All scholars would agree, however, that intense messianic speculation became more common among some Hasidic leaders by about 1800; see Scholem, 179. Regardless of the more specific question of messianism, it remains clear that already in its early period Hasidism began to develop a model of leadership that can appropriately be termed royal. This model usually involved dynastic mechanisms for the transfer of leadership. (On the development of the dynastic model during Hasidism's 1st century, see David Assaf, *The Regal Way: The Life and Times of Rabbi Israel of Ruzhin* [Stanford Series in Jewish History and Culture; Stanford: Stanford University Press, 2002] 47–68). Further, it focused on particular leaders who, like an ancient Near Eastern monarchs, served as an axis mundi. See Arthur Green, "The *Zaddiq* as *Axis Mundi* in Later Judaism," in *Essential Papers on Kabbalah* (ed. Lawrence Fine; New York: New York University Press, 1995) 291–311.

10. For a highly readable treatment of the different styles of leadership in each community, see Amnon Levi (*The Haredim* [Jerusalem: Keter, 1989) 150–64, 176–77 [Hebrew]), who also notes the tendency among Mitnagdim in recent decades to exalt certain *rashei yeshiva* in a manner that begins to approach the royal model of the Hasidim. On the even more extreme movement among recent Mitnagdim toward insistence that scholars are the ultimate leaders, see Haym Soloveitchik, "Migration, Acculturation, and the New Role of Texts

genetic succession.) For our purposes, then, the adjective "hasidic" will betoken not only an emphasis on prayer but a inclination toward royal or messianic models of leadership. The adjective *mitnagdic* will suggest an elitist view of learning and a strong emphasis on the honor due to those devoted to it—an elitism with paradoxically democratic implications, because any person,[11] regardless of birth, can aspire to learning.

In light of all this, we can phrase our original question in a new way: is the book of Psalms fundamentally a hasidic or mitnagdic book? At first blush, the answer seems obvious. The Psalter is, after all, a book of prayers. The exuberant hymns, with their cries of "Praise Yah!" (e.g., Psalms 29, 33, 95, 114, 117); the songs of thanksgiving, which disclose the strong connection between the person praying and the God who answered their cries for help (e.g., 18, 30, 32, 116, 118); the personal laments, which are rooted in the worshiper's intimate sense of connection with God (e.g., 3, 4, 5, 71, 77); the communal laments, whose aggrieved tone reflects the very presumption of closeness between community and deity (e.g., 44, 60, 74, 90, 123)—all these genres, which together account for the vast majority of texts in the Psalter,[12] represent a religiosity of feeling, not a religiosity rooted in the intellect. Each genre encourages an individual or a community to address a personal God directly. Furthermore, the adjective *hasidic* as I intend it here hints at the central role a royal figure plays in maintaining the connection between God and nation. Consequently, the royal psalms (e.g., 2, 18, 45, 72, 110) also establish the appropriateness of the adjective *hasidic* in characterizing the Psalter. The Zion psalms (e.g., 46, 48, 76) similarly underscore the importance of the royal family whose palace is on Mount Zion and who sponsor the Temple located there. To be sure, some psalms are not really prayers and have no connection to royalty—to wit, the wisdom psalms (e.g., 37, 49, 112). This category, however, represents a small fraction of the texts found in this book.[13] If the contents of any biblical book deserve to be called hasidic, surely that book is the Psalter.

---

in the Haredi World," in *Accounting for Fundamentalisms: The Dynamic Character of Movements* (ed. Martin Marty and R. Scott Appleby; Chicago: University of Chicago Press, 1994) 197–235, esp. pp. 216–21.

11. Or, in the actual world of Mitnagdim, any male.

12. In the mentioned examples, I refer to a few randomly selected from each genre for the benefit of nonbiblicists.

13. The identification of wisdom psalms is a matter of some controversy, but even by the broadest definitions they amount to less than a tenth of the psalms found in the Psalter. On this issue, see Avi Hurvitz, *Wisdom Language in Biblical Psalmody* (Jerusalem: Magnes, 1991 [Hebrew]); R. N. Whybray, "The Wisdom Psalms," in *Wisdom in Ancient Israel. Essays in Honour of J. A. Emerton* (ed. John Day et al.; Cambridge: Cambridge University Press, 1995) 152–60; Roland Murphy, "A Consideration of the Classification, 'Wisdom Psalms,'" *VT* 9 (1963) 156–67; J. Kenneth Kuntz, "Wisdom Psalms and the Shaping of the Hebrew Psalter," in *For a Later Generation: The Transformation of Tradition in Israel, Early Judaism, and Early Christianity (Essays*

This portrayal applies well to the vast majority of psalms. But the canonical *book* of Psalms as we have it in the Hebrew Bible may be more than the sum of its parts. As a result, the question of how the Psalter is presented must be raised as its own question, distinct from a discussion of the individual texts this anthology contains. One can ask the same question about psalms and Psalms and receive different answers for each, because the way psalms are organized into Psalms may spin the psalms in a surprising way. The most prominent way to give any collection of material a particular identity that one might not have discerned from its contents alone is in the way it is either introduced or summed up. This phenomenon is well known in narrative literature. Adele Berlin has pointed out the importance of an abstract or introductory remark that begins many narratives.[14] These often provide crucial guidance for the reader. For example, without the brief abstract in Gen 22:1, we would not know that the events narrated in that chapter are a divinely ordained test. One would have a very different reading of the story of the binding of Isaac if it began with the sentence

> Now, after these things, God said to Abraham, "Abraham!" and Abraham said, "Here I am," And He said, "Take your son."

rather than what we in fact read in Genesis,

> Now, after these things, *God tested Abraham*, saying to him, "Abraham!" and Abraham said, "Here I am," and He said, "Take your son."

The same may be said of the first poem in any anthology of poetry: the introduction can serve as an abstract for all that follows. I would like to argue that Psalm 1 presents, or re-represents, the Psalter in an original and rather surprising way: as a mitnagdic book.

The poem that opens the Psalter is an odd psalm; indeed, it is not really a psalm at all.[15] It is not addressed to God (as the laments and thanksgiving psalms are), nor does it speak of him in the third person (as is the case with many psalms of praise). Its topic is not God, at least not directly. Rather, its topic is God's *torah*, which may mean God's instruction generally or may refer to a specific document that contains such instruction, such as the Pentateuch. In fact, it probably means both; while the term *torah* may include something general, the phrasing of the psalm presumes that *torah* is found in a particular text. This becomes evident in the psalm's

---

in Honor of George Nickelsburg) (ed. Randal Argall et al.; Harrisburg: Trinity Press International, 2000) 144–60, esp. pp. 146–49. On the characterization of Psalms 1, 19, and 119 as Torah psalms rather than wisdom psalms, see James Luther Mays, "The Place of the Torah-Psalms in the Psalter," *JBL* 106 (1987) 3–12.

    14. Adele Berlin, *Poetics and the Interpretation of Biblical Narrative* (Winona Lake, IN: Eisenbrauns, 1994) 102.

    15. The same point was made by Whybray, "The Wisdom Psalms," 155.

second verse, according to which the happy person is one who takes delight in God's *torah*, reading (יהגה) it day and night. The verb הגה at the end of that verse is often translated with the English verb "meditate on," which may suggest to the English reader an exclusively mental activity (and hence one that need not be connected to a particular text). Nevertheless, nearly all attestations of the verb הגה in the Hebrew Bible refer to a physical act that involves one's mouth and one's vocal cords; the verb does not refer to pure ratiocination. Certainly, the pigeon and lion who perform the act of הגהing in Isa 38:18 and Isa 31:4 are making a soft low sound, not merely cogitating (they are cooing and growling respectively). The physicality of the act is clear in most of its occurrences with human beings as its subject: see, for example, Ps 115:7, where the throat is mentioned as its organ, just as hands are the organ of touching and legs of walking; Ps 71:24, where it is the tongue that performs the הגהing; and Josh 1:8, where it is the presence of the Book of the Torah in Joshua's mouth that allows him to הוגה it. (The evidence of this last verse is especially significant, given its many parallels with Ps 1:2, to which we will return later.) Several texts do identify the mind (לב) as the organ of this activity (Isa 33:18), yet most of these also put the verb alongside words indicating verbal expression, such as the verbs דִּבֶּר or הִבִּיעַ or nouns referring to parts of the mouth such as פה and שפה (e.g., Isa 58:13; Prov 15:18, 24:2). The meditation described by the verb הגה, then, is not the silent act that the word *meditation* may conjure up for many contemporary speakers of English, an act that is thought to be deeply spiritual or rational. Rather, it is something done aloud, perhaps very softly but nonetheless physically. Its connection with the mind (לב) shows that this physical act can involve contemplation or learning as well.[16] (The traditional Yeshivah rather than the Quaker meeting would be the place to see the activity Psalm 1 has in mind.)

This being the case, the *torah* to which Ps 1:2b refers consists not only of abstract ideas but of specific words that can be enunciated; in other words, it is a text. It is impossible to decide whether the text of which the author of Psalm 1 speaks is more or less identical to our Pentateuch (like the תורה to which Ezra–Nehemiah and Chronicles refer) or consists of some predecessor text, such as the book of Deuteronomy or some early edition thereof (to which the book of Kings refers when it used the term תורת משה);[17] further, it is possible that the author of the psalm meant the

16. One might compare the comment of Rabbi Simeon bar Yoḥai quoted above from *y. Ber.* 1:5 (3b), where studying is presumed to be an activity that one performs with one's mouth; reading or contemplating a text is done out loud. Study involves mouth and mind simultaneously.

17. Both ibn Ezra and Gunnel André note the similarity of vocabulary in Ps 1:1–2 and Deut 6:4–9, on the basis of which they suggest that the psalmist alludes to that passage from

term in one way while the editor who put the psalm at the head of the Psalter (if that editor was not also the author of the psalm) meant it in some other way. What remains clear, however, is that, as the introduction to the Psalter, our psalm refers us to another text; the book of Psalms begins by putting itself in relation to a book called Torah, whatever that Torah may be.

That editorial act has two implications. First, as many scholars including Meir Weiss, Claus Westermann, Joseph Reindl, and Gerald Wilson have noted, the editor who placed this paean to Torah-study at the head of the Psalter suggests a radically new vision of that anthology and its setting. While individual psalms are prayers, which one uses in cultic settings (including but not limited to the Jerusalem Temple), the Psalter that begins with Psalm 1 is a textbook, to which one turns for guidance and instruction. One recites or sings a psalm; one reads or studies the book of Psalms.[18] In short, Psalm 1 attempts to convert the book of Psalms into another form of Torah. It suggests that one ought to learn this text, just as one learns the Pentateuch. By intimating that one can receive teaching from the Psalter, Psalm 1 also makes the somewhat surprising move of transforming prayers

---

Deuteronomy. See Gunnel André, "'Walk,' 'Stand,' and 'Sit' in Psalm 1:1–2," *VT* 32 (1982) 327; Stefan Reif, "Ibn Ezra on Psalm I 1–2," *VT* 34 (1984) 232–36. This reference specifically to Deuteronomy (and not to other books) might suggest that the author of Psalm 1 regards the Torah as Deuteronomy.

18. So far as I know, this approach to the canonical function of Psalm 1 was first expressed, rather in passing, both by Meir Weiss, "The Way of Torah in Psalm 1," in *Miqra'ot Kekhavvanatam* (Jerusalem: Mosad Bialik, 1988) 111 [Hebrew] (originally published in the journal *Ma'ayanot* 6 [1957]); and by Claus Westerman, *Praise and Lament in the Psalms* (trans. Keith R. Crim and Richard N. Soulen; Edinburgh: T. & T. Clark, 1981) 253 (first published in German in 1964). This insight is developed in greater depth by Joseph Reindl, "Weisheitliche Bearbeitung von Psalmen: Ein Beitrag zum Verständnis der Sammlung des Psalters," *VT* 32 (1981) 333–56, esp. pp. 339–41; and by Gerald Wilson, *The Editing of the Hebrew Psalter* (SBLDS; Chico, CA: Scholars Press, 1985) 143, 204–7. Reindl pays particular attention to the form-critical question of setting, noting the difference between the setting of psalms and the setting of the Psalter. For brief treatments of the canon-shaping role of Psalm 1, see also Brevard S. Childs, *Introduction to the Old Testament as Scripture* (Philadelphia: Fortress, 1979) 513; Johannes Marböck, "Zur frühen Wirkungsgeschichte von Ps 1," in *Freude an der Weisung des Herrn. Beiträge zur Theologie der Psalmen. Festgabe zum 70. Geburtstag von Heinrich Groß* (ed. Ernst Haag and Frank-Lothar Hossfeld; Stuttgarter biblische Beiträge 13; Stuttgart: Verlag Katholisches Bibelwerk, 1986) 207–22, esp. p. 211; J. Clinton McCann, "The Psalms as Instruction," *Interpretation* 46 (1992) 117–28, esp. p. 119. Other scholars have made the slightly different suggestion that Psalm 1 attempts to present the Psalter as a wisdom collection, or at least a collection related to wisdom, or that Psalm 1 encourages the reader to read the Psalter in the prism of wisdom. See Johann Maier, "Psalm 1 im Licht antiker jüdischer Zeugnisse," in *Altes Testament und christliche Verkündigung: Festschrift für Antonius H. J. Gunneweg zum 65. Geburtstag* (ed. Manfred Oeming and Axel Graupner; Stuttgart: Kohlhammer, 1987) 353–365, esp. p. 365; Whybray, "The Wisdom Psalms," 155; Kuntz, "Wisdom Psalms," 150–51.

into instruction. What one might have regarded as a human's words to the deity become a form of divine revelation to humanity.[19] (One might object to the suggestion that Psalm 1 transforms prayer into learning, arguing that the phrase יהגה בתורתו in verse 2 might refer to prayerful recitation of the Torah. In that case, Psalm 1 would attempt to make the Torah into a prayer book rather than Psalter into a study book. However, the verb הגה is almost never used to refer to an utterance made in prayer. In the few cases where it does, it means to articulate a particular idea in the context of a prayer, not to sing or chant.[20] Similarly, one might refer in English to a person "uttering God's praises," but this does not mean that the word *utter* by itself suggests a liturgical context. Further, the object of the verb in Ps 1:2 is "T/torah," which definitively places the phrase יהגה בתורתו in a context of study, because "torah" means "instruction, that which is studied.")

The second implication following from the placement of Psalm 1 involves the shape of the canon. What does it mean to begin the book of Psalms—and hence the Ketuvim as a whole—by praising the Torah and recommending its study? The answer to this question becomes sharper when we realize that the phrasing found in Ps 1:2 also appears in the very first chapter of the Nevi'im.[21]

19. On this conversion of human response into divine revelation, see also Childs, *Introduction*, 513–14; Wilson, *Editing*, 206; McCann, "The Psalms as Instruction," 119. Already in the 10th century, Saadia Gaon viewed the Psalter as a revealed text rather than a humanly authored one. In light of the canon-shaping role of Psalm 1, it becomes clear that the attempt to convert the Psalter into a revelatory text is much older than Saadia; Saadia's seemingly radical reading in fact reflects the *peshat* of Psalm 1, or at least the *peshat* of Psalm 1's editorial role. On Saadia's view of the Psalter, see Uriel Simon, *Four Approaches to the Book of Psalms* (trans. Lenn Schramm; Albany, NY: State University of New York Press, 1991) 2–5. An intermediate position on the essential nature of the Psalter is held by ibn Ezra, who (reworking the rabbis' view) regarded some though not all of the psalms as composed by David writing not as an individual but as a prophet, so that parts of the Psalter is revealed, but not in the same way as the Pentateuch. See Simon, *Four Approaches*, 127–216, 314–17, 330–33. (These medieval Jewish views of the Psalter may have even earlier antecedent, incidentally. Early Muslim views of the Psalter in several ways resembled those later articulated by Saadia and Ibn Ezra. See Jacob Lassner, *Demonizing the Queen of Sheba: Boundaries of Gender and Culture in Postbiblical Judaism and Medieval Islam* [Chicago: University of Chicago Press, 1993] 108 and references there.)

20. The only strong examples are Pss 35:28 and 62:7. In three cases (Ps 62:7, 77:13, and 143:5) the verb refers to the worshiper's utterance describing divine works. In these cases, the verb is always parallel to some form of זכר (= "mention"), so that the verb הגה does not itself denote prayer but refers to a verbalization of some idea that happens to occur in the context of prayer.

21. On the significance of this parallel, see Alexander Rofé, "The Piety of the Torah-Disciples at the Winding-up of the Hebrew Bible: Josh 1:8; Ps 1:2; Isa 59:21," in *Bibel in jüdischer und christlicher Tradition: Festschrift für Johann Maier zum 60. Geburtstag* (ed. Helmut Merklien et al.; Frankfurt: Anton Hain, 1993) 78–85, esp. pp. 81–82; and, at slightly greater length, idem, "The Move towards the Study of Torah at the End of the Biblical Period: Joshua 1:8; Psalm 1:2; Isaiah 59:21," in *The Bible in Light of Its Interpereters: Memorial Volume for Sarah Kamin* (ed. Sara Japhet; Jerusalem: Magnes, 1994) 622–28, esp. pp. 624–26 [Hebrew].

This book of Torah (הַתּוֹרָה) should never leave your mouth; learn it through recitation day and night (וְהָגִיתָ בּוֹ יוֹמָם וָלַיְלָה) so that you will carefully observe everything written in it. Then your way will succeed, and you will achieve understanding. (Josh 1:8) [The righteous individual] takes delight in Yhwh's Torah (בְּתוֹרַת ה'), learning His Torah through recitation night and day (וּבְתוֹרָתוֹ יֶהְגֶּה יוֹמָם וָלַיְלָה). (Ps 1:2)

Especially when viewed alongside each other, these verses have a clear message. The former asserts the subservience of the text that begins with Joshua 1, which is to say, the whole of Nevi'im, to the Five Books of Moses. The latter proclaims the subordination of Psalms, and with them all of Ketuvim, to the Five Books. [22] The two verses work together to shape the canon, dividing it into the unequal parts known from later Jewish tradition. Within Scripture, Torah is what really matters; the remaining material is worthwhile insofar as it can serve as an adjunct or spur to studying and observing the Torah. [23] (The canon-formative role these passages play, incidentally, is clearly a late development. Rofé points out that 1:8 is an addition to the original text of Joshua 1. It is bracketed by a *Wiederaufnahme*; note the parallel of לְמַעַן תַּשְׂכִּיל בְּכֹל אֲשֶׁר תֵּלֵךְ in Josh 1:7b and אָז תַּצְלִיחַ אֶת־דְּרָכֶךָ וְאָז תַּשְׂכִּיל in Josh 1:8b. [24])

In short, Psalm 1 fosters a particular sort of piety, which I have called mitnagdic, and it fosters a particular view of the Scripture, which we might simply call Jewish. It attempts to put the book of Psalms and by extension the phenomenon of prayer in their place. That place, to be sure, is important; the Psalter remains a part of Scripture, and prayer remains part of the religious experience of the ideal Jew. But that place is also secondary: Psalms is less important that the Pentateuch, and prayer is less important than study. The phrasing in 1:2 is especially important for understanding how appropriate the term *mitnagdic* is for this psalm. The ideal person

22. The last passage in the Nevi'im makes the same point; see Mal 3:22. (One might see the reference to Elijah in 3:23 as a response which attempts to defend prophecy after the lower ranking it received in 3:22. This defense reserves an eschatological role for prophecy, even if, in the here-and-now, prophecy has surrendered its role to Torah.) The beginning of Proverbs may have a similar function; see Scott Harris, "Proverbs 1:8–19, 20–33 as 'Introduction,'" *RB* 107 (2000) 205–31.

23. On this characterization of the Jewish canon, see John Barton, *Oracles of God: Perception of Ancient Prophecy in Israel after the Exile* (London: Darton, Longman, & Todd, 1986) 21.

24. Further, even the reference to Torah in 1:7 is probably secondary; the LXX reads not the MT's "carefully observe all this Torah that My servant Moses commanded you" but merely "carefully observe what Moses my servant commanded you." Later scribes specified that Moses' commandments to Joshua were not only oral but were also found in the written Torah (that is, the Pentateuch, or perhaps Deuteronomy). Even later scribes then added v. 8 to clarify that one can observe the Torah by internalizing its commands through studying it aloud day and night. See Rofé, "Piety," 78–80; and idem, "Move," 622–24.

never moves away from Torah study according to that verse, because the Torah that is his delight and desire is on his mind and in his mouth all the time.[25] This is precisely the sort of study that Simeon bar Yoḥai presents as a sadly unrealizable ideal in the passage from *y. Ber.* 1:5 (3b) cited above and that contemporary mitnagdim have come strikingly close to realizing after all.[26]

Of course, the viewpoint reflected in the editorial placement of Psalm 1 as the introduction to the Psalter is not the only one possible. Other scriptural attempts to characterize that anthology seem to have been suggested in ancient times as well. I will briefly review a few of them.

Just as an introduction sums up a work, so too does a conclusion. In this light, the contrast between the first and last poems in the Psalter could hardly be more striking.[27] Psalm 150 focuses on prayer; and within the realm of prayer, it focuses on praise. (The rather tendentious name by which the Psalter is known in Hebrew, תהילים, "Songs of Praise," picks up on the same characterization of the anthology, which is of course by no means limited to songs of praise.) The final chapter of the Psalter is not concerned with Torah study, with recitation or meditation. Indeed, it is not concerned with words at all. Rather, Psalm 150 calls on all living creatures (כֹּל הַנְּשָׁמָה) to praise God through music. Conspicuous in its absence as the psalm specifies the types of music with which to praise God is singing. The whole world should praise God with trumpets and harps, with drums and cymbals—but not, apparently, with the voice. The logocentrism of Psalm 1 is challenged by the non-verbal music of Psalm 150. This summation, then,

25. On the ceaseless nature of study as envisioned by this psalm, see also Weiss, "The Way of Torah," 126.

26. On the emphasis of a life of nearly uninterrupted Torah study in contemporary mitnagdism, see Haym Soloveitchik, "Migration, Acculturation," 216–17. He also notes that the trend in this direction among Israeli Hasidim for reasons that are as much practical as ideological.

27. On the contrast between the two, see especially Walter Brueggemann ("Bounded by Obedience and Praise: The Psalms as Canon," *JSOT* 50 [1991] 63–92, esp. p. 66), who notes, "One would mistake neither of these two Psalms for a routine poem which might turn up anywhere in the collection. It is probable that both Psalm 1 and Psalm 150 have been carefully selected (or created) and placed as they are, in order to provide a special framing for the collection, and to assert the issues that should inform one's reading and singing of the Psalms. The perimeters of the collection thus are *obedience* (Psalm 1) and *praise* (Psalm 150)." Wilson critiques Brueggemann's reading of Psalm 1's role: "The reader is never counseled to 'keep, follow, or obey' the Torah but only to find delight in constant meditation on it. Certainly, canonical wisdom was capable of enjoining its listeners to obedience. . . . Psalm 1 seems rather to encourage an attitude of constant delight in, and meditation on, the Torah as the guide to life rather than to death." See Gerald Wilson, "The Shape of the Book of Psalms," *Int* 46 (1992) 129–42, esp. pp. 136–37. Wilson is correct to critique Brueggemann on this point, but the contrast to which Brueggemann draws our attention remains deeply significant, even if it is better characterized as a contrast between learning and praise or between mitnagdic and hasidic modes of religiosity.

posits a hasidic view of the book that is in tension with its mitnagdic introduction. Further, the two psalms mention different religious artifacts, thus
deepening the contrast between them. Psalm 150 opens with a reference
to God's holy place, which either means the Jerusalem Temple or (if one
sees the word קָדְשׁוֹ as meaning God's heavenly abode, a reading that the
last half of the line supports) at least hints at it. The only locus of religious
meaning mentioned in Psalm 1, on the other hand, is the text of the Torah.
Here again, we find a contrasting set of religious values. One psalm emphasizes the importance of sacred place and perhaps implies the importance
of royalty who sponsor it; the other psalm regards the holy as a function of
the sacred word, open to any who are willing to study it.[28]

Another attempt to characterize the Psalter may appear in Psalm 2.
Like Psalm 1, Psalm 2 seems to play an introductory role; Psalms 1 and 2
stand apart from all the other poems found in the first division or חמֵשׁ of
the Psalter in that neither has a לדוד superscription.[29] It is possible that
Psalm 2 can be taken as an introduction to the first division of the Psalter, just as Psalm 1 is an introduction to the Psalter as a whole.[30] Alternatively, Psalm 2 may once have been the introduction to the Psalter, to which
Psalm 1 was subsequently added as another, rather different, introduction.[31]
(Some support for this speculative suggestion may come from the ancient
tradition, known from some manuscripts of the MT and the New Testament, which numbers what we call Psalm 2 as Psalm 1, leaving what we
call Psalm 1 without a number.[32]) If one can imagine, at least for purposes
of argument, a Psalter that began with Psalm 2, one finds a very different

---

28. On the democratizing trend of study implied in Psalm 1, see Rofé, "Piety," 81, and
idem, "Move," 625.

29.   Wilson points out that the two apparent exceptions, Psalms 10 and 33, are in fact
no exceptions at all, because these psalms are simply continuations of the poems found in
Psalms 9 and 32, respectively, both of which have a לדוד superscription. See Wilson, *Editing*,
155; and the similar argument in Jesper Høgenhaven, "The Opening of the Psalter: A Study of
Jewish Theology," *SJOT* 15 (2001) 169–80, esp. p. 173.

30.   Similarly, Psalm 145 may be the conclusion of the last division of the Psalter; its first
and last verses contain the characteristic language of the doxologies that conclude the four
earlier divisions (בר"כ and עולם). The five hymns of praise in Psalms 146–50 would then be a
concluding set of hymns that cap off the Psalter as a whole. For this view of Psalms 146–50,
see Wilson, *Editing*, 185; and idem, "Shape," 132–33.

31.   See idem, *Editing*, 204; Patrick D. Miller, "The Beginning of the Psalter," in *The Shape
and Shaping of the Psalter* (ed. J. Clinton McCann; JSOTSup 159; Sheffield: JSOT Press, 1993)
83–92, esp. p. 85; Gerald Sheppard, *Wisdom as Hermeneutical Construct: A Study in the Sapiential-
izing of the Old Testament* (BZAW 151; Berlin: de Gruyter, 1980) 139–41.

32.   For a listing of the relevant MT manuscripts, see Wilson, *Editing*, 207. Some manuscripts of Acts 13:11 cite Ps 2:7 as 1:7. It must be admitted that the reference in some manuscripts of Acts might imply not that what we usually call Psalm 1 is unnumbered but that
what we usually call Psalms 1 and 2 are a single Psalm. The opinion in *b. Ber.* 9b–10a of Rabbi
Yehuda son of Rabbi Shimon ben Pazzi, who numbers what we know as Psalms 19 and 104 as

conceptualization of the anthology. Psalm 2 is a royal psalm, and hence as an introduction it emphasizes David's connection to the Psalter. (For this reason, it is an appropriate prelude to the first division, which is the most Davidic of the five divisions in that it has by far the highest proportion of psalms with a לדוד superscription.) The difference between Psalms 1 and 2 reflects a dichotomy that was central to ancient Israelite religion, that between writers deeply committed to the royal family and writers not enthused by the monarchy. Biblical literature frequently wrestles with the question, does God's relationship with Israel flow primarily through the king or through priests and scribes? This question reflects a tension between people who looked toward David as the ideal Israelite in communion with God and those who looked toward Moses as that ideal. For example, first Isaiah was deeply committed to the Davidic monarchy, insisting on its unique and eternal right to the throne. Deutero-Isaiah, on the other hand, rejected the possibility of the renewal of the Davidic monarchy after the exile, viewing God as the only king of Israel; according to this prophet, the whole Israelite nation enjoys the status of a royal family.[33] The literature found within the deuteronomic history is similarly mixed. 2 Samuel 7 represents the apogee of the pro-Davidic viewpoint as it promises David that his descendants will never be removed from the throne, thus presenting God as an advocate of the monarchy. On the other hand, texts such as 1 Samuel 8 regard the monarchy as an unfortunate if unavoidable concession to human frailty. Similar dichotomies appear throughout the canon. The Chronicler consistently idealizes David, and Zech 12:8 comes close to imagining an apotheosis of the Davidic king. On the other hand, texts such as Num 12:6–8 and Deut 34:10–12 regard Moses as the most extraordinary man in Israelite (perhaps human) history. It is no coincidence that the same tension appears at the very beginning of the Psalter. The first introduction to the book looks toward Moses and the mode of religiosity he represents as the best guide for one who will read the Psalms. The second introduction insists that readers should think of David as they sing his songs.[34]

---

18 and 103, respectively, might be taken as additional support for this numbering, though the Gemara there understands this tradition different (see note 00 below). See also Høgenhaven, "Opening," 170–71.

33. See my *Prophet Reads Scripture: Allusion in Isaiah 40–66* (Contraversions; Stanford: Stanford University Press, 1998) 84–88, 112–19, 154.

34. In arguing that these two texts contend with each other, I regard them as separate texts. On the other hand, many scholars argue that Psalms 1–2 are a single unit, which therefore provide a single, if complex, introduction, to the Psalter. The view that Psalms 1–2 is a unified text is already evident in *b. Ber.* 9b–10a. It is based on an inclusio that links them together: note that the word אַשְׁרֵי appears in the first line of Psalm 1 and the last line of Psalm 2. See Miller, "Beginning," 85; and, for further verbal links between these psalms, Marböck, "Frühen Wirkungsgeschichte," 211; Kuntz, "Wisdom Psalms," 152. For an especially comprehensive review of the evidence (including patristic sources not cited in other discussions) and

One additional attempt to present the Psalter may be noted. In the Septuagint, the Psalter ends with a poem not found in the MT, Psalm 151. A fuller Hebrew text of this psalm is known from the Dead Sea Scrolls in 11QPs[a]. The first part of this text (vv. 1–3 in the LXX, which roughly correspond to lines 3–8 in 11QPs[a] column 28) focuses on David as singer whose lyre and songs praise God's creation; the next lines (LXX 151:4–7 and 11QPs[a] 28:8–14) describe David as God's anointed (that is to say, His messiah) and as a heroic warrior. The earlier verses in Psalm 151 stress themes similar to Psalm 150; the latter stress themes similar to Psalm 2. This text, then, deftly combines in a single conclusion[35] two aspects of what I am terming the hasidic apprehension of the Psalter: the emphasis on song and the emphasis on royalty. A Psalter that concludes with Psalm 151 emphasizes the same musical and messianic themes found in a Psalter beginning with Psalm 2 and ending with Psalm 150.

---

secondary literature on this issue, see Høgenhaven, "Opening," 169–72. On the basis of this apparent unity, Sheppard attempts to read the unified text that is now Psalms 1–2 as functioning together to form a single introduction to the Psalter (see Sheppard, *Wisdom*, 136–44), an attempt that I do not regard as holding together. In spite of the verbal connections between these two psalms, the distinct nature of each psalm should not be overlooked. In particular, Psalm 1 begins and ends with its own inclusio that marks this text as a unit (דרך // רשעים, דרך רשעים), as noted by Robert Alter, *The Art of Biblical Poetry* (New York: Basic Books, 1985) 116. For a defense of reading Psalm 1 as its own text (rather than just part of Psalm 1–2), see J. T. Willis, "Psalm 1: An Entity," *ZAW* 91 (1979) 381–40. It seems unnecessary to me to attempt to interpret away the manifest tension between what clearly were (as even Sheppard acknowledges, 139–41) originally two separate texts. Rather, we might note the dialectic that has been created by the placement of these two texts, a dialectic that is not explicitly resolved in the Psalter. For another approach that acknowledges these tensions without artificially resolving them, see Miller, "Beginning," 88–92. For another example of an attempt to resolve these sorts of tensions (in this case, between Psalm 1 as introduction and Psalm 150 as conclusion), see Brueggemann, "Bounded," 68–86. Brueggemann's resolution is, to my mind, clearly artificial, even as it is artful; it presents a compelling theological reflection on the relationship among various psalms, though there is no evidence that the editors of the Psalter intended this particular harmonization. The same may be said of Høgenhaven's attempt to read Psalm 1 in light of the allegedly eschatological elements of Psalm 2. He suggests that these texts form a unified introduction to the Psalter, which emphasizes Mosaic torah and eschatological expectation. This reading summarizes the main theme of each psalm and attributes it to the other, and then declares them a unity because the combined psalm contains both themes. Of course, one could put many other psalms together and produce a similar result. The crucial question regarding this thesis (even if one accepts Høgenhaven's assumption that Psalm 2 deals with the eschaton at all) was already raised by Frantz Delitzsch, as Høgenhaven notes (p. 179 n. 29); unfortunately, Høgenhaven does not succeed in responding to it.

35. In fact, this text probably combines two originally independent poems, one found in lines 11QPs[a]28:3–12 (corresponding, roughly, to LXX 151:1–5), the second in lines 13 and following (corresponding, roughly, to LXX 151:6–7). This becomes clear from the inclusio linking 11QPsa[a] 28:3–4 with 11QPsa[a] 28:11–12. (This inclusio is lost in the abbreviated version in the LXX.) The two poems may have been combined to create a psalm with strong elements of both sides of David, the musical/religious and the heroic/political.

We have seen, then, that ancient editors suggested two different views of the Psalter. In so doing, they created an unresolved debate within the canon. Is David the epitome of a Jew's connection to God, or does Moses take first place even in a Davidic collection? Is the highest way to the deity to be found in song or in study? It is significant that voices on behalf of both viewpoints appear; while Psalm 1 may be said to have superseded Psalm 2 as the primary introduction, Psalm 150 still gives the hasidic stance the last word—at least for someone who has followed Psalm 1's mitnagdic advice and studied the whole Psalter as a textbook.

Precisely the same debate appears in the midrash to Psalm 1 in *Midr. Tehillim.*[36] Indeed, only in light of this debate among various editors of the Psalter are the opening sections of the midrash to Psalm 1 comprehensible. That midrash begins by linking the happy man described in Ps 1:1 with David and goes on to point out that David instituted the 24 watches of priests and Levites (*Midr. Tehillim* 1 §1). This teaching is based on 1 Chronicles 24, but its connection to Ps 1:1 might seem baffling: What has the long bureaucratic list in 1 Chronicles 24 to do with the wisdom saying in Psalm 1:1? In fact, however, this teaching comes to bear on what might be called the canonical debate (that is, the debate implied by the juxtaposition of Psalms 1 and 2 as introductions or by the juxtaposition of Psalms 1 and 150 as introduction and conclusion). More specifically, *Midr. Tehillim* 1 §1 addresses David's relationship to Moses. One might have regarded the priestly and Levitical offices as inherently Mosaic in nature, not only because Moses was a Levite and his brother the ancestor of the priests but also because Moses established both institutions and gave the laws concerning their responsibilities (see, for example, Leviticus 8 and Numbers 18). *Midr. Tehillim* begins, however, by reminding us that it was David who instituted the priestly and Levitical offices as they functioned in the First and Second Temples. In other words, the initial section of *Midr. Tehillim* comes to answer an implied question, which is the same question suggested by the editorial juxtaposition of Psalm 1 and Psalm 2: who is more important, Moses or David?[37] We should pause to note the irony of the answers

---

36. Two recensions exist, but the differences between them do not affect my argument. All subsequent references are to the Buber edition (Solomon Buber, ed., *Midraš Tehillim, Which Is Called Šōḥēr Ṭôb* [Vilna: Romm, 1891]). For an overview of the textual history, see Isaac Kalimi, "*Midrash Psalms Shocher Tov*: Some Theological and Methodological Features and a Case Study—the View of God," in *God's Word for Our World. Theological and Cultural Studies in Honor of Simon John De Vries* (ed. J. Harold Ellens, D. L. Ellens, R. P. Knerim, and I. Kalimi; JSOTSup 389; London: T. & T. Clark, 2004) 63–76, esp. pp. 63–65.

37. To be sure, the themes we see in this section are not unique within *Midr. Tehillim*. As Esther Menn points out, *Midr. Tehillim* frequently goes "far beyond the biblical sources themselves in portraying Israel's greatest king as a founding figure for its holiest site"; see Esther Menn, "Prayerful Origins: David as Temple Founder in Rabbinic Psalms Commentary (*Midrash Tehillim*)," in *Of Scribes and Sages: Early Jewish Interpretation and Transmission of Scripture*

provided by the Psalter and the *Midr. Tehillim*, respectively. The final form of David's Psalter puts Moses (more precisely, Torah) first; but the midrash, composed by the rabbinic sages who regarded themselves as inheritors of Moses' mantle, puts David first. Thus, the sages' first comment on Psalm 1 attempts to overturn the viewpoint of that psalm. The rabbis created a hasidic homily on a mitnagdic text—which in turn attempted to displace the most natural understanding of the Psalter as hasidic![38]

Immediately thereafter, the midrash presents a debate concerning who is permitted to sit in the presence of God (*Midr. Tehillim* §2). Citing 2 Sam 7:18, Rabbi Ḥiyya teaches that no one other than a Davidic king may sit in the Temple courtyard (that is, in the presence of God), a teaching supported by additional traditions coming through Rabbi Ammi from Rabbi Simeon ben Lakish. The midrash points out that even in heaven the angels must stand in the presence of God, which makes the exception granted to Davidic kings even more remarkable. Speaking in his own name. Ammi then denies that Davidic kings were permitted to sit in God's presence, explaining that 2 Sam 7:18 ("And David came and sat [וַיֵּשֶׁב] in God's presence") should be understood to mean merely that David leaned against a wall while standing, or perhaps that David set his mind (יָשֵׂב) toward intense and focused prayer.[39] The midrash then asserts that it was not the king but the high priest who was permitted to sit in the Temple courtyard, as evidenced by 1 Sam 1:9: "And Eli the priest was sitting on his chair at the doorpost of God's Temple."

(ed. Craig Evans; London: Continuum, 2004) *77–89, esp. p. 77. Thus, this passage fits a larger pattern found later in this work. Similarly, the comparison between Moses and David found in *Midr. Tehillim* 1 §1–2 occurs elsewhere in this work; see Menn, 81, and references there. It remains important to aks why these themes are brought forward in a comment on Psalm 1, which seems to deal with neither David nor the Temple.

38. One of their last comments on Psalm 2, interestingly, moves in the other direction (see *Midr. Tehillim* 2 §2). There, Rav understands Ps 2:12 to be a commendation of Torah study—even though Psalm 2 is clearly concerned with royalty, not sagacity. Something similar occurs in 4Q174 (= 4QFlor). The section of this *pesher* that deals with Ps 2:1–2 seems, so far as we can tell from the fragment available, to connect the discussion of the messiah or annointed one in Psalm 2 with בחירי ישראל באחרית הימים, which no doubt refers to the sect itself, its Zadokite leadership, and its Torah-meditating membership. (For this understanding of ישראל בחירי, see especially Yigal Yadin, "A midrash on 2 Sam. vii and Ps i–ii [4QFlorilegium]," *IEJ* 9 [1959] 95–98, esp. p. 98 and n. 30.) In other words, there is an attempt here to insert into the psalm's discussion of the Davidic messiah the theme of the sectarian vision of law and learning—to convert the Davidic into the Toraitic or Mosaic. This tendency is also evident a few lines earlier (lines 11–12), where references to the Davidic messiah in 2 Samuel 7 and Amos 9:11 give occasion to mention not only the Davidic messiah but the priestly sage who stands at his side. On the interpretive nature of the pesher, see also Marböck, "Frühen Wirkungsgeschichte," 217–19; Maier, "Psalm 1," 356; and George Brooke, *Exegesis at Qumran: 4QFlorilegium in Its Jewish Context* (JSOTSup 29; Sheffield: Sheffield Academic Press, 1985) 86–97 and 114–19.

39. On the contradiction between Rabbi Ammi's first and second statements, see Buber, *Midraš Tĕhillîm (Buber)*, 1–2 nn. 8 and 14.

At first glance, this discussion on the right to sit in the presence of the Most High seems tenuously connected to Ps 1:1, on which it purports to comment. The teaching that only Davidic kings may sit in the Temple court is based on 2 Sam 7:18 and need not mention Psalm 1; in fact, most attestations of this saying do not do so, even in cases where they do mention 2 Sam 7:18.[40] But the teaching's relevance to our psalm becomes clear in light of the debate among the editors of the Psalter discussed above. *Midr. Tehillim* 1 §2 is unique among the many rabbinic attestations of the teaching in question: this is the only passage that uses the teaching in question to set up a comparison between David and Eli.[41] The significance of this comparison becomes clear when we recall that Eli is a member of Moses' family. In the standard rabbinic view, he is descended from Moses' brother, Aaron.[42] Thus, the comparison made in *Midr. Tehillim* picks up on the antithesis between Psalm 1 and Psalm 2—that is, between a mitnagdic or sapiential outlook and a hasidic or royalist one. The comparison implies the question: who is of the highest status, David and the kings descended from him or Moses and the priesthood related to him? As is the case in the canonical Psalter, the competition between these polarities is not resolved in the midrash; two answers to the question are presented without either one being rejected. The citation of a rabbinic teaching concerning 2 Sam 7:18 in a midrash on Ps 1:1 might have seemed a nonsequitur, but the application of this teaching here turns out to be deeply connected to the debate sparked by the editorial role of Psalm 1. Put differently: the first unit in

40. See *b. Soṭah* 40b, *b. Soṭah* 41b, *b. Yoma* 25a, *b. Yoma* 69b, *y. Pesaḥ* 5.10 (7d), *y. Yoma* 3.2 (4b), *y. Soṭah* 7.7 (8a). An exception is *Midr. Sam.* 27 §1–2, which contain an extremely abbreviated form of the midrash as found *Midr. Tehillim*.

41. The one text that comes close to making this sort of comparison is *b. Qidd.* 78b. When quoting the tradition that only Davidic kings may sit in the Temple court, this passage notes an apparent exception in 1 Sam 3:3: Samuel sleeps at the temple in Shiloh. Because Samuel was Eli's disciple, his successor, and a fellow Levite (according to rabbinic interpreters who follow 1 Chr 6:17–23 in this matter), this passage might be taken to set up a comparison if not between David and Eli then at least between David and an Eloid. However, see Rashi ad loc.

42. Some modern biblical scholars believe that the Eli was in fact a direct descendant of Moses himself; see Julius Wellhausen, *Prolegomena to the History of Ancient Israel* (trans. Black and Menzies; New York: Meridan, 1957) 142–43; and Frank Moore Cross, *Canaanite Myth and Hebrew Epic: Essays in the History of the Religion of Israel* (Cambridge: Harvard University Press, 1973) 195–217. The Chronicler implies that Eli was descended from Aaron in 1 Chr 24:3 (cf. 1 Sam 22:9–20), and the rabbis follow this view. Either way, the connection of any high priest to the theme of Torah is clear. In a dichotomy between Torah and Psalter, study and prayer, or Sinai and Zion, Eli clearly aligns himself with Torah, study, and Sinai whether he is an Aaronide or a Mushide. That Eli represent an antithesis of Zion is even clearer in light of his connection to Shiloh; cf. Psalm 78, which regards Shiloh as a competitor to Zion, because Zion's rise resulted from Shiloh's fall.

Midr. Tehillim 1 §2 comments not on Ps 1:1 but on the implication of Psalm 1 as introduction and hence on the Psalter's relationship to the Torah. The issues raised by the editorial placement of Psalm 1 recur as the midrash progresses. The last part of *Midr. Tehillim* 1 §2 compares David and Moses:

> "For this is the Torah of man" (2 Sam 7:18). What man? The greatest of the prophets, or the greatest of kings? The greatest of the prophets was Moses, as it is written, "Moses went up to God" (Exod 19:3), and the greatest of kings was David. You find that whatever Moses did, David did. Moses brought the Israelites out of Egypt, and David brought the Israelites out of subjugation to foreign kingdoms.[43] Moses fought a war against Sichon and Og, and David fought a war against all around him . . . Moses reigned over Israel and Judah . . . and David reigned over Israel and Judah. Moses split the sea for Israel, and David split the rivers for Israel . . . Moses built an altar, and David built an altar. This one officiated at a sacrifice, and the other one officiated at a sacrifice. Moses gave the five books of the Torah to Israel, and David gave the five books of Psalms to Israel . . . Moses blessed Israel, saying "Happy are you!" (Deut 33:29), and David blessed Israel, saying "Happy is the man" (Ps 1:1).

The connection of this teaching to Ps 1:1 is not in question, because the passage ends with a reference to this verse. At the same time, its placement near the beginning of *Midr. Tehillim* is telling. Like the two teachings it follows, its subject is, this time explicitly, a comparison of Moses and David. Here again, we find the midrash grappling not so much with the wording of the verse in question but with the issue raised by the editors of the Psalter. Whereas the first teaching in the midrash (1 §1) exalts David over Moses and the second (beginning of 1 §2) presents two opinions, one exalting Davidic kings over all other created beings and the other exalting a Mosaic priest over all other beings, this tradition equates David and Moses. In a rabbinic context, a teaching such as this is perhaps surprising, the more so in an interpretation attached to our mitnagdic or Mosaic psalm.

The midrash to Psalm 1 moves on to other themes in subsequent sections, but it occasionally comes back to our debate. In §5, Rabbi Pineḥas opens a teaching by quoting the line "From the elders I gain learning" (Ps 119:100). He goes on to note a historical chain involving the opening and

---

43. So the standard printed edition. The text of the Buber edition (which follows most of the manuscripts; see Buber's note ad loc.) reads "subjugation of exile." This reading makes little sense, because the Israelites were not in exile immediately prior to David's time. William Braude notes Felix Perles' suggestion that one read "subjugation to Goliath" (גלית) rather than גליות). See William Braude, trans., *The Midrash on Psalms* (Yale Judaica Series; New Haven, CT: Yale University Press, 1959) 2:397 n. 10.

closing words of biblical blessings: God blessed Abraham "with *all* things" (Gen 24:1); of Abraham we read in turn, "*all* he had he *gave* to Isaac" (Gen 25:5); Isaac began his blessing to Jacob with the words, "May God *give* you the dew of heaven" (Gen 27:28), a passage that ends with the words "Isaac *called* Jacob and blessed him" (Gen 28:1); the narrative of Jacob's blessing of his sons begins with the words, "Jacob *called* his sons" (Gen 49:1) and ends with the words, "*This* is what their father said when he blessed them" (Gen 49:28); Moses picked up the chain in his final blessing to Israel, which is introduced with the word, "*This* is the blessing that Moses spoke to all Israel" (Deut 33:1), and he ended the blessing with the words "*Happy* are you, O Israel" (Deut 33:29). David finishes the chain, beginning his book with the words "*Happy* is the man" (Ps 1:1). One might argue that, because David is the culmination of the chain, he represents its apogee and enjoys a place of honor greater than those who come before, including Moses. (Indeed, as the last link he is chiastically paired with God.) On the other hand, the whole teaching begins with a verse from Psalm 119, which emphasizes the value of learning from one's forebears. Thus the teaching may be intended to stress that what David did was merely an imitation of the great ones before him; moreover, Ps 119:100 emphasizes elders and learning, a motif that underscores a mitnagdic trope. [44]

A comparison of the Psalter to the Torah occurs slightly later in our text, in *Midr. Tehillim* 1 §8. There we are told that David expressed the hope that his book would not be read like the books of Homer. He wishes, rather, that people will read it and meditate on it. By doing so, they will merit reward as though they had studied the mishnaic tractates concerning leprosy and concerning impurity that results from the presence of a dead body in a dwelling (two of the most difficult and technical parts of the Mishna). The locus of value assumed by this comment is Mosaic law; David's own book can only aspire to match its value. On the other hand, this comment at least suggests that one might be able to gain the sort of merit associated with Torah study through recitation of Psalms, which puts the Psalter on the same level as Torah—at least if the Psalter is studied as a mitnagdic text.

The midrash addresses the relation between prayer and study directly in 1 §16, which comments on Ps 1:2 ("But he takes delight in Yhwh's Torah, studying His Torah day and night"). Rabbi Eliezer asserts there that

44. My comment on the significance of Ps 119:100 assumes that Rabbi Pineḥas understands this verse as the rabbis usually do, and as I translated it above. That reading of the verse suggests a devolution from generation to generation, reflecting the idea that whatever value later figures have is derived from the earlier figures on which they draw. On the other hand, the contextual and grammatical meaning of the verse suggests an ascending model of value: "I understand more than the elders." If Rabbi Pineḥas understood the verse this way, then he may have intended to exalt David above all who came before.

Israel wanted to study Torah all the time (to the exclusion of all other activities), but they did not have the opportunity to do so. God reassured them, saying that by observing the commandment of wearing *tefillin* or prayer-phylacteries, they bring on themselves merit equal to that gained by constant study. Rabbi Joshua suggests another response by God (perhaps because he was troubled by Eliezer's suggestion, which substituted a commandment observed only in the daytime for the study of Torah that should have taken place day and night). According to Joshua, the recitation of the Shema prayer in the morning and in the evening can be the functional substitute for constant Torah study. In spite of their differences, Eliezer and Joshua share a basic perspective: some form of prayer (whether non-verbal prayer through the donning of *tefillin* or verbal prayer through the recitation of the Shema) can be the moral equivalent of Torah study. Bar Qappara, however, has a very different suggestion: a person who recites two chapters from Scripture each morning and two each evening has, for all practical purposes, fulfilled the ideal of constant Torah study. Rabbi Ḥiyya explains that Bar Qappara meant not only that a person should recite the two chapters but should engage in their elucidation; the requirement, then, involves not only two chapters of Written Torah but two *halachot* or legal traditions from the Oral Torah as well. This section moves on to other matters, ending with a statement of Rabbi Naḥman in the name of Rabbi Mani: a person who praises God seven times a day (in accordance with Ps 119:164) has performed the equivalent of constant Torah study. In 1 §16, then, *Midr. Tehillim* gives voice to rabbis who assert the hasidic viewpoint (Eliezer, Joshua, Naḥman, and Mani) as well as ones who uphold the mitnagdic view (Bar Qappara, Ḥiyya). While the last word comes from one of the former, no definitive resolution is reached.

Midr. Tehillim, in short, begins by addressing precisely the same question implied by the redactional setting of Psalm 1: Is the Psalter fundamentally a hasidic or mitnagdic book? The midrash directs our attention to two aspects of this polarity: the dichotomy between king and priest or sage and the dichotomy between prayer and study. It provides a range of answers to the implied question. In so far as it includes voices that value David over Moses or at least put them on an equal footing, it undermines Psalm 1's attempt to transform the Psalter into a mitnagdic anthology. At the same time, it allows for a variety of rabbinic opinions to be expressed on the issue. Thus the midrash to Psalm 1 reenacts the juxtaposition evident in the final form of the Psalter, which begins with a mitnagdic voice in Psalm 1, moves directly to a hasidic voice in Psalm 2, and ends with another hasidic voice in Psalm 150.

In this essay, I have attempted to draw a comparison between the explicit discussions of the rabbis in *Midr. Tehillim* 1 and the implied discussions of the redactors who placed Psalms 1, 2, and 150 in their canonical locations (and also the implied discussion of the redactors who placed Psalm 151 in its location in the LXX or its Vorlage). This sort of comparison may provide an example of, or a model for, the creation of Jewish biblical theology. Whereas some Protestant (especially Childsean) models for biblical theology emphasize the work of the final redactors (and hence attempt either to harmonize the tension between Psalm 1 and Psalms 2 and 150[45] or to privilege the voice of what we think is the final redactor[46]), a Jewish biblical theology should put no particular emphasis on the redactor.[47] Thus, the message of the redactor who made Psalm 1 the abstract for the Psalter is not definitive for a Jewish exegete. But the questions implied by the redactional placement of Psalm 1 emerge as Jewishly interesting for two reasons. The first of these is the fact that rabbinic exegetes picked up on those questions, even as they sometimes answered it in ways differing from the proposal of Psalm 1 itself. The second is the fact that the questions with which the redactors and *Midr. Tehillim* are concerned are addressed not only in the midrash to Psalm 1 but in many other parts of rabbinic and postrabbinic Jewish literature, usually in formulations that do not refer to Psalm 1 itself (for example, in the Talmudic passages quoted at the outset of this essay). In other words, it is not merely the work of the redactors but postbiblical Jewish tradition that must guide an attempt to generate a Jewish biblical theology, and in this particular case, Jewish tradition clearly used the ancient debate among the psalms' redactors as a starting point for continuing and extending the redactors' discourse.[48]

45. E.g., see Sheppard, *Wisdom*, 136–44.

46. See Wilson, "Shape," 137–38. Wilson argues there that in light of the placement of Psalm 1, "the psalms are no longer to be sung as human response to God but are to be meditated upon day and night as the source of the divine word of life to us." Building on this conclusion, he further maintains the final redaction of the Psalter must have occurred after the year 70 C.E.: "It is difficult for me to understand how such a move from performance to meditation could have taken place during a time in which the temple was in operation and the psalms in constant public worship. To appropriate these performance pieces for private meditation would seem to necessitate a period of considerable time in which Temple worship was interrupted and there was little hope of reestablishing it." This reasoning is flawed. We need not assume the rigid either/or dichotomy on which Wilson's conclusion is built. That the Psalter is to be studied does not mean that it cannot be used liturgically. Indeed, even a post-70 dating of the psalter would still assume both uses, even thought the liturgical use would occur now in synagogues rather than the Temple. Similarly, the Psalter could have been both studied and chanted while the Temple still stood.

47. Cf. my "Scroll of Isaiah as Jewish Scripture, or, Why Jews Don't Read Books," in *Society of Biblical Literature 1996 Seminar Papers* (Atlanta: Scholars Press, 1996) 225–42; and, more briefly, my "Revelation at Sinai in the Hebrew Bible and Jewish Theology," 423. Some Christian thinkers express similar qualms about the canon criticism and its theological application; see, for example, James Barr, *Holy Scripture: Canon, Authority, Criticism* (Philadelphia: Westminster, 1983) 49–74.

48. In the particular case under discussion, the rabbinic answers largely follow in the path of the biblical answers, because the rabbinic answers, like the redactors' answers, can be

A description of this particular crossgenerational discussion is especially representative of Jewish biblical theology. In the end, neither the Psalter nor *Midr. Tehillim* provides a definitive answer to the questions at hand. Both contain hasidic as well as mitnagdic voices, and any reading of the Psalter's final form or of the midrash that privileges one perspective over another is a reflection of the reader, not of the texts themselves. One could, for example claim that the first psalm is the most important and hence that the Psalter is ultimately mitnagdic; but one could just as easily argue that the last Psalm is conclusive, and therefore the Psalter is hasidic. Similarly, Jewish tradition in its widest senses never fully resolves the debate concerning prayer and study or the controversy regarding the most ideal model of leadership. While the Talmuds clearly lean in one direction, many alternative voices are preserved in their pages, and even more appear in aggadic rabbinic literature outside the Talmuds. Further, we have seen that later forms of Judaism continue the debate; it is significant that Hasidism, which began by emphasizing one of these sets of values in the 18th century, moved within a few generations to a sort of rapprochement with the other, even as the Mitnagdim produced thinkers who valued direct contact with God and messianism. The biblical redactors, then, did not so much provide an answer as an agenda concerning what issues are to be pondered. Consequently, a Jewish biblical theology need not—in fact, should not—set for itself the goal of definitely stating what the Bible says; rather, it should look for what the Bible invites us to attend to, and it should examine how rabbinic and later Jewish literatures pick up that invitation. It is by attending to the same issues and by turning them over and turning them over again, that Jewish biblical theology can become part of the all-encompassing discussion that is Torah.

---

readily classified as either hasidic or mitnagdic. It is also possible, however, that postbiblical thinkers will continue to address the biblical questions while providing new sorts of answers. In questions of theodicy, for example, the rabbinic doctrine of postmortem reward and punishment and the Lurianic idea of divine self-restriction or *ṣimṣūm* are only barely adumbrated in biblical texts.

14

Reflections on Job's Theology

MOSHE GREENBERG

Job is a book not so much about God's justice as about the transformation of a man whose piety and view of the world were formed in a setting of wealth and happiness and into whose life burst calamities that put an end to both. How can piety nurtured in prosperity prove to be truly deep-rooted and disinterested and not merely a spiritual adjunct of good fortune ("God has been good to me so I am faithful to Him")? Can a man pious in prosperity remain pious when he is cut down by anarchical events that belie his orderly view of the world? The book of Job tells how one man suddenly awakened to the anarchy rampant in the world, yet his attachment to God outlived the ruin of his tidy system.

Job is a pious believer who is struck by misfortune so great that it cannot be explained in the usual way as a prompting to repentance, a warning, let alone a punishment (the arguments later addressed to him by his friends). His piety is great enough to accept the misfortune without rebelling against God: "Should we accept only good from God and not accept evil?" (2:10). But his inability, during seven days of grief in the company of his silent friends, to find a reasonable relation between the misfortune and the moral state of its victims (himself and his children) opens Job's eyes to the fact that in the world at large the same lack of relation prevails (9:22–24, 12:6–9, 21:7–34). Until then, the crying contradiction between the idea of a just order and the reality of individual destinies had, because of his prosperity, hardly been visible to Job. He may not have been as simple as his friends, but neither was he more perceptive than Elihu, who, at the end (chaps. 32–37), offers those above-mentioned explanations of misfortune. But Job now knows their absurdity and their inadequacy to save a reasonable divine order according to human standards of morality.

The prologue of the book, telling of Satan's wager and the subsequent disaster that befell Job, has been a scandal to many readers. But the

Author's note: This essay is slightly revised by the editor, I. Kalimi, from M. Greenberg, *Studies in the Bible and Jewish Thought* (Philadelphia: Jewish Publication Society, 1995) 327–33. Thanks go to the editor and to the Jewish Publication Society for permission to republish this essay.

prologue is necessary, first of all, to establish Job's righteousness. To depict the effect of dire misfortune that demolishes the faith of a perfectly blameless man in a just divine order is the author's purpose. The book is not merely an exposition of ideas, a theological argument, but the portrayal of a spiritual journey from simple piety to the sudden painful awareness and eventual acceptance of the fact that inexplicable misfortune is the lot of man. Without the prologue, we would lack the essential knowledge that Job's misfortune really made no sense; without the prologue, the friends' arguments that misfortune indicates sin would be plausible, and Job's resistance to them liable to be construed as moral arrogance. The prologue convinces us from the outset of Job's integrity; hence, we can never side with the friends. For Job is a paradigm.[1] He personifies every pious man who, when confronted with an absurd disaster, is too honest to lie in order to justify God. The author must convince his readers that Job's self-estimation is correct and that therefore his view of moral disorder in God's management of the world is warranted. That is one purpose of the prologue.

Satan's wager and God's assent to it dramatize a terrible quandary of faith: a pious man whose life has always been placid can never know whether his faith in God is more than an interested bargain—a convenience that has worked to his benefit—unless it is tested by events that defy the postulate of a divine moral order. Only when unreasonable misfortune erupts into a man's life can he come to know the basis of his relation to God, thus allaying doubts (personified here by Satan) that both he and others must harbor about his faith. To conquer these doubts by demonstrating that disinterested devotion to God can indeed exist is necessary for man's spiritual well-being; God's acquiescence in Satan's wager expresses this necessity. The terrible paradox is that no righteous man can measure his love of God unless he suffers a fate befitting the wicked.

The speeches of Job reveal the collapse of his former outlook. For the first time in his life, he has become aware of the prevalence of disorder in the government of the world. In his former state of well-being, Job would hardly have countenanced in himself or in others a death wish; in his misfortune, however, he expresses it vehemently (3:11–23). Could Job, in his prosperity, have appreciated the anguish of victims of senseless misfortune, or could he have regarded God as an enemy of man (7:17–21, 9:13–24, 16:9–14)? Job would previously have responded to despair of God as his friends and Elihu responded to him in his misery and despair. For Job's friends were his peers ideologically no less than socially; he belonged to their circle both in deed and in creed. A chasm opened between him and them only because of a disaster that Job alone knew to be undeserved.

---

1. "He never was or existed," says a Talmudic rabbi, "except as an example" (*b. Bab. Bat.* 15a).

Job's pathetic appeals for a bill of indictment (10:2, 13:18ff., 23:1ff., 31:35–36) belong to the context of the neat, orderly system in which he had once believed. One wonders whether such repeated affirmations of his innocence are not aimed as much toward his friends as toward God, in an effort to break down their complacency. But because his friends neither have undergone his suffering nor share his confidence in his own righteousness, they will not question the validity or give up the security of their system.

Though Job never tires of denouncing the inadequacy of his former concept of the divine government (a concept to which his friends still adhere), his complaints are addressed to God. The orderly fabric of his life has been irreparably rent, yet his relation to God persists. We shall soon consider how that could be.

The outcome of the drama is that the collapse of a complacent view of the divine economy can be overcome. For Job, this came about through a sudden, overwhelming awareness of the complexity of God's manifestation in reasonless phenomena of nature. Job's flood of insight comes in a storm (סערה)—we may suppose, through the experience of its awesomeness. One may compare and contrast the midrashic wordplay that has Job hearing God's answer out of a "hair" (שערה), from contemplation of a microcosm. The grand vista of nature opens before Job, and it reveals the working of God in a realm other than man's moral order. Job responds to and thus gets a response from the numinous presence underlying the whole panorama; he hears God's voice in the storm. The fault in the moral order—the plane on which God and man interact—is subsumed under the totality of God's work, not all of which is reasonable. Senseless calamity loses some of its demoralizing effect when morale does not depend entirely on the comprehensibility of the phenomena but, rather, on the conviction that they are pervaded by the presence of God. As nature shows, this does not necessarily mean that they are sensible and intelligible.

It has been objected that God's speeches (chaps. 38–41) are irrelevant to Job's challenge. God—the objection runs—asserts his power in reply to a challenge to his moral government. But this sets up a false dichotomy. To be sure, God's examples from nature are exhibitions of his power, but they are also exhibitions of his wisdom and his providence for his creatures (38:27; 39:1–4, 26). Through nature, God reveals himself to Job as both purposive and nonpurposive, playful and uncanny, as evidenced by the monsters he created. To study nature is to perceive the complexity, the unity of contraries, in God's attributes, and the inadequacy of human reason to explain his behavior, not the least in his dealings with man.

For it may be inferred that, in God's dealings with man, this complexity is also present—a unity of opposites: reasonability, justice, playfulness, uncanniness (the latter appearing demonic in the short view). When Job recognizes in the God of nature, with his fullness of attributes, the very same God revealed in his own individual destiny, the tumult in his soul is stilled. He has fathomed the truth concerning God's character; he is no longer tortured by a concept that fails to account for the phenomena, as did his former notion of God's orderly working (42:1–6).

If God is a combination of divergent attributes and is a cause of misfortune, why does Job not reject him? `What had Job known of God in his former happy state? He had known him as one who confers order and good. Basking in his light, Job's life had been suffused with blessings (29:2–5). No later evidence to the contrary could wipe out Job's knowledge of God's benignity gained from personal experience. Job calls that former knowledge of God a "hearing," while his latter knowledge, earned through suffering, is a "seeing" (42:5); that is, the latter knowledge gained about God is to the former as seeing is to hearing—far more comprehensive and adequate. Formerly, Job had only a limited notion of God's nature—as a benign, constructive factor in his life, "good" in terms of human morality. At that time, any evidence that ran against this conception of God was peripheral: it lay outside Job's focus. He assumed that it too could somehow be contained in his view of the divine moral order, but nothing pressed him to look the uncongenial facts in the face.

But misfortune moved the periphery into the center, and the perplexity that ensued is a testimony to Job's piety, for he was not transformed by senseless misfortune into a scoffer—a denier of God—but, instead, he was thrown into confusion. His experience of God in good times had left on him an indelible conviction of God's goodness that clashed with the new, equally strong evidence of God's enmity. Though one contradicted the other, Job experienced both as the work of God, and did not forget the first (as did his wife) when the second overtook him.

The author of Job had a dedication to theological honesty and a passion to teach the reality of God's relation to man that are unique in the Bible.[2] Job cannot rest after the collapse of his old outlook until he has come to a better one, more congruent with the facts of experience. How highly the author prizes right knowledge of God is revealed by his final estimate of Job's friends. Although they argued in evident good faith in the epilogue God is angry at them and declares them in need of forgiveness (42:7–8). Wrong thinking about God is reprehensible. One might say that an aim of the author of Job is to warn men away from culpable misconceptions of this sort. After Job, God is not willing to be conceived of in the friends' terms; after Job, such views are abhorrent to him.

---

2. Qoheleth shares with Job the clear-eyed vision of a flawed moral governance of the world, but he has none of Job's anguished perplexity. This is because Qoheleth, by all appearances, never had Job's experience of the goodness of God, with which the anarchy in the world might clash. Job might well have turned cynical had he never "heard" God in his earlier days.

To the very end, Job remains ignorant of the true cause of his misfortunes, for he never learns of Satan's wager. Job appears to have found consolation in his realization of the complexity of God, but the reader knows more: he knows that Job's suffering was the result of a divine bet on Job's disinterested piety.

Why couldn't Job, like Abraham, have been told at the end that the entire event was a trial, and have heard, as did Abraham, "Now I know that you fear God" (Gen 22:12)?

From the epilogue, it is clear that God's vindication of Job's honesty, proven in his passionate recriminations against God and against his friends' simplistic theories, is more important for Job than knowing the reason for his suffering. The epilogue shows Job satisfied by the divine assurance that his friends' arguments were specious, as he had always asserted (13:7–10, 19:22–29, 42:7–9). Beyond that, God does not go in revealing to Job the cause of his suffering.

Abraham's case is not identical to Job's, for, in the end, Abraham did not sacrifice Isaac, whereas Job lost all his children and his possessions. It was dreadful enough for Abraham to learn that his God was capable of subjecting his followers to trials that brought them to the verge of disaster, even though he rescued them at the last moment. For Job to have learned that his family and his possessions had been annihilated because of a mere wager with Satan—that he had been a pawn in a celestial game— would have been far harder to accept than was the mystery of a God partly known, partly hidden, whose overall work is nevertheless good. For it is easier to bear a mixture of benignity and enmity, with their ultimate meaning clouded in mystery, than to accept cold-blooded toying with the fortunes and lives of men.

Nonetheless, the framework story says that one reason for senseless suffering is to test the motives of a pious man. This is stated only as the particular circumstance of this case and not as a general principle: One pious man, famous for his integrity, was visited with calamity for no reason other than to prove his character. That the same reason may apply to other pious men on whom senseless calamity falls is not said. But it is a possibility, one that lends a potentially heroic dimension to every such case, that is the exemplary value of the book.

Job ends up a wiser man, for he sees better the nature of God's work in the world and recognizes the limitations of his former viewpoint. The manifestation of his peace with God, of his renewed spiritual vigor, is that he reconstitutes his life. He is a vessel into which blessings can be poured; he who wished to have died at birth now fathers new sons and daughters. That, in addition to its answering the demands of simple justice, is the significance of the epilogue (which many critics have belittled as crass).

This concept of God contradicts not only that of the wisdom of the book of Proverbs (in which the principle of just individual retribution is iterated in its simplest form) but that of the Torah and the Prophets as well. These writings bear the imprint of God's saving acts, the exodus and the conquest; they represent God as the maintainer of the moral order and interpret events in terms of reward and punishment. But the Torah and the Prophets refer to the nation more than to the individual, and in their time no situation arose in which that concept failed. On the national level, Israel could always be regarded as falling short of righteousness and integrity; there were always elements within it that could rightly be reproached as deserving of punishment and, under the principle of collective responsibility established by the public covenant, of tainting the people at large with their guilt.

The later inability to find an explanation for national destiny in the Torah and the Prophets is reflected not in Job, but in the apocalyptic literature that arose in the Hellenistic period. There was no explanation in the tradition for the persecution by Antiochus IV, which singled out those loyal to God while leaving the apostates in peace. The faithful were reconciled to their suffering only because they saw it as the preordained prelude to an eventual spiritual domination of the world by the Saints of the Most High (Dan 7:27). Taking his cue from hints in the Suffering Servant passages of Isaiah (also a response to those perplexed by a topsy-turvy world in which the heathen prospered and the devotees of the Lord were humiliated), the apocalyptic visionary of Daniel perceived the suffering of the righteous as a necessary phase in a determined sequence of universal salvation. Thus, he lent a significance to the reasonless suffering of his community that was outside the categories of ordinary justice.

Is the retention in the biblical canon of Proverbs alongside Job, or the Torah and the Prophets alongside the apocalypses of Daniel, just thoughtless conservatism?

The religious sensibility apparently absorbs or even affirms the contradictions embodied in these books. That may be because these contradictions are perceived to exist in reality.[3] One can see in individual life as in collective life a moral causality (which the religious regard as divinely maintained; indeed, as a reflection of God's attributes): evil recoils on the evildoers, whether individual or collective; goodness brings blessings. At the same time, the manifestation of this causality can be so erratic or so delayed as to cast doubt on its validity as the single key to the destiny of people and nations. Hence, the sober believer does not pin his or her faith solely on a simple axiom of the divine maintenance of moral causality, but neither will he or she altogether deny its force. No single key unlocks the

---

3. On this issue in the Hebrew Bible, see also I. Kalimi, "The Task of Hebrew Bible / Old Testament Theology: Between Judaism and Christianity," *Early Jewish Exegesis and Theological Controversy: Studies in Scriptures in the Shadow of Internal and External Controversies* (Jewish and Christian Heritage 2; Assen: Van Gorcum, 2002) 135–59, esp. p. 141.

mystery of destiny: "Within our ken is neither the tranquility of the wicked nor the suffering of the righteous" (Mishnah, *Abot.* 4:17), but, for all that, the sober believer does not endorse nihilism. Wisdom, Torah, and Prophets continue to represent for him one aspect of causality in events that he can confirm in his own private experience. But this is one aspect only. The other stands beyond his moral judgment, though it is still under God: namely, the mysterious or preordained decree of God, toward which the proper attitude is "Though he slay me, yet will I trust in him" (Job 13:15, Qere).

Fear of Annihilation and Eternal Covenant: The Book of Esther in Judaism and Jewish Theology

Isaac Kalimi

I. The Book of Esther
and the Dead Sea Scrolls' Community

Among the bulk of about 800 manuscripts from the eleven caves of Qumran, which include approximately 200 biblical manuscripts (the majority are partial copies), the book of Esther is completely missing.[1] There is not even a small fraction of the 167 verses of the 10 chapters of Esther to be found![2]

We do not have any concrete evidence, that is, a written document, that expresses the position of any member of the Qumran community toward the book of Esther. However, several assumptions have been made about the absence of Esther at Qumran, as I have discussed elsewhere.[3] Nonetheless, the absence of the book of Esther altogether from among the Dead Sea Scrolls *cannot be a model* representing the general attitude of the Jewish people toward the book. One must keep in mind that the whole

---

1. This is also the case with the book of Nehemiah, unless we assume that this book was combined with the book of Ezra (as it was considered, indeed, by many other sources later on; see I. Kalimi, *The Reshaping of Ancient Israelite History in Chronicles* [Winona Lake, IN: Eisenbrauns, 2005] 8 n. 28; idem, *Zur Geschichtsschreibung des Chronisten* [BZAW 226; Berlin: de Gruyter, 1995] 7–8 n. 26; idem, *The Book of Chronicles: Historical Writing and Literary Devices* [BEL 18; Jerusalem: Bialik Institute, 2000] 9 n. 28 [Hebrew]), from which three fragments have been found.

2. See S. White Crawford, "Has *Esther* Been Found at Qumran? 4*Qproto-Esther* and the *Esther* Corpus," *Revue de Qumran* 17 (1996) 307–25, esp. pp. 307, 325; idem, "Esther, the Book of," *Encyclopedia of the Dead Sea Scrolls* (ed. L. Schiffman and J. VanderKam; 2 vols.; Oxford: Oxford University Press, 2000) 1:269–70.

3. For a brief survey of the various opinions, see C. A. Moore, *Esther: Translated with an Introduction and Notes* (AB 7B; Garden City, NY: Doubleday, 1971) xxi–xxii; S. White Crawford, "Esther, the Book of," 269; I. Kalimi, "The Book of Esther and the Dead Sea Scroll's Community," *Theologische Zeitschrift* 60 (2004) 101–6.

community of Qumran was comprised of, probably, no more than several hundred members![4] This small isolated Jewish community was, as a matter of fact, a marginal *minority* among the Jewish people at the late Commonwealth era. The *majority* of Jewish people, however, had a very different approach this fascinating book.

II. THE PLACE OF THE BOOK OF ESTHER IN JUDAISM AND JEWISH THEOLOGY

1. The Place of Esther in Judaism[5]

Despite the forethought of some rabbis toward the book of Esther,[6] it has canonized and achieved a respectful place among the hagiographical books of the Hebrew Bible. According to a *beraita* (that is, external Mishnah) in the Babylonian Talmud (*Bab. Bat.* 14b), most of the oldest codices, and the printed editions of the Hebrew Bible, the book of Esther appears before the late historical books, Ezra, Nehemiah, and Chronicles,[7] and in many cases even before the book of Daniel.[8] Esther was translated into Greek (probably at the end of the 2nd century B.C.E.), and six legendary additions (altogether, 107 verses) were attached to it. Certainly, these testify to the popularity of the book in the late Commonwealth era, at least among the Jewish Hellenistic communities.[9] Moreover, in his *Jewish Antiq-*

---

4. This assumption is based generally on the archaeological remains at Qumran. As of today, the exact number in the Qumranic community is unknown. However, what is known is that the cemeteries of the community hold about 1,100 tombs. These served the community for more than 200 years. Unfortunately, Roland de Vaux, who excavated the site, never published the final report of the data. See J. C. VanderKam, *The Dead Sea Scrolls Today* (Grand Rapids: Eerdmans, 1994) 14–15.

5. This part of the chapter is a revised and expounded version of my article in *Theologische Zeitschrift* 59 (2003) 193–204.

6. See Babylonian Talmud, *Meggilah* 7a: "Rabbi Samuel ben Judah said: Esther sent to the Sages saying, 'Commemorate me for future generations.' They replied, 'you will incite the ill will of the nations against us.' She sent back reply: 'I am already recorded in the chronicles of the kings of Media and Persia.'" For the absence of the book of Esther from among the Dead Sea Scrolls, see I. Kalimi, "The Book of Esther and the Dead Sea Scrolls' Community," 101–6.

7. This is contrary to the Christian Bible, in which Esther is located after Ezra, Nehemiah, and Chronicles. See I. Kalimi, "The Book of Esther in Christian Tradition," forthcoming.

8. For the comparison of the codices, see L. B. Paton, *A Critical and Exegetical Commentary on the Book of Esther* (ICC; Edinburgh: T. & T. Clark, 1908) 1–3.

9. For the brief description of the additions, their secondary feature, original language, date, and authorship, see C. A. Moore, *Daniel, Esther and Jeremiah: The Additions: A New Translation with Introduction and Commentary* (AB 44; Garden City, NY: Doubleday, 1977) 153–72; I. Kottsieper, *Zusätze zu Ester* (ATDA 5; Göttingen: Vandenhoeck & Ruprecht, 1998) 109–207; S. White Crawford, *The Additions to Esther—Introduction, Commentary and Reflections* (NIB 3; Nashville, TN: Abingdon, 1999) 945–72.

uities (*Antiquitates Judaicae*), Josephus Flavius devoted an extensive section to recounting Esther's narrative (*Ant.* 11.184–296). Various rabbinic writings—*halachic* (that is, Jewish religious law) as well as *aggadic* (that is, the homiletic and nonlegalistic exegetical texts)—flourished around Esther. In the Mishnah, the Jerusalem Talmud, and Babylonian Talmud, a special tractate was dedicated to it—*Masechet Megillah*. This tiny book is not lacking from the Tosefta (that is, the supplement to the Mishnah) and is the subject of a special homiletical collection (*Midrash Esther Rabbah*), two major Targums (that is, Aramaic translations), and a central place in the Purim liturgy. The central place of Esther in Judaism emerges especially when one compares it with a similar story about another heroine—Judith—and the book named after her—the book of Judith—which are completely ignored in Josephus's writings as well as in the entirety of rabbinic literature. This fact is emphasized all the more against the background that many Jewish religious aspects are mentioned in the book of Judith (name of God, prayers, Judith's righteousness, and so on)[10] but are totally nonexistent in the book of Esther.[11]

Moreover, several sages expressed the view that "Esther was composed under the inspiration of the holy spirit" (*b. Meg.* 7a).[12] Other rabbis are even of the opinion that "this scroll was given (literally: stated) to Moses at Sinai," and they bridged the hundreds of years that separate the age of Moses from that of Esther by saying, "There are no considerations of early or later in the Torah" (*y. Meg.* 1.5 [7a]). Rabbi Simeon ben Lakish (ca. 300) considered the holiness of Esther to be at the same level as the holiness of the Torah, that is, greater than the books of the Prophets and any other book in the Hagiographa/Writings. He maintained that, in time to come, all the books of the Bible would be annulled except the Five Books of Moses and the book of Esther (*y. Meg.* 1.5 [7b]). This means that, even in the Messianic era, hatred of Jews and the miraculous existence of the Jewish people should be remembered!

In addition, the rabbis portrayed Queen Esther very positively. Contrary to the Qumran community, they did not rebuke her for intermarriage with a non-Jewish man and her decree to fast on Passover;[13] rather they attempted to find some excuses for her behavior (*b. Sanh.* 74b; *b. Meg.* 15a). The Sages glorified her righteousness and modesty (*b. Meg.* 10b; 13b), and she was counted among the seven prophetesses who prophesied to Israel: Sarah, Miriam, Deborah, Hannah, Aevigail, Huldah, and Esther (*b. Meg.*

10. See, for example, Jdt 5:17; 8:4–6; 12:7; 16:22 (Judith's righteousness); 5:18; 8:8, 11–27; 10:5; 12:1–5, 19; 16:22 (her prayers).

11. On this issue, see also below in this study.

12. For the English translation, see M. Simon, *Megillah: Translated into English with Notes, Glossary and Indices* (London: Soncino, 1938) 35–36.

13. See, in detail, Kalimi, "The Book of Esther and the Dead Sea Scrolls' Community."

14a). Accordingly, Esth 5:1 ("And it was the third day, and Esther clothed herself in royalty") was expounded by Rabbi Elazar in the name of Rabbi Hanina: "This teaches that Esther was clothed in the divine spirit" (*b. Meg.* 15a). Moreover, the Sages praised Mordecai no less than Esther:

> Mordecai in his generation was equal to Moses in his. . . . Just as Moses stood in the breach . . . so did Mordecai, as it is written, "Seeking the good of his people and speaking peace to all his seed" (Esth 10:3). . . . Some say he was equal to Abraham in his generation. Just as our father Abraham allowed himself to be cast into a fiery furnace and converted his fellowmen and made them acknowledge the greatness of the Holy One, blessed be He . . . so in the days of Mordecai men acknowledged the greatness of the Holy One, blessed be He, as it says (Esth 8:17): "and many of the people of the land became Jews," and he proclaimed the unity of God's name and sanctified it. (*Esther Rabbah* 6.2)[14]

In medieval times, several commentaries were dedicated to the book of Esther, such as the Arabic commentary of Rav Saadia Gaon (882–942), *Ketab Alainas* ("The book of Society"), of which only some fragments remain. The comprehensive and complete commentary to the book of Esther has been written by the prominent Karite commentator, Japhet ben Ali Halevi (Basra [Iraq] and Jerusalem, active ca. 960–1005).[15] Well known are the commentaries on Esther that were composed in northern France, such as those of Rabbi Shelomo Yitzchaki (Rashi; 1040–1105) and Rabbi Samuel ben Meir (Rashbam; 1080–1160). It is especially worthwhile to mention the two commentaries of Rabbi Abraham ibn Ezra (1089–1164)[16] and the commentary of Rabbi Levi ben Gershom (Ralbag; 1288–1344) from Provence.[17] It should be emphasized that Rabbi Moshe ben Maimon (Maimonides; 1135–1204) composed a commentary only on one biblical book: the book of Esther.[18] He reinforced the above-mentioned statement of

14. For the English translation, compare M. Simon, *Midrash Rabbah Esther* (3rd ed.; London: Soncino, 1983) 73–74.

15. On Saaidia Gaon and Japhet ben Ali Halevi and their literary and exegetical activities, see I. Kalimi, *The Retelling of Chronicles in Jewish Literature: A Historical Journey* (Winona Lake, IN: Eisenbrauns, 2009) 191–97 and references there to earlier secondary literature. Ben Ali's commentary on Esther is published recently by M. G. Wechsler, *The Arabic Translation and Commentary of Yefet ben 'Eli the Karaite on the Book of Esther* (Leiden: Brill, 2008).

16. On ibn Ezra's commentaries on Esther, see M. Gómez Aranda, *Dos Comentarios de Abraham ibn Ezra al Libro de Ester: Edición Crítica, Traducción y Estudio Itroductorio* (Madrid: Instituto de Filologia, 2007).

17. On this issue, see B. D. Walfish, *Esther in Medieval Garb: Jewish Interpretation of the Book of Esther in the Middle Ages* (Albany, NY: State University of New York Press, 1993).

18. See J. J. Revlin, *The Commentary on the Book of Esther by Maimonides* (Jerusalem: Krynfiss, 1950 [Hebrew]). The commentary was written originally in Arabic and printed for the first time in Livorno: Antonio Santini, 1759.

Resh Lakish concerning the everlasting existence of the *Megillah*.[19] In forthcoming generations, the book of Esther was not neglected at all. We should mention, just for example, the important commentary of Rabbi Abraham Saba, who was among the Jews expelled from Spain (1492) and Portugal (1497),[20] and the three commentaries of Rabbi Eliyahu of Vilna (the Vilna Gaon, 1720–97; *Peshat* [the plain, literal meaning], *Remez* [an allusion, a hint at the deeper meaning], and *Sod* [a "secret" mystical meaning] of the text).[21] The Gaon stresses that the miracle related in the book of Esther (Purim) is ranked much greater than that of Hanukah, though the last one was an extremely great wonder.[22] It is noteworthy to mention that very same opinion was already stated by Rabbi Judah Loew ben Bezalel (the Prague Maharal, 1520[?]–1609)[23] in his introduction to *Or Hadash* dedicated to *Megillat Esther*.[24] Moreover, the first commentary of Rabbi Meir Libush ben Yechiel Michal (Malbim; 1809–79) was on the book of Esther (ca. 1845).

Scenes from the book of Esther were recurring subjects in Jewish poetry and art. For instance, Rabbi Yehudah Halevi (1086–1142) composed a lengthy and beautiful ballad on the book of Esther (*Mi Kamochah*, "Who is like You"), which became a part of the Shabbat's liturgy prior to Purim in the Sephardic synagogues.[25] Scenes from Esther's narrative have been painted as early as mid 3rd century in Dura Europos's synagogue. Continuous interest in the theme of Esther is still being expressed artistically as of today.[26]

It appears, therefore, that alongside the Pentateuch and Psalms, Esther—the "Torah of Purim"—is one of the most popular of biblical compositions among the Jews, nearly at the level of *micro-biblia*.

19. See Maimonides, *Mishneh-Torah, Hilchot Megillah*, chap. 2, halacha 18.

20. See Rabbi Abraham Saba, *Eskol Hakofer: 'al Hegilat Ester* (Drahobitshi Zupnik, 1903 [Hebrew]).

21. See Rabbi Eliyahu of Vilna, *Megillat Esther* (2nd ed.; Jerusalem: Yeshivat Tiferrat Hatalmud, 1991 [Hebrew]).

22. See the Vilna Gaon's commentary (*Peshat*) on Esth 1:2 (ibid., 16–18); and his commentary on *B. Ḥul.* 139b.

23. On the birth date of Maharal, see B. L. Sherwin, *Mystical Theology and Social Dissent: The Life and Works of Judah Loew of Prague* (London: Associated University Presses, 1982; repr., Oxford: Littman Library of Jewish Civilization, 2006) 187–89.

24. For the paragraph from *Or Hadash*, see A. Karib (ed.), *Selected Writings of Rabbi Judah Loew ben Bezalel* (vol. 1; Jerusalem: Mossad Harav Kook, 1960) 186–91, esp. pp. 189–90 [Hebrew].

25. See I. Zemorah, ed., *Complete Poems of Rabbi Jehudah Halevi* (Tel Aviv: Machbarot Lesifrot & Mesada 1955) 176–180 [Hebrew].

26. For Esther's story in poetry, art, music, songs, and so on, see P. Goodman, *The Purim Anthology* (Philadelphia: Jewish Publication Society, 1960).

2. The Place of Esther in Jewish Theology

What accounts for the great popularity of the book of Esther among the Jews, for its highly valued position and much admired figures? Was its appeal only due to its dramatic story, lively descriptions, sharp irony, clear and beautiful style (themes that are commonly shared with several other biblical compositions) that attracted Jewish audiences through the generations, or is there some other explanation for this? Indeed, one can interpret the words of Resh Lakish and Maimonides against the background of the verse: "and these days of Purim shall not fail from among of the Jews, nor the memorial of them perish from their seed" (Esth 9:28). However, something far beyond a *halachic* expounding of a scripture has made the book of Esther so popular. The book has an important and unique message for the Jewish people at all times and all places, a message that places it in a central position of Jewish theology, thought, and self-definition. Let us turn our attention to this point in some detail.

a. The Fright of Total Antnihilation

Several Scriptures in the Hebrew Bible reflect the fact that the Israelites embraced a traumatic fear of their complete extermination. Generations were terrified for their very existence and feared that complete annihilation would befall the nation. This inner hidden fear is exemplified in several accounts. It is rooted, presumably, in the horrific story of the *Aqedah* (the binding of Isaac) in Gen 22:1–14. After several promises (Gen 12:7; 15:4–5, 7–21) and long-awaited hope, the 100-year-old Abraham and 90-year-old Sarah had only one son (Gen 18:10–15, 21:5). Yet God commanded Abraham to take the beloved one and "offer him . . . as a burnt offering[27] upon one of the mountains" (v. 2). Only at the last moment before Abraham's knife slaughtered Isaac, the angel of the Lord ordered: "Do not lay your hand on the lad" (v. 12). The very founders of the Israelite nation are portrayed as near victims of extermination. Later on, the fear of annihilation is reflected in Jacob's prayer: "O save me from the power of my brother, from Esau! *I am afraid of him attacking me and overpowering me, slaying and slaying us all, the mother with the children*" (Gen 32:12). It emerges also in Jacob's reaction to Simeon and Levi's devastation of Shechem: "You have undone me, you have brought me into bad odor among the natives, the Canaanites and Perizzites; my numbers are few, and *they will muster to attack me, till I am destroyed, I and my family!*" (Gen 34:30). Indeed, the author of the story stresses that only God's interference saved Jacob's family from annihilation: "As they rode off, a panic fell upon the surrounding towns, and no one pursued the sons of Jacob" (Gen 35:5). Later on, Pharaoh could

---

27. It is striking that some old English versions have "holocaust" here in place of "a burnt offering"; see *The Oxford English Dictionary* (20 vols.; Oxford: Claredon, 1933) 5:344.

not tolerate the Israelites, because they were "too many and too mighty" (Exod 1:8). He put them "under captains of the labor gangs, to crush them with heavy loads" and had executed the newborn male Israelite children already on the birth stool (Exod 1:16). He ordered all his people "to throw every son born to the Hebrews into the Nile" (Exod 1:22). Once again, only direct interference by God saved the Israelite children from death and redeemed them from Egyptian slavery and oppression "by a series of tests, by signal acts, by war, by sheer strength and main force, with awful terrors" (Exod 1:17–20; chaps. 2–15; Deut 4:34).

The deep hatred toward Israelites and strong will to see their complete devastation is reflected not only in the biblical descriptions of "Pharaoh the enslaver" (Ramesses II?), but also in some extrabiblical sources. In Hymn of Victory, the so called "Israel Stele," from the fifth year of Pharaoh Merneptah II (1224–1114 B.C.E.), the first mention of "Israel" outside the Bible is marked by deep abhorrence: "*Israel is laid waste, his seed is not.*"[28] Several hundred years later, Mesha, king of Moab (ca. mid-9th century B.C.E.), recounts his rebellious actions against the Kingdom of Israel and states: "As for Omri king of Israel, he humbled Moab many years, for Chemosh was angry at his land . . . but I have triumphed over him and over his house, while *Israel has perished for ever!*" (the Moabite Stone, lines 4–7).[29]

The horrible, deep fear of complete destruction lingered among Israelites a long time, and one of its clearest expressions is reflected in Psalm 83:

> Do not keep silent, O God; do not hold your peace and be still, O God. For, behold, your enemies make a tumult; and those who hate you have lifted up the head. They have taken crafty counsel against your people, and consulted against your hidden ones. *They have said, Come, and let us cut them off from being a nation; that the name of Israel may no longer be remembered.* For they conspire together with one accord, they make an

---

28. See *Ancient Near Eastern Texts Related to the Old Testament* (ed. J. B. Pritchard; 3rd ed.; Princeton: Princeton University Press, 1969; hereafter, *ANET*) 378a. Most probably, "Israel" in this inscription refers to a group of people or tribe(s), because the word is written with the determinative of people rather than land. See J. A. Wilson's note in *ANET* 378 n. 18. See also A. F. Rainey, "Israel in Merneptah's Inscription and Reliefs," *IEJ* 51 (2001) 57–75. Rainey concludes: "this expression is clearly meant to indicate that Israel has been annihilated like a plant whose seed/fruit has been destroyed. . . . Israel was evidently one group among many *Shasu* who were moving out of the steppe land to find their livelihood" (ibid., 74–75). It is worthwhile to note that similar idioms are used also toward the Peoples of the Sea in Ramesses III's inscription from Temple of Medinet Habu at Thebes: "Those who reached my frontier, *their seed is not,* their heart and their soul are finished forever and ever." See *ANET* 262.

29. See H. Donner and W. Röllig, *Kanaanäische und Aramäische Inschriften*, vol. 1: *Texte* (3rd ed.; Wiesbaden: Harrassowitz, 1971) 33, no. 181. For the English translation, see W. F. Albright in *ANET* 320a; J. C. L. Gibson, *Textbook of Syrian Semitic Inscriptions*, vol. 1: *Hebrew and Moabite Inscriptions* (Oxford: Clarendon, 1973) 75–76.

alliance against you. . . . They said, let us take possession for ourselves
of the pastures of God. (vv. 1–6, 13)

Some scholars have attempted to expound this psalm against a special
event in the history of Israel in the biblical period. Briggs, for example,
dated it to the time of Nehemiah, "for deliverance from the conspiracy
made against Israel by the neighboring nations with purpose of extermi-
nating him."[30] Others suggested that the psalm refers to the story about
the attack of Jehoshaphat by the Moabites, Ammonites, and Meunites
(2 Chronicles 20), or of Uzziah by Philistines and Arabs (2 Chr 26:6–8), or
even of Judas Maccabeus by neighboring peoples (1 Maccabees 5).[31] However, because we do not know any warlike circumstances in which all the
nations mentioned here were allied against Israel, and "since it is more
doubtful whether the specified nations existed at all at one and the same
time, and since, moreover, neither an actual campaign is discussed nor any
concrete measures of defense are envisaged, but mention is made only of
enemies plots against God and his people, we shall have to refrain from
any purely historical explanation of the psalm."[32] It looks, as already assumed by Friedrich Nötscher, that the account of the nations and alliances
is "poetically and freely composed."[33] This psalm expresses, therefore, the
Israelites' fear of national annihilation by the surrounding pagan nations, a
fear that emerges from other biblical texts as well. Here, the psalmist leaves
it up to God to destroy all Israel's foes.[34]

Indeed, the Israelites' feeling of complete annihilation on the one
hand and the deep and complete trust in God's redemption on the other
are reflected once more in Psalm 124 (which is dated relatively late):[35]

> If it had not been the Lord who was on our side, let Israel now say; If it
> had not been the Lord who was on our side, when men rose up against

---

30. See C. A. Briggs and E. G. Briggs, *A Critical and Exegetical Commentary on the Book of Psalms* (ICC; 2 vols.; Edinburgh: T. & T. Clark, 1907) 2:217. See Neh 2:19, 4:1–2, 6:1–9.

31. See, for instance, R. Kittel, *Die Psalmen übersetzt und erklärt* (KAT 13; 6th ed.; Leipzig: Scholl, 1929) 277–78: "Das findet zumeist seine so gut wie sichere Erklärung durch die Beziehung auf 1 Mak 5."

32. See A. Weiser, *The Psalms: A Commentary* (OTL; Philadelphia: Westminster, 1962) 562.

33. See F. Nötscher, *Die Psalmen, Die Heilige Schrift in deutscher Übersetzung* (Echter-Bibel; Würzburg: Echter Verlag, 1947) 168: "Der Dichter ist kein Historiker. So ist es wohl möglich, dass hier im Ps keine bestimmte Lage mit geschichtlicher Treue geschildert, sondern eine Anzahl von Völkern dichterisch frei zusammengestellt wird, deren Feindseligkeit in Geschichte und Gegenwart sich geäußert hatte oder typisch war. Zudem redet der Dichter nur von bösen Plänen der Gegner (4–6), ohne zu sagen, ob wirklich zur Ausführung gekommen sind." This assumption is adopted also by H.-J. Kraus, *Psalms 60–150: A Commentary* (Minneapolis: Fortress, 1989) 161.

34. This understanding is preferable to that of Weiser's, who offered to interpret the psalm "in the light of a cultic situation." See Weiser, *Psalms*, 562–63.

35. See Briggs and Briggs, *A Critical and Exegetical Commentary on the Book of Psalms*, 2:452; Kraus, *Psalms 60–150: A Commentary*, 441 and references to other earlier secondary literature.

us; Then they would have swallowed us up alive,[36] when their wrath was kindled against us; Then the waters would have overwhelmed us, the stream would have gone over our soul; Then the proud waters would have gone over our soul.[37] Blessed be the Lord, who has not given us as a prey to their teeth. Our soul has escaped as a bird from the snare of the fowlers; the snare is broken, and we have escaped. Our help is in the name of the Lord, who made heaven and earth.

It is impossible even to suggest any specific historical event in the history of ancient Israel as the background for this text. Accordingly, it seems, once again, that the psalmist reflects the general fear of annihilation.[38]

b. Esther's Reply to the Fear of Complete Annihilation

The book of Esther is probably one of the last links in the long chain of biblical texts on the above-mentioned phenomenon. In fact, it relates that, because of a personal conflict that Haman had with Mordecai, he wanted to "destroy all the Jews . . . throughout the whole kingdom of Ahasuerus" (Esth 3:6). He wrote, "Letters were sent . . . to all the king's provinces, giving orders to destroy, to kill, and to annihilate all Jews, young and old, women and children, in one day!" (Esth 3:13; see also 7:5, 9:24). It means immediate and complete genocide of the entire Jewish people wherever they may be found. Once again, the old fear that accompanied the Israelites/Jews became clear and real.

It is worthwhile to note that Haman stated here the classic lies about the Jews: "There is a certain people scattered abroad and dispersed among the people in all the provinces of your kingdom; and their laws are diverse from all people; neither keep they the king's laws: therefore it is not for the king's profit to suffer them" (Esth 3:8). Indeed, the first part of Haman's words is clear and reflects a historical reality, because the Jews were scattered all over. The last part of his words, however, that by keeping their own particular religious laws and cultural identity the Jews become separatists who ignore the collective social laws, is completely false, and his conclusion that, therefore, the Jews's existence is worthless is totally satanic. This accusation has been used as a prototype by many Jew haters through the ages. For instance, the advisers of Antiochus VII Sidetes (133 B.C.E.) supported this view when they desired to exterminate the Jews of the Hasmonean

---

36. Compare this metaphor to Jer 51:34.

37. This verse should not be considered a gloss (contra Briggs and Briggs, *A Critical and Exegetical Commentary on the Book of Psalms*, 2:452–53). This verse is used as a switch point between the first part of the psalm (vv. 1–4) and the second part of it (vv. 6–7), as its chiastic structure with the earlier verse testifies:

אזי המים שטפוני / נחלה עבר על נפשנו (v. 4)

אזי עבר על נפשנו / המים הזידונים (v. 5)

38. The conditional words, *if* and *when*, and the word *then* testify, indeed, to the general nature of this psalm rather than to any particular historical event.

Kingdom: "They [the Jews] alone of all nations do not take part in social intercourse with other nations, and regard them all as enemies" (Diodorus Siculus [the Greek historian of the 1st century B.C.E.], *Bibliotheca Historica* 34:1; see also Josephus *Ant.* 13.245).[39] We find something similar in the book of Daniel. Here, Daniel was accused that by praying God three times a day he violated the king's law, and therefore he had been thrown to the lion's den, from which he was saved miraculously (Dan 6:2–25).[40]

Nonetheless, in the earlier crises, God interacted directly on behalf of his beloved chosen people. Now, the book of Esther relates that, even in times when the direct interference of God is unseen (and clear and unusual miracles are extremely rare, in the ages of *hester panim*, that is, "hidden face"), God will still help his people and redeem them. This is, presumably, the central theological topic (*die Mitte*) of the book of Esther: God will save his people in any case at any time and place, directly and indirectly, by extraordinary miracles or by acting "behind the history" (or, if you wish, "behind the curtain"), while the particulars of his acts are hidden and invisible. To cite Mordecai, "relief and deliverance will arise for the Jews from another source" (Esth 4:14).[41]

In order to present this main theological feature much more effectively, the author of Esther creates a "theology" without mentioning *Theos* or any theological theme: he never alludes to a religious law or cult, institution or

39. For the English version, see R. Klein, *Josephus with an English Translation* (LCL 7; Cambridge, MA: Harvard University Press / London: William Heinemann, 1966) 350–51, esp. note c. It is worthwhile to mention that the fear under review emerges also in *b. Mak.* 24a, where Rab (3rd century C.E.) expresses his fear that the prediction "And you shall perish among the nations, and the land of your enemies shall eat you up" (Lev 26:38) might yet be fulfilled.

40. In the modern times, this kind of argument is used by anti-Jewish writers in various places. For example, in 1815, the German historian, Christian Friedrich Rühs, wrote an article in *Zeitschrift für die Neueste Geschichte, Völker- und Staatenkunde* called "Über die Ansprüche der Juden an das deutsche Bürgerrecht" (reprinted as a separate booklet; Berlin: Realschulbuchhandlung, 1816). Rühs claimed that the Jews—being a scattered among the nations, forming a separate state controlled by the rabbis—are not qualified for citizenship, which requires unity of sentiment, language, and faith. Further, he argued: "If the Jews would like to become citizens of the country without giving in their Judaism, they contradict their citizen's obligations, which generally it is impossible to harmonize. Nobody can serve two masters at the same time! In fact, it is a sharp contradiction that the citizen of a Jewish 'country / empire' will be also, at the same time, the citizen of a Christian country." Compare his *Die Rechte des Christentums und des deutschen Volkes: Verteidigt gegen die Ansprüche der Juden und ihrer Verfechter* (Berlin: Realschulbuchhandlung, 1816); and J. F. Fries, *Über die Gefährdung des Wohlstandes und Charakters der Deutschen durch die Juden* (Heidelberg, 1816). The latter recommended that German rulers treat the Jews as Pharaoh had (p. 23).

41. Worth mentioning here is the literary manifestation of this theological feature—including paraphrasing Esth 3:13—in the modern story "The Act of Rabbi Gadiel the Infant," by the Israeli writer, S. J. Agnon, *Elo veElo* (Complete Writings of Samuel Joseph Agnon, 2; Jerusalem: Schocken, 1978) 416–20 [Hebrew].

custom (except the mention of fasting, Esth 4:15). On the other hand, he refers frequently to a variety of banquets and feasts (*mishteh*, 20 times). [42] He neglects mentioning God's name in any form, either the general one such as "*El*"/"*Elohim*," or the national / Israelite *tetragramaton*, "[word of] four letters," "JHWH." [43] Again, this absence is highlighted particularly by the frequent mention of the "King (of Persia)" (190 times), "Ahasuerus" (29 times), and some 30 other figures' names. [44] Thus, the attention that the book's audience has given to God's silence shows, as stated by Michael V. Fox, "that the silence speaks louder than the whole string of pious prayers and protestations." [45] Therefore, all the efforts of the ancient translators and exegetes to integrate the name of God—or any other religious aspects—into the book are missing this cardinal theological character of Esther. For example:

1. The so-called Greek A-text, the First and Second Targums on Esth 4:14, Josephus, *Ant.* 11.227, and *Midrash Esther Rabbah* 8.6 [46] all have the name of God in this verse, "For if you keep silence at such a time as this, relief and deliverance will rise for the Jews from another quarter." [47]

---

42. See Esth 1:2–9, 2:18, 3:15, 5:4–8, 7:1–9, 8:17, 9:17–19. On this motif in the book of Esther, see M. V. Fox, *Character and Ideology in the Book of Esther* (2nd ed.; Grand Rapids: Eerdmans, 2001) 156–58.

43. Meinhold refers to the acrostichon JHWH in Esth 5:4bα: ‏יבוא המלך והמן היום אל‎ ‏המשתה‎. See A. Meinhold, "Esther/Estherbuch," *Religion in Geschichte und Gegenwart*, vol. 2: C–E (4th ed.; Tübingen: Mohr Siebeck, 1999) 1594–97, esp. p. 1596. One can add also something similar in Esth 7:7: ‏כי כלתה אליו הרעה‎. The question is, however, if these features were used at all in the time of the composition of Esther. If the answer is positive, still the name appears in hidden form!

44. Generations of commentators and theologians attempted to explain this phenomenon; for example, Steinthal stated that the "author's avoidance of the name of God is due to the fact that he is a skeptic." Scholtz was of the opinion that the avoidance is due to the author's residence in Persia. Paton argued that the book of Esther was meant to be read at the annual merrymaking of Purim, an occasion when people drink a lot of wine. "On such occasions, the name of God might be profaned, if it occurred in the reading; and, therefore, it was deemed best to omit it altogether." See Paton, *The Book of Esther*, 94–96, and there are references to the works of Steinthal and Scholtz. Recently, Berlin repeated the explanation of Paton (without mentioning him); see A. Berlin, *Esther: A Commentary* (Mikra Leyisra'el; Jerusalem: Magnes / Tel Aviv: Am Oved, 2001) 4 [Hebrew].

45. Fox, *Character and Ideology*, 244.

46. Cf. Midrash Psalms *Shocher Tov* 22.5. See S. Buber, *Midrash Tehillim* (Vilna: Reem, 1891; repr., Jerusalem: Wagschal, 1977) 182 [Hebrew]; for the English translation, see W. G. Braude, *The Midrash on Psalms* (YJS 13; vol. 1; New Haven, CT: Yale University Press, 1976) 301).

47. Indeed, LXX, *Vetus Latina*, the Vulgate, and the Syraic version of the verse are not leading in this direction (see also Rabbi Abraham ibn Ezra's commentary on Esth 4:14). See I. Kalimi, "The Task of Hebrew Bible / Old Testament Theology: Between Judaism and

2. The Septuagint, *Vetus Latina* ("Old Latin"), and the First and Second
Targums on Esth 6:1 write: "That night *God* took away the King's
sleep," in place of Masoretic Text: "That night the King's sleep fled."[48]

It is hard to imagine that the name of God appeared in Esther's original text
and simply somebody took it out. Thus, the appearances of God's name in
these texts should be considered late theological misinterpretations of the
Scriptures by the translators and writers. Furthermore, the six Greek "additions" to the book of Esther (for example, Prayers of Mordechai and Esther) should also be understood in the same way. These "additions," mainly
intended "to strengthen the book's religious character (so additions A, C,
and F), and . . . the absence of religious element . . . of the Hebrew version,"
also fail to foresee the ultimate goal of the book of Esther.[49]

The basic theological concept of Esther is not entirely innovative. It
is probably an outcome of similar theological lines, already expressed in
the Pentateuch. Thus, for example, the idea of the "hidden face of God" at
times in Israelite history can be found in Deuteronomy 31:

> And the Lord said to Moses, "Behold, you shall sleep with your fathers;
> and this people will . . . break my covenant which I have made with
> them. Then my anger shall be kindled against them in day, and I
> will forsake them, and I will hide my face from them, and they shall be
> devoured, and many evils and troubles shall befall them; so that they
> will say in that day, Are not these evils come upon us, because our God
> is not among us? And I will surely hide my face in that day because of
> all the evils which they shall have done." (vv. 16–18)[50]

In the same book, the ultimate divine redemption of Israel is also stated

---

Christianity," *Early Jewish Exegesis and Theological Controversy: Studies in Scriptures in the Shadow
of Internal and External Controversies* (Jewish and Christian Heritage 2; Assen: Van Gorcum,
2002) 142 n. 20.

48. See also *b. Meg.* 15b. It is worth noting that the LXX reads "the Lord" (*ho kurios*) in
Esth 6:1, whereas the A-text is using the expression "the Powerful" (*ho dunatos*).

49. The quotation is from Moore, *Daniel, Esther and Jeremiah: The Additions*, 153. For this
purpose of the "additions," see also his commentary, *Esther*, xxxii–xxxiii. The same should be
said of Josephus, *Ant.* 11.231–32, 234, which describes Esther's prayers to God and also Mordecai's; and *Targum Sheni* on Esther, which models Mordecai and Esther as faithful to the Torah
(on this source, see B. Ego, "God as the Ruler of History: Main Thematic Motives of the Interpretation of Megillat Esther in Targum Sheni," *JAB* 2 [2000] 189–201). Similarly, one must
consider also all the midrashic literatures that insert various religious aspects into the biblical
story of Esther.

50. Note that, already the talmudic sages related the book of Esther to this passage in
the book of Deuteronomy (specifically with v. 18), though in their own unique midrashic approach, based on both the spelling and sound of the Hebrew words אסתר and אסתיר. See *b. Ḥul.*
139b: "Where is *Esther* indicated in the Torah?—[In the verse,] "and I will surely hide [אסתיר]
my face" (Deut 31:18).

in the Song of *Haazinu* (that is, "give ear," Deut 32:1–43), which Moses was directed to compose (Deut 31:19):

> He [God] shall relent regarding His servants [Israel], when He sees that enemy power progress, and none is saved or assisted. . . . For I [God] lift up my hand to heaven, and say, I live forever. If I whet my glittering sword, and my hand takes hold on judgment; I will render vengeance to my enemies, and will requite those who hate me. . . . Rejoice, O you nations, with his people; for He will avenge the blood of his servants, and will render vengeance on His adversaries." (Deut 32:35–36a, 40–41, 43)[51]

III. CONCLUSION

1. The Theological Message of Esther

The absence of God's name from the book of Esther does not mean that the author has no interest in theological issues. On the contrary, his message is intended for Jews in general and for those in the Diaspora in particular, that God is devoted to Israel.[52] Every generation has its "Haman,"[53] but God is always there to keep his promise and help his people, directly (such as in the redemption from Egypt, by taking them *out* of the land), or indirectly, while acting silently "behind the curtain" (such

---

51. See also Deut 4:25–31, 30:1–10; 1 Kgs 8:44–53.

52. Contrary to Nehemiah, for instance (see Neh 1:1–2, 6), the land of Israel and Jerusalem do not receive any special attention in Esther. See, in detail, J. D. Levenson, *Esther: A Commentary* (OTL; Louisville, KY: Westminster John Knox, 1997) 14–16. However, *Targum Sheni* to Esther fills in this "lacunae" in the biblical text by ascribing a prayer to Esther, who says: "inhabitants of Jerusalem move in their graves because You gave their sons to be slaughtered." *Midrash Esther Rabbah* 8.3 speaks about the promise that Ahasuerus made to Esther: to build the Jerusalem Temple if she will have a son.

The concept of God's devotion to Israel is entirely different from that suggested by some scholars, that is, that the purpose of the scroll is to provide Purim (or "Mordechai's Day," as it is named in 2 Macc 15:36) with an etiological-historical background in order to justify the festival (see, e.g., Berlin, *Esther: A Commentary*, 3–5). This is true for the present form of the scroll. I am of the opinion, however, that the institution of Purim was not an original part of the salvation narrative. See Fox, *Character and Ideology*, 156 n. 5, 255–61; R. Rendtorff, *The Old Testament: An Introduction* (Philadelphia: Fortress, 1991) 271.

53. Indeed, the Jews actualize the biblical story of Esther by identifying their own day's enemy with Haman. So, for instance, *Targum Sheni* identifies Haman as one who represents the entire pagan-Christian world that persecutes Jews and the victory over Haman as a prototype of Jews' overcoming their enemies. See B. Ego, *Targum Scheni zu Ester: Übersetzung, Kommentar und theologische Deutung* (TSAJ 54; Tübingen: Mohr Siebeck, 1996) 240–42, and there earlier bibliography. In his commentary on *Megillat Esther*, Rabbi Abraham Saba drew on his and his nation's terrible experiences when Jews were expelled from Spain. See Rabbi Abraham

as in the redemption *in* the framework of the Persian Empire, without any "new exodus"). The author trusts, seemingly, that God's covenant with Israel is everlasting, for "the Lord . . . is God, the faithful God who maintains *covenant loyalty* (שומר הברית והחסד) with those who love him and keep his commandments, to a thousand generations" (Deut 7:9).[54] He holds the prophetical promise, such as: "For this is as the waters of Noah to me: as I have sworn that the waters of Noah should no more go over the earth, I swore that I would not be angry with you nor rebuke you. For the mountains shall depart, and the hills be removed; but my *loyalty* (וחסדי) shall not depart from you, neither shall the *covenant* of my peace (וברית שלומי) be removed, says the Lord that have mercy on you" (Isa 54:9–10), and "For just the new heavens and the new earth that I will make will endure before Me—the words of the Lord—so will your [Israel's] offspring and your name endure" (Isa 66:22). Because the existence of the Jewish people is everlasting, he believes, the extermination of the Jews in any form and at any time and place is unbearable to God. He is confident that "Israel *is* holy to the Lord,[55] the first fruits of his harvest, all that devour him shall offend: evil shall come upon them" (Jer 2:3).[56]

This is the central theme emerging from the book of Esther for everyone, Jews and non-Jews. In other words, the story of Esther sends the message that is expressed later by the Sages in the Passover Haggadah:

Saba, *Commentary on Esther*; and the essay of A. Gross, "The Reflection of Spain and Portugal Expulsions in a Commentary on Megillat Esther," *Proceedings of the Ninth World Congress of Jewish Studies* (Jerusalem: World Union of Jewish Studies, 1986) division B, 1:153–58 [Hebrew].

54. Compare 1 Kgs 8:23 and especially Neh 1:5, 9:36.

55. Christian translators and commentators deliberately changed the original Hebrew text and write: "Israel *was* holy to the Lord, and the first fruits of his harvest" (Jer 2:3). See, for example, KJV, RSV, *Luther Bibel*, and *Zürcher Bibel* ad loc.; as well as W. Rudolph, *Jeremia* (HAT 12; Tübingen: Mohr Siebeck, 1947) 10; J. A. Thompson, *The Book of Jeremiah* (NICOT; Grand Rapids: Eerdmans, 1980) 159; J. Schreiner, *Jeremia 1–25,14* (NEB; Würzburg: Echter, 1981) 18 ("Heiliger Besitz *war* Israel dem Herrn"); R. P. Carroll, *Jeremiah: A Commentary* (OTL; Philadelphia: Westminster, 1986) 118; W. McKane, *A Critical and Exegetical Commentary on Jeremiah* (ICC; 2 vols.; Edinburgh: T. & T. Clark, 1986) 1:26; P. C. Craigie, P. H. Kelley, and J. Drinkard, *Jeremiah 1–25* (WBC 26; Dallas: Word, 1991) 22. These scholars are biased by the Christian anti-Jewish theology, which holds that the Christians—rather than the "heretical Jews" or "talmudic Jews"—are the direct continuation of "biblical Israel."

56. Consequently, the book of Esther cannot be considered "the most secular book of the Bible," as claimed, for instance, by Berlin (*Esther: A Commentary*, 3). Three decades earlier, Fohrer doubted the religious and theological value of Esther, considered the book even "less a sacred document than a secular book." He ends that "it is the produce of a nationalistic spirit, seeking revenge on those that persecute the Jews, which has lost all understanding of the demands and obligations of Yahwism, especially in its prophetical form" (G. Fohrer, *Introduction to the Old Testament* [Nashville: Abingdon, 1968] 255). This is the conclusion of a leading German biblical scholar/theologian on Esther after the Holocaust! For a detailed discussion on the Christian attitude toward Esther, see Kalimi, "The Book of Esther in Christian Tradition."

והיא שעמדה לאבותינו ולנו שלא אחד בלבד עומדים עלינו לכלותנו
אלא שבכל דור ודור עומדים עלינו לכלותינו והקב״ה מצילנו מידם

And it is this same promise which has been the support of our ancestors and of ourselves, for not one only has ["Hamans"] risen up against
us, but in every generation some have arisen against us to annihilate
us, but the Most Holy, blessed be He, has delivered us out of their
hands.[57]

Next, I would like to evaluate briefly the theological view of Esther
against the background of the Jewish historical reality, at least in the past
millennium, to compare the theology with the history (§III.2). Finally, I
review the post Shoah reading of Esther among the contemporary Jews
(§III.3).

2. The Historical Reality

Tragically, "relief and deliverance" has not characterized the Jews' bit-
ter and long Exile, as predicted by the author of the book of Esther. Thus,
here are some examples: in 1096 the crusaders slaughtered thousands of
the Rhineland's Jews ("Cross or Death!") and demolished their flourishing
communities. In the expulsions from Spain (1492) and Portugal (1497), all
the diplomatic efforts did not make up for the cruel acts of the "Hamans."
Instead of "and many of the people of the land became Jews" (Esth 8:17),
thousands of Jews were forced to be baptized, to become Christians. For
the others, there were no "joy and gladness, a feast and a good day" (Esth
8:17) as in Esther, but there were humiliating death or expulsion. In 1648–
49, about 100,000 Jews were massacred in Poland and around 300 Jewish
communities totally destroyed. Furthermore, there were horrific devastation of the Iranian Jewish communities, for example, in Tabriz (end of 18th
century) as well as forced conversions to Islam in Mashhad (1839), and horrible pogroms in Barporosh (= Babol, Iran, 1865)[58] and disastrous massacres
in Damascus (1840) and Kishinev (1903, 1905).

---

57. It is noteworthy that the rabbis of the Haggadah interpreted Deut 26:5, "A wander-
ing Aramaean was my father," as follows: "Go forth and inquire what Laban the Aramaean
intended to do to our father Jacob. While Pharaoh decreed the destruction of the males only,
Laban sought to uproot the whole, as it is said: 'An Aramean had nearly caused my father to
perish.'" See also Targum Onqelos on Deut 26:5.

58. Because the destiny of Iranian Jewry is relatively unknown, I would like to cite the
following studies: A. Netzer, "The Fate of the Jewish Community of Tabriz," in *Studies in
Islamic History and Civilization in Honour of Professor David Ayalon* (ed. M. Sharon; Leiden:
Brill, 1986) 411–19; idem, "Persecution of Iranian Jewry in the 17th Century," *Pe'amin* 6 (1980)
32–56 [Hebrew]; idem, "The History of the Forced Converts of Mashhad according to Ya'kov
Dilmaniyan," *Pe'amin* 42 (1990) 127–56 [Hebrew]; idem, "The Jews in the Southern Coast of

During the Second World War (1939–45) all the worst fears of the Jews became realities in the ghastly *Shoah* (Holocaust). Once again, "relief and deliverance" did not emerge for the Jews from any source, and Esther's theological view did not turn into reality. To cite Rabbi Zera's expression, "a miracle does not take place on every occasion" (*b. Meg.* 7a).[59] It seems that God's presence was totally removed.

3. Theology, History, and Us: Post-Shoah Reading of Esther

Yet, the question that rises is, are we, the post-Shoah readers of the book of Esther, still supportive of Esther's theological message? Or, in the words of Exod 17:7, "is the Lord among us, or not?"[60]

Of course, each of us is entitled to conclude the answer from her or his own religious viewpoint and understanding. Nevertheless, there are three main approaches among the contemporary Jews toward this issue.

One approach is characterized as theodicy, that is, justification of God and all his actions in history: whatever the All-Merciful does is for good (כל דעביד רחמנא לטב עביד, Babylonian Talmud, *Berachot* 60b, and on 60b–61a, it stated in Hebrew: כל מה שעשה הקב"ה הכל לטובה). The Shoah happened for our misbehavior. Thus, we should keep the Torah commandments better, improve our treatment of each other, and so on. This approach leads, in fact, to more religious fundamentalism.

Another is of the opinion that the absence of God in the Shoah shows that there is no God whatsoever! This approach leads, therefore, to total secularism.

The third and most common approach takes the "middle road," that is, despite of all the horrible historical experience of the Jews, it seems that the central theological message of Esther is still valid. After all, עם ישראל חי, "The Jewish people are alive!" We are entitled to ask hard questions but still to continue to hold our religious belief, to cite Jer 12:1, "O Lord, you are just, but I will dispute with you!" Why? How could you let this happen?

---

the Caspian Sea, 1: Jews in Mazandaran until the End of the 19th Century," in *Society and Community: Proceedings of the Second International Congress for Research of the Sepharadi and Oriental Jewish Heritage 1984* (ed. A. Haim; Jerusalem: Mesgav Yerushalayim, 1991) 85–98 [Hebrew].

59. *B. Sanh.* 65b relates: "Rabbah created a man, and sent him to Rabbi Zera. Rabbi Zera spoke to him, but received no answer. Thereupon he said unto him: 'you are a creature of the magicians. Return to your dust.'" In this way, Rabbah tried, presumably, to demonstrate to Rabbi Zera that 'a miracle *does* take place occasionally,' because he can create a man! This is in contrast to Rabbi Zera, who had told Rabbah, "A miracle *does not* take place on every occasion").

60. Cf. Deut 31:17b: "So that they will say on that day, are not these evils come upon us, because our God is not among us?"

Nevertheless, I am in the opinion that after the terrible genocide of the European and part of the North African Jews, the Jewish community must read differently the book of Esther in particular and the Hebrew Bible in general. This reading should not stoop to either fundamentalist theodicy or fall into depression and denial of God, uprooting him from among us. It should read Scripture critically but also with responsibility to current and coming generations, with belief but still open mindedly. It should strive to reveal timeless religious and humanistic values and create renewed hopes for the benefit of all.

The Book of Daniel:
The Strange End of Biblical Theology

PETER J. HAAS

The book of Daniel is an odd book to be in the Jewish Scriptures. It is, to begin with, the only book of the "Hebrew" Scriptures to be written not in Hebrew but in large part in Aramaic, aside from the letters and other documents cited (presumably) verbatim in Ezra–Nehemiah. But of more interest from the perspective of theology is the fact that this is the only book of clearly apocalyptic character to be included in the canon. The Book of Daniel, like all apocalyptic books, purports to be from an ancient seer who several hundreds of years prior to the book's publication revealed the course of history, which is just unfolding at the time of the readers. A whole variety of apocalyptic books appeared in the Judaic communities of Late Antiquity. Some of these appear in the Septuagint and some in the Christian Scriptures.[1] Among these are the books of Enoch, 3 and 4 Esdras, Baruch, Jubilees and 2–4 Maccabees. In addition, a host of other apocryphal books emerged from the nascent Christian community, including a number of apostolic apocrypha, Pauline apocrypha, Apostolic Constitutions, and the so-called *Sibylline Oracles*. Of all this vast literature, however, only this one representative of the vast apocryphal genre made it into the Hebrew canon. The questions to be addressed below are why this book was included in the Jewish canon at all, why it is placed where it is. My premise in what follows is that the very inclusion of this book in the canon and its particular placement offer clues as to how the final redactors attempted to frame our reading of the whole.

It should be noted at the outset that, although the genre of the book, apocalyptic literature, has come to be recognized as a distinct literary phenomenon in the Judaism of Late Antiquity, it does bear some relationship to what went before.[2] The general idea of predicting the future through

---

1. On this, see Klaus Koch, "Stages in the Canonization of the Book of Daniel," in *The Book of Daniel: Composition and Reception* (ed. John Collins and Peter Flint; Leiden: Brill, 2001) 2:421–46. See also Collins's chapter on the book of Daniel, *The Apocalyptic Imagination: An Introduction to Jewish Apocalyptic Literature* (2nd ed.; Grand Rapids: Eerdmans, 1998) 85–115.

2. See, for example, the seminal study of John Collins, ibid. Also the discussion of D. S. Russell in *The Method and Message of Jewish Apocalyptic* (Philadelphia: Westminster, 1964) 104.

visions and/or dreams is hardly new. The Tanakh, for example, is full of revelations that come to the worthy individual through dreams, visions or other media: the forewarning to Noah about the flood, for example, or the dream interpretation abilities of Joseph. In these cases, however, the events foreseen dealt with the immediate future or with the personal lives of the recipient. We do find later a shift to broader prophetic visions in later biblical times, when prophets such as Isaiah, Jeremiah, and Ezekiel made predictions about impending geopolitical events such as the rise and fall of major world empires, especially as these events touched on Israelite or Judean foreign policy. Some scholars see this period leading up to and including the Babylonian Exile as the time when the first seeds of the later apocalyptic were planted. But even here, the visions are fairly limited in scope, geographically and temporally. Apocalyptic is different in that it deals with events on a cosmic scale, addressing the whole course of history and even the underlying structures of the cosmos within which that history is played out. The apocalyptic literature, then, is thematically and substantively different in scope from what went before.

It is generally agreed among scholars that apocalyptic thinking took shape in the context of the social and political upheavals caused by the conquest of Judea in the 6th century and its subsequent subservience under Babylonian, Persian, Hellenistic, and finally Roman hegemony. This history of occupation by foreign and "pagan" powers created a cognitive dissonance between the self-understanding of the Judean people as enjoying a special covenantal relationship with the Creator of the world, on the one hand, and their political, social, and religious impotence on the other.[3] How was it that the chosen people of the Most High God could be defeated and dispersed, the holy city of Jerusalem laid waste, and the Temple, where the divine spirit had chosen to dwell, be reduced to little more than a local shrine? The vast energy of the Judaism of Late Antiquity was generated by a dire need to address this dissonance.

This tension between theology and reality could be relieved in one of three ways. One was simply to declare the covenant over. Gestures in this direction can be seen as early as the prophet Jeremiah and became standard in Christian supercessionism. Such a view, of course, amounts to the end of Judaism (or as the Church would have it, to transfer the title "Israel" from the Jews to another people). The second is to declare that Judea's humiliation is a divine response to the sins of the Jewish people. In this view, continued faithfulness and repentance will eventually lead to an ending of powerlessness, defeat and exile and a return to Judean power and suc-

---

3. See Paul D. Hanson, *The Dawn of Apocalyptic* (Philadelphia: Fortress, 1975); a brief overview of his view, and others such as Otto Ploeger's notion that apocalyptic views were born in particular religious "conventicle," can be found in Russell, *Method and Message*, 26–32.

cess. There was at least some precedent for this in the destruction of the First Temple and its rebuilding some 65 years later. The problem by Late Antiquity was that, not only did the rebuilding of the Temple not restore Jerusalem to its former glory, but the defeat and dispersion of the Judean people never fully ended. In fact, this final step in the redemption of Israel seemed, if anything, to be receding rather than approaching. This left only the third response, which was to see all the humiliation of the Temple, the holy city, and the chosen people to be but the temporary effects of a larger divine scheme or plan in which God still ruled and the ultimate victory of Judea was assured in the fullness of time. In this view, the covenant was not yet over, and the final glorious triumph of Israel still promised and assured. Matters simply had to work themselves out. It is this last tack that defines the apocalyptic genre.

In literary terms, the apocalyptic writings generally draw on the prophetic tradition as noted above. The central difference is that, instead of specific pronouncements dealing with the short term, the apocalyptic literature depicts its visions as granted to ancient figures who perceived the grand flow of all history, including the (temporary) period of Israel's humiliation at the hands of the evil nations. One of the earliest apocalyptic books, for example, claims to describe the visions of Enoch, a son of Cain, who already at the start of human history was given insight into the divine blueprint of history, a blueprint that culminates in a day of judgment for the evil ones and the final vindication of the faithful in Israel. The book of Daniel is similar in intent if somewhat less grandiose. Daniel lived not at the beginning of human history but at the time of the Babylonian Exile (early 6th century B.C.E.) and talks about political events that were just then unfolding at the time of the Seleucid rule over Judea some 400 years later. What links the two books is the conviction that Israel's situation was a part of a much larger, mythological drama that included the victory of the Jews over their foes. As one of the great experts on apocalyptic literature, John Collins neatly summarizes matters: "The visions of Daniel are not, of course, mere reflections of the historical crisis. They are highly imaginative constructions of it, shaped as much by mythic paradigms as by the actual events. Fundamental to the perspective of Daniel is the belief that events are guided by higher powers, expressed through the mythological symbolism of the beasts."[4] Thematic similarities include the urgent expectation of the end of earthly conditions in the immediate future, periodization and determinism, and activity of angels and demons.[5] There are even some literary parallels between Enoch and Daniel.[6] For all these reasons, Daniel

---

4. Collins, *Apocalyptic Imagination*, 114.
5. Taken from the summary of Koch's list in ibid., 12.
6. Such as the image of the deity seated on a throne in *1 En.* 14:20 and Dan 7:9–10; see Martha Himmelfarb, *Ascent to Heaven in Jewish and Christian Apocalyptic* (New York: Oxford

is treated as an apocalyptic book, in the same genre as *Enoch*, despite the relative modesty of its visions.

Another defining aspect of the apocalyptic literature is that it not only provides insight into the large-scale scope of history but also provides insight into the mechanics of that history and sometimes even supplies prayers and other formulas by which the adept can manipulate the cosmos so as to attain additional insight, gain immortality, or achieve some other worthy end. As regards this type of late Jewish apocalyptic, Itamar Gruenwald noted, "All in all, when these secrets and oaths used in the creation of the worlds and which are operative in sustaining it are mentioned in Jewish postbiblical writings, they reflect a significant change in the religious attitude. Not only do the apocalypticists believe in the possibility that such secrets are accessible to man—at least on certain conditions which will be discussed later on—but the knowledge of these secrets opens the way for man's understanding of divine justice."[7]

With this larger context in mind, we turn to a more detailed look at the Book of Daniel itself. The book can be divided into two roughly equal parts.[8] The first six chapters are written mostly in Aramaic (beginning in 2:4) and tell the story of a young man who was carried away to Babylonia by Nebuchadnezzar, presumably as part of the conquest of the land of Israel around the year 586 B.C.E. This young man and his compatriots are loyal believers in the Judean God ("the God of Heaven," or the "God Most High"),[9] and Daniel is called on several times to interpret dreams of the king. In this regard, the figure of Daniel is strikingly reminiscent of Joseph. Like Joseph, he is carried off as a prisoner to a foreign land and there manages to have himself saved by properly interpreting a dream of the ruler. Both Daniel and Joseph are subsequently raised to the rank of one of the supreme overlords of the land. In chap. 4, Daniel even makes a seven-year prediction about Nebuchadnezzar (in which the king becomes a wild beast), thus echoing the dream of seven years of abundance and seven years of famine as related in the Joseph cycle. Eventually, a new Babylonian king arose who knew not Daniel and who was talked into deposing Daniel, who ended up in the famous den of lions, a possible parallel to the enslavement of the children of Israel in Egypt. To complete the parallel, Daniel miraculously survives, just as Joseph's descendants are eventually freed from their slavery.

It is the second half of the book that is of most interest here. This portion of the book returns us to the Daniel of the earlier period of Nebu-

University Press, 1993) 17, 58–61.

7. Itamar Gruenwald, *Apocalyptic and Merkavah Mysticism* (Leiden: Brill, 1980) 12.

8. A good discussion of the complexities of the composition of the book can be found in D. S. Russell, *Method and Message*, 48–49.

9. NJPSV.

chadnessar's reign and has this young Daniel talk, generally in first-person, not about developments pertinent to Nebuchadnezzar but rather about the rise and fall of great empires in the grand sweep of history.[10] Here is where the book of Daniel really breaks away from the normal pattern of previous biblical stories of dream interpretations, visions, and prophecies and enters the realm of apocalyptic literature. The revelations in this chapter refer to events that are to happen some 400 years later, namely, the rise and fall of Seleucid control over Judea in the first half of the 2nd century B.C.E. Moreover, these chapters have the interpretation provided specifically by an angel, who usually appears in a dream or vision. In chap. 9, an even more radical step is taken in that the dream framework is dispensed with entirely and Daniel is addressed directly by the angel Gabriel.

As one might expect even from the brief description above, the literary history of the book turns out to be somewhat complex. The first few (Aramaic) chapters were written, according to current scholarly consensus, around the middle of the 3rd century B.C.E. Here we have a seer who interprets dreams during the Babylonian Exile. The point is not the dreams or their content per se but the ability of faithful Jews to survive the pressures of exile (as did Joseph and, in a different way, Esther). The second half of the book, however, is clearly about the visions and their application to geopolitical events contemporary with the time of their authorship. Given the details and historical accuracy of these prophecies, we can confidently date these chapters to the years of the mid-160s B.C.E.[11] Given the repetitions and other details, it is also possible to see as many as four distinct authors represented in these chapters.[12] It should be noted, however, before proceeding that, despite this complexity, some scholars have seen the book as displaying a kind of underlying unity, suggesting that its authorship, or at least its redaction, can be ascribed to one master. It is possible, for example, to see chaps. 2–7 as forming a chiasm, with the later chapters (8–12) sequenced to mirror that structure.[13]

This purported internal complexity, especially as regards the later chapters of the book, suggests that what we have before us is a core work (or legend) dealing with a particular ancient seer (Daniel), a core that was subsequently taken up by a circle of followers and "updated" as time went

---

10. However, Nebuchadnezzar's dream in chap. 2 does stretch out into the distant future.

11. See Michael Knibb, "The Book of Daniel in Its Context," in *The Book of Daniel: Composition and Reception* (ed. John Collins and Peter Flint; 2 vols.; Leiden: Brill, 2001) 1:16.

12. See, for example, H. L. Ginsberg's *Studies in Daniel* (New York: Jewish Seminary of America Press, 1948). Also Rainer Albertz, "The Social Setting of the Aramaic and Hebrew Books of Daniel," in *The Book of Daniel: Composition and Reception* (ed. John Collins and Peter Flint; 2 vols.; Leiden: Brill, 2001) 1:175.

13. John Goldingay, "Daniel in the Context of OT Theology," in *The Book of Daniel: Composition and Reception* (ed. John Collins and Peter Flint; 2 vols.; Leiden: Brill, 2001) 2:642.

by so as to address contemporary events as they unfolded. Along these lines, it should be pointed out that there are also some possibly even later additions found in the Greek version of the book as well as some fragments from Qumran.[14] If the book was indeed the result of this kind of chain of traditions, then it must be seen as the attempt by a circle of writers or "Daniel-devotees" to keep their heroic seer relevant.

These sorts of "updatings" of earlier works are of course not entirely unprecedented in biblical literature. This process appears to be responsible for chaps. 40–55 in Isaiah (so-called "Second Isaiah") and for the material that follows, often labeled "Third Isaiah." A similar process might have been at work in the later chapters of Ezekiel as well. In both of these cases, the impulse came from followers of the main figure (Isaiah, Ezekiel) who wanted to show that "their" prophet was still valuable and worthy of reading. What makes the book of Daniel different from the above is that it is not an immediate product of the followers of Daniel but was composed hundreds of years after the assumed date of its central character. This kind of reappropriation of a much older biblical figure in a narrative or as an author is completely unknown in the earlier biblical literature itself (except possibly as regards Moses), although it is altogether common among writers of Late Antiquity, who give us all manner of pseudepigraphic books. This pseudepigraphic character is another element that makes the book like other apocalyptic works and distinguishes it from the other books of the "Hebrew" canon.

This raises the question as to why Daniel of all people was chosen as the lead figure. One possibility I have already suggested is that there was some kind of sect or cult of Daniel followers who were committed for whatever reason to keeping his heritage alive. It may in fact have been his obscurity that made him attractive, especially if his visions were held to be a kind of revelation only open to a limited number of initiates. After all, unlike Isaiah or Ezekiel, Daniel was hardly an establishment figure. The choice of an obscure character, as opposed to someone like Enoch or Moses, would make sense for a cult-like Judaic mystery religion that regarded its wisdom as limited to a few adepts. This group may have seen itself, like Daniel, in fact like Judaism itself, as a small and apparently insignificant character in the grand scheme of things but one that, in the end, turns out to be the guardian of the Truth and the favored of the divine. I will return to this connection with Hellenisitic mystery religions in due course.

---

14. 4Q243–245; see Florentino Garcia Martinez, *The Dead Sea Scrolls Translated: The Qumran Texts in English* (2nd ed.; Leiden: Brill / Grand Rapids: Eerdmans, 1996) 288–89. That these and other writings might represent a "Daniel tradition" is proposed by D. S. Russell in his *Divine Disclosure: An Introduction to Jewish Apocalyptic* (Minneapolis: Fortress, 1992) 45. VanderKam and Adler note that this kind of scribal tradition is part of the sociology of Gnosticism. See James VanderKam and William Adler, eds., *The Jewish Apocalyptic Heritage in Early Christianity* (Minneapolis: Fortress, 1996) 152.

Whatever its literary and social genealogy, it is clear that the book of Daniel is premised on a particular view of history. The idea is that history is neither a random series of events coming one after the other with no rhyme nor reason nor a matter of specific divine interventions along the way to punish or reward faithful communities. Rather, history is taken by the authorship of Daniel, as by apocalyptic writers in general, as a massive drama moving in all its complexity in a certain logical and (at least to some) knowable direction toward a preordained end. For the apocalyptic literature as a whole, this movement was not entirely random but was the result of a cosmic battle between two forces, one of Good, which would ultimately prove triumphant, and the other of Evil destined for short-term victory but final defeat. This way of thinking about history as the arena of combat between binary oppositions can be traced back to Persian Zoroastrianism.[15]

Persian religion was deeply dualistic. It conceived of history as reflecting a grand cosmic struggle between the Good, represented by the god Ahura Mazda, and Evil, represented by the deity Ahura Mainyu. This scheme of things was revealed to Zoroaster, or Zarathustra, by Ahura Mazda, who charged the prophet with explaining this struggle to his people and telling them that the time had come for them to choose sides. Choosing to side with the good deity, Ahura Mazda, might have its difficulties and disappointments according to the vagaries of the war, but ultimately the good would triumph over the evil, and those who had thrown their lots in with Ahura Mazda would find their reward in the hereafter. Correspondingly, those choosing to side with evil might enjoy pleasure and triumph now, again depending on the vagaries of the struggles, but would ultimately have to face their just punishment at some point in the afterlife.

There are three facets of this conceptualization of history that bear pointing out. One is that this is not merely the normal ancient Mediterranean notion that a battle between peoples was also in some way a battle between their gods. The Persian view, rather, was of a cosmic battle between two opposing forces—Good and Evil—in which all of the universe was caught up. Second, human beings had their own role to play in this fight, and in fact winning over the human soul might well be conceived as one of the goals of this combat. Third, the nature of this struggle, and the way humans fit in, was neither a matter of common knowledge nor attainable by normal reason. Rather, the grand scheme of history, and of human destiny, was knowable only through special insight afforded to a divinely selected spokesperson. If we hold that not all people should receive this knowledge, or are even able to understand it, then, we can see that the Zoroastrian myth bears within itself the seed for the later religious movements we collectively call Gnosticism, namely, the revelation

15. On this see also, Collins, *Apocalyptic Imagination*, 29–33.

of the true state of affairs (that is, "gnosis") to a prophet, seer, or sage who is then charged with divulging this information to (certain) humans.[16] In a slightly different permutation, this form of religiosity can be seen also in the widespread phenomenon of Hellenistic mystery religions, in which some secret knowledge or ceremony, shared only among initiates, leads to purity, immortality, deep insight into the nature of reality, or some other such desideratum. In short, there is little doubt that the basic cosmological schema of Zoroastrianism, through its subsequent Gnostic and mystery-religion permutations, became a widespread form of religious organization and practice in Hellenistic times. In this milieu, we should hardly expect the Judeans to be exempt. It is of course a matter of some debate as to how widespread dualistic Gnostic views permeated Judean thought, but the continuing production of apocalyptic works indicates that cosmological views of this sort did indeed influence some significant segments of the Judean religious community.

There is general consensus that Zoroastrianism first received a Judean theological expression in the book of *Enoch*, usually dated to the second half of the 3rd century B.C.E. In this work, we find all of the basic elements that define apocalyptic literature. An ancient, in this case prehistorical, figure, Enoch, is told about (or actually brought up to heaven to witness) the larger structure of all of history. In his case, he sees a rebellion by some of the angels (loosely based on Gen 6:1–4) under the leadership of one Azazel (who later became the prototype of the Christian Satan). It is this rebellion that sets up the dualism between the good God, who created the world, and the divine forces of evil. By the Hellenistic period, this dualistic cosmology had become the basis of a growing number of Judaic apocalyptic works. One set of examples of the power of this way of thinking among Judeans at roughly the time of the composition of Daniel is provided by the Dead Sea Scrolls. The theology of a cosmic struggle between good and evil is clearly articulated in the *War Scroll* (1QM), which depicts a battle between Good and Evil, or to use its terminology, between "the Sons of Light" and the "Sons of Darkness."[17] Other scrolls reflect this thinking, although in more standard form, for example, the "Pesharim," which read earlier prophetic books such as Nahum and Habakkuk as though they were talking in their day about the much later Roman occupation that the Qumran community was experiencing. The Pesher on Habakkuk, for example, explicitly announces that God told Habakkuk to write down "what would happen to the final generation."[18] In fact one could push this even fur-

---

16. An analysis of the Jewish apocalyptic roots of Gnosticism can be found in VanderKam and Adler, *Jewish Apocalyptic Heritage*, 150ff.

17. See also the *Community Rule* or *Manuel of Discipline* found at Qumran, column 1.

18. Beginning of column 7. See Gruenwald, *Mysticism*, 21. Gruenwald summarizes matters this way: "Some of their writings in fact were eschatological commentaries to Scripture,

ther. Insofar as the kind of knowledge presented in the scrolls (whether of battle, proper law, or the understanding of ancient prophetic books) is taught (or revealed) by a special seer (that is, the Teacher of Righteousness) and is made available only to members of the sect, we can see the Dead Sea Scrolls as describing a kind of Judaic gnosticism or mystery religion.

It is with this Gnostic-like background in mind that we return to our questions about the canonization and location of the book of Daniel. We have before us two questions: why was the book included in the canon at all, and, given that it was included, why was it put among the prophets in the Septuagint and among the writings in the Hebrew Bible? The first question (How are we to explain the inclusion of this book in the Hebrew canon?) takes on special significance in light of the possibility mentioned above that it represents the tradition of a specific cultic sect or esoteric community. If this were the case, it would suggest that the process of canonization was a complicated one in which various groups or interests struggled to have their scrolls or their writings included. The parties and politics involved in the canonization process are still very poorly understood. But whatever the political and religious forces behind its inclusion, what we do know is that the book of Daniel achieved a kind of canonical status, at least among some groups, very early on. One possibility for its inclusion in the canon is suggested by the fact that it is already to be found among the Dead Sea Scrolls, and so regarded as significant by at least that group within a relatively short time of its final composition.[19] The reason may well have been connected to its claim that history was about to conclude with the victory of the Maccabees and that Israel (or at least the faithful of Israel) and Israel's deity would soon enjoy glorious justification. We also know that there was certainly a burst of apocalyptic/messianic interest at this time, which generated not only the book of Daniel but also the books of Maccabees and the eschatological speculations of the Qumran community.[20] What is curious in this scenario is that, in the wake of the failure of the Hasmoneans to inaugurate the messianic promise, the Qumran community became marginalized and the books of Macabees remained outside the Jewish canon, but the book of Daniel nonetheless retained its special status. Josephus in the 1st century unquestionably regarded Daniel as fully part of the Jewish Scriptures. He apparently even held it in high regard, remarking that "if anyone be so very desirous of knowing truth, as not to wave such points of curiosity, and cannot curb his inclination for

---

and in them they believed to have uncovered the exclusive inner meaning and terms of reference of the biblical text." See ibid., 20.

19. Klaus Koch, "Canonization of the Book of Daniel," 2:432.

20. Koch shows that when Rome established itself in Judea, a new wave of apocalyptic literature appeared that took on patterns established in Daniel, a literary tradition that eventually included even the gospels; see ibid., 432–33.

understanding the uncertainties of futurity, and whether they will happen or not, let him be diligent in reading the book of Daniel, which he will find among the sacred writings."[21] Even the later rabbinic literature reveals not even a hint of debate over the assignation of canonical status to Daniel, as opposed to books such as the Song of Songs, or Wisdom of Jesus ben Sirach. One reason may be that the book does not talk explicitly either about an imminent defeat of the Romans (as do some of the Pesharim at Qumran), nor does it deal overtly with the Maccabees (as do the books of Maccabees). In other words, the very symbolic character, obscurity, or non-specificity of the book's imagery may have been its saving feature, opening it to the possibility of constant reinterpretation as historical events unfolded in unforeseen ways. That the book has this possibility of reinterpretation is powerfully demonstrated by the fact that it is still read by some Christians as a relevant apocalypse today, some 2,000 years later.

Maybe some clue as to its inclusion and what that inclusion should mean can be gleaned from its placement. As noted earlier, the Septuagint clearly regards the book as prophetic, placing it among the major prophets, that is, on par with Isaiah, Jeremiah, and Ezekiel. In the Jewish tradition, however, it is located in the Writings, just after the five *megillot* and just before the final histories (Ezra, Nehemiah, and Chronicles). This placement does serve to downplay its prophetic or apocalyptic character and to present it as more of a history. Several theories have been advanced to account for the relatively lower status accorded to the book in the Jewish tradition. One explanation is that, by the time the book was written in the 2nd century B.C.E., the collection of "Prophets" had already been completed, so Daniel was thus thrown in with other later writings. This explanation of course ignores the fact that the Septuagint does have the book among the prophets. It is also the case that not all the books in "the writings" necessarily postdate the collection of the prophets. Given these pieces of evidence, it would appear more likely that the book was originally considered to be prophetic (as its location in the Septuagint suggests) and was only later "demoted" to the Writings by the protorabbis, who were creating their own canon in opposition to what emergent Christianity was doing. I will return in a moment to the question as to what theological considerations might have led to this decision.

Before returning to what I claim to be the Jewish theological reading of the book, I want to return to its placement in the Septuagint. The Septuagint tradition does make some sense. After all, Daniel does function as a prophet, at least in a certain sense, and some of the visions in the Book are indeed reminiscent of the rhetoric and visions in other prophets: the

21. The quotation is from *Jewish Antiquities*, 10.10.4. See also his references to Daniel in *Jewish Antiquities*, 10.10.6 and 11.8.5.

appearance of the deity as a man, or even an old man, the existence of angels, the importance of fire and so forth.[22] Thus, the inclusion among the other prophets makes a certain literary sense. But what is one to do with a book such as this that was understood to be predicting a certain outcome in the mid-2nd century B.C.E. when these outcomes did not come to pass? Several possibilities suggest themselves. One is to drop the book from the canon entirely. Its early acceptance, as well as its ability to be reinterpreted, may have precluded this option. A second, apparently chosen by the early Church, is to keep the book as a valid prophecy, but to interpret it in such a way that it can be seen to speak to the triumph of the New Israel, i.e. Christianity. This option was obviously not open to the Judean opponents of Christianity. This leaves a third possibility, apparently taken up by the framers of the Hebrew canon, namely, to retain the book, but to move it out of "Prophets" and into a more historical context (i.e., along with other historical novellas such as Esther, Job, and Ruth), thus diluting its prophetic power. What results, then, is a book of teachings that still has significance but that is not to be regarded as really prophetic. If the above analysis is valid, then the retention and location of Daniel should throw some interesting light on the theological forces at work during the canonization process.

Let me now turn to some of the theological implications of having the book in the Hebrew Scriptures at all. It was of course clear to Jewish thinkers in Late Antiquity that the Judaism that was taking form in Roman times was not the same religion described in the Bible, which was entirely centered around the Temple cult in Jerusalem. This was most obviously true for diaspora communities and eventually became starkly true even to Jews living in Judea once the Temple was destroyed. We know from the literature that this divergence from the Biblical model was a topic of some considerable political and theological debate. There were of course segments of the community who, even after the destruction, envisioned a return to the "golden age" of biblical religion, including a reenthronement of the Davidic dynasty and a return to Temple offerings (hence, the revolt of Simeon bar Kochba, with its strong Temple symbolism). For groups such as these, the Tanakh provided a normative model for the ideal community, a blueprint to be followed for reconstructing the perfect Israel. For others, the Tanakh was more a collection of laws, rules and norms to be followed by all Israel, even in the absence of the Temple. Such is the apparent ideology of the Mishnah and subsequent rabbinic Judaism. A third group treated Tanakh as primarily a sourcebook of oracular prophecy, secret knowledge, and coded revelation in which the properly initiated could find a "wisdom"

---

22. A list of such similarities with other prophets, especially Isaiah and Ezekiel, can be found in Gruenwald, *Mysticism*, 31.

not available to commoners. In short, the Hebrew scriptures were an en-coded "gnosis," not a book meant (mainly or solely) to prescribe certain practices. We see this approach to Tanakh especially in the mystical tradi-tions, which persist well into our times. This is also the view of the early Christian community. The early Christians clearly assumed that history is part of God's plan and that ultimately God, through the divine appearance on earth as the incarnate word, would triumph over evil (or Evil) and bring salvation to those who understood and accepted this by faith. For them, these Scriptures were to be read as an extended parable or analogy. For this community, the book of Daniel was prophetic precisely because it could be read as foreseeing this victory of the true Israel over all evil. On this view, the precise details were less important than the overall idea.

It is entirely possible that, by pushing for the acceptance of the book of Daniel into the canon, its partisans were trying to do in their way exactly what their nascent Christian rivals were doing in theirs, namely, turning the Tanakh into a Gnostic type document in which the secrets of history were encoded and on occasion revealed to those who had the proper discern-ment. But the victory predicted in the book as read by the early Christian community was not the victory as understood by the Jews, that is, the glori-ous return of the Temple, the priesthood, and/or the independent dynasty of David. Rather, it is the victory of the new Israel, that is, the Catholic Church. In the environment of deep internal schisms and debates within Hellenistic Judaisms, it is easy to envision that the Christian appropria-tion of Daniel's visions for their own ends is precisely what made the book dangerous for the proto-rabbis. This would account for their removal of the book from its original prophetic frame, thus blunting its power for use by early Christian-Jewish apologists. This move can be placed in a much larger context. Early Christianity, as noted above, continued to regard the apocalyptic genre as important and so went on to produce and canonize (or partially canonize) a whole range of apocalyptic works. Emergent rabbinic Judaism correspondingly sidelined apocalyptic speculation by "demoting" Daniel to writings, by preventing other apocalyptic writings from being included in the Tanakh, and, as we shall see, by eventually ruling out all claims to private revelations.

It is in the context of this Christian understanding of Daniel (and so other apocalyptic books) that we can make sense out of Porphyry's attack on the book. According to Jerome in his commentary, the neo-Platonist philosopher Porphyry declared that the book of Daniel was not prophecy at all but was written in Seleucid times and therefore contains not proph-ecy but rather description. Porphyry's critique, of course cuts right to the quick of early Christian apologetics. If Daniel (and by implication other apocalyptic literature?) is not prophecy, then it is a worthless piece of late propaganda. More basically, of course, Porphyry is likely trying to undercut the whole character that the canonization of the book of Daniel as prophet gives to the Christian Old Testament. If all such prophecy is hogwash, then Christianity is no more than what it seems to be, a late religion trying to establish roots. In this, Porphyry may be sharing a sentiment with the early rabbis about the "prophetic" character of Daniel.

This theological struggle and the decisions it engendered had long-term reverberations within both communities. With the inclusion of the "Old Testament" into the Christian canon, the notion of the Jewish Bible as oracular in Daniel's sense took firm hold in early Christianity. The "Old Testament" became a book of prophecy, not law. The question of the nature of the Bible remained much more controversial among Jewish leaders. We can see this controversy being played out hundreds of years later in the famous debate between Joshua and Eliezer over the oven of Akhnai.[23] In this debate, heaven declares Eliezer ben Hyrcanus to be correct about a certain point of law, but the declaration of the heavenly voice is ruled out of order because "the Law is not in Heaven." In other words, private revelation is dismissed in favor of public debate and reasoned logic. This set the tone for virtually all of subsequent rabbinic literature. Another example of this attitude is the rather ambivalent attitude adopted by normative rabbinic Judaism toward mystical speculation. This attitude is reflected in numerous ways over the following centuries. We find, for example, both a paucity of citations by the Talmudic rabbis from the mystical literature and cautions about studying it, such as we find, for example, in Mishnah *Hagigah* 2:1: "They do not expound upon the laws of prohibited relationships (as listed in Leviticus 18) before three persons, the world or creation Genesis 1–3) before two, or the Chariot (based on Ezekiel 1) before one, unless he was a sage and understands of his own knowledge."[24] This text is taken up and discussed in the Gemara without compromising its essential message.[25]

Apocalyptic and mystical forms of Judaism did of course continue to exist. We catch glimpses of them in what we today regard as the more marginal books of the Judaisms of the middle and late first millennium: the mystical books of *Maaseh Bereshit* and *Maaseh Merkavah*, for example, or the fact that portions of the "Damascus Rule" were originally found in the Cairo Geniza, indicating the existence of a "Qumran" sect that persisted for hundreds of years after the abandonment of the Qumran site itself. Hints of apocalyptic and messianic speculations also appear in numerous

---

23. *B. Baba Metsia* 59b.

24. Translation from Jacob Neusner, *The Mishnah: A New Translation* (New Haven, CT: Yale University Press, 1988) 330. "The creation and "the Chariot" refer respectively to creation mysticism and Merkavah mysticism.

25. For a more detailed look at how the rabbinic literature reacted to the mystical tradition, in particular "Merkavah" mysticism, see Gruenwald, *Mysticism*, 75.

midrashic works. [26] But ultimately, as we know, it was the rationalistic strain of rabbinic Judaism that won out. Daniel remained in the Tanakh, but as a sort of anomaly, a book that bears little linguistic, stylistic, or theological relationship to anything else in the rabbinic Jewish canon.

In the preceding, I have tried to offer one theological reading of the inclusion of the book of Daniel among the "Writings" in the Tanakh. As a book of apocryphal writings, Daniel stands out in the collection of Hebrew Scriptures. Both its inclusion and its placement offer clues, although no definite answers, as to what was in the minds of the redactors. The book itself has of course continued to be a focus of discussion and a source of proof-texts within rabbinic Judaism. Its attempt to introduce apocalyptic thinking into post-Temple Judaism, however, failed. If the above speculation is accurate, then the biblical book of Daniel gives us an important but subtle message of how we are, and are not, to read the Hebrew canon theologically.

26. See, for example, Yehudah Even-Shemuel's excellent collection and commentary in his *Midrashe Ge'ulah* (Jerusalem: Bialik Institute, 1954).

Index of Authors

Index of Scripture

Deuterocanonical Literature

New Testament